THE READER'S JOYCE

For David and Alice

THE READER'S JOYCE

Ulysses, Authorship and the Authority of the Reader

Sophie Corser

EDINBURGH
University Press

Edinburgh University Press is one of the leading university presses in the UK. We publish academic books and journals in our selected subject areas across the humanities and social sciences, combining cutting-edge scholarship with high editorial and production values to produce academic works of lasting importance. For more information visit our website: edinburghuniversitypress.com

© Sophie Corser 2022

Edinburgh University Press Ltd
The Tun – Holyrood Road
12(2f) Jackson's Entry
Edinburgh EH8 8PJ

First published in hardback by Edinburgh University Press 2022

Typeset in 10/12.5 Adobe Sabon by
IDSUK (DataConnection) Ltd, and
printed and bound by CPI Group (UK) Ltd,
Croydon, CR0 4YY

A CIP record for this book is available from the British Library

ISBN 978 1 4744 8143 4 (hardback)
ISBN 978 1 4744 8144 1 (paperback)
ISBN 978 1 4744 8145 8 (webready PDF)
ISBN 978 1 4744 8146 5 (epub)

The right of Sophie Corser to be identified as the author of this work has been asserted in accordance with the Copyright, Designs and Patents Act 1988, and the Copyright and Related Rights Regulations 2003 (SI No. 2498).

CONTENTS

Acknowledgements	vi
Abbreviations and Editions	viii
Introduction: Against Joyce	1
1 The Life and Death of the Author	12
2 'Critical propaganda': The Critics and Joyce, 1918–80	39
3 The Homeric Question	67
4 'Victory to the critic'? The Critics and Joyce, 1970 to Today	102
5 Joyce's Reader	138
6 'The James Joyce I knew': Legacies and *Travesties*	173
Conclusion: The Reader's Joyce	196
Bibliography	202
Index	221

ACKNOWLEDGEMENTS

Many people helped me write this book, in many different ways, and it is my pleasure to be able to thank some of them here. I always read acknowledgements, looking often for hints of the situation in which someone managed to get a book written. This one came together across a handful of fixed-term teaching and research contracts and in rented flats and houses in London and Dublin. Thanks go first, therefore, to friends from shared homes and shared offices, for giving advice, lending books, and listening.

I am incredibly grateful to the Leverhulme Trust for funding that gave me time to focus on turning a PhD thesis into a monograph, and for the opportunity to do so in Dublin. I am also grateful to the Irish Research Council for their generous support. Sections of Chapter 3 appear in *Modernism/modernity*, vol. 28 no. 2 (April 2022), and I would like to thank the journal editors for their permission to include that work here.

I'd like to thank the academic and professional staff at Goldsmiths, University of London, at University College Dublin – particularly the Humanities Institute – and at University College Cork. Thank you also to the students I was lucky enough to teach at Goldsmiths, the librarians at the National Library of Ireland, and the excellent staff at Kings College Hospital, London, and the Mater Hospital, Dublin.

Thank you to my PhD examiners, Jeri Johnson and Scarlett Baron, for the rigour and detail with which they read my thesis, and for suggestions that helped to shape this book. Thanks go also to Edinburgh University Press – particularly Jackie Jones, Susannah Butler, Ersev Ersoy, Fiona Conn and Caitlin Murphy – for making this project possible (and for being so supportive and flexible along the way), Geraldine Lyons and Amanda Speake for their copy-editing and indexing, and to my anonymous readers for such positive, careful, and useful responses.

For essential tips, corrections, advice and/or reassurance at different stages, I'd like to thank Peter Adkins, Natasha Periyan, Isobel Hurst, Terence Killeen, Sam Slote, and Annabel Corser. For her positive enthusiasm, huge thanks go to Leah Flack. For being my classicist guide, a fantastic and generous reader, and excellent friend, thank you Stephanie Nelson. Without you, I might not have believed I had anything useful to say about Joyce and Homer.

I've read a lot of Joycean acknowledgements, and one name pops up everywhere with good reason: Anne Fogarty, thank you, for your endless support as I wrote this book. Your notes and suggestions from proposal through to chapter drafts have been invaluable, as has your wisdom on when best to keep going and when best to stop. Further deep gratitude goes to another glorious Joycean woman, a dream PhD supervisor: Lucia Boldrini. How do I thank you for well over a decade of support and understanding, in work and life? This work would simply not exist without you. You are my academic inspiration, and so much more.

While Joyce studies has provided me with a topic to write on, it has also, more importantly, provided many friends. If you've made me laugh at a Joyce event: thank you. My thanks and love go especially to Katie Mishler, Michelle Witen, Stephanie Boland, and Victoria Lévêque, for your warmth, your friendship, and for the privilege of being able to read and hear your gorgeous, exacting work.

I have learnt so much from my friends and would like to particularly thank two wonderful writers and readers for their encouragement during a late, fraught stage of drafting chapters, and for much more besides. My heart Leila Essa, thank you for being there from contract signing onwards (and for our sunny front steps in Stoneybatter). And Livia Franchini, thank you for the gift of your detailed and generous ways of thinking and caring.

Love and thanks go to Elaine, Phoebe, Mindy, Mike, Emma, Britt, Beth, Laura, Jacob, Ryan, Arne, Seán, Jake, Stephan, Tobi, Sophia, Jamie, Ben, George, and many other friends. My love and gratitude go also to my parents David and Alice, to whose memories this book is dedicated, and to Lizzie, Annabel, Ben, and Jim. To my baby niece and nephew, Ari and Jago: thank you for bringing so much joy to our lives. And finally, special thanks and love go to James: for giving me so much to be grateful for, and to look forward to.

ABBREVIATIONS AND EDITIONS

References are to the following editions unless otherwise indicated. The following abbreviations are used in citations where necessary:

WORKS BY JAMES JOYCE

FW	*Finnegans Wake*, ed. Finn Fordham, Robbert-Jan Henkes, and Erik Bindervoet (Oxford: Oxford University Press, 2012) (by page and line number)
P	*A Portrait of the Artist as a Young Man* (London: Penguin, 1974) (by page number)
U	*Ulysses*, ed. Hans Walter Gabler with Wolfhard Steppe and Claus Melchior (London: The Bodley Head, 2008) (by episode and line number)

WORKS BY ROLAND BARTHES

'Author'	'The Death of the Author', in *Image-Music-Text*, trans. Stephen Heath (London: Fontana, 1977), 142–8
'Text'	'From Work to Text', in *Image-Music-Text*, 155–64
'Reading'	'On Reading', in *The Rustle of Language*, trans. Richard Howard (Berkeley and Los Angeles: University of California Press, 1989), 33–43
S/Z	*S/Z*, trans. Richard Miller (Oxford: Basil Blackwell, 1990)
'Writing'	'Writing Reading', in *The Rustle of Language*, 29–32
Zero	'From *Writing Degree Zero*', trans. Annette Lavers and Colin Smith (1977), in *A Roland Barthes Reader*, ed. Susan Sontag (London: Vintage, 2018), 31–61

INTRODUCTION: AGAINST JOYCE

Ulysses is infamously unread. Yet this reputation, every reference to it, and each time it puts off a potential reader, constitute indirect readings of Joyce's 1922 novel. It's elitist, excessive, difficult, or plain silly; not for everyone, needlessly complicated, or over-hyped; all before a glance at its first page. In *How to Talk About Books You Haven't Read*, Pierre Bayard notes with pleasure that not only has he not read Joyce, he furthermore can allude to both Joyce's texts and his not-reading of them and feel neither shame nor anxiety.[1] Bayard perpetuates a reading of Joyce: of his texts via reputation and therefore of what Joyce signifies. Complicated texts, rarely read. Responses such as these – the prerogative of any reader (direct or indirect) – also rely on and perform readings of Joyce as an author. The creator of such a difficult, labyrinthine, 'important' text as *Ulysses* must be extraordinary. Or is it that a novel by a famous, canonical 'genius' must in turn be remarkable, complex, out of reach? How do we separate the author's infamy from that of the text? Actual readings of Joyce's texts enact this same quandary: to what extent is our reading of *Ulysses* informed by how we view Joyce, and how much is our idea of Joyce dictated by what we find in the novel?

In order to respond to such questions, and show why they matter to literary criticism, we must pull at the intricate relationships between author, reader, and text – a venture which has been sidelined in both Joyce studies and the wider literary world. It has been over fifty years since theorist and critic Roland Barthes declared 'The Death of the Author' and 'the birth of the reader' ('Author', 148). While the response to and influence of his provocative 1967 polemic continues, interest has waned. It isn't easy now to completely escape the idea that the author no longer has complete control over the correct interpretation of their writing, yet literary culture continues to be the author-centric world Barthes describes and decries in his essay. Both in spite of and due to his 'unreadability', Joyce is a prime example of this. Joyce admirers have ample opportunity to indulge their fandom. We can go on Joycean walking tours of Dublin, Trieste, Zurich, Paris; we can buy bits of Joyceana such as postcards, posters, T-shirts, mugs, fingerpuppets, tea towels; we can visit the Dublin chemist Sweny's and take lemon soap home ('Sweet lemony wax' (5.512)).

This literary tourism and curio collecting overlaps in no small part with Joyce studies, an academic field which has its own calendar of summer schools, conferences, workshops, and symposia. We present research to specialists, to an audience of whom we presume not only a detailed knowledge of Joyce's texts but of his life too. Joyceans collect translations, misprints, oddities, Joyceana that's banned by the Joyce estate. We can follow up a conference paper with a pint in a pub from *Ulysses*, we enjoy knowing that Joyce preferred white wine to red, a wealthy few chase ownership of things Joyce touched. Some of this is ensured by the autobiographical nature of Joyce's texts, but is that all? What does this behaviour do, in terms of how we understand author, reader, and text? Does our Joycean paraphernalia affect the way we read *Ulysses*, the way we read its author, or is it the other way round? Is it emblematic of an attitude, or does it contribute to one?

Multivalent questions of authorship and reception have been the focus of literary theory, literary criticism, and literature itself. Works of fiction can engage provocatively with the threads and splits between authors, readers, and texts, from novels or short stories about writers (including *Künstlerromane* both autobiographical and not) to uncanny metatexts. In Muriel Spark's 1957 novel *The Comforters*, for example, Caroline Rose reckons with the possibility that she is – somehow – a character being written. As she works on a study of *Form in the Modern Novel*, she increasingly hears voices narrating her life – with an accompanying tap of a typewriter. As Caroline worries that it is '"as if a writer on another plane of existence was writing a story about us"', the interaction of what we read and Caroline hears has an increased effect on Caroline's actions, the plot in which she moves, and the form of the novel itself.[2] Laurent Binet's 2016 version of Spark's games plays less with form, rooting its fun instead in literary theory: spinning a tongue-in-cheek crime thriller out of the death of the author of 'The Death of the Author', *The Seventh Function of Language* tasks theory-informed reading with crime solving. The novel speculates that Barthes's death in 1980 was no accident, but part of an international conspiracy – and as our semiologist-turned-detective protagonist Simon Herzog does his best to read the signs and find the truth, he increasingly fears that he is 'trapped in a fucking novel'.[3] Binet's novel dramatises the reception of theory in Europe and North America, and pushes its own sequences of events to such limits that the critically trained Herzog can't help but be suspicious – just as Rose suspects strange formal games in *The Comforters*.

Binet's combination of high theory and wrongdoing has another precursor: Gilbert Adair's *The Death of the Author*, a 1992 murder mystery in which authorship is a fundamental plot point. Barthes's 'The Death of the Author', the popularity of imported literary theory in North American universities, and the scandal of theorist Paul de Man's Nazi-collaborationist past come together as sources for fiction in the novel: the theoretical death of the author spills over into homicide, and the author-protagonist's famed Theory is revealed as a ploy to 'exonerate' him for his anti-Semitic past writings.[4] *The Death of the Author* takes an interpretation of the de Man scandal – that his advocacy of anti-authorialism was driven by self-interest – and transforms it into a slippery narrative. The 'I' that controls narration in the novel and is capable of reporting events which 'followed my death by no more than a matter of days' allows for a reappraisal of authorship, theoretical volte-faces, and ethical responsibility, while retaining the intrigue of a murder mystery.[5]

Explicitly writing authors, readers, and texts into the worlds of works of fiction is one way in which literature can create an alternative space in which notions of authorship and reception can be queried. Fictionalisations of acts of authorship, or of what reading can achieve, lead us to question our own preconceived ideas of author and reader roles. Such enquiries can draw from and inform debates which take place within the texts of literary theory, but often become even more difficult to pin down as they are subject to the tropes and effects of literature. Irony, for example, has thrown sizeable spanners in the works of critics who have attempted to determine the literary theories of one Stephen Dedalus. Stephen's starring role as an oblique version of young Joyce in 1916's *A Portrait of the Artist as a Young Man* is reduced in *Ulysses*, but his tendency to spout theories of authorship remains pretty strong. Echoing Gustave Flaubert, in *Portrait* Stephen declares that 'The artist, like the God of creation, remains within or behind or beyond or above his handiwork, invisible, refined out of existence, indifferent, paring his fingernails' (215). In the 'Scylla and Charybdis' episode of *Ulysses* Stephen debates the relevance of an author's life to their work, presenting a theory about *Hamlet* to those present with him in the National Library. He defends error ('Bosh! Stephen said rudely. A man of genius makes no mistakes. His errors are volitional and are the portals of discovery' (9.228–9)), references Percy Bysshe Shelley ('In the intense instant of imagination, when the mind, Shelley says, is a fading coal' (9.381–2)), and in bits and pieces outlines his own theory. Stephen repeats himself at least once ('Said that' (9.399)), as his ideas compete with his companions' in displays of (almost unbearable) youthful macho intellectualism; they laugh at actresses playing Hamlet and wonder if anyone has argued the Dane was Irish, reference theories of Shakespeare's identity, and giggle over Buck Mulligan's 'contribution to literature' (pissing on Synge's door) (9.572).

Stephen closely reads Shakespeare's life – or what has been guessed of it – and through his life reads his works, even somehow 'all the other plays which I have not read' (9.1014–15). He claims to not actually believe his theory, however: after nearly thirty pages of discussion, he confesses so 'promptly' upon finally being asked (9.1067). The extent to which Stephen believes his own theories has posed less of a critical issue than the extent to which Joyce did: a debate which has, for some, boiled down to how much irony one reads in Joyce's presentation of Stephen; how autobiographical and how parodic; how much a mouthpiece for his own, still-held notions, and how much a joke at his younger self's expense; an authorised representative of Joyce, or an ironic figure of an author within the text. Stephen and his theories have been an enduring focus of Joycean critical work on authorship, just as *Finnegans Wake* has tended to be more commonly the subject of criticism on reading. But the ways in which *Ulysses* explores and provokes questions of authorship, and of how authors, readers, and texts relate to one another, extend far beyond Stephen's library musings. The insistent focus on Stephen in discussions of how authorship functions in Joyce's texts betrays an unswerving – if incredibly complex – weighting in favour of the author over the reader in Joyce studies. Turning to Stephen, particularly when he is read as an author-foil, displays an interest in seeking direct statements of authorial intent and strategy, rather than an interest in how the modes in which we read Joyce's texts unravel the validity of such definitive statements. *The Reader's Joyce* is not about Stephen.

Instead of an author character, *The Reader's Joyce* responds more to the invocation of an absent, unknown, and variously ideated author figure within the pages of *Ulysses*: Homer. From the ancient reception of the *Iliad* and the *Odyssey* to the present day, the name 'Homer' has triggered questions about the identity, or even existence, of the author. The presence of Homer in the background to *Ulysses* provokes and engages these same questions, as does the activity of reading prompted by the intertextuality and narrative of the novel across its pages. *The Reader's Joyce* treats *Ulysses*, accordingly, as a text that repeatedly unsettles its own relationships to the author and the reader, pre-empting and challenging the efforts of literary theory to question what we understand by author, reader, and text. My methodology could be defined as 'reading reading': this approach is an essential facet of *The Reader's Joyce*'s argument. *Ulysses* incites us to read our own readings – to ask what reading is, what it entails, where it ends. Reading reading queries our understandings of author, reader, and text; this book's method is to describe and analyse how this happens. This leads me to not only look at my own reading, but also at histories of how reading a text is informed by and constructs an author.

In order to rethink literary, critical, and theoretical notions of the relationships between the author-reader-text triad, *The Reader's Joyce* will focus on in-depth readings of *Ulysses* and its interactions with a constellation of connected texts from classical and contemporary literature to criticism, theory, and biography. Central to this approach are my analyses of the so commonly underplayed significance of Homer's *Odyssey* to *Ulysses*, and of how authority functions in the developing critical reception of *Ulysses* since its publication. Through the prisms of *Ulysses* and 'the Joyce industry', *The Reader's Joyce* seeks new perspectives on the author-reader-text triad in the wider field of literary criticism: diving into layered histories of concepts, challenges, and retreats in order to ask how we read now. This study will thus demonstrate the underappreciated significance of how intersecting literary, critical, theoretical, and biographical acts of reading construct authors.

In order to achieve this, the chapters that follow consider how approaches to authorship have changed in literary theory and criticism, how Joyce studies as a field encounters or promotes the authority of author or reader, how we read the narrative styles and intertextuality of *Ulysses*, and how Joyce's life has been read and written in Joyce studies and literature. Though only the third chapter explicitly and exclusively focuses on *Ulysses* and the unknown authorship of the *Odyssey*, the discussions of *The Reader's Joyce* repeatedly return to ideas prompted by this unexplored Homeric presence: of reading without an author, reading in search of an author, and reading that creates an author. Emphasising 'Homer' as unknown, a series of questions rather than a known authorship, uniquely enables this study to analyse how the reception of Homer is present in *Ulysses* – and probe the reception of Joyce within Joyce studies. This in turn feeds back into the central site of exploration for *The Reader's Joyce*: the text of *Ulysses*, how we read it, and where that takes us.

* * *

The figure of the author has been through a series of transformations in criticism and theory, raising and exploring issues of originality or imitation, 'genius' and inspiration, intention, ethics, and celebrity. The ethical, legal, and economic position of authors, and the role of the literary author in textual relations and critical interpretation, have shifted in remarkable ways. This complex history is the subject of the introductory Chapter 1 of *The Reader's Joyce*, as is the position of Barthes's anti-authorialism within it. Barthes's essays 'The Death of the Author' and 'From Work to Text' remove the author from the equation of how texts relate to each other – making a similar argument to Julia Kristeva in her theorisation of intertextuality. Barthes rails against the author as a closure of signification, and the author in culture and criticism, while also providing provocative and still-useful analysis of the text and the reader. Since Barthes's proclamation of 'the birth of the reader', approaches to reading in theory and criticism have also undergone a series of developments, from reader response criticism and reception theory, to much more recent definitions of 'symptomatic' or 'surface' reading.[6] The reader's role in relation to the text has varied from consumer to participant to interpreter in a multitude of iterations, while the text itself has been theorised as the product of inspiration from within or without the author, or in terms of the interrelated nature of all texts: relationships of passive influence, active reference, or an intertextuality in which the activity of the author is unimportant. Just as conceptions of the relationships between author, reader, and text have evolved, so too has the position of the critic and criticism: does the critic 'solve' the text, or 'play' with it? Is all criticism 'critique', and what does it mean to suggest we be 'post-critique'?[7] By what manoeuvres of authority do our readings of literature become critical?

A small body of work on Joyce and authorship exists, predominantly consisting of studies published after Joyce studies began to engage with poststructuralism and deconstruction. It is important to emphasise, however, that critical issues relevant to questions of authorship were explored in much earlier Joycean criticism. For this reason, the topic of Chapter 2 is the early critical reception of *Ulysses* up to 1980, from Stuart Gilbert to the field-shaping work of Hugh Kenner. A core enquiry of Chapter 2 is how the emerging characteristics of Joyce studies grew from the early question of how to read the *Odyssey* in *Ulysses*; the relationship between Homer and *Ulysses* is then the focus of Chapter 3. Rethinking this literary relationship by focusing on the 'Eumaeus' episode and Homeric scholarship, Chapter 3 establishes a new interpretation of what the Homeric presence in *Ulysses* does, and how this relates to author, reader, and text. Until recently, the bulk of our understandings of Homer and Joyce came from the 1970s and 1980s work of scholars including Kenner, Michael Seidel, and Fritz Senn; it has not been a fashionable area of Joyce studies for some time, resulting in a regrettable gap in the field that critics such as Leah Flack and Stephanie Nelson are now responding to. Flack's work on how Joyce's classicism informs his modernism, and Nelson's on time and narrative in Joyce and Homer, have provided essential fresh insight into a near-abandoned yet vital aspect of Joyce's writing. My third chapter seeks to contribute to this by showing how scholarly responses to and ideations of Homer are layered into our responses to *Ulysses*: from the influential work of F. A. Wolf to the ambiguous oddity of Samuel Butler's *The Authoress of the 'Odyssey'*. Drawing on work by classicists such as Barbara Graziosi, Chapter 3 emphasises the instability of what we mean and have meant by 'Homer' – an emphasis that has been absent from Joyce studies.

Chapter 3 shows ways in which the text of *Ulysses* can prompt us to question how readers look for, perceive, or ideate the author. Chapter 4 then brings this questioning into the realm of Joyce studies, picking up where Chapter 2 left off in an analysis of how the critical reception of *Ulysses* has understood, promoted, and created ideas of interpretive authority in terms of the author, reader, and text. It is at this point that *The Reader's Joyce* engages directly with the most influential extant pieces of Joycean work on the author, reader, and critic; on which therefore only the briefest of summaries follows here. From what remains the best-known work on the author and authority, Jean-Michel Rabaté's 1991 study *James Joyce, Authorized Reader*, to later criticism such as Aaron Jaffe's 2005 monograph *Modernism and the Culture of Celebrity*, the field of Joyce studies has tended overwhelmingly to argue for an authorial return – though, as I discuss in Chapter 4, it remains to be seen when or where the author ever 'left'. The field also displays a proclivity for keeping Stephen at the centre of work on Joyce and authorship. Stephen is the subject of much of Rabaté's study, amid its discussions of authorial authority; he is the focus too for example of Christopher Butler's 1982 essay 'Joyce and the Displaced Author', Susan Stanford Friedman's 1991 article on 'Weavings: Intertextuality and the (Re)Birth of the Author', Christine Froula's theory-heavy 1996 study of ironic autobiography in *Modernism's Body: Sex, Culture, and Joyce*, and Jaffe's analysis of modernist literary celebrity.

There are exceptions: Vicki Mahaffey's 1988 monograph *Reauthorizing Joyce* identifies multiple modes of authority in Joyce's texts, spending less time on Stephen (or, however, on authorship specifically). Paul K. Saint-Amour's 2003 work *The Copywrights*, furthermore, focuses in its Joyce chapter on the 'Oxen of the Sun' episode of *Ulysses* within the context of intellectual property law. The general trend has been, however, to embed Stephen within critical work that deals with authorship: he is a nascent-author-character, whichever way we read his relationship to Joyce. But such consistent focus on Stephen in *Portrait* and the 'Scylla and Charybdis' episode of *Ulysses* suggests that these aspects of the novels offer the most significant provocations of author questions in Joyce's texts, in turn implying that valuable engagement with authorship occurs primarily where the Joycean text is at plot and character level *about* authorship: a restriction I challenge. The arguments of Stephen-rooted studies take in much more, but Stephen is their key source. I am, however, fundamentally less interested here in what the text might explicitly tell us, via Stephen, about authorship, and more in what it might show us through the ways in which our reading responds to its stylistic, narrative, inter-, and intratextual games.

My metacritical chapters continue a long tradition in Joyce studies, which includes useful guides and overviews of criticism as well as analytical work on reception. Joseph Brooker's 2004 study *Joyce's Critics* takes perhaps the broadest look yet at the development of Joyce's critical reception, while John Nash's 2006 work *James Joyce and the Act of Reception* considers Joyce's view of reception, and how this manifests in his writing. On reading and *Ulysses* more specifically, Margot Norris's 2011 study *Virgin and Veteran Readings of*

'*Ulysses*' instead considers the different positions from which readers approach Joyce, using Possible Worlds theory to articulate how it is to be a first-time reader of *Ulysses* or an experienced critic. Norris shows the value of focusing on the reader: on what new readers can create, and how the text of *Ulysses* challenges readers to acts of inference. Norris pays attention to readers at different levels of experience and textual engagement, while Brooker looks only at critical readership. Nash, meanwhile, argues that the question of a readership is far more than that of identifying a historical, actual readership – it is also theoretical, and textual; a position which leads him to exclude critical reception from his discussions.[8] Nash's work, furthermore, is about Joyce's own view of readers, reading, and reception. By contrast, my focus is on the reader's view of Joyce, and includes critical writing as acts of reading. The way in which the field of Joyce studies perceives the author-reader-text triad in terms of authority is inferred by all acts of Joycean criticism individually and *en masse*. Furthermore, Joyce studies constitutes a history of recorded readings, which interact to varying degrees and in multiple modes with broader shifts in literary theory, criticism, and culture.

The Reader's Joyce diverges from the norms of earlier critical work on Joyce and reading by combining analysis of critical readings with readings of *Ulysses*: this combination is key, and particularly informs the explorations of the final two chapters of this study. My approach develops across Chapter 5's readings of the 'Calypso' and 'Wandering Rocks' episodes of *Ulysses* and Chapter 6's examination of written Joyces in biography and literature; together, these chapters continue to unpick the manoeuvres by which we authorise our readings in criticism, and ask how we construct Joyces. Chapter 5 considers how reading *Ulysses* can lead to conflicting ideas of the author of the pages before us, and how this relates to the questions of authority raised by Chapter 4. These questions are then brought to bear upon critical uses of biographical texts, using a comparison between the Joyce of memoir and anecdote and the Joyce of Tom Stoppard's 1974 play *Travesties*. *The Reader's Joyce* spirals through its topics: questions raised in early chapters are picked up and complicated later, and particular focuses recur and develop across my discussions of *Ulysses* and its reception, our readings, and our Joyces. I find this not just unavoidable, but vital. This study comprises both literary criticism and metacriticism, seeking to let each interact in order to approach issues from several angles – and my own activity is part of this. *The Reader's Joyce* is about reading; the shifting developments of my responses are visible across its pages.

* * *

There's a lack of standard critical terminology to use in analysis of the author, reader, and text today. Furthermore, these three terms that make up my triad of focus exist both as innocuous daily words and the sites of ferocious debate and opinion; *The Reader's Joyce* is in many ways about such debates and usages. It is not always straightforward to find and use terms that function well – that retain clarity yet also flexibility, responding to shifts in emphasis – and a little explication of mine should be valuable and help to delineate the central interests of this book. Starting with 'the reader': references to a generalised, hypothetical, or ideal figure by this title can cause problems – perhaps most pertinently where that universal reader is presumed to be white, male, straight, and financially secure, for instance. My usage is instead pointedly broad, multivalent, and mutable, referring to any figure responding to *Ulysses* and Joyce. 'The reader' varies across this study, at times including critic, theorist, biographer, author – I endeavour to make this clear throughout. On the verb 'to read', in many ways I follow Jacques Derrida's questions in his 1982 talk 'Two Words for Joyce':

> But I'm not sure that one can say 'reading Joyce' as I just have. Of course, one can do nothing but that, whether one knows it or not. But the utterances 'I am reading Joyce', 'read Joyce', 'have you read Joyce?' produce an irresistible effect of naivety, irresistibly comical. What exactly do you mean by 'read Joyce'? Who can pride himself on having 'read' Joyce?[9]

In this book I seek to revivify the debate of what it is that 'reading' can mean and do. Using too many synonyms for 'reading' runs the risk of wooliness, as the differences between, for example, 'reading' and 'interpretation' can be of high significance. At core, by 'to read' I mean to respond to a text, and thus this includes a myriad modes of response to explore and examine.

The 'Joyce' of Derrida's 'Two Words' is 'an event rather than a work or a subject or an author'.[10] How we define, imagine, refer to, construct, mutate, ignore, or deify what we mean by 'Joyce' is precisely the topic of *The Reader's Joyce*: I seek to unsettle our understandings of the way we use that name. One way to describe this is to be 'against Joyce', the phrase I have used to title this introduction. It's a nod to Leo Bersani's 1988 essay 'Against *Ulysses*', a critique of 'The community of *Ulysses* and its exegetes' in which Bersani adopts a pretty challenging position in order to better analyse *Ulysses* and its readers. Despite writing 'against' the novel, however, Bersani notes how painful it is 'to stop working on *Ulysses*'.[11] Writing 'against Joyce' plays with an idea – never popular in Joyce studies – of criticism which reads 'without' the author. Against, then, connotes a sort of preparation or defence – shielding the reader and the text from the directives of the author, from any limitations the author imposes on reading. Yet to be 'against Joyce' could also suggest being next to, leaning on, supported by. In its attempts to make 'Joyce' uncertain, *The Reader's Joyce* responds to the ways in which readers and critics position themselves in relation to Joyce. This book will challenge theoretical and critical approaches and habits which pitch reader against author: whether they do so by declaring the birth of the reader must come at the cost of the author, or by giving greater currency – however veiled – to an author's understanding of their text, over a reader's.

To refer to movements away from the author, reading without an author, and arguments or activities related to the death of the author, I use the term 'anti-authorial' in the following chapters. Though not in common usage, it is deployed by critics including Seán Burke as a convenient way to broadly denote a critical or theoretical positioning.[12] Its partner here is 'author-centric', a descriptor I use to refer to the continuing situation of academic and popular literary culture. Furthermore, I refer to 'authorship' – or more commonly 'questions of authorship' – to encompass queries surrounding the relationships between author, reader, and text. 'Authorship' here is not a reference to how the text was written, or the processes of its revision and publication (though the way in which genetic criticism functions within Joyce studies is a focus towards the end of Chapter 4). 'Authority', whether the author's or reader's, is interpretive authority in *The Reader's Joyce*: the connections forged or broken between author, reader, text. Which mode or source of authority is given most weight or credence when it comes to suggesting what the text *does* or *means*? And why? That 'why' raises the issue of intention, a sticky topic that recurs at several points in my chapters – particularly those on the field of Joyce studies.

The six chapters of *The Reader's Joyce* respond to a string of connected questions that, as I will argue, emerge from reading *Ulysses*. How does *Ulysses* encourage a reader to query or affirm the authority of the author, and how does the novel emphasise the reader's role? How do these effects function together? What is the relevance of the Homeric to such questions? How have these problems been acknowledged and responded to in the field of Joyce studies? What is the impact of an author-centric scholarly environment on reading and criticism? What bearing has Barthesian anti-authorialism on *Ulysses*? Why have enquiries like these fallen from favour? And what does it mean to claim that these questions arise from reading the text of *Ulysses* itself?

Notes

1. Pierre Bayard, *How to Talk About Books You Haven't Read*, trans. Jeffrey Mehlman (New York: Bloomsbury, 2007), 11.
2. Muriel Spark, *The Comforters* (Edinburgh: Polygon, 2017), 63.
3. Laurent Binet, *The Seventh Function of Language*, trans. Sam Taylor (London: Vintage, 2017), 268. First published in French in 2016.
4. Gilbert Adair, *The Death of the Author* (New York: Melville House, 2008), 96.
5. Adair, *The Death of the Author*, 133.
6. For deft discussion of these terms, see Ellen Rooney, 'Symptomatic Reading Is a Problem of Form', in *Critique and Post-critique*, ed. Elizabeth S. Anker and Rita Felski (Durham, NC and London: Duke University Press, 2017), 127–52, and Stephen Best

and Sharon Marcus, 'Surface Reading: An Introduction', *Representations*, vol. 108, no. 1 (Fall, 2009), 1–21.
7. See for example Anker and Felski, and Felski's *The Limits of Critique* (Chicago and London: University of Chicago Press, 2015).
8. John Nash, *James Joyce and the Act of Reception: Reading, Ireland, Modernism* (Cambridge: Cambridge University Press, 2001), 2.
9. Jacques Derrida, 'Two Words for Joyce', in *Post-Structuralist Joyce: Essays from the French*, ed. Derek Attridge and Daniel Ferrer (Cambridge: Cambridge University Press, 1984), 145–59 (148).
10. Derrida, 'Two Words for Joyce', 146.
11. Leo Bersani, 'Against *Ulysses*', in *James Joyce's 'Ulysses': A Casebook*, ed. Derek Attridge (Oxford: Oxford University Press, 2004), 201–29 (228).
12. Seán Burke, *The Death and Return of the Author: Criticism and Subjectivity in Barthes, Foucault and Derrida*, 3rd edn (Edinburgh: Edinburgh University Press, 2008), 16 and *passim*.

I

THE LIFE AND DEATH OF THE AUTHOR

At the end of 2017, the short story 'Cat Person' was published in *The New Yorker* and swiftly shared and shared again online, gaining over 4.5 million views and inspiring myriad opinion pieces. Margot, twenty years old, has an unpleasant sexual encounter with Robert, who is in his mid-thirties. Detailing the build up to and aftermath of one awful date, the story deals with issues of consent, ambiguity, and communication; it is in the third person but is filtered through Margot's perspective, quite sparely written yet dotted throughout with occasional sharp, horrible details. It provoked sharp responses in turn. Some readers and commenters saw the piece as particularly of its time, a story for #MeToo, its perfect timing leading to its frequently referred to status as 'perhaps the most talked about short story ever'.[1] Others were more interested in its previously unknown author, Kristen Roupenian, and in how 'Cat Person' related to Roupenian and her life. Her short piece of fiction was widely misunderstood as memoir, as a non-fiction personal essay; this misreading and the need to correct it became part of the narrative around 'Cat Person'. Even when understood as fiction, the story was presumed to be autobiographical, and an intense fascination with Roupenian's private life even led to her relationship with a woman making front page news.[2]

'Cat Person', incidentally, revolves around acts of interpretation. Details are considered, interpreted, reinterpreted, Margot worries over how she is being judged, how she is being read. She imagines her date's responses, his reception of her. Towards the close of the story she tries to write a text message to Robert to say she no longer wishes to see him, and struggles to compose anything that runs no risk of being misread – that has no room for misunderstanding, no space for Robert to squeeze his own meaning into. As texts from him appear on her phone, she imagines Robert 'carefully crafting' his messages, lying on his mattress for a bed.[3] Women writers have to deal with presumptions of autobiography more often than their male counterparts – for this we can thank an undercurrent of misogyny in twenty-first-century literary and online culture. But any author can face such assumptions, and a concurrently keen interest in their personal lives. This is due to a broader, ongoing, modern attitude towards the link between an author's life and work that has its roots in romantic literary criticism.

'Cat Person' and its reception raise a complex net of questions about authorship. What is the relevance of an author's life to their work? Why does that level of relevance matter? Who owns or determines the meaning of a text? How does the gender, race, class, or sexual orientation of an author place pressure on such questions – and why? What is the reader's role in these queries? Roupenian, as Megan Garber observed online for *The Atlantic*, explained 'Cat Person' in interviews, 'its genesis, its creation process, its point', as it gained its millions of hits. Garber argues that Roupenian's emphasis on 'the craft' sought precisely to undermine accusations of autobiography, presumptions that women writers 'are not possessed of enough moral imagination to create characters who are fully fictionalized'. Yet this self-annotation also leads Garber to glibly note that 'Roupenian is an author who is, apologies to Barthes, very much alive' – with the words 'apologies to Barthes' bizarrely linking to a .pdf of Roland Barthes's 1967 essay 'The Death of the Author' in full.[4]

'The Death of the Author' holds a peculiar position in literary culture and humanities academia. For a short, fifty-year-old essay by someone who is generally agreed to have later changed their mind, it is strangely well-known outside the academy: in addition to casual references like Garber's, for example, the centenary of Barthes's birth in 2015 inspired write-ups discussing 'The Death of the Author' in national UK newspapers.[5] Though the essay had substantial impact within criticism and theory, it is now predominantly discussed and studied as a part of histories of changing attitudes to authorship, reading, and textuality – rather than as a still-useful tract. The essay, or the use of its title as a 'slogan', 'token', or 'catchphrase',[6] did not result in an abandonment of interest in authors – and though traces of its complex influence and reception remain, many have characterised it as a failure. Authors continue to enjoy a revered, exceptional status in both popular and academic culture; in this chapter, I will be to varying degrees outlining a history of this status.

This chapter functions a little like a second introduction. *The Reader's Joyce* looks at *Ulysses* and its reception in order to consider how readers construct authors. How the author has been formed, dissolved, and remoulded otherwise in literary studies and culture, and how such movements interact with *Ulysses* and its critical reception, are crucial parts of understanding what it is that *Ulysses* and our reading of it can do. The fate of the author in modern criticism and theory plays out in Joyce studies, and I will track how Joyceans create Joyces in my later chapters. Here, I will establish and then question general critical perceptions of the life and death of the author, structuring my discussions around three developments in literary criticism: how the figure of the author gained importance in nineteenth-century romanticism, how that positioning was rejected by the poststructuralism of the 1960s, and how such rejection has been received since.

A central argument of *The Reader's Joyce* is that every act of literary criticism requires a decision regarding the relationship between author, reader, and text – and that in the majority of critical acts this decision goes unacknowledged, let alone examined. This poses problems of scope and focus for this chapter, as a history of attitudes towards authors could include all literary criticism. Given my overall focus on Joyce, and particular interest in Barthes, it is appropriate to limit discussions to European and Anglo-American literary critical shifts from the late-eighteenth century onwards – though this narrowing still leaves a laughably vast scope. In writing a history of the author I must also navigate the written histories that already exist: it is a key strategy of many works of author criticism and theory to present a history of the author, which often involves revising or augmenting a pointedly identified, previously presented chronology of development. These histories and their strategies are therefore vital to understanding modern conceptions of the author. I will proceed, then, by looking at a selection of texts that have influentially theorised and historicised authorship, zooming in at useful points in order to track, question, and complicate the critical manoeuvres which led to the status held by authors today.

The triad of author, reader, text is a core tenet of *The Reader's Joyce*. My focus throughout this book is how questions about the relationships between this triad arise within literature, criticism, and theory. This is why Barthes's 'The Death of the Author' features so prominently: it remains the most explicit and yet ambiguous exploration of author, reader, and text – and moreover it implies that it is this triad itself which provokes the stance of the essay. Barthes's anti-authorialism forms the centre of this chapter for the importance it places on the reader and the text, and for its continuing – if overlooked – significance to literary studies. Our understanding of the points of connection between author, reader, and text remains unsettled.

A Brief History of the Author

'The author is a modern figure, a product of our society' ('Author', 142). It is far from simple to trace this claim from Barthes's 'The Death of the Author'; to track the history of what has been and what is now meant by 'author', of the shifting understandings of the role, function, activity of authors. Differing histories exist, and diverge precisely because they are each the product in turn of an author. Tracing these multiple histories, however, offers a richer understanding of what led to the anti-authorialism that was (by some) so explicitly demanded from the 1960s onwards in the European and American academy – and helps to contextualise not only the debates around the death of the author, but also the ways in which we currently perceive authorship. In this section I offer a chronology of the author: moving from the eighteenth century towards Barthes's polemic, and keeping my eye on the subjectivity inherent in authored histories of authorship (insofar as I can, while writing my own). I'll draw on three perspectives of how modern notions of the author emerge, broadly figured as authorial, critical, and economic. These include the development – often by literary authors – of ideas of the author as original, inspired genius; critical arguments linking the author's life and work; and interrelated shifts in the financial pressures and legal rights of authors. Combining these different narratives of authorship enables me to present a complex impression of the author – the figure against which Barthes reacted with a counter-narrative of anti-authorialism. The modern author develops in romantic doctrine and in response to a shifting economic position, surviving recognisably even into modernist reactions to romanticism. As I'll argue, the ways in which the author is described tend towards the contradictory and deflective: a potent character who is invisible yet key to the text, a divine creator rooted in the very mortal demands of the market. Yet this effective model persistently endures.

In the late eighteenth and nineteenth centuries our understandings of inspiration underwent a marked transformation. Romanticism relocated inspiration from the divine external to the fundamentally internal: the author ceases to be the emissary of the Hellenic Muse, moves beyond medieval Christian notions of authorship as an expression of a divine truth, and overcomes Renaissance and neoclassical ideas of the writer as, in Martha Woodmansee's description, 'always a vehicle or instrument'.[7] Percy Bysshe Shelley's 1821 tract 'A Defence of Poetry', for example, crucially marries inspiration and originality: 'the mind in creation', Shelley claims, 'is as a fading coal with which some invisible influence, like an inconstant wind, awakens to transitory brightness: this power arises from within, like the colour of a flower which fades and changes as it is developed'.[8] The author now has what they need to write within themselves, the same power seen in nature's transformational abilities. The discourse of the original genius profoundly changes the relationship between the author and a Christian God from special communication to comparison. While analogies for the poet as creator existed in Renaissance thought, they lacked this reach or ambition. The romantic author now imitates; now creates. And, as inspiration from within replaces inspiration from without, the writer becomes 'a unique individual uniquely responsible for a unique product'.[9]

For authors at this time were also becoming self-sufficient in more prosaic terms. The romantic original genius has the isolation and privacy required to perform great acts of creativity: the end of patronage in the eighteenth century brought such independence to authors. The newly independent author, however, still needed to make a living. A developing notion of an isolated, anti-political, outsider author was a product of the dilemma caused by the end of patronage and the rise of booksellers. As Robert Folkenflik and Michael McKeon argue, this figure was, in turn, key to an increased interest in authors themselves; as writers and subjects of literature.[10] McKeon characterises the shift 'from a system of aristocratic patronage to a system of capitalist publication and exchange' as a 'liberation' for writers, as 'freedom', to be 'read in acknowledgement of one's own intrinsic literary worth'. The bond between the individual and their work was strengthened, as the individual was remunerated by good sales. This system of 'private genius confirmed by its public reward',[11] of authorship within the capitalist marketplace, calcified the link between the writer and the work. The image of the work as the expression of the writing subject also contributed to a heightened cultural fascination with authors, and the popularity of writers and artists 'as heroes'. Folkenflik neatly summarises the way in which authorship changed during the romantic period:

> I can best mark the shift which came about by observing that in the Renaissance Tasso wrote *Gerusalemme Liberata* and Milton wrote *Paradise Lost*; but in the late eighteenth century and the early nineteenth, Goethe wrote *Torquato Tasso* and Blake wrote *Milton*.[12]

Interest swings away from explanations of 'the ways of God to men' – towards the ways of authors.

As the author became a more popular subject for literature, the importance of the author's life and personality to their work was also increasingly asserted by romantic critics. In his classic 1953 study of romantic theory, *The Mirror and the Lamp*, M. H. Abrams details the complex theoretical manoeuvres which transformed the way we read literature. The change was dramatic: from a pre-romantic approach, in which an author's personality was of no interest, to the enduring appeal of the romantic attitude. Abrams' 'romantic extremist' believed that 'the proper key' could 'penetrate to the reality behind the appearance', not only to understand a text better but to 'come to know an author more intimately than his own friends and family; more intimately, even, than the author, lacking this key, could possibly have known himself'.[13] The evolution of this critical attitude stems, in some histories, from a disagreement between the Friedrichs Schiller and Schlegel, over their seemingly intrinsically incompatible deifying readings of Shakespeare. Schiller sees the poet nowhere in the work: 'Like the Deity behind this universe, he stands behind his work;

he is himself the work, and the work is himself.' The author, in Abrams's summation, 'like God, is not visible in his work'. Schlegel, however, reads *Hamlet* and insists that 'the spirit of its author is at its most visible'. 'It has often been remarked', he claims, 'that the original impress of his individual manner is unmistakable and inimitable' (Abrams, 238–9).[14] Schlegel finds a solution, resolving these opposing readings within an argument relying on a comparison between the author and the divine creator – that would prove persuasive. He imports readings of Paul's Epistle to the Romans, 1.20, into literary criticism: 'For the invisible things of him from the creation of the world are clearly seen, being understood by the things that are made, even His eternal power and Godhead.' Schlegel renews 'the Renaissance metaphor of the poet as creator, with its implicit analogy between God's creation of the world and the artist's making of a poem', as a method for literary analysis. This analogy then allows literature to be seen as, in Abrams's words, 'a disguised projection of its author' (Abrams, 239–40).[15] Reading Giovanni Boccaccio, Schlegel can now find that 'everywhere the feeling of the author – even the innermost depths of his most intimate individuality – gleams through, visibly invisible' (241).[16]

An increasingly enthusiastic critical focus on the individual personality of the author developed, based on a paradoxical defence in which being unable to see the author in the work proves the author is everywhere within it. And similar approaches grew elsewhere. In England, John Keble 'independently' reached the same position as Schlegel; Abrams even credits Keble as 'the founding father' of a system of criticism in which literature is treated as veiled autobiography (257 and 261). Oddities of this foundational period of author-centric critical methods include similarities between a critic and their topic: between a critic's Milton and that critic himself, or between Keble's Homer, Keble's Walter Scott, and Keble (Abrams, 248–61). Thomas Carlyle's collection of lectures *On Heroes* neatly betrays the habits of the age: alongside work on the heroic in mythology, religion, and history, two lectures address 'The Hero as Poet' and 'The Hero as Man of Letters'. His method, Folkenflik fumes, 'with its facile shifts from factual to fictive worlds, is subject to some of the worst excesses of nineteenth-century biographical criticism'.[17]

The afterlife of these romantic methods is complicated by Gustave Flaubert's use of the 'visibly invisible' author-god doctrine to defend authorial impersonality, and the ways in which modernism picked up such ideas. 'The author in his work', Flaubert writes in a much-referenced 1852 letter, 'ought to be like God in the universe, present everywhere, and visible nowhere'. Detailing this, he continues: 'Since art is a second nature, the creator of this nature ought to act in analogous ways, so that one may feel in all its atoms, and in every aspect, a hidden, infinite impassibleness.'[18] Stephen Dedalus's rehashed Flaubertian fingernail-paring artist and T. S. Eliot's 'Impersonal theory of poetry', where poetry is 'an escape from emotion; [. . .] an escape from personality', have served as totemic models of modernist impersonality as a reaction against the excesses of romanticism.[19] Impersonal re-framings of the author do not, however, remove or reduce the author's importance. The Flaubertian and Dedalean authors are still very much 'like God'. Eliot's proposed authorial disappearance is only made possible by an author's maturity, or even exceptionalism.[20] Furthermore, as Loren Glass has argued, the well-developed public personas of modernist authors somewhat undermine their statements of impersonality.[21] The image of the romantic, solitary, original genius lingers even now in popular culture, and – to a certain extent – persists in literary criticism. This image infers a fundamental connection between the author and the work, encouraging a view of literature as the expression of an individual whose life and personality are thus of high relevance to critic or reader.

The relationship between author and work is also enshrined in law: the concepts of intellectual property and copyright ensure that, for a certain length of time, the author and their heirs own the work. These modes of ownership also have origins in romanticism and its intellectual context. The ideas of originality and genius expressed by Shelley in 1821 appear earlier in Edward Young's 'Conjectures on Original Composition', in terms of property. In her landmark work on the topic, Woodmansee examines how Young's 1759 letter promotes an originality inextricably linked to a poet's genius, and made possible through ownership. The author's 'works will stand distinguished; his the sole property of them; which property alone can confer the novel title of author', Young writes. Ownership makes 'author'; originality permits ownership.[22] And 'owning' one's work facilitates writing as a viable profession, free from patronage. As Carolyn Guertin and Paul K. Saint-Amour have also proposed, the formation of intellectual property law not only solidified romantic attitudes to authorship, but contributed to them. Saint-Amour picks at a myth within copyright, in which authors 'win the laurel of intellectual property through the creation of *original expression*'. In practice, copyright does not live up to such standards: 'originality' in legal terms is of a far lower standard than that held by the romantics.[23] From the twentieth century onwards, furthermore, laws have been adjusted to promote the interests of corporations rather than authors.[24] Saint-Amour believes copyright does far more than reimburse labour: 'instead, it has been enlisted in the projection and consecration of a model of the self as original genius'.[25] Copyright made authors the legal owners of their work. This contributed fundamentally to the shifts towards independence I've outlined above, but also emphasised literature as something to be owned and therefore fiscally valued. Authorship and literature are thus absorbed within the systems of capitalism, an individualist creation of a product, a commodity with a value determined by market demand and competition.

The enduringly romantic author finds inspiration within, and thus the personality, opinions, and life of the author can explain the work. This literary work is legally tied to the author's life – the copyright terms of the European Union and the US, for example, extend seventy years past the author's death – and the ownership of the work by the author and heirs continues to reassert the notion that works of literature are the individual expression of original genius. It is against this romantic and capitalist model of authorship that Roland Barthes explicitly positions 'The Death of the Author' in 1967: responding to 'the epitome and culmination of capitalist ideology, which has attached the greatest importance to the "person" of the author'. 'The *author*', he continues, 'still reigns in histories of literature, biographies of writers, interviews, magazines':

> The image of literature to be found in ordinary culture is tyrannically centred on the author, his person, his life, his tastes, his passions [. . .] The *explanation* of a work is always sought in the man or woman who produced it, as if it were always in the end, through the more or less transparent allegory of the fiction, the voice of a single person, the *author* 'confiding' in us. (143)

Barthes pinpoints the connection between 'capitalist ideology' and the activity of seeking explanations from the author: between capitalist authorship as ownership, and broadly defined romantic attitudes. He responds with his own history of anti-authorialism, a move against authority and the establishment resonating with the iconoclasm of May 1968.

Barthes's history places Stéphane Mallarmé's writing at the root of the author's death, investing great significance in Mallarmé's 'Crisis in Verse':

> The pure work implies the disappearance of the poet-speaker who yields the initiative to words animated by the inequality revealed in their collision with one another; they illuminate one another and pass like a trail of fire over previous stones, replacing the audible breathing of earlier lyrical verse or the exalted personality which directed the phrase.[26]

The 'poet-speaker' has disappeared, not remaining 'visibly invisible', or 'present everywhere, and visible nowhere' – but yielding, replaced by language. The speaker's voice and control are emptied out of the text, 'to reach that point', Barthes reads, 'where only language exists, "performs", and not "me"'. Mallarmé's entire poetics consists in supressing the author in the interests of writing' ('Author', 143). What begins with Mallarmé – that 'it is language which speaks, not the author', that attempts must be made to disrupt the relationship between the author and the text – Barthes tracks through Valéry, Proust, the Surrealists, and 'recently' linguistics (143–5). This sequence has in turn been pulled apart with some fervour. In *The Death and Return of the Author*, for example, Seán Burke labels it 'palpably false', taking particular umbrage with the placement of Mallarmé as both '*author* [. . .] of the author's disappearance', and a 'shield' for 'a more difficult and serpentine history'. Burke declares the death of the author to be one result of a clash within French academia, between structuralism's prioritisation of language and the subjectivity privileged by phenomenology.[27] Barthes's history locates the death of the author within the developments of literature, while Burke's alternative is firmly embedded in the academy.

THE AUTHOR IS DEAD!

The author was rephrased, removed, or put to one side in a variety of approaches that emerged from Europe in the 1960s and 1970s – which were, with mixed results, picked up by the Anglo-American academy. In the theorisation of intertextuality, the formation of deconstruction, and the work grouped together as reader response criticism, emphasis shifted broadly away from the author and towards the reader and the reader's activity. Julia Kristeva's 1966 analysis of Mikhail Bakhtin, 'Word, Dialogue, and Novel', is an important prefiguration of elements of Barthes's work. Kristevan intertextuality describes a textual system; she examines how 'each word (text) is an intersection of words (texts) where at least one other word (text) can be read', and argues that 'any text is constructed as a mosaic of quotations; any text is the absorption and transformation of another'. Kristeva's work is not as caustically focused on the author as Barthes's, though 'The writer', she suggests, 'becomes an anonymity, an absence, a blank space'.[28] That same year, Jacques Derrida gave his lecture 'Structure, Sign, and Play in the Discourse of the Human Sciences', at Johns Hopkins – a vital step in the development and reception of deconstruction. In 'Signature, Event, Context', Derrida progresses the de-centring described in that early lecture, pronouncing 'To write is to produce a mark that will constitute a sort of machine which is productive in turn, and which my future disappearance will not, in principle, hinder in its functioning.' Writing, he continues, is 'an iterative structure, cut off from all absolute responsibility, from *consciousness* as the ultimate authority, orphaned and separated at birth from the assistance of its father'.[29] In its privileging of language and text, deconstruction has been characterised as anti-authorial. Varying readings of Derrida's famous statement '*il n'y a pas de hors-texte*' contribute to this: 'there is nothing outside the text' has been a common translation, corrected by Chris Baldick as closer to 'language cannot take us outside itself'.[30]

In the next decade a variety of critical approaches developed and were subsumed under the labels 'reader response criticism' and 'reader response theory'. Work by Louise Rosenblatt, David Bleich, Stanley Fish, and Wolfgang Iser focused on the active reader and their role in the text, foregrounding effect: 'what literature *does* and not what it *means*'.[31] The involved and imaginative reader in reader response criticism does not, however, rely upon or cause the absence of the author: Iser, for example, describes 'two poles' in a literary work that relate to the author and reader, and are both of 'vital importance'.[32] Though it is now rarely referred to or used as a specific approach to literature, elements of reader response criticism have been absorbed by the academy.[33] Reader response criticism does not devalue the author: the author is put to one side, the question of their authority left unasked.

From the wealth of theory and criticism characterised as turning away from the author, the subject, the centre, essays by Barthes and Michel Foucault stand out for their direct engagement with the specific question of the author. Foucault's *'Qu'est-ce qu'un auteur?'*, 'What is an Author?', delivered as a lecture and published in 1969, is known best for its concept of the 'author-function'. It's a wildly different piece of writing from Barthes's 'The Death of the Author': most pertinently, in Foucault's discussions the reader is almost entirely absent. What marks Barthes's work apart from that of Foucault and others at this time is the way in which he explicitly phrases his prioritisation of the reader as being utterly reliant on a movement away from the author, and enabled by the qualities of text itself. It is for this reason, this portrayal of author, reader, text, that I focus so heavily on Barthes's anti-authorialism in this book – and why I will consider his essays in such detail here. I will then return briefly to Foucault, before considering the reception of anti-authorialism in the next section. In my readings below I will revivify discussions of Barthes's 'The Death of the Author', responding to critics who find its style and arguments reductive or contradictorily authoritative. Closely examining the style and form of 'The Death of the Author' along with 'From Work to Text' and *S/Z*, I will show how Barthes's theory of text deserves further attention – and set up this book's discussions of its relevance to reading Joyce.

'The Death of the Author' was published first in an English translation by Richard Howard in 1967 in the multimedia magazine *Aspen*, and then in French as 'La mort d'auteur' the following year in *Manteia*.[34] It followed Barthes's earlier work *Le degré zéro de l'écriture* and *Mythologies*, published in 1953 and 1957. It is a provocative, ambiguous essay, developing Mallarmé's prioritising of language over author in order to argue that 'writing is the destruction of every voice, of every point of origin' ('Author', 142). It is often paraphrased with its famous and final point – that 'the birth of the reader must be at the cost of the death of the author' (148)[35] – but doing so not only overlooks the complex rhetoric and style of the essay, but also the equivocation throughout. Whether the death of the author has occurred, is occurring, or must occur is unclear; it appears to have never been alive within a text, but is still to experience a cultural death. The vague figure of 'the modern scriptor' is outlined as an alternative to the author: where the author precedes a text, the scriptor is 'born' with it and 'traces a field without origin – or which, at least, has no other origin than language itself, language which ceaselessly calls into question all origins'

(145–6). However, the 'scriptor' is undeveloped, near-abandoned in the essay, as Barthes moves on to make his central claims on the interconnection between author, text, and critic:

> To give a text an Author is to impose a limit on that text, to furnish it with a final signified, to close the writing. Such a conception suits criticism very well, the latter then allotting itself the important task of discovering the Author (or its hypostases: society, history, psyché, liberty) beneath the work: when the Author has been found, the text is 'explained' – victory to the critic. Hence there is no surprise in the fact that, historically, the reign of the author has also been that of the Critic . . . (147)

The author is asserted above as the creation of criticism, even as a tool for the critic: it is the critic and the act of criticism that benefits from the 'conception' of the Author. Furthermore, the idea of tyranny lingers in the power-inflected concepts of 'victory' and 'reign'; here a tyrannical authority held by the author and absent with the scriptor.

Though this authorial authority is identified earlier in the essay as something functioning in a wider sense of 'ordinary culture', it becomes now situated with the critic and the critic's author; shifting from a cultural interest in authors phrased in doomsday terms to a more serious analysis of the author as a structural aspect of literary criticism. Barthes continues:

> In the multiplicity of writing, everything is to be *disentangled*, nothing *deciphered*; the structure can be followed, 'run' (like the thread of a stocking) at every point and at every level, but there is nothing beneath: the space of writing is to be ranged over, not pierced; writing ceaselessly posits meaning ceaselessly to evaporate it, carrying out a systematic exemption of meaning. (147)

Deciphering, piercing; disentangling, running. Barthes begins to establish what activities should and should not respond to writing, developing his position in opposition to a certain kind of critical activity:

> In precisely this way literature (it would be better from now on to say *writing*), by refusing to assign a 'secret', an ultimate meaning, to the text (and to the world as text), liberates what may be called an anti-theological activity, an activity that is truly revolutionary since to refuse to fix meaning is, in the end, to refuse God and his hypostases – reason, science, law. (147)

The author becomes something used by the critic to exert authority, to promulgate a myth of 'ultimate meaning' that critics have claimed to mine from the depths of a text. For Barthes this is at odds with the nature of text: as language resists fixed meanings and 'question[s] all origins', there is no ultimate meaning, final signified, or authorial explanation.

The style of 'The Death of the Author' is as provocative and demanding as its central concept. Peggy Kamuf observes Barthes's 'polemical style, favouring reductive summary and rapid judgements to any more patient procedure', but allows that this positioning is perhaps the necessary tactic of 'a spokesman representing to a broader readership'.[36] In *The Death and Return of the Author* Burke snipes instead that 'What is presented is not offered as though it were open to question' – critique he extends to 'modern anti-authorialism' as a whole – and reads Barthes's references to prior authors as a reliance on authorial authority that undermines the essay (16). Susan Sontag responds to Barthes's style across his work, suggesting it might be productively contextualised: 'Intellectual terrorism', she argues, 'is a central, respectable form of intellectual practice in France – tolerated, humoured, rewarded'. The contradictory authority with which Barthes expresses his arguments against authority could fall in amongst Sontag's listing of 'ruthless assertion and shameless ideological about-faces; the mandate of incessant judgement, opinion, anathematizing, overpraising; the taste for extreme positions, then casually reversed, and for deliberate provocation' as examples of the forms of discourse in which Barthes's own sits comfortably and charmingly.[37] Though she does not refer explicitly to 'The Death of the Author' or even Barthes's later contradiction of its arguments, Sontag's defence does outline a stylistic lineage in which to potentially place Barthes's inflexible didacticism. If we do look specifically at the style and structure of 'The Death of the Author', moreover, we can further unsettle accusations of 'ruthless assertion' or invocations of authority within Barthes's forms of phrasing. To do so, we need to consider the essay's structure in terms of Barthes's concept of text.

Without an author, a text is limitless: devoid of a 'final signified'. Multiplicity is inferred in the preferred activity of disentangling over deciphering, and made explicit where Barthes connects his positioning to literary relations and intertextuality. Notions of an active reader and open-ended text form the most substantial argument of 'The Death of the Author':

> We know now that a text is not a line of words releasing a single 'theological' meaning (the 'message' of the Author-God) but a multi-dimensional space in which a variety of writings, none of them original, blend and clash. ('Author', 146)

The text becomes not only open-ended, but of open, multiple, and far-reaching origins:

> The text is a tissue of quotations drawn from the innumerable centres of culture [. . .] the writer can only imitate a gesture that is always anterior,

> never original. His only power is to mix writings, to counter the ones with the others, in such a way as to never rest on any one of them. (146)

The characteristics of text reduce the status, the 'power' of the author. 'The Death of the Author' opens with a sentence from Balzac's *Sarrasine*; Barthes now returns to reread it anew, and determines a definition of writing, of the text, in terms of the reader:

> Thus is revealed the total existence of writing: a text is made of multiple writings, drawn from many cultures and entering into mutual relations of dialogue, parody, contestation, but there is one place where this multiplicity is focused and that place is the reader, not, as was hitherto said, the author. (148)

The reader is the counterpoint to the text, not the author. Barthes's essay continues, with a particularly ambiguous application of the impersonal to the reader:

> The reader is the space on which all the quotations that make up a writing are inscribed without any of them being lost; a text's unity lies not in its origin but in its destination. Yet this destination cannot any longer be personal: the reader is without history, biography, psychology; he is simply that *someone* who holds together in a single field all the traces by which the written text is constituted. (148)

The impersonal reader is not developed further, a little like the 'modern scriptor'. Despite this vague element, it is clear that the relationship between reader and text takes precedence, and crucially – if paradoxically – both relies on and affirms the absence of the author.

Barthes elaborates the theory of text, of a text's relation to other texts and to both author and reader, in *S/Z*, his 1970 study of *Sarrasine*. The text – 'a tissue' in 'The Death of the Author' – becomes in *S/Z* 'like a piece of Valenciennes lace' and 'a braid (*text, fabric, braid*: the same thing)' of voices or codes (160). When Barthes published 'The Death of the Author' he was at an early stage of writing *S/Z*, best known for the delineation of 'writerly' and 'readerly' texts – a division closely linked to the concept of active reading. In *S/Z*, the 'writerly' text is preferred as it 'make[s] the reader no longer a consumer, but a producer of text', while the 'readerly' text leaves the reader idle, 'intransitive' (4). 'Writerly' texts maintain 'the plurality of entrances, the opening of networks, the infinity of languages', and are '*ourselves writing*' (5). Barthes defines an 'ideal text', the ultimate 'writerly' text: 'a galaxy of signifiers, not a structure of signifieds; it has no beginning; it is reversible; we gain access to it by several entrances, none of which can be authoritatively declared to be the main one'. He continues, arguing that 'systems of meaning can take over this absolutely plural text, but their number is never closed, based as it is on the infinity of language' (5–6). 'Writing Reading', an essay Barthes published the same year as *S/Z*, defends the elaborate dissection of *Sarrasine* by naming it a description of reading: an analysis of text is thus an analysis of reading, and the reader firmly established as a necessary part of the text.

The theory of text develops even further, and with particular fine detail, in Barthes's 1971 essay 'De l'oeuvre au texte', 'From Work to Text', published in *Revue d'esthétique*. Defining 'the Text' as 'a methodological field', and in opposition to the 'work', Barthes describes how while 'the work can be seen (in bookshops, in catalogues, in exam syllabuses), the text is a process of demonstration, speaks according to certain rules (or against certain rules); the work can be held in the hand, the text is held in language' (157). In agreement with Kristevan intertextuality, for Barthes 'The Text is plural.' And in accordance with what began in 'The Death of the Author', he details this multiplicity: 'Which is not simply to say that it has several meanings, but that it accomplishes the very plural of meaning: an *irreducible* (and not merely acceptable) plural' ('Text', 159). Barthes develops what this means in terms of what can be done with a text, and affirms again the aptness of the word 'text' to contain these qualities:

> The Text is not a co-existence of meanings but a passage, an overcrossing; thus it answers not to an interpretation, even a liberal one, but to an explosion, a dissemination. The plural of the Text depends, that is, not on the ambiguity of its contents but on what might be called the *stereographic plurality* of its weave of signifiers (etymologically, the text is a tissue, a woven fabric). (159)

Such woven pluralities are constant in text, which is and has always been 'woven entirely with citations, references, echoes, cultural languages (what language is not?), antecedent or contemporary, which cut across it through and through in a vast stereophony'. Barthes clarifies that the intertextual that allows for this 'is not to be confused with some origin of the text' – crucially, 'to try and find the "sources", the "influence" of a work, is to fall in with the myth of filiation; the citations which go to make up a text are anonymous, untraceable, and yet *already read*: they are quotations without inverted commas'. 'Filiation', he makes clear, is a process that only functions in 'the work' (160). The text, instead, 'reads without the inscription of the Father' (161): the intertextuality of all texts is inextricably linked to the impossibility of fixing origins or processes of attribution.

'From Work to Text' and 'The Death of the Author' come together as Barthes explains that the images or metaphors for work and text are *'organism'* and '*network*' respectively, and that therefore 'no vital "respect" is due to the Text: it can be *broken*'. The text, he continues, 'can be read without the guarantee of its father' ('Text', 161). Another substitute for the author emerges at this point in the essay, as Barthes allows that while an author might return in the text, 'he does so as a "guest"':

> If he is a novelist, he is inscribed in the novel like one of his characters, figured in the carpet; no longer privileged, paternal, aletheological, his inscription is ludic. He becomes, as it were, a paper-author: his life is no longer the origin of his fictions but a fiction contributing to his work . . . (161)

The reader is again the figure of importance: the text 'asks of the reader a practical collaboration' (163). As in 'The Death of the Author', in 'From Work to Text' the plurality of text is focused on reception not origin; the fundamental relationship is that of active reader with text. Where the work is 'the object of a consumption', the text 'decants the work (the work permitting) from its consumption and gathers it up as play, activity, production, practice'. Barthes demands that writing and reading are joined 'in a single signifying practice' by the text ('Text', 161–2). This refers perhaps again to the 'capitalist ideology' the author's death undermines: the text disrupts the process of consumption and disposal implied in the work, and is thus removed from the capitalist systems of the literary marketplace. Stating finally that 'The theory of the Text can coincide only with a practice of writing' (164), Barthes insists that the text relies upon the activeness of the reader, the reader playing, no longer a passive consumer but a part of the production. Significantly, unlike the labels 'readerly' and 'writerly' which seem to apply to different kinds of writing, here the work can be treated as text: can become text through the reader's play. Reading and writing are united 'in a single signifying practice', which further attests to the absence of authority in the author or 'father'. It is the active reader and the intertextual text that defies this authority.

So, let's return to the provocatively dogmatic positioning and style of 'The Death of the Author'. Does it express authority, stake its claims as closed to questioning, reduce its arguments to summary? Do references to Mallarmé et al. form a contradictory invocation of authorial authority, filiation, influence? Fractured paragraphs, loose ends, briefly put bold statements, and swiftly made citations can be read, instead, as a formal echo of the essay's content – contributing to its overall efforts. Michael Moriarty defends 'The Death of the Author' along similar lines, suggesting that through citation it does not rely on the authority of named authors, but rather embodies the concept of the text as a tissue of quotations. He identifies Barthes's uses of spiral and fragment: the spiral 'returns to its point of departure, but at a higher level, producing hitherto absent meanings from the same words, and thus manifesting the inexhaustibility of discourse', while the fragment 'prevents the discourse cohering into the continuous utterance of a single subject: it de-authorizes discourse'. The writer of 'The Death of the Author' 'simply brings forth words from the great dictionary of culture' and these words 'simply refer interminably to other words'.[38] The style of Barthes's essay works to underscore its message, rather than close that message to investigation.

In 'The Death of the Author' and 'From Work to Text' the reader and their reading are free and unconstrained, responding to an infinite text. The essays combined define the author as a closure of signification. What *else* the author is, is explored in Foucault's lengthy 1969 essay 'What is an Author?'. Though implicitly phrased as a response to declarations of the 'event' of the 'disappearance or death of the author', Foucault names Barthes only for his notion of *écriture* in *Writing Degree Zero*.[39] The context of the essay is stated as one in which the author has already disappeared, but as 'The Death of the Author' is not directly cited we must presume this is something that has occurred beyond the confines of Barthes's tract – yet the title asks what an author 'is', in the present tense, implying the author exists. Was the death of the author an immediate effect of Barthes's essay (published so shortly before Foucault's), or had it occurred already? 'What is an Author?' has none of the determined demands for authorial demise that we find in Barthes: though Foucault refers to 'the empty space left by the author's disappearance', he also does not want 'the subject' to be 'totally abandoned', yet intriguingly suggests 'We can easily imagine a culture where discourse would circulate without any need for an author' ('What is an Author?', 121, 137, and 138).

Foucault's focus is 'the singular relationship that holds between an author and text' (115). The reader is notably absent from his essay, and the author or writer is again the central figure (despite their death or departure). He details the author 'as a privileged moment of individualization', yet 'set[s] aside a sociohistorical analysis of the author', such as:

> how the author was individualized in a culture such as ours; the status we have given the author, for instance, when we began our research into authenticity and attribution; the systems of valorization in which he was included; or the moment when the stories of heroes gave way to an author's biography; the conditions that fostered the formulation of the fundamental critical category of 'the man and his work'. (115)

Woodmansee, Folkenflik, McKeon, and Saint-Amour's work elaborates aspects of this itemised chronology of status and conditions, and responds to the complementary ideas of Walter Benjamin's 1934 essay 'The Author as Producer'. 'Before I ask', Benjamin queries, 'what is a work's production *vis à vis* the production relations of its time, I should like to ask: what is its position *within* them?'[40] Foucault's essay is informed by the process and context of individualisation he refers to, though it was left to these more recent critics to pick up and detail that process. 'What is an Author?' is concerned instead with the author as a function, first finding that the name of an author is 'unlike a proper name' but a referent 'to the existence of certain groups of discourse and [. . .] to the status of this discourse within a society and culture' – before establishing that 'the function of an author is to characterize the existence, circulation, and operation of certain discourses in society' ('What is an Author?', 121–4). Foucault summarises how the 'author-function' operates within 'legal and institutional systems', its changeability across cultures, and the 'series of precise and complex procedures' that connect writings to writers (130–1). The author is again characterised as dependant on a mode of criticism or response:

> these aspects of an individual, which we designate as an author (or which comprise an individual as an author), are projections, in terms always more or less psychological, of our way of handling texts: in the comparisons we make, the traits we extract as pertinent, the continuities we assign, or the exclusions we practice. (127)

Here the definition, or use, of the author in the text is described in terms of 'explaining', echoing Barthes but stopping short of claiming the author places a limit on the text or reading.

The broad shift in focus towards the reader that emerged in the mid-twentieth century was phrased explicitly by Barthes as being reliant on movements away from the author – and as enabled by the qualities of text. In the decades since, and in the reception of anti-authorialism, the concept of the death of the author becomes a significant issue. The triad of author, reader, text that Barthes identifies fell out of focus, but it remains valuable. The project of *The Reader's Joyce* is to examine the activity of reading *Ulysses* in terms of how it engenders a reassessment of this triad – and I will treat *Ulysses*, accordingly, as a text that repeatedly unsettles its own relationships to the author and the reader. In the next section I will examine how the relationships between the reader's practice, intertextuality, and the death of the author were rethought and lost sight of: how elements were absorbed, while others were discarded. Aspects of this will recur in my analysis of Joycean criticism, and will be challenged by my readings of *Ulysses*.

Long Live the Author!

Across the 1980s and 1990s, the texts and impact of a homogenised death of the author were reassessed, most effectively in terms of ethical and political objections to removing the author from critical consideration. It is important to note however, before looking at this reception, that the author-centric version of 'ordinary culture' and literary criticism that Barthes presents in 'The Death of the Author' was not a completely accurate picture of the late 1960s, nor was the author everywhere considered 'privileged, paternal, aletheological'. The developments I examined in the previous section were not the first in European or Anglo-American academia to attempt a movement of emphasis away from the author: New Criticism, Russian Formalism, and Prague Structuralism also sought, to varying degrees, a displacement of the author. Barthes represents a culture 'tyrannically centred on the author', a misleading position Burke reads as an attempt to add 'a greater urgency' to 'The Death of the Author' (*The Death and Return of the Author*, 25). New Criticism and its attendant anti-intentionalism was well-established in North American literary studies by the 1960s. In their flagship 1946 essay 'The Intentional Fallacy', W. K. Wimsatt and Monroe C. Beardsley set the course for a generation of New Critics with an attitude which does not look to the author for interpretation or explanation: demanding 'Critical inquiries are not settled by consulting the oracle', and that the author's intention is 'neither available nor desirable'.[41] The author, however, is ignored rather than removed in New Criticism – and the reader's responses and activity are of little interest.

In his work on the reception of the death of the author, Burke argues that the context of New Criticism and its attendant version of anti-authorialism in the American academy was key to the way in which the tenets of poststructuralism were adopted. He describes the attendees of the 1966 Johns Hopkins symposium, 'The Languages of Criticism and the Sciences of Man', with faintly patronising hindsight: these critics were 'completely ill equipped' for Derrida and the other radical participants. With little knowledge of phenomenology and less of structuralism, they were faced with methodologies which sought to move past both (175). Burke details the reversals of younger phenomenology-aligned critics and the similarities of 'new' approaches to the old New Criticism, claiming that 'Fragments of a specifically directed, rigorous, and highly technical critique have been put to the service of a freeplaying literary criticism eager to sideline the question of the author rather than to debate and contest the issues it raises' (177). What this forms is a crucial aspect of Burke's own critical position in 1992, the year he published *The Death and Return of the Author*: he complains that critics behave as if Derrida, Barthes, and Foucault have '*achieved*' the author's death, that 'the texts of the death of the author remain closed to investigation, revision or critique', that 'the author-question has largely been lost' (179 and 17).

Burke is guilty of just what he derides Barthes for: adding urgency to his approach by offering an inaccurate picture of the critical or cultural scene. *The Death and Return of the Author*, a classic study that is now in its third edition, was not an outlier in 1992. It was rather evidence of an increased engagement with the question of the author across the 1980s and 1990s – and an increased, often concomitant rejection of anti-authorialism (even earlier, critics such as E. D. Hirsch and Wayne C. Booth sought to reinstate the author, or an idea of the author, in the 1960s).[42] Kamuf's *Signature Pieces: On the Institution of Authorship*, for example, gathered together several of her essays in 1988; in far-reaching work on authorship, gender, and signature, she engages directly with many of the texts of Burke's study. Jack Stillinger's *Multiple Authorship and the Myth of Solitary Genius* approached the question of plural, editorial authorship in 1991, and Michael Moriarty's study *Roland Barthes* was published that same year. Moriarty is a rare voice in unqualified support of Barthes at this time, warning that 'The Death of the Author' is 'one of his easiest pieces to misread', while noting 'the eclipse of the author in Barthes' work is merely temporary'.[43] Academic interest in authorship also played out across journal articles and chapters through the 1980s and early 1990s: in, to give only a handful of examples, work I've discussed by Woodmansee, Folkenflik, and McKeon; Alexander Nehamas's extended work on 'the postulated author' in 1981 and 1986 articles, in which he argues that 'No reading can fail to generate an author'; and Colin McCabe's historicising 1991 chapter 'The Revenge of the Author'.[44] McCabe links the death of the author to modernism; a strategy not unrelated to Burke's reading of the similarities between New Critical and Barthes-influenced removals of the author (given the strong links typically seen between New Criticism and the modernist ideas of writers such as Eliot).[45] To challenge the death of the author, McCabe relies on relationships between modernism, Barthes, and poststructuralism more generally that were promoted by writers like Peter Ackroyd. Ackroyd's highly enthusiastic 1976 study *Notes for a New Culture* helped to introduce poststructuralist ideas to UK academia, as did MacCabe's own late 1970s writings.[46] Ackroyd cites Barthes's prioritisation of language to argue that 'borrowing from the modernist tradition is very much in evidence'; MacCabe also finds 'borrowing', but relates this with negative inflection to Barthes's 'classless, genderless, completely indeterminate reader'.[47]

Burke's *The Death and Return* is therefore more a general trend writ large, rather than the first reopening of a closed discussion. The majority of those writers who engaged critically with anti-authorial theory from the 1980s onwards tended to do so in order to resist the death of the author – and Burke's overriding aim is similarly to reveal the author's death as inherently unsound. His study is heavily invested in theory and philosophy rather than literature, from his opening prologue on Paul de Man to his concern that arguments against the death of the author have been – and will become again – arguments against theory itself. Burke argues that the de Man revelations – that he had written for a collaborationist newspaper in Nazi-occupied Belgium between 1940 and 1942 – shed new light on his later, influential anti-biographical and anti-authorial stances. The resultant scandal and reception show, Burke continues, 'how the principle of the author most powerfully reasserts itself when it is thought absent' – a summary of the focus of *The Death and Return* as a whole (8). Burke locates the return of the author in the work and reception of Barthes, Foucault, and Derrida, seeking to undermine the efforts of anti-authorialism and correct what he sees as misreadings. Barthes, he claims, has been misunderstood; he actually sought 'the closure of representation', not the death of the author (41–6).

The main thrust of an overwhelming majority of work within literary studies since the 1980s and 1990s has returned to the author, or declared the author suffered no 'death' in the first place. Theorists and practitioners of historicist, political, or identity-related approaches to literature tend towards systems of analysis in which the connection between author and text is vital. Context-rich critical methodologies now dominate the field of literary studies, and as the context of the author is given importance so too, sometimes, are an author's life, personality, and opinions on their own texts. In some areas, it has been of real political importance to return to a position where the author is part of literary analysis: feminist literary theory and criticism, for example, has moved through several critical shifts regarding the author question. Early anti-authorial poststructuralist roots, with concomitant claims that the author as a concept is embroiled within the patriarchy (and therefore a death of the author is required),[48] clashed with a necessary focus on the author, origins, the processes of writing, and the context of that writing. Nancy K. Miller's direct 1986 reappraisal of the Barthesian death of the author, building on her germane observation that 'women have not had the same historical relation of identity to origin, institution, production that men have had', reworks the metaphors of web, textile, lace that have been used by poststructuralist and deconstructive critics: 'the question of identity' is closed, she argues, in theories that prefer the web to the spider, the lace to the lacemaker.[49] She proposes, instead, an 'arachnology', in which we should 'put one's finger – figuratively – on the place of production that marks the spinner's attachment to her web'.[50] Miller's arguments underpinned Susan Stanford Friedman's work on intertextuality five years later; Friedman observes that the author has already returned in the way Barthesian and Kristevan intertextuality has been altered within critical usage, and that Miller's emphasis on the connection of spinner to web should be adopted beyond the field of feminist literary criticism.[51] A little more recently, Rita Felski has tried to temper this strong feminist shift towards the figure of the author by suggesting that authorship is only 'one strand in the weave of the text rather than a magic key to unlocking its mysteries'.[52] But how possible is it to maintain such a middle ground in critical practice, and what allows for such balance?

Direct critical engagement with the death of the author over the last twenty years has been limited, with particular exceptions in the field of celebrity studies.

Loren Glass's and Aaron Jaffe's 2004 and 2005 studies of modern authorial self-fashioning focus on conscious constructions of self by authors as celebrities. The author returns again: not explicitly in terms of biographical positivism nor as a means to close the interpretations of literary texts, but in the unequivocal promotion of the idea that what an author 'is' can be controlled, or authorised, by the author. It is telling that in this most recent sustained work on literary authorship, the most valid opinions on the topic are apparently those of literary authors. Other work on the author question, let alone the Barthesian death of the author, has been rare: beyond contained interventions in a handful of disparate studies dotted across queer theory, intention, digital media, and fan fiction, the field of literary studies has consigned to history Barthes's analysis of author, reader, and text.[53] In her 2020 work *Hooked: Art and Attachment*, Felski very briefly suggests the loose concept of an 'author-text' as what 'critics care about'. The 'author-text' is a 'composite' of life and text: admired style, biographical details, bits of interviews, and even, with living authors, 'a fleeting exchange of looks at a bookstore signing'.[54] It's a perceptive, pragmatic description of what leads critics to keep working on, or in Felski's terms, to be attached to certain authors. It does not, however, examine the broader cultural and academic urge towards authors – nor consider how this 'author-text' functions within, contributes to, or is itself influenced by criticism.

The author retains a position of authority in literary criticism, the academy, and culture. I'm not the first to point out that we continue to arrange research specialisms, conferences, academic studies, societies, and online groups around the author; we give the author space in magazines, documentaries, interviews, biographies, and at 'in conversation with' events. I enjoy Stephen Donovan, Danuta Fjellestad, and Rolf Lundén's incredibly careful description of the author today, who 'continues to thrive with undiminished if not unchallenged power'.[55] The challenges are not to be denied, but what effect have they had? Academia continues to use the names of theorists as shorthand for entire, complex critical approaches and the associated authority of such approaches. An author's notes and drafts are highly valued in the academy – these written records of authorial thought processes provide the heavy lifting of many influential works of literary criticism in recent years. Literary authors' opinions are sought by the media on any number of topics, and particularly on their own work.

Though still predominantly unacknowledged, the popular view that the author to some extent owns meaning does persist within and without literary studies. Jeremy Hawthorn has plucked a cursed example from Woody Allen's 1977 film *Annie Hall* to illustrate this presumed ownership: a scene in which Allen's comedian character is stuck in a cinema queue near some man loudly interpreting several films, pieces of literature (including Joyce, natch), and works by Marshall McLuhan. Allen disagrees with the interpreter, and in a daydream-esque sequence he summons McLuhan – the real McLuhan, in person – to correct and silence him.[56] Hawthorn's reading does not go far enough, however. This scene also describes our compulsion towards the author, as Allen explicitly portrays the wish fulfilment of having the author explain the text to us in real time. Apparently, the right interpretation is the author's, and thus the critic/reader who follows the author is correct. There are right and wrong interpretations. All this raises particular problems, relevant to my own discomfort in referencing Allen here at all. The comedy of the scene rests on Allen's character's neuroticism, his inability to ignore a show-off intellectual and listen to Annie. Is there something more sinister at work, too? Allen has repeatedly been at the centre of discussions revolving around the significance of a creator's life and actions to their creations. If as director/author Allen owns the meaning of his work, controls the correct interpretation, then would he be able to silence negative readings that draw connections between the content of his films and accusations made against him?[57] The ethical issues of separating life from work have prompted perhaps the most frequent eruptions of the author question in recent popular culture, particularly if we expand 'author' to include directors, producers, comedians, artists.[58]

Contemporary versions of McLuhan-summoning abound online. Twitter has been host to passionate literary debate, allowing unprecedented immediate access to the thoughts and opinions of authors. As one of the world's best-known and most financially successful writers, J. K. Rowling's significant Twitter presence garners an immense response. She has notoriously tweeted extra-textual clarifications of *Harry Potter* characters or plot points; authorised interpretations which are re-broadcast on news blogs, online cultural magazines, and the websites and print pages of international newspapers. The interactions that have followed these authoritative statements re-enact the debates of anti-authorialism, with some users thanking Rowling for confirming their own readings or revealing the 'right' interpretation, while others lambast her for attempting to correct her audience of readers. Where her revelations have extended to the hidden sexual orientations or religious identities of several characters, the response evolved further: users questioned why Rowling had not written a more explicitly diverse set of characters in the first place, to circumvent the need for later explanation. Much more recently, Rowling has expressed views via her Twitter platform that have again raised questions of separating an author from their work, as upset and offended fans seek an understanding of whether they can hold onto emotionally important literary texts while simultaneously condemning their author.[59] Rowling's comments have had an exclusionary effect on some of her audience, and provoked readers to radically reconsider their relationship to text and author.

Have I been aping the methods of Barthes and Burke, presenting a reductively unified picture of culture's relationship to authors? I hope this chapter instead shows how contradictory and erratic the situation is. The examples I've given here, Roupenian's 'Cat Person', Allen's McLuhan, Rowling's tweets – together, crucially, with the reception of each – are situations which emphasise the points of connection between a text, its author, and the reader, and how those points relate to the level of authority we as readers and critics grant authors to interpret their own texts. Furthermore, and most importantly, these examples underscore how unsettled our understandings of or investment in such points of connection remain. At literary festivals, bookshop readings, or book prize events, audience members ask authors probing questions of method and intention: the way in which a writer's personality and life influences their work continues to be the focus of popular literary culture, and their role as arbiters of meaning continues to be asserted as an only occasionally queried default position. Where this also emerges in academia, the question 'why?' rarely follows. The academic literary spheres most focused on authorship – creative writing studies and genetic criticism – perhaps only solidify the author's control over their text, its meaning, how to read it, where it came from. The enduring popularity of fiction about authors, meanwhile, reveals cultural tastes: we are fascinated by authors and authorship, by the 'artist as hero', but we like it best seen through the lens of an author.

Looking back over this chapter, it is remarkable that statements describing ongoing romantic attitudes towards authors, written by Abrams before the arrival and reception of poststructuralist theory, endure as accurate descriptions of the general view of the figure of the author. It also strikes me how often the emphasis has been on theory as the answer to questions of authorship. It is crucial to consider that a questioning of author, reader, and text can be provoked by literature – could arise not from theoretical texts but from readers' responses to literary ones. 'The Death of the Author' remains vitally relevant – but it does not go far enough. This does not mean it should be thrown out, put to bed, left as a historical curiosity within the mores of theory. It means that we should re-engage. In the chapters that follow I will emphasise the ways in which it is the reader who places pressure on the points of connection between author, reader, and text. I will revive questions of authorship by analysing how they are prompted by literature – by *Ulysses*, a near-exaggeration of how authors, readers, and texts function. I will further examine criticism's relationship to the author, combing through the critical reception of *Ulysses* and Joyce. Ultimately, I seek to understand how the reader's authority can be protected in an author-centric environment, and how the specific example of *Ulysses* and its readers can offer valuable insight to issues common to any literary encounter.

NOTES

1. Sian Cain, 'Cat Person: the short story that launched a thousand theories', *The Guardian*, 13 December 2017 <https://www.theguardian.com/books/2017/dec/13/cat-person-short-story-that-launched-thousand-theories> [accessed 5 July 2021].

2. Dolly Alderton, 'Kristen Roupenian, author of Cat Person, is dating a woman', *The Sunday Times*, 13 May 2018 <https://www.thetimes.co.uk/article/kristen-roupenian-author-of-cat-person-is-dating-a-woman-fghsfn02g> [accessed 5 July 2021].
3. Kristen Roupenian, *Cat Person And Other Stories* (London: Vintage, 2019), 95.
4. Megan Garber, '"Cat Person" and the Impulse to Undermine Women's Fiction', *The Atlantic*, 11 December 2017 <https://www.theatlantic.com/entertainment/archive/2017/12/cat-person-is-not-an-essay/548111/> [accessed 5 July 2021].
5. Andrew Gallix, 'Roland Barthes' challenge to biography', *The Guardian*, 14 August 2015, Books Blog <https://www.theguardian.com/books/booksblog/2015/aug/14/roland-barthes-challenge-to-biography> [accessed 5 July 2021], and Lidija Haas, 'Roland Barthes: "Author, I'm Sorry"', *The Telegraph*, 12 November 2015 <http://www.telegraph.co.uk/books/what-to-read/roland-barthes-centenary-death-of-the-author/> [accessed 5 July 2021].
6. Peggy Kamuf, *Signature Pieces: On the Institution of Authorship* (Ithaca, NY and London: Cornell University Press, 1988), 7, and Jane Gallop, *The Deaths of the Author: Reading and Writing in Time* (Durham, NC and London: Duke University Press, 2011), 1 and 2. Both use the term 'slogan'; Gallop references Gayatri Chakravorty Spivak, 'Reading the Satanic Verses', reprinted in *Outside in the Teaching Machine* (Oxford: Routledge, 1993), 217–19, originally published in *Public Culture* (Fall, 1989). Kamuf also uses 'token', 5, and Gallop uses 'catchphrase', 4.
7. Martha Woodmansee, 'The Genius and the Copyright: Economic and Legal Conditions of the Emergence of the "Author"', *Eighteenth-Century Studies*, vol. 17, no. 4 (Summer, 1984), 425–48 (427). See also Seán Burke, 'Changing Conceptions of Authorship', in *Authorship: From Plato to the Postmodern. A Reader*, ed. Burke (Edinburgh: Edinburgh University Press, 1995), 5–11 (5–7).
8. Percy Bysshe Shelley, 'From "A Defence of Poetry"', in Burke, *Authorship*, 43–50 (45).
9. Woodmansee, 429.
10. Robert Folkenflik, 'The Artist as Hero in the Eighteenth Century', *Yearbook of English Studies*, vol. 12 (1982), 91–108, and Michael McKeon, 'Writer as Hero: Novelistic Prefigurations and the Emergence of Literary Biography', in *Contesting the Subject: Essays in the Postmodern Theory and Practice of Biography and Biographical Criticism*, ed. William H. Epstein (West Lafayette, IN: Purdue University Press, 1991), 17–41.
11. McKeon, 22.
12. Folkenflik, 91.
13. M. H. Abrams, *The Mirror and the Lamp: Romantic Theory and the Critical Tradition* (Oxford: Oxford University Press, 1971), 228–9. Further references to this edition are given after quotations in the text.
14. Quoting Friedrich Schiller, *Über naive and sentimentalische Dichtung*, in *Schillers Werke*, ed. Arthur Kutscher (Berlin, n.d.), vol. VIII, 128, 135, 162, and Friedrich Schlegel, *Prosaische Jugendschriften*, ed. J. Minor (Wien, 1882), vol. I, 107–9. This debate is to a certain extent re-enacted in the 'Scylla and Charybdis' episode of *Ulysses*.
15. Abrams slightly differentiates his approach from A. E. Lussky, who reads this in terms of Schlegel's concept of 'romantic irony'. A. E. Lussky, *Tieck's Romantic Irony* (Chapel Hill: The University of North Carolina Press, 1932).

16. Quoting Friedrich Schlegel, 'Nachricht von den poetischen Werken des Johannes Boccaccio', *Jugendshriften*, vol. II, 411–12.
17. Folkenflik, 93.
18. Gustave Flaubert, *Correspondence*, ed. Eugène Fasquelle (Paris, 1900), vol. II, 155. As quoted by Abrams, 262.
19. T. S. Eliot, 'Tradition and the Individual Talent', in *Selected Prose of T. S. Eliot*, ed. Frank Kermode (London: Faber, 1975), 37–44 (40 and 43).
20. Eliot, 40. Loren Glass discusses this aspect of Eliot in *Authors Inc: Literary Celebrity in the Modern United States, 1880–1980* (New York and London: New York University Press, 2004), 6.
21. Glass, 6.
22. Edward Young, 'Conjectures on Original Composition in a Letter to the Author of Sir Charles Grandison', in *English Critical Essays. Sixteenth, Seventeenth, and Eighteenth Centuries*, ed. Edmund D. Jones (London: Oxford University Press, 1975), 289, and Woodmansee, 430–1.
23. Paul K. Saint-Amour, *The Copywrights: Intellectual Property and the Literary Imagination* (Ithaca, NY and London: Cornell University Press, 2003), 3–7.
24. Carolyn Guertin, *Digital Prohibition: Piracy and Authorship in New Media Art* (London: Continuum, 2012), x and 9, and Saint-Amour, 4-6.
25. Saint-Amour, *The Copywrights*, 7–8.
26. Stéphane Mallarmé, 'From "Crisis in Verse"', in Burke, *Authorship*, 51–3 (51).
27. Burke, *The Death and Return of the Author: Criticism and Subjectivity in Barthes, Foucault and Derrida*, 3rd edn (Edinburgh: Edinburgh University Press, 2008), 8–14. Further references to this edition are given after quotations in the text.
28. Julia Kristeva, 'Word, Dialogue, and Novel', in *Desire in Language: A Semiotic Approach to Literature and Art*, ed. Leon S. Roudiez, trans. Thomas Gora, Alice Jardine, and Leon S. Roudiez (New York: Columbia University Press, 1980), 64–91 (66 and 74). This essay was written in 1966, but first published in 1969.
29. Jacques Derrida, 'Signature Event Context', trans. Samuel Weber and Jeffrey Mehlman, in *Limited Inc* (Evanston, IL: Northwestern University Press, 1988), 1–23 (8). This translation first appeared in *Glyph* 1 (Baltimore, MD: Johns Hopkins University Press, 1977).
30. Derrida, 'The Exorbitant. Question of Method', in Burke, *Authorship*, 117–24 (118); Chris Baldick, *Criticism and Literary Theory from 1890 to the Present* (London: Longman, 1996), 172.
31. Wolfgang Iser, *The Act of Reading: A Theory of Aesthetic Response* (London and Henley: Routledge and Kegan Paul, 1978), 53. (This translation has no named translator: it is owned by Johns Hopkins 1978, from 1976 *Der Akt des Lesens. Theorie Ästhetischer Wirkung*.)
32. Iser, *The Act of Reading*, 21.
33. For a detailed account, see Patricia Harkin, 'The Reception of Reader-Response Theory', *Composition and Communication*, vol. 56, no. 3 (February, 2005), 410–25.
34. *Aspen* no. 5 and 6, 'The Minimalism issue', was a box containing three essays, several phonograph recordings, poems, musical scores, cardboard models, a reel of film, and advertisements. It was dedicated to Stéphane Mallarmé, and was edited by

Irish critic and artist Brian O'Doherty. <http://www.ubu.com/aspen/aspen5and6/index.html>
35. In Howard's translation, 'cost of' is rendered as 'ransomed by'.
36. Kamuf, 8.
37. Susan Sontag, 'Writing Itself: On Roland Barthes', in *A Roland Barthes Reader*, ed. Sontag (London: Vintage, 2000), vii–xxxviii (xxxiv).
38. Michael Moriarty, *Roland Barthes* (Cambridge: Polity, 1991), 101–2.
39. Michel Foucault, 'What is an Author?', in *Language, Counter-Memory, Practice: Selected Essays and Interviews*, ed. Donald F. Bouchard, trans. Bouchard and Sherry Simon (Ithaca, NY: Cornell University Press, 1977) 113–38 (117). Further references to this edition are given after quotations in the text.
40. Walter Benjamin, 'The Author as Producer', in *Understanding Brecht*, trans. Anna Bostock (London: Verso, 1998), 85–103 (87).
41. W. K. Wimsatt and Monroe C. Beardsley, 'From "The Intentional Fallacy"', in Burke, *Authorship*, 90–100 (99 and 90).
42. E. D. Hirsch Jr, *Validity in Interpretation* (New Haven, CT: Yale University Press, 1967), Wayne C. Booth, *The Rhetoric of Fiction*, 2nd edn (Chicago and London: University of Chicago, 1961, 1983).
43. Moriarty, 2–3.
44. Alexander Nehamas, 'What an Author Is', *The Journal of Philosophy*, vol. 83, no. 11, Eighty-Third Annual Meeting American Philosophical Association, Eastern Division (November, 1986), 685–91 (690), and 'The Postulated Author: Critical Monism as a Regulative Ideal', *Critical Inquiry*, vol. 8, no. 1 (Autumn, 1981), 133–49; Colin MacCabe, 'The Revenge of the Author', in *Subject to History: Ideology, Class, Gender*, ed. David Simpson (Ithaca, NY and London: Cornell University Press, 1991), 34–46. Other related articles and chapters from this period include Clara Claiborne Park, 'Author! Author! Reconstructing Roland Barthes', *The Hudson Review*, vol. 43, no. 3 (1990–1), 377–98; William H. Gass, 'The Death of the Author', *Salmagundi*, no. 65 (Fall, 1984), 3–26; Denis Hollier, 'Foucault: The Death of the Author', *Raritan*, vol. 5, no. 1 (1985), 22–30; Theresa Enos, 'Reports of the "Author's" Death May Be Greatly Exaggerated but the "Writer" Lives on in the Text', *Rhetoric Society Quarterly*, vol. 20, no. 4, 'Essays in Honor of George Yoos' (Autumn, 1990), 339–46.
45. In Louis Menand and Lawrence Rainey's introduction to *Modernism and the New Criticism*, volume seven of *The Cambridge History of Literary Criticism*, they urge caution of the link implied by the text's title: 'Although it is a commonplace to assimilate modernism and the New Criticism to one another, sometimes treating the latter as if it were merely a more systematic, more philosophical, or more academic articulation of formalist undercurrents within modernism, much is lost in assigning to either term the kind of monolithic coherence such a claim presumes.' *Modernism and the New Criticism*, ed. A. Walton Litz, Louis Menand, and Lawrence Rainey (Cambridge: Cambridge University Press, 2000), 1–14 (3).
46. Peter Ackroyd makes this claim himself: *Notes for a New Culture* (London: Alkin Books, 1993), 8–9.
47. Ackroyd, 115, and MacCabe, 'The Revenge of the Author', 38.
48. For the 'death of the author' position, see for example Toril Moi, *Sexual/Textual Politics: Feminist Literary Theory* (London: Methuen, 1985), 63.

49. Nancy K. Miller, 'Changing the Subject: Authorship, Writing, and the Reader', in *Feminist Studies / Critical Studies*, ed. Teresa de Lauretis (London: Palgrave Macmillan, 1986), 102–20 (106), and 'Arachnologies: The Woman, The Text, and The Critic', in *The Poetics of Gender*, ed. Miller (New York: Columbia University Press, 1986), 270–95 (271).
50. Miller, 'Arachnologies', 288.
51. Susan Stanford Friedman, 'Weavings: Intertextuality and the (Re)Birth of the Author', in *Influence and Intertextuality in Literary History*, ed. Jay Clayton and Eric Rothstein (Madison: University of Wisconsin Press, 1991), 146–80.
52. Rita Felski, *Literature after Feminism* (Chicago: University of Chicago Press, 2003), 91. See also Cheryl Walker, 'Feminist Literary Criticism and the Author', *Critical Inquiry*, vol. 16, no. 3 (Spring, 1990), 551–71.
53. Including Gallop, *The Deaths of the Author* (2011); Kaye Mitchell, *Intention and Text: Towards an Intentionality of Literary Form* (London: Continuum, 2008); John Farrell, *The Varieties of Authorial Intention: Literary Theory Beyond the Intentional Fallacy* (Cham: Palgrave Macmillan, 2017); Aaron Jaffe, *Modernism and the Culture of Celebrity* (Cambridge: Cambridge University Press, 2005); Glass, *Authors Inc* (2004); Guertin, *Digital Prohibition* (2012); R. Lyle Skains, *Digital Authorship: Publishing in the Attention Economy* (Cambridge: Cambridge University Press, 2019); Judith Fathallah, *Fanfiction and the Author: How Fanfic Changes Popular Cultural Texts* (Amsterdam: Amsterdam University Press, 2017).
54. Felski, *Hooked: Art and Attachment* (Chicago: University of Chicago Press, 2020), 116–17.
55. 'Introduction: Author, Authorship, Authority, and Other Matters', in *Authority Matters: Rethinking the Theory and Practice of Authorship*, ed. Stephen Donovan, Danuta Fjellestad, and Rolf Lundén (Amsterdam and New York: Rodopi, 2008), 1–19 (13).
56. Jeremy Hawthorn, 'Authority and the Death of the Author', in Donovan et al., *Authority Matters*, 65–88 (65).
57. For excellent discussions of the Allen problem, see Dahlia Grossman-Heinze, 'The witch hunt is coming for you, Woody Allen', *Bitch*, 27 October 2017 <https://www.bitchmedia.org/article/woody-allen-witch-hunt> [accessed 5 July 2021] and Claire Dederer, 'What Do We Do with the Art of Monstrous Men?', *The Paris Review*, 20 November 2017 <https://www.theparisreview.org/blog/2017/11/20/art-monstrous-men/> [accessed 5 July 2021].
58. While within the academy, Burke considers the ethical responsibilities of authors in terms of legacy in his 2008 study *The Ethics of Writing: Authorship and Legacy in Plato and Nietzsche* (Edinburgh: Edinburgh University Press, 2008), a continuation of his discussions of authorial return.
59. Lesley Goodman discusses the specific instance of Rowling and her fans in terms of 'disappointment' in her 2015 article 'Disappointing Fans: Fandom, Fictional Theory, and the Death of the Author', *The Journal of Popular Culture*, vol. 48, no. 4 (August, 2015), 662–76. Since 2015, such negative feelings have only increased.

2

'CRITICAL PROPAGANDA': THE CRITICS AND JOYCE, 1918–80

> There was some concern expressed two years ago when the *JJQ* was started that after a year or two there would be a dearth of manuscripts of publishable quality dealing with Joyce.
> Thomas F. Staley, *James Joyce Quarterly*, 1965.[1]

Joycean critics have long written about Joycean criticism. Such self-reflexive tendencies are apparent in the number of published metacritical studies, appearing as early as 1956 with Marvin Magalaner and Richard M. Kain's *Joyce: The Man, The Work, The Reputation* – which boldly set out mid-century to tell us 'what the twentieth century has thought of this strange Irishman over the years'.[2] Reception studies, edited volumes collecting or responding to 'classic' pieces of criticism, and round-ups or critiques of Joycean theoretical work have followed, with one obvious reason for such surveys being the volume of existing critical work on Joyce's texts: disproving wonderfully the 1965 note that opens this chapter.[3] Since that early worry, the size and growth of the field has been repeatedly complained about – with each critical complaint further increasing the field.[4] Studies of studies help readers navigate an intimidating mass of criticism, but can also serve their own critical purposes: arguing for the re-canonisation of an overlooked work, reappraising established ideas, evaluating a particular mode or modes of criticism, or outlining patterns in previous critical thought. In this vein, the aim of this chapter and its partner, Chapter 4, is to analyse the ways in which the field of Joyce studies has engaged with questions of authorship, reading, and textuality. In order to do so, my examination is built on close readings of critical texts: of queries and presumptions, uses of language, emerging habits, repeated linguistic or analytical tics. Critical norms, such as an impulse to correct and the basis one has for doing so, indicate attitudes to the author, reader, and text – and the relationships between all three.

I will here look back at a selection of key early works of *Ulysses* criticism, Joyce's involvement in critical exegeses, and the resultant habits that form in critical works which predate or preclude Joyce studies' engagement with literary theory from the 1970s and 1980s onwards; Chapter 4 will investigate the Joycean response to theory. The division of material for these chapters cannot be strictly chronological: I am qualifying 'predate' with 'or preclude' to indicate the blurry overlapping of 'pre'- and 'post'-theory within the Joycean critical sphere. In this chapter I will explore the reception of critical works from Stuart Gilbert's Joyce-authorised monograph *James Joyce's 'Ulysses'*, published in 1930, up to and including Hugh Kenner's 1980 study *'Ulysses'*. I draw a line from Gilbert to Kenner, in opposition to suggestions that the post-war criticism of *Ulysses* can be split into two paths: one following Frank Budgen and the other Gilbert, with Kenner and Richard Ellmann representative of each. The importance of the Homeric – and therefore the reappraisal of Gilbert – in Kenner's readings of *Ulysses* are of equal value to Kenner's Budgen-ordained focus on Bloom. Kenner's Homeric focus is also one reason why his foundational work looms large here and throughout *The Reader's Joyce*.[5]

There are too many men in the following pages. Queer women were instrumental in seeing *Ulysses* reach publication: without Sylvia Beach, Adrienne Monnier, Margaret Anderson, and Jane Heap, the male critics I consider below might not have had a text to critique.[6] Women scholars made significant contributions during the period of Joyce studies I am focusing on: by the 1960s, Margaret Solomon and Adaline Glasheen were publishing important work on *Finnegans Wake*, and in the following decade Hélène Cixous and Margot Norris were amongst the first to radically consider Joyce with French theory. As in literary studies more broadly, however, women working on Joyce were in a minority in this period (and beyond). The particular delineations of my chapter's scope – work specifically on *Ulysses*, predating or precluding literary theory – leave an even more predominantly male pool of critics. I could have chosen a different set of parameters for my topic. But much of the writing I examine below formed the foundations of the field of Joyce studies; these are the approaches that later critics continued or railed against, and the ongoing role of this early work is too often now overlooked.

I am arranging my discussion of studies by Gilbert, Harry Levin, Richard M. Kain, A. Walton Litz, David Hayman, and Kenner around three focal points: how critics responded to the emphasis Gilbert placed on the Homeric schema, the critical conflation and separation of Stephen Dedalus and Joyce, and the ways in which early critical works prefigure later theoretical approaches. Hovering in the background of all three foci is Joyce's role in Gilbert's study, an involved authorial presence found also in the schema given to Carlo Linati, in Frank Budgen's 1934 work *James Joyce and the Making of 'Ulysses'*, and in 1929's *Our Exagmination Round his Factification for Incamination of Work in Progress*. By concentrating particularly on Joyce's involvement and the effects of authorially authorised criticism; readings of the relationships between Joyce, Stephen Dedalus, and the Arranger; and the resultant habits of Joycean criticism, I will establish the manner in which criticism of *Ulysses* quickly became as much about *how* to read the text as it was about the text itself, and – as criticism is an act of reading – became self-reflexive. Through this rereading of critical developments I argue that Joyce studies grew into a discipline with a corrective urge yet an openness to multiplicity, and that these traits can be traced back to the reception of the Homeric in *Ulysses* and Joyce's own role in that reception.

How to read the author in Joyce studies is rarely asked by Joycean critics; Hugh Kenner is an occasional exception, here discussing Gilbert and other early critics:

> The trouble Joyce took to get *Ulysses* explicated while making the explications seem to come from other men resembles Dedalus' trouble over his wings: a contrivance to negate the side-effects of an over-successful contrivance. It is behind Val[é]ry Larbaud and Stuart Gilbert and Frank Budgen that the artist disappears, nail-file in hand. It was they, at his behest, who equipped the great affirmation of meaninglessness with meaning. We have been carrying on their work ever since [. . .] And Joyce, despite the most diligent biographical effort, has meanwhile ascended on unexpected wings into the air and out of sight.[7]

Kenner makes a playful link between the author who meddles in criticism – who meddles with reading – and the author described by Stephen in *A Portrait of the Artist as a Young Man*. Joyce sticks his oar in there too: in Budgen's *James Joyce and The Making of 'Ulysses'* readers are admonished by Joyce's complaint that '"Some people who read my book, *A Portrait of the Artist* forget that it is called *A Portrait of the Artist as a Young Man*"', emphasising 'as a young man'.[8] Budgen's study defends the importance of Bloom, not Stephen, in *Ulysses*, and does so with the author's stamp of approval. The presence within early Joyce studies of authorially approved readings of *Ulysses* leaves subtle traces, and this is a key reason for returning to Gilbert in this chapter, and Budgen in Chapter 6, where I will discuss biography in Joyce criticism. Joyce's involvement complicates the roles of critics, and muddies the question of how we should read *Ulysses* – a text which so completely refutes the idea of there being any one 'right' reading. These authorial traces are preserved, and Joyce studies overwhelmingly turns away from examining them. From the early works which form the foundations of the field, to the continuing boom of new critical texts, every piece of Ulyssean criticism involves an implicit decision on how to read the relationship between the author and the text of *Ulysses*. Reading *Ulysses* informs, and is informed by, these decisions.

For Us, or For Joyce: How Important is Homer Anyway?

In '*Ulysses*, Order, and Myth', published in *The Dial* in November 1923, T. S. Eliot cites two earlier critical responses to *Ulysses* as preludes to his defence of Joyce's 'mythical method'.[9] Pointedly retorting, Eliot's essay lauds Valéry Larbaud and derides Richard Aldington; Larbaud's 1921 lecture is a 'valuable paper', while Aldington's review is just 'pathetic solicitude for the half-witted' (Eliot, 175 and 176). First given as a lecture in Paris, December 1921, then published in the *Nouvelle Revue Française* in April 1922 and in an English translation by Eliot in *The Criterion* that October, Larbaud's Joyce-authorised reading identifies the 'key' to *Ulysses* as 'on the cover', its titular relationship to the *Odyssey*.[10] Richard Aldington's review of *Ulysses*, 'The Influence of James Joyce', published in *The English Review* in April 1921, sees Joyce as 'a prophet of chaos', ignores 'the parallel to the *Odyssey*', and as a result 'seems to [. . .] fail by this oversight' in Eliot's view (175). Aldington's 'oversight' is matched, and furthered, in the better-known opinions of Ezra Pound: viewing Joyce's Homeric 'correspondences' as 'chiefly his own affair, a scaffold, a means of construction, justified by the result, and justifiable by it only'.[11] Aligning himself with Larbaud and positioned against Pound and his kind, Eliot refuses the idea that the mythical parallel is 'an amusing dodge, or scaffolding erected by the author for the purpose of disposing his realistic tale, of no interest in the completed structure' (175). He defends and promotes the 'mythical method' as 'simply a way of controlling, of ordering, of giving a shape and a significance to the immense panorama of futility and anarchy which is contemporary history' (177). However, Eliot's article and its arguments that this method is 'a step toward making the modern world possible for art' could not halt less positive reactions to *Ulysses* (178). In the chapter 'An Analysis of the Mind of James Joyce' in his 1927 work *Time and Western Man*, Wyndham Lewis eloquently accuses *Ulysses*: 'It is a suffocating, mœtic expanse of objects, all of them lifeless, the sewage of a Past twenty years old, all neatly arranged in a meticulous sequence.'[12] The importance of the *Odyssey* is dismissed, and the matter in Joyce's composition luridly described:

> So rich was its delivery, its pent-up outpouring so vehement, that it will remain, eternally cathartic, a monument like a record diarrhoea [. . .] he

collected like a cistern in his youth the last stagnant pumpings of victorian anglo-irish life [. . .] then when he was ripe, as it were, he discharged it, in a dense mass, to his eternal glory.[13]

Corrective methods were needed, both to cement the importance of the *Odyssey* to *Ulysses* and improve the novel's reputation. In 1930 Stuart Gilbert wrote *James Joyce's 'Ulysses'* with the encouragement and assistance of Joyce himself: the study 'contains nothing', Gilbert prefatorily insists, 'to which he did not give his full approbation; indeed there are several passages which I directly owe to him'.[14] Sharing with the public a schema of correspondences, including a list of Homeric episode titles, Gilbert also turns to a named Joycean precursor, Victor Bérard, in his detailing of Joyce's methods and his attempts to establish that 'James Joyce is, in fact, in the great tradition which begins with Homer' (43). Katherine Mullin depicts the efforts of Joyce, Gilbert, Larbaud, and Pound as a protest against the legal battles *Ulysses* faced – battles with censorship she also argues Joyce 'anticipated, provoked, and, eventually, profited from';[15] Patrick A. McCarthy similarly reads Gilbert's study as 'intended to be an essay in critical propaganda, with an elaborate exegetical apparatus whose main purpose was to demonstrate the rationality, and therefore the respectability, of *Ulysses*'.[16] Joyce's involvement has been further characterised as a manipulation rather than collaboration: from the idea that Joyce 'talked his friend Stuart Gilbert into writing the study', to viewing Joyce's suggestions – including the significance of Bérard – as 'elaborate practical jokes'.[17] Michael Seidel sums up the extreme: 'Gilbert is seen as a dummy who moves his lips in synchronization with his master's trickster voice.'[18]

In the first half of *James Joyce's 'Ulysses'* Gilbert addresses many aspects of reading *Ulysses*, but most specifically the 'fragments of a theme or allusion' which 'have to be assimilated in the reader's mind to arrive at complete understanding' (36). He looks at themes such as metamorphosis, return, and paternity, and draws attention to Bérard and Giambattista Vico – attempting to align Joyce's writing methods with those of the writer of the *Odyssey*. Translating Bérard, he suggests we can think of Joyce, like Homer, as 'a skilled arranger' (87). Going into more depth than Larbaud, Eliot, or any other early defender of the Homeric in *Ulysses*, Gilbert endeavours to establish the link between the *Odyssey* and Joyce's novel as so strong, and so important, that it can no longer be overlooked by critics or readers. His firmly positive study (unsurprisingly complimentary, given who peered over his shoulder) shifts in its second half to read *Ulysses* episode by episode, quoting it extensively and so giving access to a text that was, in 1930, quite hard to come by. This access did, however, come at the price of wading through what McCarthy reads as a 'pedantic tone' and 'the humourless reverence' of biblical exegesis;[19] Vivienne Koch makes perhaps the earliest noises of frustration over such exegetical listings of correspondences, in 1944.[20] The significance of Gilbert's study lies not only in its successful dissemination of the schema, with its correspondences assigning organs, arts, colours, symbols, technics, characters and a Homeric title to each episode. I see its relevance also in the critical tendencies it provoked in both opposition and agreement, the responses it garnered to the author-critic relationship between Gilbert and Joyce, and the openly author-authorised status of the schema itself.

One critical tendency provoked by Gilbert – though he inherited it himself from Eliot – is the urge to overturn previous critical conclusions; a corrective attitude which searches for the 'right' reading. The trend for correcting or moving away from Gilbert's arguments begins most notably and influentially with 1941's *James Joyce: A Critical Introduction* by Harry Levin, who roundly rejects the prioritisation of the mythical in *Ulysses*. Though written and published after Joyce's death, the study was undertaken by Levin at Joyce's suggestion.[21] It markedly places Joyce's texts within a literary context, attempting to ease the difficulties of *Portrait*, *Ulysses*, and *Finnegans Wake* by relating them to larger ideas and trends within the writings of others: 'The more we study him, the less unique he seems; and the more he seems to have in common with other significant writers of the past and of the present.'[22] Levin specifically seeks authorial intentions in *James Joyce*, pondering for example whether Joyce might wish 'to impose a private pattern upon the chaos of his experience' (20), yet arguing against the importance of the once private, now public, pattern of the schema. He identifies two 'keys' with which to read *Ulysses*: 'the map' and 'the myth' (66). The latter is thoroughly discounted. 'The closeness of the correspondences between his Irish characters and their Hellenic prototypes is a point that can be, and has been, heavily laboured', he begins, before making his best-known conclusion regarding the correspondences: 'They are not there for us, but for Joyce' (72 and 75). Levin does acknowledge that 'No serious reader can afford to neglect' the Homeric scheme, 'but he need not take it quite so seriously as Gilbert takes Joyce' (228). Levin's pointed turn away from what can be read as a published authorial intention – the importance of the schema – and his suggestions to not take Joyce too seriously sit oddly with the otherwise explicitly author- and intention-focused aims of *James Joyce* (and I will pick this up in the final section of this chapter). The significance of Levin's study in the development of *Ulysses* criticism lies predominantly in how later critics read the directive of 'not there for us': querying whether a reader can, in fact, neglect the mythic framework of the novel. Levin's suspicious treatment of the Homeric scheme diminishes the authority of Gilbert's study, leading to works that look elsewhere for explanation. Two that specifically cite Levin are Richard M. Kain's *Fabulous Voyager*, which looks at a variety of predominantly non-literary printed paraphernalia such as newspapers; and A. Walton Litz's *The Art of James Joyce*, which digs into

Joyce's worksheets for answers and initiates a strong genetic critical presence in the arena of Joycean criticism.

In 1947's *Fabulous Voyager* Kain investigates the factual texts woven into *Ulysses* and implicitly questions the boundaries of fiction within the novel. Naming Joyce 'the most bitterly attacked and grossly misunderstood of modern writers', he states his purpose to 'evaluate' Gilbert's exegesis, implied to be one such gross misunderstanding.[23] This questioning of Gilbert's approach and the correspondences is apparent even at a structural level of Kain's study. Rather than moving through the text episode by episode or huge theme by huge theme (cf. Gilbert and Levin), he works through crucial pieces of novelistic concern: such as facts discernible without the schema, from time, date, weather; to local events, news, races, bets; pamphlets, theatre performances, even schooners; and does so using maps, newspapers, and directories to aid his reading. His disagreement with Gilbert is incrementally detailed: he summarises the Homeric correspondences in ten lines, labelling some of the associations 'arbitrary'; on 'the symbolic interpretation of *Ulysses*' he concludes Joyce 'appears to grow increasingly independent of his classical source as the story goes on'; and listed correspondences are 'never limited' to one episode (40, 46, and 42). Developing this last objection, Kain argues that some of the correspondences of the schema are pointless – targeting the schematically assigned colour of 'Calypso': 'The color orange is not even mentioned' (42).[24] The overall impression of Kain's study, however, is not as an attack on Gilbert or the 'mythical method' – yet it does refute the usefulness of that approach. In its detailed re-enactment of a reading without recourse to the schema, *Fabulous Voyager* confirms the possibility of finding information such as the date and time in the text itself, and it also establishes the relevance to *Ulysses* and its readers of other texts beyond the *Odyssey* and the schema: the *Freeman's Journal* and *Evening Telegraph*, maps of Dublin, and *Thom's Directory*. Kain's enthusiasm for this new mode of reading the novel runs through his field-changing study, as he investigates how 'Upon four pages of newsprint Joyce has erected the foundations of his fictional world!' (61). Kain prompted decades of Joycean investigation into newspapers, maps, and directories, a method which expands understandings of the novel's relationship with texts beyond the realm of 'highbrow' literature, and the games it plays with the fictive/factual divide.

Similarly turning to external texts in a movement away from the Odyssean correspondences advocated by Gilbert, in *The Art of James Joyce* (1961) Litz instead reads Joyce's notes and manuscripts. Though also explicitly aligned with Levin and the 'not there for us' approach, there is a crucial difference between Litz's and Kain's methods: both in many ways look at how *Ulysses* was formed, but while Kain's focus is on the resultant way in which we read the novel, Litz is interested in the writing, not the reading, of *Ulysses*. His recourse to Joyce's worksheets to overturn the authorially authorised importance of the

Homeric schema constitutes a return to the author himself, in an effort to prove him wrong. Litz focuses particularly on the revisions and additions of Joyce's writing process, with extended reference to unused notes in the worksheets. Thus he finds evidence to argue that though 'Invaluable to Joyce [. . .] the correspondences with the *Odyssey* do not provide a major level of meaning in the completed work. Ezra Pound was right.'[25] Litz details the prevalence of Homeric references in the worksheets and the deletions that occurred before the text was published, illustrating Joyce's removal of certain explicit referents. His focus on the revision process does some work to undermine what McCarthy outlines as a particular difficulty of Gilbert's presentation of the schema: 'the implication that the plan predated the novel'. McCarthy confidently informs us 'Joyce wanted to encourage' via Gilbert an understanding that 'the Homeric correspondences were incorporated into the text fairly early [. . .] for it made the parallels seem an integral part of the book's texture'.[26] By detailing the additions and removals of the drafting processes of *Ulysses*, Litz argues instead that exhibiting the 'mechanical nature' of Joyce's compositional process emphasises 'the mechanical nature of those ordering principles which give *Ulysses* its superficial unity, and which sometimes obscure the deeper unity of the novel' (27). Litz clarifies his conclusion: 'The artistic effects [Joyce] sought to achieve while reworking the early episodes and writing the later ones do not depend on our conscious recognition of the analogies he was strengthening' (52). Using a new methodology, Litz re-evidences an opinion of the Homeric as 'an amusing dodge': 'Joyce, in revising *Ulysses*, ran the danger of placing disproportionate emphasis on the *schema* of the novel' (52). Litz's study is a fairly negative critique, peppered with unfavourable opinions of Joyce's abilities, beyond this idea that the author misjudged his own revisions of *Ulysses*. Litz's reading of the 'neutral patterns, arbitrary scaffolds' that 'tend to exist for their own sake, *imposing* order rather than reflecting it', is one of the earliest instances of manuscript or archival work in Joyce studies (123). Here, curiously, Litz implements this mode of analysis in order to unsettle the claims of an authorised worksheet, the schema.

Gilbert's study and the Homeric elements of *Ulysses* were, however, reclaimed. In his Joycean texts written between the 1950s and 1980s Hugh Kenner seeks an influential reappraisal of Gilbert and the mythical method. *Dublin's Joyce*, published in 1956, marks a significant return of Ulyssean criticism to the Homeric. From the eleventh chapter onwards of this far-ranging study Kenner explores how 'the Homeric situation – Homer's world – is *in Joyce's text*, because Joyce found it in Dublin',[27] how the Homeric correspondences in *Ulysses* are both comic and serious, and how the universal nature of the *Odyssey* is appropriate for *Ulysses* and has the effect of establishing it within a tradition. Kenner makes the relationship between *Ulysses* and the *Odyssey* less eccentric and less intimidating in a variety of ways (for example emphasising the intricate relationship between *Ulysses*, the *Odyssey*, and *Hamlet*), and exhibits how it can aid rather than stymy reading the text: a critical first. He sees value in Gilbert's schema, but points out that the lists of correspondences cannot be expected to explain all – plotting a middle ground between Gilbert and Levin (*Dublin's Joyce*, 225). Kenner's treatment of Gilbert might best be characterised as affectionately mocking: on Joyce and his critics, he suggests Joyce 'also appears to have taken revenge in the most elaborate legpull of his career: he permitted [. . .] Stuart Gilbert, to believe that his useful book was the authorized exposition of *Ulysses*' (361). Kenner enjoys 'Mr. Stuart Gilbert's timid acknowledgement that Bloom "is no servile replica of his Homeric prototype, for he has a cat instead of a dog, and a daughter instead of a son" (Joyce playfully altering a few trifles in the interests of variety)', while affirming that the variations from the Homeric are 'neither capricious nor mechanical' (182). Amongst extended exploration of the Homeric parallels, he argues that 'the fundamental correspondence is not between incident and incident, but between situation and situation', and that this 'has never gotten into the critical tradition' (181). Kenner ultimately marries the arguments of his predecessors:

> the reader should reflect that the object of reading the book is not to reconstruct the schema [. . .] It is not a set of answers to a puzzle; [. . .] It was, while the book was a-writing, *affair de cuisine*; its usefulness to the reader who happens to have access to it now that the book is completed should consist in helping him focus his apprehension. (225)

Kenner's reclamation of the Homeric is developed throughout his later work on Joyce, and from the 1970s and 1980s was taken up by critics including Michael Seidel and Fritz Senn; particularly his way of viewing the Homeric parallels 'ironically'.[28] A Kenner-esque mid-way point is plotted, for example, in Seidel's comment in 1976's *Epic Geography* that 'A scaffold is a dispensable structure once the building is built. But if the process of building is as important as the result, the scaffold never disappears.'[29] An about-turn, the very act of critical reappraisal, is thus one legacy of Gilbert's *James Joyce's 'Ulysses'*.

The reception of both Gilbert's study and his advocacy of the Homeric schema has resulted in a variety of tendencies within Joyce studies. Writing in the early 1990s, McCarthy observes that 'The pervasiveness of Gilbert's influence [can] be seen in the way some of his working assumptions, and even specific observations, have come to be regarded as common property and are often repeated without attribution to their original source'[30] – a phenomenon I view as being in part explained by the way criticism, for a time, turned so absolutely away from Gilbert's study. Given what we know of Joyce's involvement, there is an added significance to how we understand that 'original source'. Elements of Gilbert's authorially authorised study persist in *Ulysses* criticism, and continue to be either unattributed or unexamined. Joyce's 'critical propaganda' did not establish how to read *Ulysses*; it secured instead that 'how' as a central, ongoing question of Joyce studies. The idea of the Homeric in *Ulysses*, as argued for by Gilbert and the schema, was, in Kenner's words, 'either haggled over in detail, or brushed aside as a nuisance' (*Dublin's Joyce*, 181). Joyce's role in this has been largely ignored, and this early phase of Joyce criticism has not been included in more recent discussions of the relationship between the author and criticism. Gilbert, Levin, Kain, Litz, and Kenner explore questions of authorship: in terms of the author, the author's intentions, the author's worksheets, or the author's jokes, what matters to the critic or reader? What does it mean to 'take seriously' the author's comments on his own work? In the wake of Gilbert's study there emerged a focus on how to read Joyce's texts, and a corrective impulse within Joycean criticism formed in part by a movement away from the author's suggestions. In trying to decide how best to read Joyce's texts, however, some critics turned to a Joyce within the text: Stephen Dedalus.

'The mind that informs Ulysses': Stephen and the Arranger

Gilbert's treatment in *James Joyce's 'Ulysses'* of the relationship between Stephen and Joyce is complicated and contradictory. 'Stephen Dedalus', he warns, 'represents only one side of the author of *Ulysses*, the juvenile, self-assertive side, unmodified by maturer wisdom'. Gilbert finds it easier to believe a Bloom could create a Stephen than the other way around, and criticises a 'polemist' for using Stephen as a model for Joyce's personality (105–7). Despite this, Gilbert quotes Stephen's words from *Portrait* – 'The personality of the artist passes into the narration itself, flowing round and round the persons and the action like a vital sea', and 'Old father, old artificer, stand me now and ever in good stead' – in a way which assigns them with an explanatory authority in discussions of *Ulysses* (P, 214 and 253; q. Gilbert, 23 and 101). Gilbert stops short of referencing the rest of Stephen's musings on the 'personality of the artist'; the first quotation is taken from the passage that culminates in his Flaubertian theory of impersonal authorship. Levin, however, refers explicitly to Stephen's ideas – continuing and developing a method of using his pronouncements in discussions of the aesthetics of *Ulysses* or of Joyce.

Gilbert's warnings go unnoticed. Levin's greater endeavour is to read Joyce's intention, expressed in the preface of his study:

> With writers, there is always what Henry James called 'the figure in the carpet,' a pattern woven into the warp of historical necessity by the woof of artistic intention, which it is the task of criticism to discover and set forth. With Joyce, this figure has been obscured by a luxuriant profusion of language and detail but it is nonetheless implicit in everything he wrote. (viii)

In his attempt to read authorial intention, Levin conflates Stephen and Joyce. Levin justifies his use of Stephen's words by reading *Portrait* as 'based on a literal transcript of the first twenty years of Joyce's life. If anything, it is more candid than other autobiographies' (45). He therefore allows himself to read Stephen's theory of authorship as Joyce's: 'The artist, like the God of creation, remains within or behind or beyond or above his handiwork, invisible, refined out of existence, indifferent, paring his fingernails' (*P*, 215; referenced by Levin, 45). Levin's reading of Joyce in 'The Artist' section of his study relies on a romantic approach to authorship, seeking explanation for the complexities of text in the personality of the writer – and reading earlier work as a direct record of the writer's aesthetic views. Stephen's late-romantic impersonal author conveniently serves Levin's purposes.[31]

As Morton P. Levitt observes of Levin's study, it 'is needlessly limiting' to read Joyce's words as autobiographical; the creation of a 'biographical myth' is 'directly at odds' with Levin's arguments against the schematic scaffolding – arguments which allow us to see 'a Joyce beyond his own myth'.[32] In a statement which reveals his own attitude to the life-art relationship in Joyce's work, Levitt suggests that 'Given time and greater distance, any reader of Joyce can learn to note and then bypass the artist's often trivial life and go on to the real life, his art.'[33] I will explore Joyce studies' treatment of the life-art relationship and its uses of (auto)biography in Chapter 6; what is pertinent here is not the use of Stephen's life as Joyce's life as a key to the text, but rather the use of Stephen's aesthetic views as Joyce's aesthetic views as a key to the text. Levin is one of many; as Kenner notes in *Dublin's Joyce*, 'Most critics [. . .] have reached in the *Portrait* for a clue' (167).[34] Levin does, however, attempt to justify his reading of Stephen as a direct mouthpiece for Joyce; other critics use his words without comment. Kain, for example, uses words from *Portrait* to detail Joyce's biography in an early section of *Fabulous Voyager* (11–16) – later in the study, however, he queries 'But is Stephen the author of *Ulysses*?' His brief argument is based on a reading of personalities: 'The identification of Joyce with Stephen has often been made, but the creator of Bloom is far more tolerant than Stephen.' Kain also references, without naming Budgen, Joyce's reminder 'that the *Portrait* was entitled the portrait of the artist as a *young* man' (210–11). It is Kenner, however, who is credited with separating the two: a significant development in Joyce studies, but also an elaboration of Gilbert's warnings.

Looking back, in his 1987 preface to the Morningside edition of *Dublin's Joyce*, Kenner claims he had to separate Stephen and Joyce: that Stephen's 'limitations' were 'sufficient to make it implausible that an extrapolated Stephen had managed to write them' (xii). Where Levin and others read candidness in *Portrait*, in *Dublin's Joyce* Kenner reads pastiche, parody, and irony. He, like Levin, refers to an earlier version – here *Stephen Hero* – but advises that 'by the time he came to rewrite the *Portrait* Joyce had decided to make its central figure a futile *alter ego* rather than a self-image'. Kenner moves on to '*Ulysses*, which neither Stephen nor any extrapolation of Stephen could have written' (137). In his chapter 'Baker Street to Eccles Street' Kenner compares Bloom with the narrating Watson and Stephen with the narrated Sherlock Holmes, confirming his view of Stephen as created, not creator, within the domain of *Ulysses* (161–78). He pushes this even further by the chapter's end, arguing that 'Bloom, immersed in this sensate world [of *Ulysses*], is the father of Stephen exactly as the Watsonian Conan Doyle is the father of Sherlock Holmes' (170). In the intervening analytical steps, Kenner begins to explore a narrating, pseudo-authorial presence in *Ulysses* that is related to Bloom rather than Stephen. He begins by arguing it is 'essential' to see *Ulysses* as 'a huge and intricate machine clanking and whirring for eighteen hours'. Kenner finds a 'thinking machine' that is 'mechanical and craftsmanlike and unreflective' behind the novel – if one were looking for an 'auctorial personality'. 'Joyce', he argues, 'has been at great pains to build up this persona behind his book [. . .] it is behind *that*, rather than behind the obvious façade of the work, that the author stands indifferent, paring his fingernails'. Unusually didactic once more, Kenner demands 'It is essential to the total effect of *Ulysses* that it should seem to be the artefact of a mind essentially like Bloom's, only less easily deflected; a mind that loses nothing, penetrates nothing, and has a category for everything' – though Bloom, he adds carefully, is not a 'disguise of the author' but a 'low-powered variant on the mode of consciousness that imparts substantial form to the book' (166–7). Having linked this machine to the mind of Bloom rather than Stephen, Kenner refers his readings back to the conclusions of Wyndham Lewis: 'One of the prime exhibits of that book is an analysis of the mind that informs *Ulysses*, which Lewis unfortunately mistook for the mind of James Joyce' (168).

Kenner did not convince all: *Dublin's Joyce* is attacked in S. L. Goldberg's 1961 work *The Classical Temper* for Kenner's 'remarkably boring' reading of a machine-like presence beneath the narrative of the novel.[35] His argument that 'One of Joyce's greatest creations is the character of this sardonic impersonal recorder, that constantly glints its photoelectric eyes from behind the chronicle of Bloomsday' holds no water with Goldberg, who spends twenty pages of his study disagreeing with Kenner (*Dublin's Joyce*, 167–8). *The Classical Temper* further (if indirectly) opposes *Dublin's Joyce* by extending Levin's argument that the Homeric correspondences are 'there for Joyce', not the reader. Goldberg claims that though the Dublin setting, details of physicality, and Homeric and symbolic catalogues 'all have their function; yet they seem to have mattered to Joyce far more than their function warrants': that their 'treatment' is 'projected from some unease in the author himself' and 'his tendency to rely on purely verbal arrangements of his material, which so weakens his encyclopaedic scheme that it often remains little more than an arbitrary and empty ordering gesture'.[36] Given his use of the anti-Homeric buzzword 'arbitrary', it is fitting that

Goldberg goes on to echo Litz by increasingly detailing Joyce's limitations as a writer towards the end of *The Classical Temper*. His closing remarks demand that 'it is to the active, the dramatic, that we should look, rather than the passive, the ingenious, and the purely verbal'.[37] To further establish the differences between Goldberg's and Kenner's approaches, we need only look at Kenner's later work and his continuing emphasis on the crucial impossibility of separating form from content, of anything being 'purely verbal'. Kenner does not lose sight of the distance between Stephen and 'The omniscient showman-narrator in *Ulysses*, "paring his fingernails"' (*Dublin's Joyce*, 45–6):[38] in *Joyce's Voices* he reads in *Ulysses* a narrative voice which 'flaunts skills such as Stephen covets' (72). Kenner's continued focus on the uncanny mind, persona, or machine that informs *Ulysses*, or sits between its author and its narrative, is sustained by his belief in 'the showman-narrator' as 'one of the most extraordinary masks in literature' (*Dublin's Joyce*, 46).

Kenner's strategy of reading narrative and structure in search of what controls the text of *Ulysses* prioritises language, character, and enjoyment of the narrative. The Arranger, Kenner's text-based solution to a search for a pseudo-author in the text, is a narrative device that forms a climax to his developing readings of *Ulysses*. It is also, however, a device first named by David Hayman (and neither Hayman nor Kenner notice that the term 'arranger' is first used by Gilbert). But we can trace the evolution of the Arranger in Kenner's work from the separation of Stephen and Joyce, through Kenner's focus – following Budgen – instead on Bloom as the central figure, his insistence that there can be no separating of form and content in *Ulysses*, and the critical attention he pays to the significance of the Homeric and of the physicality of the novel as a printed and bound book. *Flaubert, Joyce and Beckett: The Stoic Comedians* and *Joyce's Voices* were published in 1962 and 1978 respectively, forming vital pieces of critical housekeeping in Kenner's development of what was to become the Arranger. In *The Stoic Comedians* Kenner reads *Ulysses* as the dramatic rewriting of the *Odyssey* from an oral epic to a printed book, focusing therefore on the importance of the book form to the novel. Kenner explores the simultaneously finite and permanent nature of a printed and bound book, and how an awareness and exploitation of this nature can be read in the text.[39] A caveat can be found early in his preface when Kenner outlines his scope to be Flaubert, Joyce, Beckett, 'and the books they contrived, or had their contrivances contrive'.[40] Echoing the machine lurking beneath the narrative in *Dublin's Joyce*, this also reaches forwards to Kenner's identification of a conniving contrivance in the form of the Arranger. *Joyce's Voices*, which further reaches forward to Kenner's Arranger, was in fact published eight years after David Hayman's naming of the 'arranger' in his 1970 monograph *'Ulysses': The Mechanics of Meaning*.[41] *Joyce's Voices* is most often cited for its development of 'the Uncle Charles Principle': a way of reading confusions in narrative voice, allowing the narrative idioms of a character to infiltrate the third person narration (17–18). Curiously, though Kenner's study is an in-depth unravelling of narrative voice in *Ulysses*, the term Arranger does not appear in *Joyce's Voices*.

Continuing to focus on the importance of the book as a physical object, and establishing within his argument that nothing in the novel is anything but 'purely verbal', Kenner's reading in *Joyce's Voices* is once more affected by the Homeric. He discusses two narrators of *Ulysses*, linking his analysis back to a Homeric invocation of the Muse, and the multi-narrator form of the *Odyssey*. Arguing that Joyce 'commences *Ulysses* [. . .] as a sort of duet for two narrators, or perhaps a conspiracy between them', Kenner describes 'one voice perhaps better informed about stage-management, the other a more accomplished lyrical technician' (67). He continues, detailing how 'Fulfilling one office of the Muse in periodically elevating the style, this second narrator has served an apprenticeship on *A Portrait of the Artist as a Young Man* and become a virtuoso of the Uncle Charles Principle' (71). While the first voice 'attends to [. . .] housekeeping', the second's 'responsibility is to the sensation reported rather than to the locked and cherished phrase' (71 and 72). Kenner harks back to his suggestion in *The Stoic Comedians* – that the physical book resting in the hands of the reader is of concern to the reading – in a comment that, in 'Aeolus',

> The narrator is letting us know that he is there, and that he will not necessarily remain content to serve the needs of the narrative [. . .] No, he is *reading* the narrative, and reserves the privilege of letting us know what he thinks of it.

Kenner continues, adding irresistible characterisation and clearly having fun:

> He is an ironic, malicious figure, this second narrator [. . .] arranging the strategic presence of banana peels or helping weave the network of coincidence [. . .] He has written a great many books before this one, he will have us know, and arranged a great many pantomimes. (75)

One narrator 'tries to get on with the business of the book', while the other increasingly 'snatches the pen' (77 and 78). In his later study *'Ulysses'*, Kenner credits Hayman with coining the phrase 'arranger'. It is puzzling then, that in this earlier examination of an arranging, weaving narrative presence, neither the term nor Hayman's study is cited.

In *The Mechanics of Meaning*, Hayman identifies a need for order 'in the narrational strategy and the evolution of a nameless creative persona or "arranger"', using 'the term "arranger" to designate a figure or a presence that can be identified neither with the author nor with his narrators, but that exercises an increasing degree of overt control over increasingly challenging materials'.[42] He continues: 'It is in small effects that this presence is first felt, in stylistic ticks or rather rhetorical gestures' (88–9). 'Gradually and with calculated stealth this invisible but consistently locatable speaker will be metamorphosed into the artist-God as cosmic joker', Hayman details, claiming that 'By the book's second half he will have become a creature of many faces but a single impulse' (92–3). Hayman's Arranger 'calls attention to his ingenuity' (100), and though it is not to be identified with the author it has some manner of tangential link to authorial authority. He references the Stephen-mused 'artist-God', but changes it into a cosmic joker – a move not dissimilar from Kenner's fingernail-paring 'showman-narrator'. Hayman later revisits the Arranger in the 1982 edition of *The Mechanics of Meaning*, in which he assesses the fate of the Arranger in the hands of other critics – with particular focus on Kenner.

Published in 1980, Kenner's *'Ulysses'* emphasises the fun of the Homeric and the usefulness of difficulties of reading, building its arguments in tandem with the changing episodes of the novel. Outlining principles of narration – of how the parallactic narrative structures in *Ulysses* are tied to the way the narration is affected by the characters it presents – Kenner works through the novel, reading and offering explanations for unnarrated gaps. He links unwritten scenes to Bloom and exhibits how what is *not* narrated develops Bloom's character as much as, if not more than, what is. In 'Sirens' he marks the Arranger's explicit presence in the phrase 'As said before', which reaches back to the opening line of the 'Calypso' episode.[43] Arguing that 'Some mind, it is clear, keeps track of the details of this printed cosmos', of the events 'mimed in words arranged on pages in space', a mind which 'enjoys a seemingly total recall for exact forms of words used hundreds of pages earlier, a recall which implies not an operation of memory but access such as ours to a printed book, in which pages can be turned to and fro', Kenner credits Hayman with the naming of the Arranger.[44] Arguably, Kenner's debt is less to Hayman than to his own earlier work in *The Stoic Comedians* on the myriad ways in which *Ulysses* is aware of its physical form. Reaching back too to the 'craftsmanlike' machine of *Dublin's Joyce*, and showing clear links to *Joyce's Voices*, Kenner's Arranger appears to be the fruition of his own explorations of what lies between the narrative of *Ulysses* and its author, coinciding with rather than developing Hayman's construction. We have again the two narrators of *Joyce's Voices*, one Muse, one 'housekeeper'. Such a link is tacitly encouraged by phrases lifted directly from Kenner's previous study, describing the Arranger as 'snatching the pen from his anonymous colleague' – as the second narrator from *Joyce's Voices* 'snatches the pen' – and 'just this side of being malicious' – as the second narrator is an 'ironic, malicious figure' (*'Ulysses'*, 67). His Arranger, increasingly busying himself as the novel moves through 16 June 1904, is more a continuation of Kenner's critical thought than a response to Hayman's construct.

In 'Ten Years After Thoughts', added to the 1982 edition of *The Mechanics of Meaning*, Hayman argues that Kenner makes too much of the role of the Arranger: he suggests that 'Perhaps it would be best to see the arranger as a significant, felt absence in the text, an unstated but inescapable source of control.' Hayman worries over Kenner's use of the term, seeing Kenner's construct as a narrative voice, which therefore diminishes its innovation (122–3). Hayman also dislikes a broader application of the idea of the Arranger across the novel; on the narrative voices that record behaviour and scenes and objects, Hayman comments 'Clearly, both of these help reassure the reader adrift in this strange new medium, this unpredictable narrative space. Both fade with the coming of the late-afternoon and evening hours; neither need be attributed to a capricious arranging presence.' He continues, arguing that 'the attempt to generalize further the arranged component of the text weakens the concept of arranger. The latter becomes the sum of the narrative process rather than a component of it: the distinction between narrator and arranger is virtually eliminated.' Hayman declares that 'Instead of going that far, we should probably think of the arranging presence as subtly penetrating the fabric of the narrative at a variety of points and in a variety of ways' (124). There is a marked difference between each critic's construct: where Kenner implies a link between the increased activities of the Arranger and Bloom, Hayman does no such thing. Kenner's Arranger is a continuation of his reading style, linking formal oddities and the minds of the characters: on the increasing presence of the Arranger perceived in the elaborate styles of the later episodes, in *'Ulysses'* he comments:

> And now we are in a position to understand that Joyce has not forgotten his former criterion of fidelity to the rhythm of his characters' thoughts. For, if the book seems for some hours temporarily adrift, that reflects Bloom's state, adrift, too, putting in time, neither free to go home nor sure how long to stay away. (101)

Kenner continues, observing that 'The new stylistic complications, too, which tend rather to screen than to clarify the chain of events, correspond to a span of time he won't want to discuss with Molly' (101). As something greater than a 'component', more active, and in more control throughout *Ulysses* than Hayman would allow, Kenner's Arranger plays a far greater role than Hayman's.

A thread runs from Kenner's reading of an ironised Stephen to his proposed Arranger. Clear links back to Stephen are seen also in Kenner and Hayman's use of the phrasing of Stephen's authorial theory (a nail-file bearing God-like artist) to refer to a narrating presence, rather than to the author. These links are further established by Kenner's continued, if complicated, emphasis on the relationship between the Arranger and Bloom – which has its roots in his turn from Stephen. Despite the occasional didacticism of *Joyce's Voices*, Kenner's critical mode does not claim to have solved anything once and for all. Michael Patrick Gillespie's assessment of Kenner's work on *Portrait* in *Dublin's Joyce*, perhaps referring in part to his separation of Stephen and Joyce, reflects not only his style but also that style's legacy in Joyce studies: 'Kenner's argument does not simply serve to advance his own views about Joyce's writings; rather, it makes us more aware of our own.'[45] His view of Stephen did not close the topic: critics continue to find themselves prompted by Kenner to discover their own perspective, and not everyone sees Stephen as ironically as Kenner does. As I will touch on again in Chapter 6, this is in part due to a continuously varied response to the autobiographical in Joyce's texts. Given its anecdotal style, in Chapter 6 I will discuss Budgen's *The Making of 'Ulysses'* – though it is here worth marking two of Joyce's assertions via Budgen. We are reminded to note the youth of Stephen (and thus the distance between Stephen and Joyce), and to focus on Bloom (suggesting difficulties will be answered by paying attention to Poldy). In his *'Ulysses'*, Kenner even confirms his debt to Budgen: thanking him for his pioneering of 'the centrality of Bloom' (5). Kenner's Arranger is touched somewhat by the relevance of Budgen's study to Kenner's Bloom-centric approach, and his elaboration of Gilbert's warnings against simple Stephen-Joyce links and readings of Bloom as more capable of creating Stephen than vice versa. Significantly, the theory of the Arranger is indebted to approaches recommended by two authorially authorised studies.

'The half-erased writing of our predecessors': Corrections, Intentions, Authority

The Arranger and the Uncle Charles Principle are readings of narrative informed by character: the roots of the Arranger lie partly in a shift of focus from Stephen to Bloom, and the Uncle Charles Principle suggests that confusing moments of narration are in fact character-inflected, an elaboration of free indirect discourse. Using characters to explain a stylistic choice or difficulty is one more critical mode owed to Gilbert, who defends the hyper-referential style of the novel by pointing at the saturation of Stephen and Bloom's minds with 'literary sources' and 'literary habits' (82). These are examples of finding solutions or explanations within the text itself, a well-established habit of Joycean criticism that endures despite demands to search also for help beyond the pages of the novel. In this last section, I will bring together earlier threads of my discussion to look at the other trends, habits, and shifts we can see in early *Ulysses* criticism which implicitly or explicitly convey attitudes to the author, the reader, and the text – and to the relationships between all three. First, however, I wish to highlight some intriguing instances of phrasing in these critical texts. Kenner echoes Gilbert's reading and declares in *Dublin's Joyce* that 'As Bloom's mind is a compost of objects, so is Stephen's a fabric of quotations', within his discussion of Stephen as a parody of a writer (174). Kain, meanwhile, looking briefly at *Finnegans Wake*, explores an idea of history and its writings as layered: 'The pages of history rapidly pass from view, and each generation, in turn, writes its records. But the pages are palimpsests on which we can barely trace the half-erased writing of our predecessors' (213). This layering shifts later in *Fabulous Voyager*: 'In *Ulysses* thoughts, characters, events, hopes, fears, and memories are woven into an intricate strand, constantly changing color with the changing moods of the principal figures' (226). Kenner's and Kain's phrasing is oddly evocative of Barthes's formulations, of texts formed of mixed writings and tissues of quotations. The text as woven, as fabric, is not original to Barthes; as he himself points out, its etymological roots are clear. With Barthes this idea of a text being 'woven entirely with citations, references, echoes, cultural languages' forms an argument against origins, against 'the myth of filiation' ('Author', 146 and 'Text', 160). Even if we set aside these connotations, Kenner and Kain still highlight the textuality of *Ulysses*.

Early on, a discernible shift in the aims of Ulyssean criticism gradually emerged: whether a move towards a more realistic outcome, or a sea change in notions of what literary criticism should try to achieve. This, again, is revealed in turns of phrase. Gilbert indicates what a reader must do in order 'to arrive at complete understanding' (36). Kain notes an aspect of the text 'has never been fully interpreted' (21). The motif of a 'key' or of 'keys' is used by both Larbaud and Levin – a metaphor with a long history in the study of texts, carrying the implication that a text can be unlocked, even solved. An attendant concern is that of intention, as we can see in Levin's desire to fully comprehend authorial intent and belief in the possibility of such an endeavour. Litz shares such faith, arguing that 'The action of the book is immediately accessible, and this provides the reader with an incentive for the careful study necessary to comprehend Joyce's full intent' (*The Art of James Joyce*, 125). Full, total, complete understanding aided by the discovery of a distinct, concrete intent gives way in time to more attainable aims of pluralism. As the number of studies increases, and with them the unavoidable coexistence of multiple readings, the way in which Joyce's texts resist 'complete understanding' – their polysemy – becomes itself a focus of criticism.

Acknowledging or foregrounding the wealth of possible readings of *Ulysses* also prioritises the reader. These early studies pay increasing attention to the reader rather than the author; we can even see this by identifying a contradiction in *James Joyce: A Critical Introduction*. Despite his stated aim to grasp the author's intention, Levin bases his movement away from an authorially authorised 'key' – the schema – on the argument that it is 'not there for us, but for Joyce'. What is 'for us', the reader, is more important than that which is 'for Joyce'; Levin's study does not explain how or why what could be classed as a statement of intent (the schema), or a doubling of that statement (Gilbert's study) are discounted in the search for 'the figure in the carpet'. By arguing that what is relevant to the author is irrelevant to the reader, Levin's approach undermines his own stated aims. Kain's *Fabulous Voyager* also focuses on the reader: its re-enactment of how they might search for and find information in *Ulysses* displays an interest in that very activity. Though not explicitly stated in his study, his efforts begin to show how *Ulysses* can make us aware of our own reading. Coupled with the work of Kenner, Kain's approach suggests that the activity of reading is itself relevant to *Ulysses*. Kenner is explicit in his focus on reading: his theories of Ulyssean narrative, emphasis on the physicality of the text, and use of the text to fill in its gaps, all explore the question of *how* we read *Ulysses* – his study *'Ulysses'* is further structured in such a way that his arguments develop as his discussion moves through the episodes of the novel, mimicking the growing adeptness we (might) feel as we work our way forwards and backwards from 'Telemachus' to 'Penelope'. The Arranger and the Uncle Charles Principle are as much about reading as they are writing; they offer strategies to navigate *Ulysses* and encourage playful, suspicious, even disrespectful readings.

An increased need to recognise and consider a wealth of possible readings and the relevance of the actual reading experience develops in these early years, and as it does so a contradictory corrective urge is established in Joyce studies. As I explored earlier in this chapter, the *raison d'être* of Gilbert's study was to correct some of the first critics of *Ulysses*. Gilbert confirms this:

> we who admired *Ulysses* for its structural, enduring qualities and not for the occasional presence in it of words and descriptive passages which shocked our elders, were on the defensive, and the pedant's cloak is often a convenient protection against the cold blasts of propriety. (12)

Ulysses had to be rescued from Aldington and Lewis by Eliot and Gilbert. Gilbert responds to and even pre-empts negative criticism of the novel, in general evasions,

> Some critics of *Ulysses*, while accepting the work as a whole, accuse defects in this passage or that, in the technique of one episode or another, and blame the author for leading us around unnecessary *détours*; it is often [. . .] precisely in the offending passages that the text is at its most significant. For no passage, no phrase in *Ulysses* is irrelevant . . . (59)

and in more specific suggestions: 'It will be observed that there is no corresponding "Organ of the Body" for the first three episodes. The explanation of this is probably that these episodes deal exclusively with the acts and thoughts of Stephen Dedalus' (42). The literary mind of Stephen silences complaints that the novel is too referential, accusers who see an uncontrolled outpouring are shown the regimented schema, and any gaps in the schema are there for good reason too. This aspect of Gilbert's critical legacy is established by his critical opponents: enter Levin's own correcting approach. Righting critical wrongs is entrenched: Levin tut-tuts over the emphasis Gilbert places on the schema, Litz backs up this correction by delving into worksheets and notes, and Kain not only disagrees with Gilbert but also laments previous criticism more generally: 'Just as Shakespeare has often been ruined for schoolboys, so Joyce's brilliant insights into the dilemmas of modern civilisation are too often smothered under a moraine of footnotes' (2), a useful claim echoed by critics preceding and following (adding yet more footnotes).

Kenner's salvaging of Gilbert, and the reinstatement of the Homeric in Joycean critical thought continued by others, is itself corrective. Kenner's reclamation of the mythic in *Ulysses* comes with careful adjustments: he is not repeating Gilbert, but reassessing. He does, however, therefore replicate Gilbert's corrective mode: both generally in his Homeric work and more specifically in his references to Wyndham Lewis. Kenner pointedly corrects Lewis at least twice in his studies, and these corrections form the basis of his innovative readings of Joyce's narratives. Kenner amends Lewis's misreading of 'the mind that informs *Ulysses*' and revises the way in which previous critics read Stephen as Joyce, developing – as I have argued – both rectifications in his theory of the Arranger. Similarly, in *Joyce's Voices* Kenner frames the Uncle Charles Principle as a direct response to another of Lewis's misreadings: 'Scanning *A Portrait of the Artist as a Young Man* fifty years ago, the eye of Wyndham Lewis was caught by what seemed an inadvertency of diction in a book not quite, as he thought, "swept and tidied".' What Lewis spots is the word 'repaired': 'uncle Charles repaired to his outhouse but not before he had greased and brushed scrupulously his black hair and brushed and put on his tall hat' (*P*, 60; q. *Joyce's Voices*, 16–17).

> Lewis thought that in catching Joyce writing 'repaired' he had caught him off guard. 'People,' he said, '*repair* to places in works of fiction of the humblest order.' He was characterizing Joyce as a humble scrivener who kept himself from dropping into cliché by not wholly incessant vigilance. But the normal Joycean vigilance has not faltered here. (17)

Combining this with other readings, Kenner establishes his argument of 'invisible quotation marks' in the narration: 'something new in fiction, the normally neutral narrative vocabulary pervaded by a little cloud of idioms which a character might use if he were managing the narrative' (17). Where other critics find error, Kenner finds innovation. He further uses the principle to explain the opening naturalism of the novel, reading it as linked to both the presence of the characters Buck Mulligan and Stephen, and the expectations of the reader opening and beginning to read the book; a correction substantially developed by Karen Lawrence in her 1981 study *The Odyssey of Style in 'Ulysses'*. Lawrence reads the early naturalising style through the changing modes of the second half of the novel to reveal and explore 'the arbitrariness of all styles', and further voices some of the earliest critical scepticism over the relevance of Stephen's theories of authorship (she is also one of the first Joyceans to look at Barthes).[46]

A gentler description of this critical tendency would be 'collaborative'; as Kenner describes, looking back fondly at *Dublin's Joyce* in 1987,

> We draw on a kind of collective and evolving awareness of the text, something I've watched develop among Joyceans over forty years. Joyceans are readers of Joyce who keep in touch, by article or book or letter, and each Joycean helps form the conscience the rest rely on. So we none of us now read the same *Ulysses* Stuart Gilbert read in 1930; nor, for that matter, do I read the same *Ulysses* I was reading in 1950. (*Dublin's Joyce*, xiii)

I characterise these early critical endeavours as 'corrective', however, to highlight their underlying preservation of a belief in a 'right' reading of *Ulysses*, which itself connotes a prospect of 'complete understanding'. Even if I tone down this view and concede that these corrective early critical studies are not offered 'instead of' what precedes them but as 'better than' them, I still come up against an implicit hierarchical attitude to readings – a sort of one-upmanship[47] that is perhaps how all literary critics are trained to write, but which undermines polysemy. Though these inherent paradoxes were not explored at the time, the developmental mode of Joyce criticism formed by layers of remedial critical studies established a self-reflexive tendency. At its origins, criticism of *Ulysses* had to respond to previous criticism, in a manner beyond the basic critical due diligence of locating one's work in the field; and this response became more and more of a focus. This places an increased emphasis on the activity of reading *Ulysses*, as an analysis of criticism is an analysis of other readings. The polysemantic text of *Ulysses* provokes myriad readings, and so criticism becomes a space in which *how* we read *Ulysses* assumes increasing importance.

In these early critical works much of the expressed or suggested attitudes to the relationships between authors, readers, and texts – and to the role of the critic – revolve around questions of intention. McCarthy wonders whether Gilbert's 'status as an authorized interpretation seems less important to a generation that has come to be suspicious about author's statements regarding their intentions' – a query that tells us as much about McCarthy's 1991 context as it does about critical attitudes earlier in the twentieth century, and somehow also misses the point.[48] 'Intention' is not a dirty word to many of the critics discussed above, and its discovery is often expressed clearly, for example by Levin in 1941 and Litz in 1961, as the aim of their work. As I have begun to explore, the oddity of Levin is the coincidence of his pro-intention stance and his refusal of 'an authorized interpretation'. In *The Art of James Joyce*, meanwhile, Litz relies on (and perhaps establishes) a perceived greater authority of worksheets over schema in his search for intention – but complicates this in a rarely cited confession in his preface:

> I have long since relinquished the comforting belief that access to an author's workshop provides insights of greater authority than those produced by other kinds of criticism [. . .] Indeed it now seems to me that the controlling design – the 'figure in the carpet' – lies always in plain view, not in the dark corners explored by the genetic or biographical critic. (v)

Litz contradicts the authority of biographical or genetic criticism (little affecting the growing popularity of genetic methods in the decades that followed) but retains the explicit aim he shares with Levin: to seek the artist's design.

Kain, meanwhile, moves away from such objectives in his 1947 study. This is clear in his focus on the reader and the reader's activity, but it is also suggested in a choice of phrase: discussing certain aspects of 'Calypso' Kain notes that 'Gilbert would have us believe [. . .] [these] are not accidental' (41). He refutes what Gilbert presents as intentional – either due to a distrust of Gilbert, a disinterest in the author's intentions, or a treatment of those intentions with the 'suspicion' McCarthy finds in later critical responses. Kenner does not shy away from discussing intention either, though it is an occasional rather than overriding critical concern. In *Dublin's Joyce* Kenner reads the Homeric correspondences 'inflected with a pathetic divergence of intention' (186). He develops this in *'Ulysses'*: not, however, by suggesting more knowledge of that intention, but by defending the impossibility of knowing it. 'In giving the *Odyssey* priority, the title does not tell us how the *Odyssey* is present: retrieving its marks is our doing', he argues:

> It is this compliance with our collaboration, this symbiosis of observer with observed, that marks the radiant novelty of *Ulysses*. Whatever tasks we may set ourselves with its aid, we are oddly liberated from an anxious sense of living in the great Taskmaster's eye, confined by the intentions of the author. He kept his intentions, so far as he could, out of sight, suppressing even the Homeric episode-titles, and much, he saw to it, must emerge that he did not intend. (*'Ulysses'*, 155)

Kenner presents *Ulysses* as a text in which there is no need for readers or critics to concern themselves with the author's intention, as we have our own important role to play; a text to be read without the guarantee of the father, to use instead Barthes's words. This is described by Kenner, however, in terms of what Joyce 'did' ('so far as he could'). The result is a paradoxical assertion that I will repeatedly address across *The Reader's Joyce*: that we cannot read the author's intention in *Ulysses* because the author did not intend that to be possible – and that furthermore the author intended (or 'saw to') the potential for unintended effects.

Reappraising Kenner in 1991, Gillespie tries out multiple labels: successfully showing how Kenner's work resists such categories (while revealing the concerns of a Joycean in the early 1990s). Claiming Kenner's approach as 'a useful guide to any scholar, whatever his or her particular theoretical predilections', he argues, 'long before writers like Jacques Derrida called into question traditional linear critical responses, Kenner had been deconstructing Joyce's works. Yet in doing so, he has resolutely avoided the linguistic accoutrements adopted by many of the most outspoken proponents of poststructuralism.' Applying some linguistic accoutrements and now a 'New Critic' label, Gillespie suggests that

> Even when he most overtly exercises his New Critical tendencies, it would be a mistake to dismiss Kenner's methodology or his findings anachronistic. Like the best of the recent critical approaches, Kenner's methods remind one of the power inherent in words and of the power inherent in the reader's signification.

Finally, he reaches out to two more theoretical modes: 'Such an openness demonstrates implicit affinities with contemporary theories of reader response and with current gestures toward a methodology of phenomenological interpretation.'[49] In 1987 Kenner observes, looking back at the early critical works of Gilbert, Budgen, Levin, and Kain – as well as Gorman's biography – 'That the key to the books is the man and what he lived through was a post-Romantic dogma then seldom questioned. We've since swung all the way clear to deconstructible text – an excessive correction' (*Dublin's Joyce*, xi). Joyce is often very present and knowable in Kenner's work: he cannot be described as an anti-authorial critic. Furthermore, despite the evident similarities between aspects of his work and the poststructuralist ideas of writers like Barthes, Kenner places himself in opposition to those ideas. In '*Ulysses*' he clearly restates his belief that 'On nothing is *Ulysses* more insistent than on the fact that there is no Bloom there, no Stephen there, no Molly there, no Dublin there, simply language.' The reader and author are 'co-creators', he continues, but tries to clarify: 'This is not to say, with Barthes in *S/Z*, that our reading of any book is essentially our doing. Words are prior to us, communal, entangled in human experience, registered in other books and in dictionaries' (156) (Barthes might, however, agree with the latter). Kenner's critical work resists the labels and standpoints of critical theory. His analytical concerns, and those expressed by the early critics of *Ulysses*, nevertheless share common ground with the concerns of literary theorists and their followers from the 1970s onwards. These early Joyce critics engage, if indirectly, with the issue of what literary criticism should aim for – critiquing the mode of criticism itself, one aim we can see in literary theory's reforming streak. They also engage – again, not always explicitly – with questions pertinent to analyses of literary origins, of the role of the reader, the nature of text, and the relationships between all three: the questions grappled with in the authorial theorising of the writers explored in my previous chapter. The shift from 'what was the author trying to do?' to 'how do we read this?' is prompted by *Ulysses* criticism and *Ulysses* itself.

These early works of criticism display the impact of Gilbert's *James Joyce's 'Ulysses'*, a study authorially authorised by Joyce. Gilbert's legacy of corrective criticism emphasises a trait of all literary criticism: to reassess, find something new, position one's reading in relation to others. This inherent characteristic begins to be writ large in early Joyce studies because the rudimentary question of *how* one can or should read *Ulysses* continues to require attention. Joyce's interventions, however we view them – and depending on how much intention-mining we can stomach – did not clarify how to read *Ulysses*, but instead ensured the ongoing provocation to answer the question. This focus, and the attendant self-reflexivity of Joycean criticism, are also the results of the text itself. The difficulty of *Ulysses* and its demands to be reread not only provoke critics to query how the text is to be read; the difficulty and demands of the text also themselves become topics for criticism. Joseph Frank in 1945 argues that 'Joyce cannot be read – he can only be re-read', and that despite the 'burdens placed on the reader' he 'proceeded in the assumption that a unified spatial apprehension of his work would ultimately be possible'.[50] Edmund Wilson, five years later, compares the book's difficulty and our need to 'revisit it' to 'a city, where we come more and more to recognize faces, to understand personalities, to grasp relations, currents and interests'.[51] The impossibility of discussing *Ulysses* without discussing the activity of reading informs Joyce studies from its earliest years. And as suggested by Frank's response, the question of *how to read the author* is caught up in that of *how to read the text*. Looking for help, some critics turn to the text's composition – and as Seidel mentions in his defence of the schema, 'if the process of building is as important as the result, the scaffold never disappears'. Joyce guaranteed the importance of process when *he* turned to Gilbert. Traces of the ongoing entanglement of Joyce's involvement in the conclusions and practices of early critics are still present in studies written decades after his death, as is the implicit question of *how to read the author*. Meanwhile, a tiny minority of Joyceans began to respond to new theoretical approaches to literary texts.

French theory started to appear in Joyce studies in the 1970s (as did some further overdue cracks in the male domination of the field), most notably with Hélène Cixous's *L'Exil de James Joyce ou l'Art du remplacement*, a 1972 study translated into English in 1976, and Margot Norris's 1976 *The Decentred Universe of 'Finnegans Wake': A Structuralist Analysis*. Cixous and Norris explored psychoanalytic and poststructuralist approaches, and were part of a small group which grew in number and impact as Joyce studies moved into and through the 1980s. The work of Hayman and Kenner exists concurrently to these developments: both critics refer to these shifts in later editions of their work, but go no further than brief prefatory mentions. Much of Joyce studies carried on regardless, critical heads not turned by new methods or ideas. These non-theoretical, or 'pre'-theoretical studies proliferated beyond and in spite of the arrival of theory in Joycean criticism: Richard Ellmann's *'Ulysses' on the Liffey* in 1972, Clive Hart and David Hayman's edited volume of episode-by-episode essays *James Joyce's 'Ulysses': Critical Essays* in 1974, Marilyn French's *The Book as World: James Joyce's 'Ulysses'* in 1976, Charles Peake's *James Joyce: The Citizen and the Artist* in 1977, among many others.[52] While Kenner's concerns in particular overlap with those of various literary theoretical approaches, the other works I've discussed also confirm that many of the issues occupying the theorists and theoretical critics of the 1970s and 1980s were already present in Joyce studies: issues such as the role of criticism, the polysemy of text, the activity of reading, the relevance of intention, playfulness, intertextuality, the potential within language, and who or what lies behind the text. Early critical works reached differing conclusions riddled with contradictions, and rarely discussed these issues explicitly – but they were being attended to.

The *Odyssey* is one text of the many that we address when reading *Ulysses*, joined by countless other works of literature, and the factual written sources explored by Kain and those who followed him. Whether engaged in critical analysis or reading only for pleasure we are also obliged to address the schemata appended to nearly every edition of the novel, and various annotations or footnotes. We note the existence of other versions of *Ulysses* when we check errata in the backs of our copies, or turn to other editions. Reading further – closer, yet more widely – we must address yet more texts to assist our endeavour: a constellation of 'satellites',[53] or so-called guide books. When we open a work of criticism, we encounter a layered history of readings, a palimpsest attesting to the novel's resistance to being pinned down. We can trace key characteristics of Joyce studies – self-consciously corrective criticism, a focus on reading itself, and a strange and complex relationship to the author – back to the fundamental, early, and unanswered question of how to read the *Odyssey* in *Ulysses*.

NOTES

1. Thomas F. Staley, 'Notes and Comments', *James Joyce Quarterly*, vol. 3, no. 1 (Fall, 1965), 1–2 (1).
2. Marvin Magalaner and Richard M. Kain, *Joyce: The Man, The Work, The Reputation* (New York: New York University Press, 1956), v.

3. Including: Michael Patrick Gillespie and Paula F. Gillespie, *Recent Criticism of James Joyce's 'Ulysses': An Analytical Review* (2000); Joseph Brooker, *Joyce's Critics: Transitions in Reading and Culture* (2004); *Re-Viewing Classics of Joyce Criticism*, ed. Janet Egleson Dunleavy (1991); Geert Lernout, *The French Joyce* (1990); Alan Roughley, *James Joyce and Critical Theory: An Introduction* (1991).
4. Which increases again, when such complaints are commented on (here, and Brooker, *Joyce's Critics*, 3).
5. See Brooker, *Joyce's Critics*, 97–100, and Jeri Johnson's introduction to *Ulysses* (*Ulysses: The 1922 text*, ed. Johnson (Oxford: Oxford University Press, 2008), xvii–xviii), both cf. Litz, 'Pound and Eliot on *Ulysses*: The Critical Tradition', in *'Ulysses': Fifty Years*, ed. Thomas Staley (1972; repr. Bloomington: Indiana University Press, 1974), 5–18.
6. See, for example, Joseph Valente, 'Joyce's (Sexual) Choices: A Historical Overview', in *Quare Joyce*, ed. Valente (Ann Arbor: University of Michigan Press, 1998), 1–16 (13–14). Valente also names the influential queer figures Janet Flanner, Djuna Barnes, and Natalie Barney.
7. Hugh Kenner, *Joyce's Voices* (Berkeley, Los Angeles, and London: University of California Press, 1978), 62–3. Further references to this edition are given after quotations in the text.
8. Frank Budgen, *James Joyce and The Making of 'Ulysses'* (Bloomington: Indiana University Press, 1961), 60.
9. T. S. Eliot, '*Ulysses*, Order, and Myth', in *Selected Prose of T. S. Eliot*, ed. Frank Kermode (London: Faber, 1975), 175–8 (178). Appeared in *The Dial*, November 1923. Further references to this edition are given after quotations in the text.
10. Valéry Larbaud, 'James Joyce', in *James Joyce: The Critical Heritage*, ed. Robert H. Deming, 2 vols (London: Routledge and Kegan Paul, 1970), 252–62 (260).
11. Ezra Pound, 'Paris Letter, *Ulysses*', May 1922, in *Early Writings: Poems and Prose*, ed. Ira B. Nadel (London: Penguin, 2005), 334–41 (338). Appeared in *The Dial*, June 1922.
12. Wyndham Lewis, *Time and Western Man* (London: Chatto and Windus, 1927), 108.
13. Lewis, 109.
14. Stuart Gilbert, *James Joyce's 'Ulysses'* (London: Faber, 1960), 12. Further references to this edition are given after quotations in the text.
15. Katherine Mullin, *James Joyce, Sexuality and Social Purity* (Cambridge: Cambridge University Press, 2003), 203.
16. Patrick A. McCarthy, 'Stuart Gilbert's Guide to the Perplexed', in *Re-Viewing Classics of Joyce Criticism*, ed. Janet Egleson Dunleavy (Urbana and Chicago: University of Illinois Press, 1991), 23–35 (25).
17. R. Brandon Kershner, 'Intertextuality', in *The Cambridge Companion to 'Ulysses'*, ed. Sean Latham (New York: Cambridge University Press, 2014), 171–83 (174), and William Schutte, *Joyce and Shakespeare: A Study in the Meaning of 'Ulysses'* (New Haven: Yale University Press, 1957), quoted in McCarthy, 30.
18. Michael Seidel, *Epic Geography: James Joyce's 'Ulysses'* (Princeton, NJ and Guilford: Princeton University Press, 1976), xvi.
19. McCarthy, 30 and 29.

20. Vivienne Koch, 'An Approach to the Homeric Content of Joyce's *Ulysses*', *Maryland Quarterly*, vol. 1 (1944), 119–30.
21. Harry Levin, 'Preface to the Revised Edition', in *James Joyce: A Critical Introduction* (Norfolk: New Directions, 1960), vi–xx.
22. Harry Levin, *James Joyce: A Critical Introduction* (Norfolk: New Directions, 1941), viii. Further references to this edition are given after quotations in the text.
23. Richard M. Kain, *Fabulous Voyager: James Joyce's 'Ulysses'* (Chicago: University of Chicago Press, 1947), 5. Further references to this edition are given after quotations in the text.
24. The Blooms' 'orangekeyed chamberpot' sits unnoticed by Kain in the Eccles Street bedroom, beside a sprawled book, waiting for Bloom to stub his toe (4.330).
25. A. Walton Litz, *The Art of James Joyce: Method and Design in 'Ulysses' and 'Finnegans Wake'* (London: Oxford University Press, 1961), 21. Further references to this edition are given after quotations in the text.
26. McCarthy, 30.
27. Kenner, *Dublin's Joyce*, Morningside Edition (New York: Columbia University Press, 1987), 180. Further references to this edition are given after quotations in the text.
28. McCarthy, 31.
29. Seidel, xv.
30. McCarthy, 24.
31. In the later edition of *James Joyce: A Critical Introduction*, however, Levin adjusts some of his readings of *Portrait*, toning down his treatment of the novel as straightforward autobiography. Morton P. Levitt, 'Harry Levin's *James Joyce* and the Modernist Age: A Personal Reading', in *Re-Viewing Classics of Joyce Criticism*, 90–105 (95–6).
32. Levitt, 96 and 98.
33. Levitt, 96.
34. Kenner becomes guilty of this towards the end of his discussion of Joyce in *The Stoic Comedians* when he argues the importance for 'Joyce' of *consonantia* and *integritas*. Stephen explores these ideas of Thomas Aquinas in *Portrait*. Kenner, *Flaubert, Joyce and Beckett: The Stoic Comedians* (London: Dalkey Archive Press and Normal, 2005), 60–6.
35. S. L. Goldberg, *The Classical Temper: A Study of James Joyce's 'Ulysses'* (London: Chatto and Windus, 1961), 107.
36. Goldberg, 300.
37. Goldberg, 312.
38. Some confusion here: Kenner sees the author hiding, paring his fingernails, behind a machine-like glinting narrative presence – which is also paring its fingernails.
39. Kenner has great fun exploring the possibilities opened up by structures of printed discourse, such as footnotes. In a mid-sentence footnote to his own diatribe on footnotes, Kenner comments: 'Some footnotes of course seem totally unrelated to the point in the text at which they are appended. They suggest an art form like the refrains in Yeats' late poems.' A footnote not much later reads 'Please pay attention' (*The Stoic Comedians*, 40 and 41).
40. Kenner, *The Stoic Comedians*, xix.

41. On typographical confusions: Hayman's term in 1970 is '"the arranger"'. I will follow Kenner in using 'the Arranger'.
42. David Hayman, *'Ulysses': The Mechanics of Meaning*, revised and extended edition (Madison: University of Wisconsin Press, 1982), 84. Further references to this edition are given after quotations in the text.
43. Though Kenner does not acknowledge it, the phrase is previously noted by Charles Peake in *James Joyce: The Citizen and the Artist*. Peake suggests the 'clumsy formula' is used to show 'the author's intention' – to emphasise the text as a 'verbal representation' (London: Edward Arnold, 1977), 230.
44. Kenner, *'Ulysses'* (London: George Allen and Unwin, 1980), 64–5. Further references to this edition are given after quotations in the text.
45. Michael Patrick Gillespie, 'Kenner on Joyce', in *Re-Viewing Classics of Joyce Criticism*, 142–54 (149).
46. Karen Lawrence, *The Odyssey of Style in 'Ulysses'* (Princeton, NJ: Princeton University Press, 1981), 9.
47. Tempting to use the term pissing contest, here.
48. McCarthy, 32.
49. Gillespie, 'Kenner on Joyce', 143, 148, and 149.
50. Joseph Frank, 'Spatial Form in Modern Literature', in *Essentials of the Theory of Fiction*, ed. Michael J. Hoffman and Patrick D. Murphy, 3rd edn (Durham, NC and London: Duke University Press, 2005) 61–73 (64). Frank is also quoted by Litz, *The Art of James Joyce* (London: Oxford University Press, 1961), 56.
51. Edmund Wilson, *Axel's Castle* (New York: Charles Scribner's Sons, 1950), 210. Also quoted by Litz, *The Art of James Joyce*, 58.
52. With Ellmann further making the Carlo Linati schema widely available.
53. McCarthy, 25. He quotes Judge Woolsey, ruling *Ulysses* was not obscene in the 1933 trial *United States* v. *One Book Called 'Ulysses'*.

3

THE HOMERIC QUESTION

Written texts and pieces of paper clutter Dublin on 16 June 1904. In transit, a 'crumpled throwaway' moves along the current of the Liffey (10.294–7, 10.753–4, and 10.1096–9); Deasy's letter is repurposed as scribbling paper for Stephen's poetic composition, later found by Bloom (3.404–7 and 13.1246–7); letters are received, written, and dwelled upon; an advertisement is placed, galleys are proofed, and Bloom 'watch[es] a typesetter neatly distributing type' (7.204); a library book requires renewal (4.360–1), but remains out of date (16.1421–2); and Bloom picks up *Sweets of Sin*, a novel which remains both in his pocket and on his mind. In 'Eumaeus', the sixteenth episode of *Ulysses* and first part of the final 'Nostos', there is something a little wrong with anything on paper or card. The sailor 'D. B. Murphy, A. B. S.' – regaling Leopold Bloom, Stephen Dedalus, and others with seafaring stories in a cabman's shelter late at night – presents 'a not very cleanlooking folded document' as his discharge papers (16.452–5), quickly followed by a postcard 'A friend of mine sent me' contradictorily addressed to a *'Señor A Boudin'* (16.471 and 16.489). The *Evening Telegraph* write-up of Patrick Dignam's funeral, read by Bloom, is peppered with errors of omission and inclusion; mistakes foretold by the pun 'tell a graphic lie' (16.1232). Even a photograph of Molly Bloom shown by her husband to Stephen is not just 'faded' but 'slightly soiled': 'an added charm' (16.1425 and 16.1465–8). Something is a little wrong too with 'Eumaeus' itself: though the text of the episode looks on the page like the straightforward third person narrative we might yearn for after the riot of

'Circe', it swiftly becomes clear that the narrative of Bloom and Stephen making their way from the brothels of Nighttown to Bloom's home on Eccles Street will not be straightforward at all. In a confusion of posturing and slip-ups, populated by characters with mistaken, false, and mislaid identities, suspicion coils through 'Eumaeus' – and faced with such an intriguing and evasive narrative, we are provoked to read suspiciously. As survivors (of sorts) of the games of previous episodes, of the geographically hopping omniscience of 'Wandering Rocks' or the melodic repetitions of 'Sirens', by the time we reach 'Eumaeus' we have some experience of reading the narratives of the novel with suspicion and of filling in narrative unknowns. But this mode of reading becomes especially pertinent in 'Eumaeus'; as is made clear by an analysis of its exploration of disguises and storytelling, and – in particular – the Homeric roots for such explorations.

Several key concerns which run throughout *Ulysses* and the *Odyssey* are at their most explicit in 'Eumaeus'. The themes of disguise, role-playing, and identity which are explored in the episode are present all through the novel and the *Odyssey*, and furthermore are constant in *Ulysses*' position as a rewriting in which intertextual roles shift and change across a disguised source text. In the *Odyssey* hidden identities are linked to the telling of stories, to lies and revelations. The same occurs in *Ulysses*, especially where Bloom is concerned, who in his extra-marital letters goes by 'Henry Flower'. This too is perhaps most explicitly realised in 'Eumaeus', by the spurious narratives within the episode and the curious narrative by which they are communicated to the reader, and by the confused and stolen identities of the episode's characters – bodied forms of lies and storytelling. Critics tend to focus on two confused identities in 'Eumaeus' – the keeper of the cabman's shelter who resembles the getaway driver of the Fenian Invincibles, and Murphy the storytelling sailor – along with their schematically assigned roles Eumaeus the swineherd and 'Ulysses Pseudangelos'. In this chapter I will instead begin by reassessing the strange relationship between Bloom and the narrative, treating the very act of questioning the narrative as a significant playful interaction of *Ulysses* with its Homeric precursor. This will enable me to not only argue for a reconsideration of how *Ulysses* rewrites the *Odyssey* – but also propose a significant new reading of how it rewrites Homeric scholarship, with far-reaching implications for how we perceive the relationship between author and reader in and beyond *Ulysses*.

In Chapter 2 I discussed the lengths to which Joyce went to establish the Homeric precursor of *Ulysses*, and the impact that questions of the role of the *Odyssey* had on early critical responses to the novel, touching upon the suggestion that one function of Stuart Gilbert's 'critical propaganda' was to establish the 'respectability' of *Ulysses* by emphasising the Homeric.[1] This reading of Gilbert is briefly addressed in more recent criticism by Katherine Mullin and Leah Culligan Flack: in *Modernism and Homer* (2015) Flack reads a pointed use of the 'cultural currency' of Homer by Joyce and others.[2] Referencing Mullin's 2003 study *James Joyce, Sexuality and Social Purity*, Flack characterises the Joyce-authorised works of Linati, Eliot, Larbaud, and Gilbert as 'a targeted public relations campaign to pre-emptively dismantle charges of formless incoherence and obscenity'.[3] The 'promotional' use by Joyce, Pound, and Eliot of Homer's 'cultural currency [. . .] intentionally obscured the complex, changing engagements with Homer that fuelled their literary and socio-political projects'.[4] Flack demands a reappraisal, joining the long line of Joycean readers I have considered who query the way the Homeric in *Ulysses* was characterised by Gilbert et al. Michael Seidel positions himself similarly, but with quite a different emphasis. In his preface to *Epic Geography*, published in 1976, he raises the unpopular opinion that Gilbert, 'the bag man for Joyce's esoterica', rather than overblowing the Homeric correspondences 'did not take Joyce's schemes far enough to reveal the extent to which some of them informed the narrative design of the novel'.[5] Hugh Kenner's work across each of the studies I discussed in the previous chapter, a number of articles, and his 1971 tome *The Pound Era* – in which he finds 'a museum of Homers' in *Ulysses*[6] – for a long time constituted the most sustained effort in Joyce studies to take 'Joyce's schemes' further.

The central enquiries of this chapter revolve around the textual provocations within 'Eumaeus' to look beyond the narrative, beyond *Ulysses* to its precursory text the *Odyssey*, and beyond the *Odyssey* to the Homeric Question. But first, a further note on the position of Homer in the field of Joyce studies today, and the decades that lie between the field's last extended engagement with Homer and the very recent work of a small group of critics. In this chapter I'll be discussing the Homeric Question, a term usually referring to areas of classical scholarship interested in questions of Homeric authorship and composition: the centuries-old and ongoing debate of, to put it simply, how the *Iliad* and the *Odyssey* came to be. There also remains a 'Homeric Question' in the field of Joyce studies however, concerning authorship, composition, and authority. This is the question of identifying how, or if, or to what extent, the *Odyssey* is relevant to *Ulysses* – or to how we read *Ulysses*. In the previous chapter I traced an entertaining back-and-forth from the earliest criticism of the novel onwards, between those who defend the usefulness of the *Odyssey* and those who contest it (with Joyce's own involvement enjoyably complicating matters). Since the early disagreements, Joyce-ordained studies, and resultant movements to and from Homer as a site of Joycean enquiry, until recently criticism by Kenner, Seidel, and Fritz Senn provided the bulk of our current understandings of the titular intertextual relationship of *Ulysses*.

An increased interest in modernist classical reception studies has caused a timely (if very contained) revival of discussions of how *Ulysses* reads Homer, seen in criticism by, most notably, Leah Flack and Stephanie Nelson. In *James Joyce and Classical Modernism* (2020), Flack defines Joyce's modernism as enabled by his engagement with the classics, arguing that Joyce turned to the classics 'not to stabilize his writings, but rather to innovate';[7] Nelson's work, meanwhile, reconsiders time, narrative, and storytelling in the *Odyssey* and *Ulysses*.[8] Beyond the exciting scholarship of a very small group of critics, however, there remains a pervasive attitude in much of Joyce studies that the relationship between *Ulysses* and Homer is either important but fully explicated, or unimportant (and thus, also fully explicated).[9] Perhaps the turn from the Homeric is one casualty of the schism some see between Irish and European Joyces[10] – it has maybe simply not been the time to emphasise shared European roots. As more recent criticism begins again to reassess the relationship between the *Odyssey* and *Ulysses*, critics rethink a stated authorial decision to associate oneself and one's writing with a previous author, a previous text. But what if that author and the authorship of that text are uncertain, even unknown? *Ulysses*, I will argue, provocatively engages with a debate over authorship and the processes of literary genesis that spans hundreds of years. The reception of Homer is present in *Ulysses*, and thus too the attendant uncertainties that led to centuries of ideated Homers. As a result, Homeric theories of genesis, composition, authorship, are relevant to *Ulysses*. By emphasising Homer as an unknown, as a series of questions rather than a known authorship, I will here examine the links between the Homeric Question in *Ulysses* and ideated authorship.

This chapter explores how 'Eumaeus' causes us to re-enact questions of authorship, and how through its rewriting of the *Odyssey Ulysses* thus provokes a questioning of the activities of authors and readers. Reading *Ulysses* closely, and tracing the ambiguous inferences of our readings, engenders these questions of authorship. My enquiries lead me to discuss a wide range of texts, but these emerge from 'Eumaeus': something of the episode points at its origins. This strategy relates to the methodology I described in the introduction to this book, and it is important to emphasise again the difference between reading *Ulysses* closely through questions of authorship, and asking such questions as arise out of close readings of *Ulysses*. It is the latter, along with its implications, that I endeavour to undertake in this study as a whole, and here in particular: it is what impels such questions, and what such interrogation does, that is the focus of what follows in this chapter. Beginning with the language of the Eumaean narrative style, I shall explore how suspicions of 'who' narrates the episode shift to 'what', as the concept of an individualised narrator becomes impossibly simplistic. Through an interrogation of the episode's treatment and awareness of printed texts, papers, or cards, I will argue for a vital development of previous readings of how the *Odyssey* is rewritten in *Ulysses* – and particularly contend that we can in *Ulysses* find traces of the Homeric poem's orality, of its shift from oral to written text, and of its unidentifiable authorship. Led thus to investigate the questions of authorship – subsumed under the umbrella term 'the Homeric Question' – which are central to certain approaches to the Homeric texts, I will posit parallels between the narrative effects of 'Eumaeus', the unknowns denoted by the name 'Homer', and the activities of authorially focused Homeric scholars, as well as suggest further resonances with theoretical approaches to the roles of authors and readers generally.

Prompted by these parallels, I will then introduce two further texts. First, I will turn to the suggestively creative authorial scholarship of Samuel Butler's 1897 *The Authoress of the 'Odyssey'*. Butler's response to the *Odyssey* plays with the uncertainties of authorship; filtering its suggestion of a Homeric authoress through a further author-persona. Though, as a text found in Joyce's Trieste library, it has been critically discussed before as an intertext through which *Ulysses* reads the *Odyssey*, many elements of this relationship, and the ways in which it has a significant impact on the narrative of 'Eumaeus', have been missed. The comfort with which these explorations sit within the thematic concerns of 'Eumaeus', its corresponding section of the *Odyssey*, and the *Odyssey* as a whole, is of great importance to my approach. I will therefore turn finally to Zachary Mason's contemporary Homeric short stories, *The Lost Books of the 'Odyssey'* (2010), which reach back to the Homeric poems and their scholarship and refigure both via the trope of self-conscious metafiction. *The Lost Books* provides a model for the fictive capacity of the Homeric Question.

My initial reading of the narrative style of 'Eumaeus' contributes to two arguments. First, that the episode contains ludic references to movements from oral narratives to printed text, from the spoken to the written; and second, that we as readers are encouraged to seek what lies behind the episode's narrative. By linking these elements via the Homeric Question, I will be able to examine how each encourages a focus on both origin and reception, originator and reader. I propose that *Ulysses* rewrites the concerns of Homeric scholarship – and that in this reworking we as readers are complicit, our manner of reading providing a further crucial link back to these debates. The presence of the Homeric Question in 'Eumaeus', in *Ulysses*, prompts ideas of reading without an author, reading in search of an author, and reading that creates an author. In what follows, I will treat *Ulysses* as an exploration of authorial and readerly roles, and argue that the Homeric intertext crucially informs the ways in which we read the novel – which in turn form our understandings of the text, its author, and our own activity of reading.

'MY EXPERIENCES, LET US SAY, IN A CABMAN'S SHELTER' (16.1231):
THE NARRATIVE OF 'EUMAEUS'

The peculiarities of narrative in 'Eumaeus' may appear subtle after the dramatic script-like form of the preceding episode, 'Circe', but instead point to a complicated and unsettling upset of narrative norms. Cumbersome phrasing and too many clauses, asides, and qualifying statements result in a style which many readers and critics find boring or tired.[11] The opening sentence has the narrative detail we might expect, but is presented in an oddly list-like yet elaborated style. The result is one too many 'ands' and a strangely described mode of 'bucking up': 'Preparatory to anything else Mr Bloom brushed off the greater bulk of the shavings and handed Stephen the hat and ashplant and bucked him up generally in orthodox Samaritan fashion which he very badly needed' (16.1–3). In 'Eumaeus' things are hit-upon or taken a shot at, sentences go on for too long or read like notes ('Funny, very!' (16.600)), and it is often unclear to whom pronouns refer. Subjects are buried by extra pieces of information and attempts at style, as a lack of logic pushes syntax to the brink of nonsense:

> But as he confidently anticipated there was not a sign of a Jehu plying for hire anywhere to be seen except a fourwheeler, probably engaged by some fellows inside on the spree, outside the North Star hotel and there was no symptom of its budging a quarter of an inch when Mr Bloom, who was anything but a professional whistler, endeavoured to hail it by emitting a kind of whistle, holding his arms arched over his head, twice. (16.24–30)

The narrative is not to be satisfied with anything as simple as 'he whistled twice' – though ten pages later 'Pom, he shouted twice' (16.401) is deemed more appropriate than 'Pom pom' – as events are over-narrated in an elaborate style. These seemingly harmless details of bad writing, clumsy narration, and overreaching style obscure the limited events of the episode, with the cumulative effect of causing a reader to ask of the narrator, 'But who?' (16.530).[12]

Though others find it tedious, the narrative is as comic as it is intriguing: we can discover great humour in the way in which the episode tries and fails. The pretensions of the narrative are revealed in an abundance of italicised imported words – *au fait, soirée, entre nous, coup d'œil, tête-à-tête, apropos, protégé, voglio, hoi polloi,* and *sangfroid* – unevenly littered through 'Eumaeus', as if the narrative only occasionally remembers to appear cosmopolitan. But its tendency to use clichéd phrases, a poor attempt at sophistication, often backfires: 'The horse, having reached the end of his tether, so to speak, halted' (16.1874). Bloom ('anything but a professional whistler' (16.29), and whose button, we are told, 'had gone the way of all buttons' (16.37)) and Stephen ('not in an over sober state himself' (16.129)) are 'our two noctambules' (16.326) – though Bloom is later upgraded to 'our hero' (16.1643) – and the sailor Murphy receives the brilliant moniker 'the communicative tarpaulin' (16.479). These modes of phrasing are so pronounced as to hint almost at a personality, what we could describe as a characterised narrative. Several cues in the episode's narrative games suggest attribution might be possible, tempting the reader of the words of 'Eumaeus' to attempt to discover 'who precisely wrote them' (16.783).

A story told twice offers a clue for the suspicious reader of 'Eumaeus'. In the right newspaper office at the right time (though unsure now of which office it was), Bloom once had a brief interaction with Charles Stuart Parnell, then leader of the Irish nationalist movement: Parnell thanked him for returning his knocked-off hat. This tale first appears as Bloom's recollection, within a passage of interior monologue:

> He saw him once on the auspicious occasion when they broke up the type in the *Insuppressible* or was it *United Ireland*, a privilege he keenly appreciated, and, in point of fact, handed him his silk hat when it was knocked off and he said *Thank you*. (16.1333–6)

This story is transformed a few pages later, narrated into over thirty lines of sentences each at least as long as the original recollected anecdote, peppered with 'fracas' and '*aplomb*', and resulting in such a confusion of detail that not only is an attempt to amplify Parnell's *Thank you* into '*Thank you, sir*' smothered but even the following clarification is necessary: 'His hat (Parnell's)' (16.1495–1528). Something of the transition from Bloom's thoughts to a narrative performance echoes the form of the episode, and suggests a culprit.

Bloom is the only character who in 'Eumaeus' speaks in the same idiom as the narrative.[13] This becomes particularly clear when Bloom's speech is juxtaposed with that of other characters:

> – You as a good catholic, he observed, talking of body and soul, believe in the soul. Or do you mean the intelligence, the brainpower as such, as distinct from any outside object, the table, let us say, that cup. I believe in that myself because it has been explained by competent men as the convolutions of the grey matter. Otherwise we would never have such inventions as X rays, for instance. Do you?
>
> Thus cornered, Stephen had to make a superhuman effort of memory to try and concentrate and remember before he could say:
> – They tell me on the best authority it is a simple substance and therefore incorruptible. It would be immortal, I understand, but for the possibility of its annihilation by its First Cause Who, from all I can hear, is quite capable of adding that to the number of His other practical jokes, *corruptio per se* and *corruptio per accidens* both being excluded by court etiquette. (16.748–60)

The awkward and syntax-muddling asides of Bloom – which are not incorrect, but are difficult to follow – are all the more apparent when compared to the natural interruptions a slightly drunk Stephen makes; his 'I understand' and 'from all I can hear' do not sacrifice the sense or logic of his point, while Bloom's asides sit uncomfortably within his sentences, excessive explanation leaving 'Do you?' hanging oddly. His question to Stephen is rendered nonsensical, in the same manner as his Parnell story is rendered dull – or, like the narrative, 'boring' (and we might also think of Bloom's inability in 'Hades' to properly tell the anecdote about Reuben J. Dodd (6.262–90)). We are encouraged to make further tentative links between Bloom's mind and the narrative of 'Eumaeus' as he thinks back to a story read in *Titbits* magazine that morning: 'suppose he were to pen something out of the common groove (as he fully intended doing) at the rate of one guinea per column. *My Experiences*, let us say, *in a Cabman's Shelter*' (16.1229–31).[14] Bloom's daydream of a hypothetical entrepreneurial endeavour is consistent with the meanderings of his thought elsewhere in *Ulysses*, particularly in the following episode 'Ithaca'. However, rather than pondering a scheme for increasing Dublin tourism (17.1720–4), Bloom here imagines writing the episode in which he himself is written.

This impulse to imply that Bloom is a part of the formation of the narrative, but not its sole perpetrator, is most explicitly explored by Kenner as an extension of free indirect speech. The appearance of the word 'literally' in *Dubliners* is crucial to Kenner's development in *Joyce's Voices* of the Uncle Charles Principle. In defence of 'Lily, the caretaker's daughter' who in 'The Dead' is 'literally rushed off her feet' and the 'repairing' Uncle Charles, the Principle allows that in Joyce's works *'the narrative idiom need not be the narrator's'*. In Kenner's reading 'repaired' is a word Uncle Charles would use, just as Lily might claim to be 'literally rushed off her feet', a 'speck of his characterizing vocabulary' affecting the third person narration.[15] It is satisfying to find 'literally' dotted about in 'Eumaeus', fulfilling its role as a pointer of narrative interpolation: though 'the civilised world' is taken 'by storm, figuratively speaking' there is also music capable of 'literally knocking everything else into a cocked hat', and Bloom can be 'Literally astounded', for example (16.607, 16.1740, and 16.1578). Kenner's reading of 'Eumaeus' elaborates this concept of 'writing about someone much as that someone would choose to be written about'. 'Eumaeus' is 'the Uncle Charles Principle *in excelsis*': Bloom is 'treated to an episode written as he would have written it', and furthermore 'it is so much Bloom's episode he even daydreams of writing it'.[16] Where others also suggest a relationship between Bloom and the narrative of 'Eumaeus', it is with a consistent carefulness of phrasing in order to avoid anything so simple as 'Bloom narrates/writes the episode'.[17]

Though stranger and more subtle than free indirect speech, the Uncle Charles Principle similarly implies a collaborative narrative. If the narrative is in some manner disguised in Bloom's idiom, playing the role of Bloom-as-author, then the reader is still left with questions. What does the disguise conceal, and who, or what, is playing the role? The Uncle Charles Principle in 'Eumaeus' does not solve an impulse for identification caused by the narrative style: it causes an inherent function of narrative to be writ large. In this episode we find a complex, teasing version of the effects of any narrative: to ask what lies behind it. Narratives beg questions. As Vladimir Nabokov points out in *Lectures on Literature*, 'Eumaeus' is full of a 'variety of synonyms for *he said*' – though to Nabokov these are only evidence of an 'elegant journalese' style.[18] '[H]e said'; 'he mentioned'; 'he commented'; 'he very sensibly maintained'; 'he added with a half laugh'; 'he informed'; 'he remarked'; 'he observed'; 'he ventured to say'; 'he appetisingly added'; 'says he'; 'repeated he'; 'he resumed'; 'he proceeded'; 'he continued'; 'he declared'; 'he stated'; 'he softly imparted'; 'he muttered'; 'he managed to remark'; 'he intimated'; and, my favourite, 'he subjoined pensively' – these are also repeated markers of the narrative act, exaggerated by their style and variation. In his 1953 work *Writing Degree Zero* Roland Barthes discusses the preterite tense of narrative: the 's/he said' function of third person narration. He argues that 'The preterite *signifies* a creation', and that 'it is a lie made manifest, it delineates an area of plausibility which reveals the possible in the very act of unmasking it as false'. Reading narrative as 'a lie made manifest' allows a reader to see the sailor Murphy's untruthful storytelling as an exaggeration of the inherent fiction of any narration. Barthes claims that 'Behind the preterite there always lurks a demiurge, a God, or a reciter'. So, 's/he said' indicates both that 's/he' has 'said', and that an other has informed us of this act. There is someone or something weaving the lie of narrative and simultaneously using it to conceal them or its self; as Barthes explains, 'this is what writing does in the novel. Its task is to put the mask in place and at the same time point it out' (46–8). Narrative can be read therefore as a disguise, as a concealed identity. Furthermore, we can read it as a form of role-playing: Gérard Genette, in *Narrative Discourse* (1980), describes narrating as 'an *act* like any other'.[19] In 'Eumaeus', then, this '*act*' is performed so badly as to draw attention to itself. And this causes us to suppose that, as I have explored above, the narrative is in some manner playing the role of Bloom on the page, while Bloom plays the role of narrator in his mind.

The narrative of 'Eumaeus' is where these two collide, in a confusion of mistaken and concealed identities, adopted roles, and disguises. The narrative maintains the thematic games of the episode, in which a man spuriously named Lord John Corley mistakes Bloom for a friend of Boylan (16.198–9); the keeper of the cabman's shelter is 'said to be the once famous Skin-the-Goat, Fitzharris, the invincible' (16.323–4); someone bears 'a distant resemblance to Henry Campbell, the townclerk' (16.661); Simon Dedalus is transformed by Murphy into a circus performer, and, when asked, Stephen Dedalus claims only to have 'heard of him' (16.379). The search for what or who is behind the narrative is in no way limited to the 'Eumaeus' episode of *Ulysses*, or even to those episodes of the novel in which a characterised narrative implies some sort of collaborative narrative effort. This search prompts Kenner (developing David Hayman's formulation), as I explored in Chapter 2, to find a non-human arranging figure at work in *Ulysses*, a presence which is neither the narrator nor the author. Kenner's Arranger reveals itself in the musical episode 'Sirens' with the words 'As said before' placed before a repetition of the opening of 'Calypso' – 'he ate with relish the inner organs, nutty gizzards, fried cods' roes' (11.519–20). It 'keeps track of the details of this printed cosmos', and has 'access such as ours to a printed book, in which pages can be turned to and fro'.[20] Across much of his Joycean criticism Kenner explores links between the ways in which *Ulysses* plays with its own printed form and questions of who or what informs the narrative of Joyce's texts. In the close readings that follow, I will respond to Kenner to argue moreover that the tensions between a self-conscious printed text and a disguised narrator or narrative are at their peak in 'Eumaeus', found in tiny mistakes and oddities which reveal a troublesome interaction between speech and writing. I am not attempting to find further evidence for an Arranger: rather, digging into these textual details enables me to show how in 'Eumaeus' the relationship between *Ulysses* and the *Odyssey* reaches a particularly self-aware pitch of intensity.

Errors and Slips in 'printed matter' (16.474)

The mourners included: Patk. Dignam (son), Bernard Corrigan (brother-in-law), Jno. Henry Menton, solr, Martin Cunningham, John Power, .)eatondph 1/8 ador dorador douradora (must be where he called Monks the dayfather about Keyes's ad) Thomas Kernan, Simon Dedalus, Stephen Dedalus B. A., Edw. J. Lambert, Cornelius T. Kelleher, Joseph M'C Hynes, L. Boom, C P M'Coy, – M'Intosh and several others. (16.1255-61)[21]

Two instances of terrible transcription lurk in the above extract of a printed text, quoted in 'Eumaeus'. The *Evening Telegraph* write-up of Patrick Dignam's funeral – attended by Bloom in the episode 'Hades' – includes M'Intosh, an embodied mishearing. A mistaken identity who wanders through the pages of *Ulysses*, the pseudonymous M'Intosh is named for his overcoat:

> – And tell us, Hynes said, do you know that fellow in the, fellow was over there in the . . .
> He looked around.
> – Macintosh. Yes, I saw him, Mr Bloom said. Where is he now?
> – M'Intosh, Hynes said, scribbling. I don't know who he is. Is that his name?
> He moved away, looking about him.
> – No, Mr Bloom began, turning and stopping. I say, Hynes!
> Didn't hear. What? Where has he disappeared to? Not a sign. (6.891–9)

M'Intosh, having found his way into print, is joined by 'the line of bitched type' (16.1262–3): '.)*eatondph 1/8 ador dorador douradora* (must be where he called Monks the dayfather about Keyes's ad)', a disaster of interpolation. In his 1987 study *The Mechanical Muse*, Kenner posits 'that "eatondph" is the grope of James Joyce's memory toward "etaoin"'.[22] Typing jumbled letters – 'etaoin' – after a mistype was a method of compositors using Linotype machines, to enable the whole line to be removed later: so we might assume that this 'line of bitched type' is either the compositor's incorrect (and perhaps therefore ignored) effort to do so, or follow Kenner and read it as Joyce's incorrect effort to imitate.[23] Bloom's thought – 'must be where he called Monks the dayfather about Keyes's ad' – refers the reader back to 'Aeolus', in which Bloom visits the newspaper offices and its printing machines which clank and 'sllt' (7.174–7). Making an adjustment to an advert for 'Alexander Keyes, tea, wine and spirit merchant', Bloom witnesses Monks, the dayfather, being called for by the foreman on an unrelated matter (7.184). On his way out Bloom passes Monks, and a typesetter working: 'Reads it backwards first. Quickly he does it. Must require some practice that. mangiD. kcirtaP' (7.205–6). A reader might presume that Bloom is seeing 'Patrick Dignam' being typeset at that very moment. However, it is just as likely that, having just left Dignam's funeral and spoken to Hynes about the write-up, Bloom is imagining 'mangiD. kcirtaP', pretending to read the name backwards as a typesetter would (particularly given his association with his father 'reading backwards with his finger' (7.206–7)). Either way, it is not clear that Bloom interrupted Monks himself, though the interruption is tied to Keyes in his memory; he is only tangentially linked to that typographical error, unlike the misprinted character he inadvertently christened 'M'Intosh'. And as the characters M'Intosh, Stephen Dedalus, and C. P. M'Coy are incorrectly included in the write-up, another character is excluded: the 'L' in Bloom's name is missing, as if in a fit of typographical revenge against the originator of the erroneous M'Intosh. Despite the galleys-checking and 'Proof fever' in 'Aeolus' (7.165), the snippet of newsprint is full of mistakes, at least one of which exposes the dangers of transferring the spoken ('macintosh') to the written and printed ('M'Intosh').

This is not the only time that the registers of speech and writing collide. Not long after reading the *Evening Telegraph* Bloom hands Stephen a slightly grubby photograph of Molly. He 'looked away thoughtfully with the intention of not further increasing the other's possible embarrassment while gauging her symmetry of heaving *embonpoint*' (16.1466–8).[24] A parenthetical anomaly in the narrative that follows suggests to a suspicious reader that 'Eumaeus' is aware of itself as a written and printed text; and therefore just as susceptible to errors caused by the interaction of the spoken and the written.

> In fact the slight soiling was only an added charm like the case of linen slightly soiled, good as new, much better in fact with the starch out.

> Suppose she was gone when he? I looked for the lamp which she told me came into his mind but merely as a passing fancy of his because he then recollected the morning littered bed etcetera and the book about Ruby with met him pike hoses (*sic*) in it which must have fell down sufficiently appropriately beside the domestic chamberpot with apologies to Lindley Murray. (16.1468–75)

The third person narrative reports – or mediates – Bloom's thoughts as they turn to Molly, and as he recalls 'I looked for the lamp which she told me', a line from Thomas Moore's 'The Song of O'Ruark, Prince of Breffni'. Bloom's mind and the narrative wander back to the morning and Molly's misreading of 'metempsychosis' in her book, present in *Ulysses* as 'met him pike hoses' only in Bloom's repeated recollections.[25] This four-word translation is accompanied by the italicised, bracketed '*sic*'. *Sic erat scriptum*. Thus it was written. Thus it was however in no way written in *Ruby: the Pride of the Ring*, as Bloom read that morning 'near her polished thumbnail' (4.338): thus, rather, it was spoken by Molly. These four words were not written in Bloom's world, but in ours. The text is referring to itself: as in 'Sirens', where the text pronounces 'As said before'. Both 'as said before' and '(*sic*)' are all the more noticeable for being placed where they are least needed: 'Mr Leopold Bloom ate with relish' is one of the most memorable formulations of *Ulysses*, and the error of 'met him pike hoses' is pretty well established earlier in the text. Furthermore, this shorthand for *thus it was written* is a solely typographical convention: it is not only not used to denote incorrect speech, it is not used within speech, or thought, or in any medium other than writing. It points to previous writing, and to its own status as written: the writing *here* refers to the writing *there* – only the writing *there* is not 'the book about Ruby', but *Ulysses*. Whatever narrates 'Eumaeus' inadvertently calls attention to its own medium of writing in an enthusiastic misapplication of a convention to exonerate a writer from blame, to assert that an error is not their own. In indicating that this is not an error made during transcription, it implies an act of transcription or copying – which in turn implies a writer, an author, a presence who knows what is wrong, yet blunders themselves.

The twice-repeated appearance in 'Eumaeus' of '£. s. d.', a purely typographical stand-in for 'pounds, shillings, pence', forms another narrative choice which highlights the very printed nature of the text (16.88 and 16.1076). There is a disjunction in the episode between spoken and printed words, and between oral and written narratives. The long, winding sentences formed of qualifying clause upon qualifying clause appear in this light to be amended as the action is narrated, as if composed aloud, stutteringly self-corrected. There is a disguised perpetrating presence in a further fictional layer of the episode, who, like Kenner's Arranger, has access to a printed text – but who, or perhaps rather which, further acts in 'Eumaeus' as an incompetent scribe. Yet the inherent risks of translating the spoken to the written occur elsewhere in *Ulysses*: there is, for example, something of the reverse of '*thus it was written*' in Bloom's world when his 'I was just going to throw it away' is heard as 'Throwaway', the horse whose name is printed in the newspaper Bloom is to discard (and who eventually wins the Ascot Gold Cup, a detail taken by Joyce from the real newsprint of 16 June 1904) (5.534).[26] In our world as readers, meanwhile, we face the Blooms' cat's transliterated meows in 'Calypso': 'Mkgnao!', 'Mrkgnao!', 'Mrkrgnao!' (4.16, 4.25, and 4.32).

In his application of the Uncle Charles Principle to 'Eumaeus' Kenner fends off those who might point out the differences between the narrative style of the episode and Bloom's thoughts and speech earlier in *Ulysses*: he argues that 'no man writes as he speaks or thinks, but more formally, and generally in longer sentences, and with elegant variations'.[27] The mis-attempt to write in a formal style of long, elegantly varied sentences is itself a signal of the transition of spoken to written, in the Eumaean version of Kenner's principle. Kenner touches upon the importance and effects of shifts from oral to printed texts in his Joyce chapter of the often overlooked 1962 study *The Stoic Comedians*, which explores the ways in which *Ulysses* is self-aware as a text printed on bound pages. Introducing his argument, he makes the following claim:

> the most profound of all Joyce's Homeric transformations is this, that the text of *Ulysses* is not organized in memory and unfolded in time, but both organized and unfolded in what we may call *technological space*: on printed pages for which it was designed from the very beginning. The reader explores its discontinuous surface at whatever pace he likes; he makes marginal notes; he turns back whenever he chooses to an earlier page, without destroying the continuity of something that does not press on, but will await until he resumes. He is manoeuvred, in fact, precisely into the role of the scholiasts whose marginalia encumbered the Alexandrian manuscripts of Homeric texts; only here is a text designed, as Homer's was not, precisely for this sort of study.[28]

Kenner reads the cat's meows and other instances where 'something living has been imperfectly synthesized out of those twenty-six interchangeable parts' as 'taut, arbitrary and grotesque' in their imperfection; part of Joyce 'playing in every possible way with the spatial organization of printed marks'.[29] Developing his reading of *Ulysses* as the *Odyssey* composed in print, Kenner underscores how 'Nothing more completely separates typographic from oral narrative than the fact that, as we turn the pages, we can literally see the end coming.'[30] It follows, then, that at the opening of the end of the novel, as the weight of pages-read are in the reader's left hand and the end is in sight – at the sixteenth episode 'Eumaeus' – such games are played with the differences between oral and printed narratives.

Walter Benjamin elaborates an effect of the printed and finite pages of a novel in 'One-way Street': 'As a life-clock ticking away the seconds like mad, the characters in a novel have, hanging over them, the page number. What reader has never once fleetingly, anxiously, glanced up at it?'[31] The threat of print to characters is clear in 'Eumaeus'. The character 'L', as I've previously noted, is absent in the newsprint of the *Evening Telegraph*; an insult to Bloom which is gamely continued by the narrative. This narrative, however, cannot keep track of its characters. In the references to Bloom following his re-christening by the *Telegraph* the joke slips up:

> L. Boom pointed it out to his companion B. A.
> [...]
> – It is. Really, Mr Bloom said
> [...]
> While the other was reading it on page two Boom (to give him for the nonce his new misnomer)
> [...]
> – There was every indication they would arrive at that, he, Bloom, said.
> [...]
> All the same Bloom (properly so dubbed) was rather surprised ...
> (16.1265–1307)

Forgetting that it has already given Bloom 'for the nonce his new misnomer', and then slipping back to 'Mr Bloom' before marking his returned 'L' – 'properly so dubbed' – the narrative errs in such a way as to suggest a lack of attention, or to form a comment on the powers of print over characters.[32]

For the characters of 'Eumaeus', of *Ulysses*, are themselves the rewritings of oral creations into printed compositions: they are unaware of their Homeric roles, of their previous incarnations. As the narrative of 'Eumaeus' is a transformed, disguised version of the narrative of the corresponding section of the *Odyssey*, so are the characters altered and disguised versions of their Odyssean counterparts. The characters are unaware of their imposed roles, just as M'Intosh is unaware of his own misnomer, and therefore that misnomer's appearance in newsprint – were he to see the article, he would have no way of knowing 'M'Intosh' referred to him (whoever he is). 'Eumaeus' weaves together threads of disguise, concealment, and mistaken identities; enticements to search behind the narrative, behind the storytelling; and explorations of the episode's own 'printedness'. This combination allows us to suspect that a concern of 'Eumaeus' is the rewriting of the *Odyssey* as *Ulysses*: that the episode's multiform explorations of disguise and revelation riff not only on the plot and themes of the parallel Odyssean text, but on its own literary transformation of both the *Odyssey* and its unknown genesis.

'Assuming he was he' (16.985): F. A. Wolf and the Homeric Question

Odysseus finally reaches Ithaca from Scheria, home to the Phaeacians. He has kept his identity concealed from Alcinous, the King of Phaeacia, and his people, revealing it only after requesting that Demodocus sings of the wooden horse at Troy. The tale of Odysseus's cunning stratagem, a wooden disguise, moves Odysseus to tears, causing the King to question his identity. Once revealed, Odysseus moves into the position of narrator and tells of his exploits across the seas. The Phaeacians then aid the final stretch of his journey to Ithaca, and once there Athena disguises Odysseus as an old beggar, 'such-like that no man shall know thee'.[33] 'His fair flesh she withered on his subtle limbs, and made waste his yellow hair from off his head, and over all his limbs she cast the skin of an old man, and dimmed his eyes, erewhile so fair.' So changed, Odysseus first visits the swineherd Eumaeus, who fails to recognise him, and declares to 'tell thee all most plainly' how he reached Ithaca. Spinning a fictitious tale, Odysseus invents himself as a tricked Cretan forced into beggars' clothes.[34]

Disguises, transformations, and stories define this section of the *Odyssey*, but these themes are present throughout the poem. Odysseus narrates whole swathes of the epic, providing a model for Genette's 'intradiegetic homodiegetic' narrative: a 'narrator in the second degree who tells his own story'.[35] The concealment of Odysseus's identity is played with right from the opening of the epic poem: it is twenty-one lines into the Greek before we even reach the name of the *andra* described as *polutropon* (a delay easily observable in English translations). Later, Odysseus is concealed variously by his own methods and Athena's, and his unveiling becomes the turning point of his violent homecoming. The Uncle Charles Principle in 'Eumaeus' can thus be read as a translation of the *Odyssey*'s withholding of its protagonist's name and, further, a translation of Odysseus's narrating tendencies, his control over sections of the narrative in the *Odyssey*. The narrative style of 'Eumaeus' is formed in the idiom of Bloom, the rewritten Odysseus of *Ulysses*. In *Epic Geography* Seidel focuses much of his attention on the sailor Murphy, the pseudo-Odyssean storyteller of 'Eumaeus'.[36] In doing so, Seidel's reading of 'Eumaeus' overlooks the parallels between the narrative games of the episode and the narrative of the *Odyssey*, an epic tale constructed of many 'he said's' in which the identity of the narrator is often masked, veiled by role-playing, a 'lie made manifest'. Narrative as a mask or an act, following Barthes and Genette, is of great relevance to the *Odyssey*, while the corresponding prompted desire to unveil what lies beneath or behind a narrative echoes *Ulysses*' rewriting of the Greek epic. Furthermore, this enticement to identify a perpetrator, a creator, forms a palimpsestial echo of the Homeric Question, a centuries-old need to identify the authorship of the *Iliad* and the *Odyssey* – to which I will now turn. The errors and slip-ups of 'Eumaeus' shadow the history of scholarship's understandings of the poems attributed to Homer: crafting thus a further layer of rewriting.

The Homeric scholar J. V. Luce cautions that 'If one is to begin to write about Homer, one must make assumptions.'[37] Understandings of 'Homer' have been and continue to be so contentiously varied that the use of Homer as a proper noun, an identifier for an individual, must itself be clarified as an assumption. Theories of single or multiple authorships, of differing authorship for the *Iliad* and the *Odyssey*, and of modes of composition have been developed and debated for centuries. A key figure in modern readings of Homeric authorship is F. A. Wolf, whose 1795 *Prolegomena ad Homerum* argues 'The Homer that we hold in our hands now is not the one who flourished in the mouths of the Greeks of his own day, but one variously altered, interpolated, corrected, and emended.'[38] Wolf proposes a Homer, or 'many Homers', responsible for several oral compositions which were brought together during a far later period.[39] This notion of 'many Homers' includes the suggestion that the poems were not completely the work of 'Homer'. Wolf's ideas, however, were not new: as the translators of the 1985 English edition of the *Prolegomena* describe, repeating Wolf's own admission,

> Classicists knew long before Wolf that Homer's text had been composed and transmitted in unusual ways. Ancients of high authority, Josephus and Cicero, suggested that the *Iliad* and *Odyssey* had been composed without writing and only put into coherent, written form by Pisistratus some centuries later . . .[40]

In their translators' introduction to the *Prolegomena* Anthony Grafton, Glenn W. Most, and James E. G. Zetzel also detail the similarities between Wolf's arguments and those of his near contemporaries, including his teacher Christian Gottlob Heyne and J.-B.-G. d'Ansse de Villoison, the scholar who in 1788 published 'the vast corpus of Venice scholia on the *Iliad*, still the richest single source for our knowledge of the working methods of ancient Homeric scholars'.[41] Both assert that the Homeric texts shifted from song to written form, pieced together later with adjustments and additions. These ideas are in the work of Giambattista Vico too: as James I. Porter outlines, in 1730's *Scienza nuova seconda* Vico reads Homer as an idea 'created by the Greeks' rather than as a person, presenting a hypothesis that Homer did not exist and 'that Homer's poems were the final product of a long tradition of oral composition and compilation'.[42] Porter entertainingly compares Vico's logic to that of 'the MacGuffin (an impossible, nonexistent and empty object the effects of which are nonetheless real)', and argues that it anticipates Wolf and the analytic approach Wolf inspired (330).

In his eleventh chapter of the *Prolegomena*, and in a style absolutely worth quoting at length, Wolf complicates the aims of some Homeric scholarship:

> But what if the suspicion of some scholars is probable – that these and the other poems of those times were not consigned to writing, but were first made by poets in their memories and made public in song, then made more widely available by the singing of the rhapsodes, whose peculiar art it was to learn them? And if, because of this, many changes were necessarily made in them, by accident or design, before they were fixed, so to speak, in written form? And if for this very reason, as soon as they began to be written out, they had many differences, and soon acquired new ones from the rash conjectures of those who rivaled one another in their efforts to polish them up, and to correct them by the best laws of the art of poetry and their own usage? And if, finally, it can be shown by probable arguments and reasons that this entire connected series of the two continuous poems is owed less to the genius of him to whom we have normally attributed it, than to the zeal of a more polite age and the collective efforts of many, and that therefore the very songs from which the *Iliad* and *Odyssey* were assembled do not all have one common author? If, I say, one must accept a view different from the common one about all these things – what, then, will it mean to restore these poems to their original luster and genuine beauty? [*sic!*].[43]

In his exploration of these difficulties, questions, and theories, Wolf finds evidence for the orality of the Homeric texts within the poems themselves. With rhetorical flourishes in Chapter XX he points out the absence in the texts of any references to writing, finding 'no evidence of even the faintest beginnings of true writing':[44]

> The word *book* is nowhere, *writing* is nowhere, *reading* is nowhere, *letters* are nowhere; nothing in so many thousands of verses is arranged for reading, everything for hearing; there are no pacts or treaties except face to face; there is no source of report for old times except memory and rumor and monuments without writing; from that comes the diligent and, in the *Iliad*, strenuously repeated invocation of the Muses, the goddesses of memory; there is no inscription on the pillars and tombs that are sometimes mentioned; there is no other inscription of any kind; there is no coin or fabricated money; there is no use of writing in domestic matters or trade; there are no maps; finally there are no letter carriers and no letters.[45]

Wolf avoids firm conclusions, as Grafton et al. observe:

> Wolf took great care not to write his exact results into the book. Wherever possible he stated his meaning by negation or approximation [. . .] And above all he refused to give definitive answers to the main Homeric questions, even though he liked at times to pretend he had them.[46]

Porter picks up the flipside of this pretence, reading 'hesitations' and 'indecision [. . .] only some of which was rhetorically staged' ('Homer', 335). For Wolf, Porter argues, 'Homer [. . .] must have been a simple and illiterate bard, but in the end he remains an unknowable cipher' (335). In the century that followed, Homeric scholarship divided over questions of multiple and single authorship – often characterised as Analysts and Unitarians – and later, in the 1930s, Milman Parry investigated more fully and coherently the 'oral formulaic composition' of the poems.[47] Though lacking in solid (or at least, clearly stated) arguments, Wolf's *Prolegomena* did establish Homer as uncertain and illiterate.

In her 2002 study *Inventing Homer: The Early Reception of the Epic* Barbara Graziosi discusses how ancient audiences responded to the *Iliad* and the *Odyssey*, exploring facets of the Homeric Question prefigured much earlier. She outlines two different traditions of etymological analysis: one which works to link Homer to a place and a biographical story, and an opposing 'important tradition [. . .] which etymologises the name "Homer" so as to show that it does not refer to an individual at all, but rather speaks of the composition of the poems as a collective effort'.[48] Graziosi focuses on F. G. Welker's nineteenth-century translation of 'Homer' as '*Zusammenfüger*' – 'compiler'.[49] More recently updated by Gregory Nagy as 'he who fits [the song] together', such translation opposes ideas of a single, creative author (Graziosi, 52).[50] Graziosi argues that even in antiquity the name was not understood simply, and that 'the two options, that Homer was originally a proper name, or that it was a symbolic one, are both possible, but neither can be proved right to the exclusion of the other' (53). The questions that have been, and continue to be, relevant to some fields of Homeric scholarship – whether an individual Homer lived and composed, or if there were instead 'many Homers'; whether the same person or persons composed the *Iliad* and the *Odyssey*; and the issue of later interpolations – have authorial implications. In his 1869 inaugural lecture Friedrich Nietzsche queries whether 'in Homer "has a person been made out of a concept [*Begriff*] or a concept out of a person?"' (Porter, 'Homer', 329). A concept, a compiler, one of many, non-existent, a genius; Homer the author is unfixed. As Thomas de Quincey quips in 'Homer and his Homeridae' in 1841, 'Some say, "there never was such a person as Homer." "No such person as Homer! On the contrary," say others, "there were scores"' (Porter, 'Homer', 330).

We can read de Quincey's 'scores' of Homers as referring both to notions of multiple authorship, and to the reception of the poems: to the host of different ideated Homers formed by Homeric scholars. Graziosi concludes *Inventing Homer* by arguing that multiple imagined Homers existed for ancient audiences too, though with different implications:

> ancient audiences did not try to discover, once and for all, who the real author of the Homeric poems was, but rather tailored new images of

the poet to suit particular contexts, or, alternatively, collected and listed several contradictory views without adjudicating between them. At the same time, the authority of this imaginary and multiform figure was real enough: rhapsodes were expected to perform his work, rather than improvise freely on a well-known story, and countless intellectuals appealed to the authority of Homer in order to establish their own. (250)

The ancient audiences Graziosi explores form their own Homers without seeking a definitive author, yet we can see that modern scholarship has also created its own Homers for its own contexts.[51] For example, in the work considered in my first chapter, M. H. Abrams details romantic readings of Homer from Coleridge's 'objective' poet to John Keble's highly-knowable author: 'Keble was not in the least deterred [. . .] by the knowledge that a number of contemporary investigators affirmed that Homer was not a person at all, but a composite myth', comments Abrams.[52] Keble's application of romantic ideas of a 'visibly invisible' author-god to Homer results, as Abrams describes, in 'a poet made patently after his own image, or at least after his own ideals. The Homer who emerges from Keble's pages is a Tory, a backward-looking romantic, and a sentimental, all-but-Christian gentleman.'[53] Keble's Homer is a genius poet, markedly different from the Homers of Wolf or Welker: his Homer responds to Keble's context and serves his purposes.

How the *Odyssey* was read is of great importance to how we read the *Odyssey* in *Ulysses*. As shifts from oral to written narratives are acted out before us in 'Eumaeus', held up in newsprint and signalled by lapses in narrative cohesion, we can discover an echo of the translation of spoken to printed epic, and a rewriting of a significant change in perceptions of the Homeric. 'As said before' becomes 'Thus it was written': the self-conscious asides of *Ulysses* enact the transition from voice to print, echoing the early suggestions of Vico or Wolf. Parry's development of understandings of Homeric oral composition in the 1930s theorised the mechanisms of oral composition; pre-Parry, the *idea* of Homeric orality would have been fully available to Joyce. Traces in 'Eumaeus' of transformations from oral to printed text are an important reference back to the Homeric Question, and more broadly problematise how texts originate. We can also read the Arranger as a 'compiler', as 'he who fits the story together', controlling the many voices and styles of *Ulysses*, and see something of a compilation in the overwhelming intertextuality of *Ulysses*, a re-versioning and stitching together of previous texts. Such a reading suggests a strange alliance between Welker and Nagy's genius-author-effacing translations of 'Homer', and Roland Barthes's definitions of the writer as one who 'can only imitate a gesture that is always anterior, never original' and of a text as 'a tissue of quotations' ('Author', 146). This reading of *Ulysses* accordingly suggests that questions of what we mean by an 'author' or a 'text' manifest both in Homeric scholarship and twentieth-century literary theory.

In her explorations of the myriad interpretations of 'Homer' Graziosi plots the appearances of and transitions between *aoidos* (bard), *rhapsodos* (rhapsode), and *poietes* (poet, 'maker': the closest to 'author') (19–20). Graziosi identifies Homer as a bard and a poet, but not a rhapsode (48), and details that 'the maker and the performer can coincide in the figure of the *aoidos*. The verb *poieo* and its cognate *poietes* become relevant when the performer, or the reader, evokes the absent author' (42). In relation to Homer, the word closest to author becomes important when the distinction needs to be made between the performer and the composer; when a gesture is required to signal an absent other, who has authored the poem performed. As Graziosi continues, 'The difference is one of perspective: the word *aiodos* belongs to the distant world described in epic poetry, the word *poietes* points towards the relationship between maker and performer as well as to what was made by the poet once and for all.' She concludes that 'by the time the name Homer first appears in our sources the distinction between author and performer is already in place. Homer emerges when the performer evokes the absent author' (48).

'Homer' can thus be understood as metonymic from its very roots of an unknown, absent author. Graziosi's investigations lead her to give her own definition of 'the author Homer' as 'the place where you establish your own special connection and interpretation' (89). Her delineation of Homer is reminiscent, as she briefly notes (18), of Michel Foucault's exploration in 'What is an Author?' of the 'author-function': 'the name of an author is not precisely a proper name among others' but rather 'points to the existence of certain groups of discourse and refers to the status of this discourse within a society and culture'.[54] The 'absent author', I'd add, furthermore reaches out again to Barthes: 'To give a text an Author is to impose a limit on that text, to furnish it with a final signified, to close the writing' ('Author', 147). If Homer is 'the place where you establish your own special connection and interpretation' then the *Iliad* and *Odyssey* can be read as texts without origin, limitless, authorless texts which allow a creativity of reading. Paradoxically, areas of Homeric scholarship use such freedoms of reading precisely to locate an author. The absent author who provokes the Homeric Question conversely allows for a method of reading strikingly similar to that advocated by Barthes – a 'birth of the reader', but here in the service of locating an author. Acts of conjecture define authorially seeking Homeric scholarship: the author or authorship of the Homeric poems is a gap to be filled, an inference writ large. Forming an author through conjecture fulfils a potential of unlimited, creative, authoritative reading.

Written Homers: Samuel Butler and Zachary Mason

Nearing the end of *Inventing Homer* Graziosi suggests that the authorial hunting of Homeric scholarship supports a broader observation: 'The analogy

God/author vs world/work has greatly influenced modern literary criticism: the good reader of the work, or the world, hopes to gain some insight into the will of the Creator' (245–6). In many respects, the way some scholars engage with the Homeric Question is by hungrily seeking an author, with little more than the texts and previous readings of the *Iliad* and *Odyssey* to aid their investigation. In doing so, certain classicists theorise an author by interpreting a text – an intriguingly creative act of reading. We can read Samuel Butler's *The Authoress of the 'Odyssey'* as a response to such Victorian scholarship; to make things even more Eumaean, the seriousness of this 1897 text remains moot. The result of his conjecture (whether tongue-in-cheek or not) is the creation of an authoress, which suggests a potential for fiction within the Homeric Question. In what follows, I will explore this potential by looking both at Butler's study and at several of the interlinked short stories in *The Lost Books of the 'Odyssey'*. The twisting games of Mason's stories enable me to highlight how fictions in which authors and readers are figured have Homeric precedence, and how creative scholarship such as *The Authoress of the 'Odyssey'* is rewritten by 'Eumaeus'. In their readings of the *Odyssey* and their engagement with Homeric scholarship, Butler's and Mason's texts encourage further consideration of theoretical questions of authorship and suggest how such questions can be wrought in fiction. These texts shed yet more light on the narrative of 'Eumaeus', and how games with ideated and constructed authors have an impact on the modes by which we read *Ulysses*.

In his 2003 introduction to Butler's *The Authoress of the 'Odyssey'*, Tim Whitmarsh views Butler's reading of the *Odyssey* (along with his translation) as a response to the elitism of classical scholarship, 'to challenge the academic establishment's monopoly on the Homeric poems'.[55] Victorian Homeric scholarship was perhaps not for everyone, but it became well known: as Porter comments, 'by the end of the century the "analysed" Homer was such a commonplace that it had percolated into popular consciousness' ('Homer', 336). Another Homer emerged at this time too, one formed by the archaeologist Heinrich Schliemann; Kenner and Edith Hall remark that it is this Homer whom (or which) Butler reacts to, or riffs on. 'The most reputable scholars are still divided on the question of whether Butler believed his own arguments, or was writing a parody of the earnest, archeologically informed Homeric hypothesis that had been such a feature of nineteenth-century scholarship', claims Hall, highlighting the unanswered question of intent at the heart of attempts to explain Butler's *Authoress*.[56] Whitmarsh reads *The Authoress* as part of Butler's lifelong resistance to authority, but such conclusions are surely tempered by Whitmarsh's opening admission that *The Authoress* remains 'one of the great mysteries of Victorian scholarship. Even to categorise it as "scholarship" begs the question' (vii). Porter describes the text meanwhile as Butler's 'curious, half-satirical and half-whimsically serious study aimed at the late-Victorian public' ('Homer', 336). The 'whimsically serious' study is a challenge for recent commentators, who can easily find serious and worthy reasons for the parody – such as Butler's belief that more should have access to the Homeric poems – yet must struggle with Butler's sillier arguments. Such difficulties were not experienced by contemporary reviewers and academics, who 'took it very much as a joke' (Whitmarsh, in Butler, ix) (though Butler's translation of the *Odyssey* was met with some outrage). Someone who did not take it as a joke, in Kenner's estimation, was Joyce a decade or so later. Kenner critiques Butler for having had too much fun at the expense of established scholars, which as a result 'put himself forever beyond their serious consideration':

> He could have been a Bentley or a Wolf, inventor of the Homer of his age. Instead he chose to be the man with the silly bee in his bonnet about a poetess, and that his most serious reader should have been James Joyce was perhaps more than he deserved to expect.[57]

Yet Kenner, consequently, takes Butler rather too seriously, reading his use of 'the archaeologists' Homer' – the Homer of Joyce's age – as crucial to Joyce: 'During [Joyce's] young manhood archaeology had been turning Homer into just such an organizer of information as the novelist had also become'.[58] As Seidel summarises, citing Kenner's speculations, 'as a novelist working on the *Odyssey* in novelistic ways, Butler provides a model for Joyce's epic translation'.[59] Though Seidel spends some time in *Epic Geography* on what he calls 'the most apocryphal, although witty, piece of blarney in the Homeric tradition', his study primarily explores the work of another 'eccentric scholar': reading Victor Bérard's unusual geography of the *Odyssey* as a precursor to Joyce's translation of the epic poem onto the spaces of Dublin.[60] Seidel takes this precursor named by Stuart Gilbert, written off by some as a joke, and argues that Bérard's idiosyncratic *Les Phéniciens et l'Odyssée* work of 1902–3 was essential to Joyce's rewriting of the *Odyssey*. Bérard and Butler sit between *Ulysses* and the *Odyssey*, both exhibiting creative responses to questions prompted by the latter. Both suggest their own geography for the *Odyssey*; it is, however, Butler's provocative construction of author-figures that has been overlooked, and that is of the most pertinence to my Eumaean investigations.

Taking a Homeric tradition of close-reading-in-search-of-an-author to its extreme, Butler defends a single authorship of the wanderings of Odysseus. 'That the finest poem of the world was created out of the contributions of a multitude of poets revolts all our literary instincts', he insists, explaining that, when reading the original Greek of the poem,

> The more I reflected upon the words, so luminous and so transparent, the more I felt a darkness behind them that I must pierce before I could see the heart of the writer – and this was what I wanted; for art is only interesting in so far as it reveals an artist.[61]

He agrees with theories that the authors of the *Iliad* and the *Odyssey* were separated by 'some generations', but his application of what he calls 'common sense' takes him far from other popular responses to the Homeric Question (5). *The Authoress* argues that the writer of the *Odyssey* was female and from Sicily, based her geography on her knowledge of her home Trapani, and 'introduced herself into her work under the name of Nausicaa' (8). In a chapter entitled 'Further indications that the writer is a woman – young – headstrong – and unmarried', Butler invokes questionable logic to argue that only a young woman would dare to undertake the writing of the *Odyssey*, and that, for instance, 'Calypso's jealousy of Penelope is too prettily done for a man. A man would be sure to overdo it' (145); in a later chapter, 'Who was the writer?' he uses close readings of a shift in tense and descriptive detail to locate the authoress in the household of King Alcinous.

The entertainingly titled chapters 'That the *Iliad* which the writer of the *Odyssey* knew was the same as what we now have', and 'The *Odyssey* in its relation to the other poems of the Trojan cycle, and its development in the hands of the authoress', develop Butler's opening claim that the authoress not only had an in-depth knowledge of the *Iliad*, but a much-read manuscript in her possession (232). Butler presents an *Odyssey* that is a written text, by a single author, with a relationship to the *Iliad* explained by him in an uncannily Harold Bloomian manner. Similar or borrowed lines are due to the authoress's 'saturation' with the previous text – an 'unconscious cerebration' – 'the spontaneous outcome of the fullness of the writer's knowledge of the *Iliad*'; while the lack of references to Iliadic events in the *Odyssey* proves the authoress guilty by omission (238 and 246). As Butler's quoted publisher friend remarks: '"let me tell you that it is our almost unvaried experience that when a writer mentions a number of other books, and omits one which he has evidently borrowed from, the omitted book is the one which has most largely suggested his own"' (251). Butler provides his own alternative reasons for the absence in the *Odyssey* of direct Iliadic reference, varying from accusations of jealousy to the supposition that the authoress perhaps knew something of Homer that we do not – for instance the poet might have beaten his wife, or run off with someone else's (247 and 251).

By identifying oddities in the *Odyssey* Butler creates a personality for his authoress, with which he then constructs authorial intentions to sanction or authorise his own conclusions. For example, he argues that at the close of the poem his authoress had to either have Odysseus kill Penelope along with the suitors, or maintain throughout that Penelope 'had been pure as new fallen snow. She chose the second alternative, as she would be sure to do, and brazened it out with her audience as best she could' (254). As Whitmarsh argues, *The Authoress* 'confronted the prejudices that lay at the core of the masculinist view of literary authorship' (xvi). Hall echoes this opinion, suggesting that Butler 'was irreverently debunking both Victorian scholarship and the patriarchal values it embodied'.[62] Butler is prompted by perceived inconsistencies in the *Odyssey* to create a characterised author-figure through which to read the poem; nonsensical gender stereotyping aside, *The Authoress* thus prefigures the effects of textual peculiarities in 'Eumaeus'.

Butler mocks 'masculinist' literary and Homeric scholarship through his authoress,[63] but also through the construction of another author-figure: the 'Butler' to whom I have referred in the last few paragraphs. This ironised figure is solemn yet flippant, angry at the methods of previous scholars yet using only 'common sense' for his own methodology. 'Though repeatedly pressed', Whitmarsh reports, 'Butler never claimed that the book was anything other than a serious contribution to scholarship' (ix). Whitmarsh writes of the 'self-fashioning' of a Butler who 'liked to refer to himself as an *enfant terrible*, even when his *enfance* was several decades behind him'. He sees *The Authoress* as 'consciously playful', and part of a broader self-conscious endeavour by Butler to create a persona and play a role (xii and viii). Despite this carefully cultivated persona within and without *The Authoress*, Whitmarsh refuses to write off the study as 'late-Victorian whimsy', arguing nothing less than that *The Authoress* helped to undermine the fundamental academic beliefs of Butler's classicist and literary contemporaries: those of the 'great poet' Homer or 'great author' in literature (xvii–xviii). Its similarities in method to straight-faced readings of Homer lead Porter to describe Butler's text as 'at the very least an extreme symptom of the age' ('Homer', 337). For the 'Butler' of *The Authoress* (and his other Homer-related writing) sees the author as the focus of literary scholarship: 'art is only interesting in so far as it reveals an artist' intimates that this persona at least believes a 'good reader' will be rewarded with a glimpse of the author (or an intimate knowledge of and surety about her actions). It is this attitude that we find rewritten into 'Eumaeus', and in our searching reading we echo the activity and focus of *The Authoress*.

There is thus more of Butler in 'Eumaeus' than only the treatment of the *Odyssey* in 'novelistic ways'. Seidel compares Butler's theories to those of Stephen Dedalus, and, in an echo of the latter's Shakespearean arguments, claims that it does not matter whether Butler believes in his authoress or not.[64] Kenner, meanwhile, argues that Butler and Joyce saw an *Odyssey* both domestic and epic: rather than Wolf who 'believed in a number of bards, making things up', he sees 'Butler, in the age of the novel, work[ing] from a different psychology of creation [. . .] using knowledge of an immediate and experienced world'.[65] While I agree with this positioning of Butler as an exceptionally important interpreter of Homer for Joyce, the relationship between Butler and Joyce goes much further. Kenner bases his arguments on his view that Joyce took Butler far more seriously than he deserved, but that reading – that Joyce took Butler at face value – flattens out the performance of Butler's text, its evasive tongue-in-cheek mode. Butler creates an authoress, *and* creates the Butler who theorises her. His narrative performance is thus a further vital link to 'Eumaeus'.

We are encouraged in 'Eumaeus' to think that if we read well enough we will be rewarded and will be able to pierce the narrative of the episode to find the narrator, unmask the demiurge behind the preterite tense, and remove the storyteller's disguise – just as many readers have believed thorough reading of *Ulysses* can identify M'Intosh, the character named for what disguises him. As I have discussed above, Kenner posits that through the transformation of the orally composed *Odyssey* to the printed pages of *Ulysses* the reader is 'manoeuvred [. . .] into the role of scholiasts whose marginalia encumbered the Alexandrian manuscripts of Homer's texts'. In our search through reading for an author-narrator of 'Eumaeus', some combination of Bloom playing the narrator in his mind and the narrative playing Bloom on the printed page dotted with oddities, we are manoeuvred rather into the role of Butler's overreaching Victorian Homeric scholar, attempting to characterise a controlling figure by availing of the strangeness of the text. Scholars form Homers in reaction to the greatness of the Homeric poems; the reader of 'Eumaeus' is prompted instead by the episode's clumsy oddness. We are trapped by the narrative hide-and-seek into a constant search for a narrative presence, which is ever beyond our reach. Yet in the absolute refusal of 'Eumaeus' to allow such a discovery our stymied readings become creative: theoretically any narrator could be argued for (de Quincey's 'scores,' even). Butler's exaggerations reveal an element of all author-seeking Homeric scholarship: critical readings which construct an origin, an authorship. In certain responses to the Homeric Question we have, again, a 'birth of the reader', and not only in the service of locating an author. Butler does not find his authoress: he creates her. A confusion of the authority of the reader and the author seeps too into 'Eumaeus', consistent with the Odyssean fun and games of mistaken identities, storytelling sailors, and a lying beggar-king.

Butler's construction of an authoress involves a creative effort in the service of a scholarly endeavour. The potential for fictive creation prompted by the figure of Odysseus as hero, narrator, and subject of the gods intermingles in Zachary Mason's *The Lost Books of the 'Odyssey'* with tropes from within and without the *Iliad* and the *Odyssey*; interlinked short stories draw as much from the activities of Homeric scholarship as they do from literature which self-consciously addresses questions of authorship. Often sinister, Mason's dark retellings echo the meta-theatrical confusion of Pirandello's 1921 play *Six Characters in Search of an Author*, which ends tragically with the deaths of two unfinished characters; or the claustrophobic, anxious worlds of Jorge Luis Borges's short fictions. *The Lost Books* contains, the preface informs us, 'forty-four concise variations on Odysseus's story', evidence of how 'the Homeric material was formless, fluid, its elements shuffled into new narratives like cards in a deck'.[66] Games of fiction, scholarship, and the author's authority start with the preface, as an authorial voice informs us that these 'variations' are a 'translation' of 'a pre-Ptolemaic papyrus excavated from the desiccated rubbish mounds of Oxyrhynchus' (vii). Described upon publication as 'Thinly posing as a literary hoax', this preface is also a foreshadowing of what follows.[67] In *The Lost Books* the relationships and boundaries between authors and readers are treated as irreverently as the stories of the Homeric poems and the centuries of scholarship devoted to them.

In 'Record of a Game' the *Iliad* and *Odyssey* become 'largely atrophied' chess primers, much altered over the years until they 'assumed an essentially literary character' (209–10). The *Odyssey* is particularly corrupted and interpolated – perhaps even 'apocryphal' – reimagined as 'a treatise on tactics to be used after the game has ended [. . .] the pieces left finally to their own devices and to entropy' (210–11). A combination of theories of a different authorship for the *Iliad* and *Odyssey*, and arguments of interpolation and a patchwork composition, this story plays both with the – certainly entropic – movements of Odysseus and his men and with the 'speculations' of Homeric scholars. By treating the literary substance and scholarly history of the Homeric poems as equally viable material for fiction, Mason presents an exaggeration that is only a step further than Butler's construction of a Sicilian authoress. In 'Fugitive', Mason allows correspondences to develop between the question of Homeric authorship and the character of Odysseus, complicating the divine control wielded over Odysseus, his frequent role as narrator, and his characterisation as silver-tongued liar – weaving authorial control and the role of the reader into the fabric of the Homeric poems. An Odysseus finds a book called the *Iliad*, the introduction of which claims that 'the epics attributed to Homer were in fact written by the gods before the Trojan war – these divine books are the archetypes of that war rather than its history'. We are told that the Trojan War keeps recurring, in an 'attempt at bringing the terror of battle into line with the lucidity of the authorial intent' (51). Authorial intent and control are thus transposed onto the gods of the Homeric scene, and romantic author-god conflations dramatised. The unknown authorship of the epics is figured into this construction as an echo of links between the authorial hunting of Homeric scholarship and the broader attitudes of literary studies. A divine authorial authority in 'Fugitive' doubles as we learn that even when the poems, 'through authorial and managerial oversights', have been seen by 'their protagonists [. . .] this has had no impact on the action or the outcome' (51–2). As 'Fugitive' continues, Odysseus, the helpless reader, finds his story repeats: trapped by the narrative of the gods, by the intentions of his author(s). He is written as an ensnared, controlled reader in stories which explore the enticements of Homeric scholarship to identify an author, and theoretical questions of authorial control: these divine authors place what Barthes would describe as a 'limit' on Odysseus's life – inescapably a text ('Author', 147).

A joke on Odysseus the liar, storyteller, and oftentimes narrator becomes in Mason's 'A Fragment' the answer to the Homeric Question:

> Odysseus, finding that his reputation for trickery preceded him, started inventing histories for himself and disseminating them wherever he went. This had the intended effect of clouding perception and distorting expectation, making it easier for him to work as he was wont, and the unexpected effect that one of his lies became, with minor variations, the *Odyssey* of Homer. (71)

The *Odyssey* is rewritten as the fruits of its protagonist's wily labour: narrator becomes author and lies become composition. This fanciful theory of authorship can be read as prefigured by the application of the Uncle Charles Principle in 'Eumaeus', where Bloom-Odysseus wields obscure, indirect, and unknown control over the narrative, imagining himself to even author the episode.[68] In Mason's 'Guest Friend', Odysseus tells Alcinous a story of a king and a wanderer walking together in an apple orchard, as the pair do the same. Narrative acts and authorial control are again twisted together, combining the mask of the preterite and Odysseus's knack for disguise and tale-telling. At a crucial moment, to save his own life, Odysseus is revealed as the narrator of the piece: 'he said' shifts to 'I tell this story' (22). Authors are written into *The Lost Books*, in a confusion of textual norms which echoes the intrusions of a work such as 'Borges and I', in which 'I do not know which of us has written this page' separates the 'I' on the page from the author, a fictionalisation of a disconnection between the author and their work, or of a questioning of how the author functions within the text.[69] Such confusions draw too on Odysseus's narrative capability and the authority of storytelling; the importance of lies, disguises, and stories in the final stretches of Odysseus's journey home; the godly control over characters' lives in the *Odyssey*; and the creative authorial-seeking of Homeric scholars exhibited by Butler's *The Authoress*.

The constructions of paradox in Mason's texts render theoretical questions about the roles of authors and readers as fiction, and thus explore the ways in which such questions materialise in the *Odyssey* and the history of its scholarship. Writing authors and readers into texts allows for subtler and less didactic wanderings through issues of authorship and reading. Genette labels such traversing of narrative boundaries 'metalepses', and explains that the effect of placing readers within a narrative is an unsettling sensation of ourselves being part of a narrative.[70] Through these metaleptic fictions we are encouraged to question our own roles as readers and how we approach the author; such questioning is relevant to both the content and form of the *Odyssey* and to the history of its scholarship. In its engagement with the unknowns of narration, authorship, transcription, and truth, 'Eumaeus' also explores authorial and reader roles. By provoking the reader into a Butler-esque disguise, and constructing an authorial, out-of-reach narrative presence, 'Eumaeus' thus engages in a highly specific manner with questions at the core of acts of literature.

Performing Authorship

Discussing translations of Homer, Porter suggests that 'At issue, in a most basic sense, is how we can communicate with the past' (341–2). If a preoccupation of Homeric scholarship rewritten in 'Eumaeus' is how we communicate with our literary past, then a related concern of the episode is how literature communicates with its predecessors: how texts can be formed of readings of previous texts. As the opening of the third and final section of *Ulysses*, the 'Nostos', or 'return', this is particularly apt: we return to both the *Odyssey* and the centuries of readings that lie between it and *Ulysses*. The clichés that dot the pages of 'Eumaeus' are a similar reminder of repetitions, pre-existing texts, words that have been said before or have been written by another. Placing Butler between *Ulysses* and the *Odyssey* emphasises the presence within *Ulysses* of not only previous readings, but unusual readings. As Flack notes, Joyce was not only 'interested in the major channels of transmission and translation of the literary tradition,' he was 'also attentive to the back roads, fragments, silences, and blank spots in literary history'.[71] And as one such back road or blind spot, Butler's *The Authoress* is strange not only in its findings, but in its style.

The Butler persona's pseudo-serious voice and elusive position continue to confuse readers, but they are perhaps not so different from the 'staged indecision' of Wolf in his *Prolegomena*. Butler and Wolf engage in authorial role-playing, withholding something of what we expect from the authors of academic texts – from the first person voice of scholarship. In Butler, the excessiveness of this becomes almost narrative: a novelist's character spouting theories of authorship. Such narrative role-playing is a further link to 'Eumaeus', as we struggle to pinpoint the creator of a puffed-up, overcomplicated, overwritten text: *The Authoress* and 'Eumaeus' can be said to have a similar narrative structure. Narrative masks are at play in the Uncle Charles Principle too, in its borrowings of characters' words, and of course in Barthes's reading of the preterite tense, 'a lie made manifest' behind which 'always lurks a demiurge, a God, or a reciter'. It is this distance between creator and voice that is exploited in a literary hoax: where an authorial persona is a fiction and a narrative persona treated as fact. Mason plays with the notion of literary hoaxes; his pretence that the 'lost tales' are real excavated documents is part of the fiction itself. There are also elements of hoax about Butler's *The Authoress*. 'Real' literary hoaxes, when exposed, disturb our perception of authorial authenticity and authority.[72] The boundaries between fiction and reality are crossed: a lie of authorship is a disruptive activity.

A literary hoax, authorial persona, narrative voice, or preterite tense points elsewhere: all are at one, hard to quantify, remove from the author. There is something of this in the *Odyssey* when a disguised Odysseus tells Penelope he has met Odysseus, doubling down in his role-playing by teetering dangerously close to the truth. This lie creates a gap in its evasions, a potent space. In this context, Porter's reference to 'the MacGuffin' when discussing Homeric scholarship takes on a particular pertinence: the MacGuffin is a blank, a space, a piece of fiction, but it has real effects within a text. We sense a gap of sorts from the very first sentence of 'Eumaeus': we confront our struggle to identify clauses and scan the words for meaning. We can still make sense of it – Bloom brushes down Stephen and returns to him his hat and stick – but something is not quite right, the sentence itself needs brushing down and bucking up. Even if we decide on how it is wrong, we are left to question why, and we increasingly experience the effects of this fecund unknown, mimicking the suspicious listeners in the cabman's shelter.

'(*sic*)' also points elsewhere, conventionally at another writer of another text: in 'Eumaeus' its misuse points instead at the fictionally incompetent author-persona of the episode's narrative (and at the unnarrated moment of Molly's misreading). The 'elsewhere' to which 'met him pike hoses (*sic*)' directs us, however, is worth further unpicking. The real novel *Ruby. A Novel. Founded on the Life of a Circus Girl* by Amye Reade, does not contain the word 'metempsychosis'.[73] Believing that its fictional counterpart *Ruby: The Pride of the Ring* does contain such a word requires a bit of a leap of faith. But it is this word that Molly misreads, or mispronounces, and her unnarrated attempt in 'Calypso' that Bloom recalls in 'Eumaeus': 'met him pike hoses'. The third person narrative of the episode – formed by the author-persona with whom Bloom has a bizarre, unquantifiable link – reports this recollection with the caveat '(*sic*)', seemingly overlooking the fact the words appear (eventually) in *Ulysses*, not *Ruby*. This narrative muddle is controlled – perhaps – by the Arranger, and ultimately by Joyce. In its reference to Molly and *Ruby*, 'met him pike hoses (*sic*)' also refers to the relationship between *Ulysses* and the *Odyssey* – as the words are an invocation of a prior text, transformed – and to Homeric scholarship – by prompting us to find who or what is responsible for this slip up. Within these five words are traces of Molly, Bloom, whatever narrates 'Eumaeus', the Arranger, and Joyce – and with these voices are rereadings or rewritings of earlier pages of *Ulysses*, two *Ruby*s (one real, one fictional), 'major channels' and 'blank spots' of Homeric scholarship, and the *Odyssey*.

'Met him pike hoses (*sic*)' is a palimpsest of fictional and real reader and author voices, a coexistence of texts and their readings – as is 'Eumaeus', and all of *Ulysses*. Ultimately, '(*sic*)' gestures towards an absent author-figure, who remains unknown, but whose effects we feel and towards whom we strive. When we hold this idea together with Graziosi's argument that 'Homer emerges when the performer evokes the absent author', we find a sense of the performative in '(*sic*)' and in 'Eumaeus' that links the episode and its oddities again back to understandings of Homer. The narrative of the episode is a performance, and refers to a blank but potent elsewhere in the way a rhapsode's performance of the *Odyssey* might. Narrative performance is in the *Odyssey* itself when Demodocus sings, when Odysseus lies, and even when Penelope weaves. It is in the Uncle Charles Principle, and the preterite tense, gesturing elsewhere, an amalgamation of character, author, the unknown; inauthenticity, hoax, fiction, and authority. Narrative performance seeps into a performance of authorship, a show put on by Butler, Wolf, and the narrator of 'Eumaeus'.

Rewriting the Homeric texts involves a rewriting of Homeric scholarship, which allows for a fictionalisation of crucial questions of authorship. The underlying presence of such questions in Homeric scholarship, and their explicit existence in fictions such as Borges's short stories, signals their constant, intrinsic relevance to literature and literary studies. We can even read the formulation of the unknown 'Homer', the name and all it connotes, as the birth of the 'author', the inception of the set of questions signalled by the term. In tracing such questions, the thematic fabric of the *Odyssey* remains undisturbed: these concerns are consistent with the act of narrative, the functions of disguise, the wit and power of language, the overarching control of the gods, and the weaving of lies. Nor do these questions jar with the games of 'Eumaeus', of the search for who tells the story or for who creates printed texts, of speech altered in writing, of pseudonyms, identities, and lies. Printed pages of curious origin are waved before the characters – the *Evening Telegraph*, the postcard, the photograph – and before us. 'Eumaeus' focuses our attention on our desire to unveil the narrative presence, to prick the bubble of performed authorship, and thus self-consciously gestures towards the previous Homeric text through which centuries of scholars have roamed to find an author. The concern of rewriting is woven through the episode, an explicit reference to a curious origin of the pages of *Ulysses*. As we search, or read, for the creator of the narrative of 'Eumaeus' we enact the entrapment of some Homeric scholars, a freedom of limitless reading conversely in the service of locating or theorising an author.

The quasi-Barthesian freedom of reading I have identified is not limited to 'Eumaeus'; nor is the way in which this mode of reading is contradictorily focused on determining or constructing an origin for the episode. Throughout *Ulysses* we enjoy an activity of reading in which we must to some extent create the text ourselves, unravelling the mass to string together occasional moments of possible, unstable, and incomplete clarity. We might even feel in control, aware of our own writing of the text in our reading, yet all the while conscious of or drawn towards the author that such a complicated intertextual novel also constantly points to in its intricacies. The fun 'Eumaeus' has with the Homeric Question – as a general idea and as it is specifically explored by Butler – constitutes a key strand of the ways in which *Ulysses* prompts us to consider how we read, what reading does, and where reading takes us. It might even cause us to query, as I will in part over the following chapters, to what extent we form our own

Joyces in response to the difficulties of the text or the demands of current critical trends: Joyces serving different critical purposes at different times. Between 'Eumaeus' and Odysseus's beggar-guise lie centuries of attempts to recognise or identify or *read* the authorship of the *Odyssey*. Our acts of reading are part of the rewriting of 'Homer' in 'Eumaeus'.

Notes

1. Patrick A. McCarthy, 'Stuart Gilbert's Guide to the Perplexed', in *Re-Viewing Classics of Joyce Criticism*, ed. Janet Egleson Dunleavy (Urbana and Chicago: University of Illinois Press, 1991), 23–35 (25).
2. Leah Culligan Flack, *Modernism and Homer: The Odysseys of H.D., James Joyce, Osip Mandelstam, and Ezra Pound* (Cambridge: Cambridge University Press, 2015), 4.
3. Flack, *Modernism and Homer*, 6. Flack references Katherine Mullin, *James Joyce, Sexuality and Social Purity* (Cambridge: Cambridge University Press, 2003), 203.
4. Flack, *Modernism and Homer*, 4.
5. Michael Seidel, *Epic Geography: James Joyce's 'Ulysses'* (Princeton, NJ: Princeton University Press, 1976), xvi.
6. Hugh Kenner, *The Pound Era* (Berkeley and Los Angeles: University of California Press, 1971), 49–50.
7. Flack, *James Joyce and Classical Modernism* (London: Bloomsbury, 2020), 5.
8. See Stephanie Nelson, 'Telling Time: Techniques of Narrative Time in *Ulysses* and the *Odyssey*', in *Reading Joycean Temporalities*, ed. Jolanta Wawrzycka (Leiden: Brill, 2017), 121–36. Nelson's monograph *Time and Identity in 'Ulysses' and the 'Odyssey'* is forthcoming (Gainesville: University Press of Florida, 2022).
9. The clearest evidence for this attitude is the paucity of published work on Joyce and Homer in the last three decades. Tim Conley's recent comment that 'Retooling Homer is the least astonishing of [Joyce's] alchemical acts' is less a hard-fought conclusion than a summary of prevailing opinions in the field. *Useless Joyce: Textual Functions, Cultural Appropriations* (Toronto: University of Toronto Press, 2017), 146.
10. Outlined neatly by Vike Martina Plock in '"The Seim Anew": Joyce Studies in the Twenty-First Century', *Literature Compass*, vol. 7, no. 6 (June, 2010), 477–83.
11. For examples of this enduring attitude (the pointing out of which is perhaps itself rather boring and tired) see Frank Budgen, *James Joyce and The Making of 'Ulysses'* (Bloomington: Indiana University Press, 1961), 249; S. L. Goldberg, *The Classical Temper: A Study of James Joyce's 'Ulysses'* (London: Chatto and Windus, 1961), 140; Richard Ellmann, *'Ulysses' on the Liffey* (London: Faber, 1972), 151; and David Pierce, *Reading Joyce* (Harlow: Pearson, 2008), 190.
12. There are more occurrences of the word 'who' in 'Eumaeus' than in any other episode of *Ulysses* (87 at my count – though I have not separated the interrogative 'who' from the relative pronoun). Pleasingly, in second place is 'Cyclops', an episode with a nameless narrator (67); third is 'Circe', the longest episode of the novel, teeming with roles and voices (54); in fourth place is the many chronologically advancing narrative styles of 'Oxen of the Sun' (46). Neatly, with regards to the suggestions of this current chapter, the episode with the fifth highest occurrence of 'who' is 'Scylla and Charybdis' (45), in which Stephen theorises (and then recants)

a strong link between Shakespeare's life and his work – though little biographically is known of the author.
13. Kenner, *'Ulysses'* (London: George Allen and Unwin, 1980), 130.
14. 'Asquat on the cuckstool' at the end of the fourth episode 'Calypso' Bloom reads *Matcham's Masterstroke* by Mr Philip Beaufoy, a story in three and a half columns in *Titbits*: 'Quietly he read, restraining himself, the first column and, yielding but resisting, began the second. Midway, his last resistance yielding, he allowed his bowels to ease themselves quietly as he read, reading still patiently that slight constipation of yesterday quite gone' (4.500–9). As the output of Mr Philip Beaufoy is aligned with the output of Bloom's bowels, it is fun to note that Richard Ellmann has argued *Matcham's Masterstroke* 'jocularly' refers to a story that is the output of a young Joyce – for *Titbits*. Ellmann, *James Joyce: New and Revised Edition* (Oxford: Oxford University Press, 1982), 50.
15. Kenner, *Joyce's Voices* (Berkeley, Los Angeles, and London: University of California Press, 1978), 17–18.
16. Kenner, *Joyce's Voices*, 21, 38, 35, and 37.
17. See, for instance, John Paul Riquelme, *Teller and Tale in Joyce's Fiction: Oscillating Perspectives* (Baltimore, MD and London: Johns Hopkins University Press, 1983), 217; Brook Thomas, *James Joyce's 'Ulysses': A Book of Many Happy Returns* (Baton Rouge and London: Louisiana State University Press, 1982), 134; and Fritz Senn, '"All kinds of words changing colour": Lexical Clashes in "Eumaeus"', in *Inductive Scrutinies: Focus on Joyce*, ed. Christine O'Neill (Dublin: Lilliput, 1995), 156–75 (173) and 'Eumaean Titbits – As Someone Somewhere Sings', in *Inductive Scrutinies*, 176–96 (176 and 177).
18. Vladimir Nabokov, *Lectures on Literature*, ed. Fredson Bowes with an introduction by John Updike (New York and London: Harcourt Brace Jovanovich, 1980), 355.
19. Gerard Genette, *Narrative Discourse: An Essay in Method*, trans. Jane E. Lewin (Ithaca, NY: Cornell University Press, 1980), 234.
20. Kenner, *'Ulysses'*, 64–5.
21. In the 1922 text Stephen Dedalus is left out, Simon Dedalus gains a BA, and Bloom's name is correct. The publication history of *Ulysses* itself exhibits the lasting effects of printed errors.
22. Kenner, *The Mechanical Muse* (Oxford: Oxford University Press, 1987), 8.
23. John Simpson details the history and technicalities of Linotype printing in his note 'Eatonph and Douradora' at Harald Beck and Simpson's online resource *James Joyce Online Notes*. He explains that 'etaoin' was a nonsense word made by running one's left hand down the keys of the composing machine, and that occasionally compositors would forget to remove these lines of 'bitched type' – which then ended up in newsprint. <http://www.jjon.org/joyce-s-words/eatondhp> [accessed 16 June 2021].
24. Molly merges in Bloom's mind and idiom with *'the beautiful woman'* of *Sweets of Sin*, who *'threw off her sabletrimmed wrap, displaying her queenly shoulders and heaving embonpoint'* (10.615–6). Just moments before finding *Sweets of Sin* in 'Wandering Rocks', Bloom surveys the 'Crooked botched print' of a copy of Aristotle's *Masterpiece*, in a foreshadowing of Eumaean errors (10.586).

25. It is partially revealed as 'Met him what?' in 'Calypso' (4.336), before being recalled in full in 'Lestrygonians' (8.112). It is later rewritten by Molly as 'that word met something with hoses in it' (18.565).
26. And another potential transformation from speech to print is greeted with suspicion: Stephen seems less than impressed by the idea of his own 'sayings' being collected by Haines, unless he might 'make any money by it' (1.480 and 1.490). He does, however, later try to sell his disingenuous theorising in 'Scylla and Charybdis': 'For a guinea, Stephen said, you can publish this interview' (9.1085).
27. Kenner, *'Ulysses'*, 130.
28. Kenner, *Flaubert, Joyce and Beckett: The Stoic Comedians* (London: Dalkey Archive Press and Normal, 2005), 35.
29. Kenner, *The Stoic Comedians*, 47. I do however think 'sllt', a noise occurring as pages are printed, is pretty perfect.
30. Kenner, *The Stoic Comedians*, 49.
31. Walter Benjamin, *One-way Street and Other Writings*, trans. J. A. Underwood (London: Penguin, 2009), 83.
32. 'New misnomer' implies that 'Bloom' is his 'old' misnomer – a reference presumably to Virag, his father's original surname, obliquely referenced in 'Eumaeus': 'Our name was changed too' (16.365–6). Bloom, furthermore, is hereafter in the novel only ever 'Bloom': either he has forfeited his 'Mr' during this bout of name-calling, or we simply know him well enough. It must be significant that his title is lost here, though, in this episode of similarly unfixed names.
33. S. H. Butcher and A. Lang, *The Odyssey of Homer: Done into English Prose* (London: Macmillan, 1924), 220. I am referring to the Butcher and Lang edition partly because Joyce 'relied mainly on the mannered translation', but mostly because I feel a 'mannered' version of the *Odyssey* sits nicely with the put-on style of 'Eumaeus'. Brian Arkins, 'Greek and Roman themes', in John McCourt, ed., *James Joyce in Context* (Cambridge: Cambridge University Press, 2009), 239–49 (240).
34. Butcher and Lang, *Odyssey*, 221 and 228–33.
35. Genette, 248.
36. Seidel, 229–32.
37. J. V. Luce, *Homer and the Heroic Age* (London: Thames and Hudson, 1975), 10.
38. Friedrich August Wolf, *Prolegomena to Homer*, trans. Anthony Grafton, Glenn W. Most, and James E. G. Zetzel (Princeton, NJ: Princeton University Press, 1985), 209.
39. Kostas Myrsiades, 'Introduction', in *Reading Homer: Film and Text*, ed. Kostas Myrsiades (Madison and Teaneck, NJ: Fairleigh Dickenson University Press, 2009), 7–18 (8).
40. Grafton, Most, and Zetzel, 'Introduction', in Wolf, 3–35 (5).
41. Grafton, Most, and Zetzel, 'Introduction', in Wolf, 7.
42. James I. Porter, 'Homer: The History of an Idea', in *The Cambridge Companion to Homer*, ed. Robert Fowler (Cambridge: Cambridge University Press, 2004), 324–43 (329–30). Further references to this edition are given after quotations in the text. Porter's chapter is based on his seminal article 'Homer: The Very Idea', *Arion: A Journal of Humanities and the Classics*, Third Series, vol. 10, no. 2 (Fall, 2002), 57–86.

43. Wolf, 69–70.
44. Wolf, 100.
45. Wolf, 101. As Grafton, Most, and Zetzel note, this argument was also made by Wolf's friend J. B. Merian (31).
46. Grafton, Most, and Zetzel, 'Introduction', in Wolf, 33.
47. Porter uses the word 'discovery', in 'Homer', 340.
48. Barbara Graziosi, *Inventing Homer: The Early Reception of the Epic* (Cambridge: Cambridge University Press, 2002), 81 and 52. Further references to this edition are given after quotations in the text.
49. F. G. Welker, *Der epische Cyclus oder die homerischen Dichter*, 2 vols, 2nd edn (Bonn: 1865–82), vol. 1, 121.
50. Gregory Nagy, *The Best of the Achaeans: Concepts of the Hero in Archaic Greek Poetry* (Baltimore, MD: Johns Hopkins University Press, 1975), 297–300.
51. It is worth nothing here that the Homeric Question does not only ponder the composition of the poems or identity of their author(s). Such scholarship can also be concerned with the audiences of Homer: for example, Douglas Frame argues that the Homeric audience is figured within the *Odyssey* by the Phaeacians, who listen to Odysseus and return him home. Douglas Frame, 'New Light on the Homeric Question: The Phaeacians Unmasked', included in 'A virtual birthday gift presented to Gregory Nagy on turning seventy by his students, colleagues, and friends', The Centre for Hellenic Studies, Harvard University <https://chs.harvard.edu/CHS/article/display/4453> [accessed 28 July 2021].
52. M. H. Abrams, *The Mirror and the Lamp: Romantic Theory and the Critical Tradition* (Oxford: Oxford University Press, 1971), 256–7.
53. Abrams, 261.
54. Michel Foucault, 'What is an Author?', in *Language, Counter-memory, Practice: Selected Essays and Interviews*, ed. Donald F. Bouchard and trans. Bouchard and Sherry Simon (Ithaca, NY: Cornell University Press, 1977), 113–38 (122 and 123). Porter, 336, invokes Foucault too when discussing Wolf.
55. Tim Whitmarsh, 'Introduction', in Samuel Butler, *The Authoress of the 'Odyssey'* (Bristol: Bristol Phoenix Press, 2003), vii–xxv (xiv). Further references to Whitmarsh's introduction to this edition are given after quotations in the text.
56. Edith Hall, *The Return of Ulysses: A Cultural History of Homer's 'Odyssey'* (London: I. B. Tauris and Co, 2008), 116.
57. Kenner, *The Pound Era*, 49.
58. Kenner, *The Pound Era*, 44.
59. Seidel, x.
60. Seidel, 183 and xiv.
61. Samuel Butler, *The Authoress of the 'Odyssey'* (Bristol: Bristol Phoenix Press, 2003), 2 (quoting an unnamed writer in *The Spectator*, 2 January 1892) and 6. Further references to this edition of *The Authoress* are given after quotations in the text.
62. Hall, 116.
63. A move arguably mirrored by Anne Enright's evergreen comment, regarding Joyce's legacy for Irish writers: 'you look at *Ulysses* and say, well, he was a girl, that was his secret'. Quoted in David Mehegan, 'For this writer, identity is subject to change', *Boston Globe*, 27 February 2008 <http://archive.boston.com/ae/books/

articles/2008/02/27/for_this_writer_identity_is_subject_to_change/> [accessed 16 June 2021].
64. Seidel, 84–5. There are of course parallels between the Homeric Question and debates which have surrounded the authorship of Shakespeare's plays. Furthermore, Samuel Butler himself tackles Shakespearean unknowns in his volume *Shakespeare's Sonnets Reconsidered* (1899), in very similar manner to that adopted in *The Authoress of the 'Odyssey'*.
65. Kenner, *The Pound Era*, 47.
66. Zachary Mason, *The Lost Books of the 'Odyssey'* (London: Vintage, 2011), vii. Further references to this edition are given after quotations in the text.
67. Charlotte Higgins, 'The Lost Books of the Odyssey', *The Guardian*, 15 May 2010 <http://www.theguardian.com/books/2010/may/15/lost-books-odyssey-zachary-mason> [accessed 16 June 2021].
68. This has precedence: *Ulysses Homer; or, a Discovery of the True Author of the 'Iliad' and 'Odyssey'* by Constantine Koliades is an 1829 argument that the King of Ithaca himself wrote the texts of Homer (Whitfish: Kessinger, 2010).
69. Jorge Luis Borges, 'Borges and I', trans. James E. Irby, in *Labyrinths: Selected Stories and Other Writings*, ed. Donald A. Yates and James E. Irby (London: Penguin, 2000), 283.
70. Genette, 236.
71. Flack, *Modernism and Homer*, 11.
72. The reactions to contemporary literary hoaxers JT LeRoy and James Frey evidence this. Each hoax was exposed with vast, emotional media attention. See Steve Rose, 'JT LeRoy unmasked: the extraordinary story of a modern literary hoax', *The Guardian*, 20 July 2016 <https://www.theguardian.com/film/2016/jul/20/jt-leroy-story-modern-literary-hoax-> and Evgenia Peretz, 'James Frey's Morning After', *Vanity Fair*, June 2008 <https://www.vanityfair.com/culture/2008/06/frey200806> [both accessed 28 July 2021].
73. Mary Power, 'The Discovery of "Ruby"', *James Joyce Quarterly*, vol. 18, no. 2 (Winter, 1981), 115–21 (121). Power notes however that 'it well could have, for it provides a description of the whole thematic process of the novel'. To make matters even more fun, Power is not able to conclusively say who 'Amye Reade' was the pen name of.

4

'VICTORY TO THE CRITIC'? THE CRITICS AND JOYCE, 1970 TO TODAY

From a discipline spanning millennia, to one just a century old: comparisons between the weight and heft of Homeric scholarship and Joyce criticism would be overdoing it a bit, though might feel reasonable to anyone facing the daunting mountain of critical writing on Joyce's texts.[1] This chapter will not offer a guide to Joyce studies, nor cut through the last fifty years of publications to show what is 'best' – but I do want to briefly observe a strange fondness in the field for what is 'worst'. Joyceans seem to love quacks, pretenders, the misled. Stories of apparently overreaching or ridiculous conference papers are circulated within certain groups at summer schools and symposia, and one pre-eminent Joycean is purportedly even now in the process of collecting Joycean quacks, spoofs, loons: to write a 'study' of them. This study will not be representative of the field at large, but its proposed existence is revelatory.

What does this Joycean tendency mean in terms of critical authority? What has happened when one scholar's approach becomes fodder for ridicule? When a reading 'fails' in the eyes of the critical mass, it could be due to a lack of authority in the work itself: it could be poorly evidenced, without invocation of the right modes of authority, a weakly made argument lacking enough supporting material to back it up. Or, it could make a claim that is 'wrong' in the eyes of the current conglomerate of Joyceans: a confidence that *they* know *that* is not what is going on in Joyce's texts. Both options situate authority with the massed critics. The field determines which modes of authorisation are necessary, as it determines what the 'right sort' of readings or approaches are. This can lead to a sense of an 'in crowd', which is also communicated at conferences, summer schools, workshops, symposia. Newcomers learn a lot about Joyce studies by listening to critical gossip, including which critics hold the power to decide who should be taken seriously or not. An established Joyce scholar might make a running joke about another's mixed metaphors for decades, and somehow the former's joke can overshadow the latter's contributions to the field.

I am not here to decry specialists, or expertise; it is my privilege to respond to other critics of Joyce, and my own readings benefit immeasurably from such interaction. What interests me is the concept of a 'bad' or 'wrong' reading, the implication then of 'right' readings, and who it is who gets to decide. I'm not the first to be fascinated by this; Umberto Eco muses on interpretation's limits and *Finnegans Wake*, for example, in work that has been picked up and elaborated on by several Joyce critics.[2] How the field of Joyce studies itself locates, creates, and manipulates the authority required to determine which readings are 'right' and which are 'wrong', however, and how that authority relates to the author, reader, or text, deserves much more attention than such issues have yet received. In this chapter I seek to address this, by considering what has happened in Joyce studies since its so-called 'boom' and up to the present day: what the field's trends and tendencies can tell us about authorial or readerly authority.

I hold on to my own criticism anecdotes too. The senior Joycean who told me, at the time only eighteen months into my PhD, 'there was nothing more to say about Joyce and Homer', as I prepared to give a paper on *Ulysses* and the *Odyssey* the next day. The *Ulysses* reading group I attended briefly, at which no one mentioned beauty or humour – only historical facts and titbits from Joyce's manuscripts and notebooks. A tour around Trieste by a Joyce scholar, who kept referring to Nora Barnacle as 'Molly' and never noticed his mistake. And a collection of instances where the intimidating position of one still-living Joyce scholar as '*the* authority' on Joyce and Homer stifled the work of newer critics: the ways in which a community of readers and researchers had perpetuated the myth of this mortal male critic's infinite knowledge on the topic had created a figure of authority who had, perhaps, said it all, leaving 'nothing more'. Maybe I am exaggerating, plucking some of the negative from an otherwise supportive, encouraging field of scholars. Maybe I am impudently but usefully following through such inferences of authority to their logical conclusion.

Published criticism and the chatter of conferences are different matters – but they do interact. The proceedings of symposia and other gatherings are often published, recording not only a selection of an event's intellectual contributions but also the editor's introductory opining on the occasion itself. As this chapter will describe with particular regard to the reception of talks given on Joyce by the 'outsider' Jacques Derrida in the 1980s, clashing accounts of academic events exist in print. Later histories of Joyce studies might reiterate or quibble with the received impressions or recollections of key conferences from those in attendance, and shifting responses to a given talk weave their way into a strand of critical reception. Big shifts in approaches often come with an attending critical history, examining how the field got to a certain point and why change is in the air (and urgently needed). These histories not only record but contribute to the developing reception of Joyce criticism, and are involved in emphasising who or what in criticism is most convincing, most relevant, most useful. Or 'best', or 'right'?

What critical histories in Joyce studies tend no longer to include is how delayed Joyce studies' engagement was with critical and literary theory, or how briefly the field dealt more specifically with theories of authorship. What did this delay of and resistance to literary theory do? What does denying or eliding that delay do? This chapter takes a broad look at Joycean criticism from the 1970s to the present, focusing on the growth of the Joyce industry, the belated impact of literary theory, and the field's current proclivities. I will here be paying some particular attention to the mixed reaction of the discipline to poststructuralism and deconstruction, but also, following on from Chapter 2, to a more general idea of theory (or capital 'T' 'Theory') as yet another provocation for Joyce studies to pay attention to its own activity and method. I will also address how later Joycean criticism has understood the relationships between author, reader, and text – and offer an account of how Joyce studies has veered away from such topics. I'll finish by considering the position of author and reader in the reigning areas of the field today, before gesturing at the argument I will develop in my final chapters: that the reader's authority needs to be re-emphasised.

In this chapter I will track how the author has been perceived, invoked, promoted, and constructed as a source of authority in Joyce studies, and examine if and how alternatives have been explored. How does the author's authority interact with reading, and how has Joycean criticism explored this connection? Primarily, my point here is to illustrate the ways in which the field of Joyce studies has examined authority as it relates to the relationships between author, reader, and text, and to argue and detail the ways in which the author remains a key site of authority. While *The Reader's Joyce* emphasises how poststructuralist theory is only one of many manifestations of questions of how author, reader, and text function, it was in its brief engagement with poststructuralist theory that Joyce studies last explicitly queried the roles of reader and author in terms of authority. This chapter examines such queries, as well as the movement – along with the wider field of literary studies – towards approaches in which the identity and historical context of the author attains great, if unexamined, significance.

In the next chapter I will pick up much of what I discuss here, relating these topics directly to the text of *Ulysses* and the way in which we read it. In order to have those textual discussions of reading and authority, I need first to analyse how such questions have been asked before. Criticism on Joyce promotes ideas of reading and authority, which feed back into the way we read the text itself. It is therefore essential to consider how such ideas have developed due to and despite differing approaches and trends in the field. In Chapter 2 I examined how Joyce studies became a self-reflective discipline, with key traits that I traced back to the reception of the Homeric in *Ulysses* and Joyce's own role in that reception. I looked at the authorial traces of Joyce's involvement in criticism, how they are preserved, and how Joyce studies has overwhelmingly turned away from examining them. In this chapter I pick up these concerns, continuing to trace those characteristics – self-conscious corrective criticism, a focus on reading itself, and a strange and complex relationship to the author – as Joyce studies encounters literary theory.

The questions of authorship – of author, reader, and text – that I explore through *The Reader's Joyce* remain unresolved in Joyce studies. In each shift in Joyce studies, in each book, chapter, article, or paper, the critic makes a choice of how to read the relationship between author, reader, and text. These choices generally go unnoticed, let alone explored: and even the studies focusing on or touching upon issues of authorship can overlook the implications of their own critical modes and tendencies. Questions prompted by this relationship are thus everywhere in Joyce studies, and yet rarely ever investigated. In this chapter I will discuss how criticism overtly or quietly signals an attitude towards the author: what various critical ideas of the author and their authority are, and how they have developed and altered and taken on new modes and approaches over time. Joyce studies lacks an extended analysis of how the field promotes or encounters the authority of reader, text, and author. By analysing how critical reception constructs authorship and the author, I will be able in this chapter to offer new ways of considering critical practice in the academy, and contribute more broadly to understandings of how different types of critical authority gain or lose credence.

A core aim of this chapter is to track Joyce studies' relationships to authority through its reception of and engagement with literary theory, in order to establish the field's concepts and practices of authority that function today. Many histories of Joyce studies and theory exist: as extended works on the Joycean reception of theory; broader studies of links between Joyce's texts and the work of a particular theory or theorist; and briefer, introductory examinations of how particular theoretical approaches have fared in the field. My focus on authority leads me to reconsider similar ground from a new angle, but also to focus on those histories themselves – how they communicate attitudes towards authority and engage with authority by promoting a particular view of developments and events. Engaging with how others have written about theory requires, as I have mentioned, dealing with 'theory' in terms both general and specific.³ I will discuss theory as a generalised challenge, following the way its critics used the term theory to denote and homogenise a variety of approaches. This massed body of theory and theoretically informed work functions in two ways in Joyce studies: first, as a perceived threat to the norm for the Joyceans of the 1970s and 1980s, and then as an apparently exhausted mode that Joyceans of the 1990s and 2000s sought to move beyond.

While many disparate literary and critical theories are included within the term 'theory' as used by its Joycean critics (and it is important to note that 'theory' is also used as a broad referent and useful shorthand by its advocates), in Joyce studies the focus has often been far more specifically poststructuralism and, even more specifically, deconstruction. It is essential in this chapter for me to engage with the particular reception of poststructuralism and deconstruction, with the Joycean response – for example – to Derrida and Derrida's response to Joyceans. The way in which Joyce studies has viewed theory in terms of authority (even as the theory in question has attempted to dissolve structures of authority), is an important, underexplored facet of how the author functions in the field. The reception of theory has played out in publications and at the conferences, symposia, and other events around which the field of Joyce studies has grown and developed – to which I will now briefly turn.

After the first Bloomsday celebrated in Dublin in 1954, a pilgrimage of Ulyssean sites by a group that repeated retellings insist were fairly booze-soaked, there appears to have been a hiatus – with celebrations cropping up again for Bloomsday 1962 on the streets of Dublin and the pages of *The Irish Times*. The first Joyce Symposium took place in Dublin in 1967; as 'An Irishman's Diary' had it, 'The Joyce posers (or symposers) [. . .] made speeches at each other.'⁴ Joyceans were apparently jeered at in pubs, and their event was characterised as 'American madness'.⁵ The Symposia rolled on, however, continuing to provide fun for onlookers and increasingly creating space for varying amounts of Joycean in-fighting.

The Fifth Symposium in Paris, 1975, at which Jacques Lacan gave a keynote, revealed a growing split within Joyce studies. Roughly pro- and anti-theory, French and American, 'traditionalists' and 'avant-gardists', the two sides 'ignored each other'.⁶ Different histories give differing reasons for this lack of communication: Bernard Benstock diplomatically suggests the language divide played a significant role, while Geert Lernout blames 'the French' for an 'unwillingness' to explain their work or their interest in new approaches.⁷ Theory-informed and theory-friendly work continued to appear at Symposia, particularly the Seventh in Zurich, 1979, and, in 1982 – separate from the huge Centennial Symposium in Dublin that year – Derrida gave a talk titled 'Two Words for Joyce', at the Centre Georges Pompidou in Paris. He made it to the main event two years later, giving one of the keynotes at the Ninth Symposium in Frankfurt. This, the 1984 Symposium, was and remains a key moment for Joyce studies. For the first time, self-defined poststructuralist approaches dominated the proceedings. Keynotes were given by Derrida and Julia Kristeva. Panels were organised with Marxist, psychoanalytic, deconstructive, and feminist critical approaches. A Women's Caucus was held, with a 'women only' policy that prompted complaints.[8] And Hans Walter Gabler presented Joyce's grandson with the first copies of *Ulysses: The Corrected Edition*. It is for Gabler, far more than Derrida, Kristeva, or the (now non-existent) Women's Caucus, that the 1984 Symposium is most frequently memorialised by many in Joyce studies today.

More Joyceans grappled productively with theoretical approaches to literature in the late 1980s, and at the Eleventh Symposium in Venice keynotes were given by Jean-François Lyotard and Umberto Eco. By the early 1990s histories of the field's encounter with theory had speedily appeared, with one – Lernout's *The French Joyce* in 1990 – demanding, already, that the field leave 'French' approaches behind and focus instead on historical context. Which an increasing number of critics did, while others continued to explore Joyce with any number of theoretical modes. All contributed to the ongoing expansion of Joyce studies, which was progressively dominated by critics absorbed by questions of history and politics, and – if a little more slowly – by the methods of genetic criticism. In the early 2000s, it appears to have seemed necessary to defend such approaches and methodologies against an imagined stranglehold of theory – and articles, overviews of criticism, and monograph introductions did so with enthusiasm. As the field of Irish Studies grew, so too was Joyce's Irishness belatedly considered – and increasingly emphasised. In 2004, Bloomsday's centenary prompted a multitude of conferences, celebrations, and publications. Historicist and genetic criticism have continued to loom large in the field of Joyce studies, more recently the latter; in 2018 the Twenty-sixth Symposium was held at the University of Antwerp's Centre for Manuscript Genetics, with two keynotes given by genetic critics and an opening lecture from Gabler. A large proportion – if not a majority – of Joycean work published in the last decade or so draws on genetic criticism: using findings from Joyce's drafts, notes, and writing processes to authorise specific, localised readings, or to give credence and heft to broader approaches.

In this chapter, I will be examining elements of the above potted history through a specific lens: which ideas of authority are and have been encountered, promoted, and constructed by Joyce critics and the field as a whole? By 'authority' I refer to what might also be termed 'interpretative authority': my interest is in which mode or source of authority is given most weight or credence when it comes to arguing what a text *does* or *means* (and how, or why). I will here be taking more of a bird's-eye view of Joyce studies than in Chapter 2, partly given the sheer quantity of published criticism in the last forty years. The following four sections will focus in turn on the early encounters of Joyce studies with literary theory, Gabler and Derrida in 1984, the extent to which Joyce criticism engaged directly with questions of the author, and the ways in which the field has continued to ask how we should read Joyce's texts. The growth of the Joyce industry very much coincided with the arrival of theory, so my scope here cannot be comprehensive: though this chapter looks at many more works of criticism than Chapter 2, it by no means considers every major work of Joyce criticism in the last forty years. Furthermore, though some specifics are vital, I will here be also looking more broadly at groups, trends, and habits. I am not attempting to undermine the work I discuss in this chapter. I am examining criticism from a particular, neglected, useful angle, and what I highlight is not a judgement of the validity of any interpretation. Where specifics are picked at and contradictions teased out, my aim is not to expose supposed failings but rather to document how difficult it has been and continues to be for Joyce studies to wrestle with questions of authority and of the relationships between author, reader, and text – and, how unresolved such questions remain.

'But this is not so different from what we have been doing for years': Joyce and Theory

Following on from the early ventures of Margot Norris and Hélène Cixous, by the end of the 1970s a small minority of Joyce critics began to engage critically with literary theory. Colin MacCabe's 1978 work *James Joyce and the Revolution of the Word* is often credited as a key forerunner in this engagement; his writing on Joyce along with his work with Stephen Heath in the film journal *Screen* are commonly also credited with importing French theory to Anglophone (particularly British) academia. *Joyce and the Revolution of the Word* wears its allegiances on its sleeve, opening with a section on 'Theoretical Preliminaries' and ranging from psychoanalysis to political conclusions via Freud, Saussure, Derrida, and Marx.[9] MacCabe's complex theoretical framework somewhat overwhelms the Joycean texts in question, and results in a confusing approach to the author. Referencing Derrida, MacCabe repeatedly situates his study as a movement away from the author as a root of meaning, and further explicitly states that his approach 'will not be to study the work as a product of the life' (12). Yet MacCabe looks specifically and directly at the author by increasingly referring to Joyce's letters (constituting a movement towards the author even when refuting their comments) and using Joyce's words reported in Arthur Power's 1974 memoir *Conversations with James Joyce* as authoritative proof of Joyce's socialism (159–65). MacCabe interprets both Joyce's letters and his reported conversations in order to prove a personal politics of the author, with which he then reads Joyce's literary texts. In his efforts to argue that 'Joyce's writing produces a change in the relations between reader and text, a change which has profound revolutionary implications', MacCabe presents a confusion of theoretical attitudes towards the author – and uses authorising methodologies not dissimilar from critics who predate or avoid the literary theories he adheres to (1).

These confusions are avoided in Karen Lawrence's important 1981 study *The Odyssey of Style in 'Ulysses'*, a theory-literate reappraisal of narrative and style that responds to Derrida, Wolfgang Iser, Edward Said, and early Barthes (texts predating 'The Death of the Author' or *S/Z*). Lawrence touches upon questions of authorship and textuality: she labels *Ulysses* 'antirevelatory', with no 'single truth'; argues Joyce's 'rhetorical masks' in the novel 'allowed the writing to be both the "me" and the "not me" of the writer'; and ponders whether 'The artist "paring his fingernails" is no longer an adequate image for the process of artistic creation.'[10] As a small but growing group of Joyce scholars began, like Lawrence, to see a critical engagement with theory as unavoidable and essential, so too did several critics begin to position themselves pointedly against their peers. Both MacCabe and Brook Thomas take on this combative, corrective tone: MacCabe, for instance, accuses Richard Ellmann's 1972 work *'Ulysses' on the Liffey* of reading the novel as 'a fixed source of fixed meanings', while Thomas (citing MacCabe) argues critics like Ellmann, Marilyn French, and S. L. Goldberg reductively 'posit a subject matter and then judge the book according to this subject matter'.[11]

Such bickering develops the ongoing enquiry of *how* to read Joyce. The Joyceans who began to ask this by turning to French theory, and its explorations of how to read any literary text, sat on one side of a developing rupture in Joyce studies. This divide deepened as theory-focused Joyceans increasingly argued further that not only are, most specifically, poststructuralism and deconstruction useful ways to approach Joyce's texts – but that there is also an intricate and significant relationship between the texts and the theory that cannot be ignored. Deconstruction refuses precisely to see literary texts as 'a fixed source of fixed meaning', seeking ways instead to reveal and preserve the instability of meaning in a text and thus avoid efforts towards critical mastery – or authority – over either text or meaning. And while Phillipe Sollers's avant-garde journal *Tel Quel* – described by Jennifer Levine as 'one of the major vehicles for French poststructuralism' – had been publishing articles on Joyce since 1960, the leading Joyce journal the *James Joyce Quarterly* only attempted to keep up with new approaches in its hodgepodge 1979 'Structuralist/Reader Response' issue.[12]

Pro-theory Joyceans worried over a delayed reception or continued absence of theory in Joyce studies, querying why the field appeared so resistant compared to the rest of the academy. Was this only a position to adopt, a way to drum up useful outrage in order to create a sense of need for theory-informed work on Joyce? It seems not, if we compare the frustrations expressed in Attridge and Ferrer's 1984 edited volume *Post-Structuralist Joyce* with Jonathan Culler's *On Deconstruction* published the previous year. In their introduction, Attridge and Ferrer complain of a 'remarkable absence of substantial change', identifying a core concept of literary critical poststructuralism to further protest that 'The realization that texts are unmasterable, and will return new answers as long as there are new questions, new questioners, or new contexts in which to ask questions, and that Joyce's texts display this characteristic more openly than most, is a thread that is barely visible' in Joyce scholarship and criticism.[13] Such observations are at odds with Culler's contemporaneous comment that 'To write about critical theory at the beginning of the 1980s is no longer to introduce unfamiliar questions, methods, and principles, but to intervene in a lively and confusing debate.'[14] Much of Anglo-American Joyce studies appears to have been cut off from – or avoiding – evolving literary critical attitudes in the broader field of the humanities. *Post-Structuralist Joyce* addressed this neglect, gathering together translated essays by Derrida, Cixous, Jacques Aubert, and André Topia (some originally from *Tel Quel*) and stressing the specific importance of poststructuralist approaches to Joyce studies. '[T]he affinity between Joyce and the theory of the Text and the Subject being elaborated in Paris is so close', Attridge and Ferrer point out, endeavouring in their introduction to establish a robust link between the two by arguing that the concerns of French theory – such as 'unreadability', 'mechanisms of [. . .] infinite productivity', the 'perpetual flight of the Subject and its ultimate disappearance', and 'strategies that attempt a deconstruction of representation' – closely echo the concerns of the texts and readers of Joyce (10).

Attridge and Ferrer spend a great deal of time on Derrida, his 'Two Words for Joyce', and his alignment of Joyce with deconstruction. 'Deux mots pour Joyce', included in the volume, is a very close reading of the words 'he war' in *Finnegans Wake*, and of Derrida's relationship to Joyce and his works. 'How many languages', he asks, 'can be lodged in two words by Joyce, lodged or inscribed, kept or burned, celebrated or violated?'[15] He describes a 'madness of writing by which whoever writes effaces himself, leaving, only to abandon it, the archive of his own effacement', then adjusts this reading to suggest an 'act of writing by which whoever writes pretends to efface himself, leaving us caught in his archive as in a spider's web'. Though Derrida speaks of authorship and the idea of Joyce as an author – discussing 'the singular *event* of his work (I prefer to talk here of an event rather than a work or a subject or an author)', for example – 'Two Words for Joyce' is best known for its approach to reading Joyce (146):

> But I'm not sure that one can say 'reading Joyce' as I just have. Of course, one can do nothing but that, whether one knows it or not. But the utterances 'I am reading Joyce', 'read Joyce', 'have you read Joyce?' produce an irresistible effect of naivety, irresistibly comical. What exactly do you mean by 'read Joyce'? Who can pride himself on having 'read' Joyce?
>
> [. . .] you stay on the edge of reading Joyce [. . .]. Is this true to the same extent of all works? In any case, I have the feeling that I haven't yet

begun to read Joyce, and this 'not having begun to read' is sometimes the most singular and active relationship I have with this work.

That is why I never dared to write *on* Joyce. (148)

According to Attridge and Ferrer, during the presentation of 'Two Words' at the Pompidou 'a leading Joyce scholar' claimed, as he 'listened carefully', Derrida's reading of 'he war' to be the same activity of any reading of the *Wake* (11). In her *James Joyce Quarterly* review of *Post-Structuralist Joyce*, Margot Norris makes an educated guess ('I would bet a fin') that the scholar overheard complaining '"But this is not so different from what we have been doing for years"' is Fritz Senn. Senn, a critic with a vocal and consistent disinterest in theory, confirms this in a 'Letter to the Editor' a couple of issues later, though he denies 'listen[ing] carefully'. He does graciously acknowledge, however, that the 'Decanians and Larridians' 'should have *their* say'.[16] This squabble rewards unpicking: what does it do, to claim that both deconstructive critics and readers of Joyce are interested in or even doing the same things? Attridge and Ferrer, on the defensive, use the comparison to strengthen new approaches; to authorise poststructuralist and deconstructive readings by claiming them as very Joycean. Senn's comparison is also defensive – but with a dismissive effect, protecting against the new. But does it write off newer approaches, muddling up the names of Derrida's and Lacan's disciples for comic effect, or does it attempt to promote an extant sophistication among Joyce scholars? 'We're already doing this, aren't we clever?' The comparison paradoxically gives strength to both sides of the argument. If a deconstructive reading is no different from how Joyce critics already read the *Wake*, then such new approaches are irrelevant, a pointless novelty in methodology. Conversely, if the similarities are so great, then deconstruction is a pertinently Joycean activity, clearly developed as Derrida, Attridge, Ferrer et al. would have it from the ways in which Joyce's output (particularly the *Wake*, they'd argue) causes one to read and be aware of one's reading – and thus requiring Joycean attention. Part of Derrida's argument in 'Two Words' is that Joyce – the event – pre-empts all. He makes the same claim regarding *Ulysses*, in his keynote at the Ninth Symposium in 1984. This manoeuvre raises vital questions concerning critical and authorial interpretative authority, as do the comparisons and discussions surrounding the validity of poststructuralist, and often specifically deconstructive, theory in Joyce studies. Anti- and pro-theory debates intensified during and in the aftermath of the Ninth Symposium, raising further issues of authority.

1984: Jacques Derrida and Hans Walter Gabler

The Ninth Symposium location of Frankfurt was a departure from the usually Joyce-related locations of the Symposia: Paris, Dublin, Trieste, Zurich. Though (as I've mentioned) accounts differ, it is generally agreed that 'a confrontation of sorts' took place thanks to an apparent new dominance of theory-inflected and theory-promoting approaches (*Augmented Ninth*, 4). This dominance must have developed swiftly: Attridge and Ferrer's complaints about an absence of attention being given to such approaches were published in *Post-Structuralist Joyce* that same year. In her essay on the history of women in Joyce studies, included in *Who's Afraid of James Joyce?*, Karen Lawrence remembers how the influences of poststructuralist and feminist theory seen in panels and plenaries 'were the news' at the Ninth Symposium (93). Benstock, in his introduction to the published proceedings, pays more attention to 'two groups' who reportedly clashed. He refers back to the 1975 Symposium in Paris to detail the tension between supporters of these two groups, refusing to name names and instead defining each side as 'for the most part, English-speaking' and 'French-speaking': 'the "revolution" in Frankfurt had its roots in Paris', where these groups 'ignored each other' (5–6). And as Lernout claims in *The French Joyce*, reading rather than recalling:

> In the proceedings of the Paris Joyce Symposium, I read between the lines that there was a genuine willingness on the part of American Joyceans to find out what the French were so excited about and an equally genuine unwillingness on the part of the French to offer that explanation. (13)

The importance of Joyce in the development, or birth, of deconstructive criticism was explicitly reasserted in the papers of the panel titled 'Deconstructive Criticism of Joyce', the discussion with Derrida during that panel, and in Derrida's address 'Ulysses Gramophone: Ouï-dire de Joyce'. The first copies of Hans Walter Gabler's new edition of *Ulysses*, a three-volume edition titled *Ulysses: The Corrected Text*, were presented to Joyce's grandson Stephen during the Symposium; this edition pushed the role of 'editor' to new extremes, and forced an appraisal of how the use of manuscripts and editorial judgement to correct the mistakes of the 1922 published text affects critics and readers. In 1985 a conference took place in Monaco with the aim to assess Gabler's edition of Joyce's text, and in 1988 John Kidd, in 'The Scandal of *Ulysses*' in *The New York Review of Books*, accused the text of being more Gabler's than Joyce's. Much of the Ninth Symposium's significance in the history of Joyce criticism lies in the reception of both Derrida and Gabler: the continued disagreements over the validity of deconstruction's claiming of Joyce's texts at its roots, and the ongoing development of editorial and genetic research by Gabler and others.

Beyond his extraordinary, extended, and dense opening address 'Ulysses Gramophone', Derrida was also the focal point of the 'Deconstructive Criticism of Joyce' panel; both for those presenting (Attridge, Christine van Boheemen-Saaf, and Jean-Michel Rabaté, with Ellen Carol Jones chairing) and those asking questions. The 'Joyce' of the panel title, and the 'Joyce' discussed by the presenters and Derrida, referred to the texts themselves – or what unites them. During this discussion, Jones informs us, Derrida stressed that 'Joyce is one of the most powerful preconditions of deconstruction, and that's why there is a privileged circulation between those two types of discourses' (Quoted by Ellen Carole Jones, *Augmented Ninth*, 78). He reportedly stated too, in an unusually direct style, that 'Deconstruction could not have been possible without Joyce' (78). 'Ulysses Gramophone' is far less direct: opening with the untranslatable 'Oui, oui, vous m'entendez bien, ce sont des mots français' and abruptly ending at 'I decided to stop here because I almost had an accident just as I was jotting down this last sentence, when, on leaving the airport, I was driving home after the trip to Tokyo', Derrida plots an appropriately parallactic path through his arguments.[17] He spoke in French for two and a half hours, pausing roughly every half an hour to allow a translator the unenviable task of giving the non-French speakers of the audience some sense of what was being said.[18] 'Ulysses Gramophone' performs a circular close reading of the word 'yes', moving from textual specifics to the specifics of Derrida's own context, of time running out and where he was when writing his presentation. His self-awareness extends to self-disparagement, which forms part of his argument: 'Incompetence as they [Joyce critics] are aware, is the profound truth of my relationship to this work which I know after all only directly, through hearsay, through rumours, through what people say, secondhand exegeses, readings which are always partial' (280).[19]

Derrida develops an idea he also explores in 'Two Words for Joyce', of being 'read in advance by *Finnegans Wake*' (150): 'Everything we can say about *Ulysses*', he argues in 'Ulysses Gramophone', 'has already been anticipated [. . .] Yes, everything has already happened to us with *Ulysses* and been signed in advance by Joyce' (281). This forms part of his reading of the 'double laughter' in *Ulysses*: one controlling and one opening the text.[20] Derrida's 'reading and [. . .] re-writing of Joyce' takes in bookshops, tourism, phone calls, aeroplanes, and even 'the Joyce international, the cosmopolitan, but very American James Joyce Foundation' (292 and 284); the circling development of his arguments proves difficult reading – let alone, we must imagine, listening. Attridge claims that, despite such difficulties, few people left as Derrida spoke: 'perhaps there was a shared awareness that this was, however incomprehensible, a landmark event in twentieth-century literary studies' ('Signature/Countersignature', 269). At least one Joycean, however, has proudly confessed in print to fleeing to a café partway through.[21]

Accounts of the unveiling of Gabler's *Ulysses* in Frankfurt differ too. Looking back in 2006, Lernout recalls a 'general feeling of excitement', but in 1986 C. George Sandulescu reports his own 'deep sense of frustration' due to what he saw as 'indifference' towards the Gabler edition at the 1984 Symposium.[22] Sandulescu arranged a conference in 1985 to address this and assess the edition, though assessments were already receiving plenty of attention elsewhere. John Kidd's well-publicised opposition to Gabler's text and the work behind it played out first in a *Washington Post* interview in 1985, and then Kidd's own eventual article 'The Scandal of *Ulysses*' in *The New York Review of Books* three years later. Kidd identifies 'literally thousands of unfortunate features of *Ulysses: The Corrected Text*', variously accusing Gabler and his team of simply doing a bad job, and of aiding 'the hopes of the Joyce estate [. . .] for a new copyright to run seventy-five years from 1984'.[23] Previous editions of *Ulysses* were reissued following the Kidd-Gabler controversy, and the 'corrected' 'corrected text' was printed in 1993 as 'The Gabler Edition'.[24] Objections died down, even to Gabler's most famous change – which provided the answer 'love' to Stephen's previously unanswered request for his mother's ghost to tell him 'The word known to all men' – and Gabler's *Ulysses* is now a standard, preferred edition, accepted and absorbed into the field. But, for a time, critics (and not just Kidd) questioned how Gabler authorised his edits, what his methods were, and where his authority came from. How, furthermore, should those who disagree with the edits of Gabler's *Ulysses* authorise their complaints? These questions are not dissimilar from those prompted by Derrida's *Ulysses* and explored in the debates surrounding links between Joyce and literary theory: how are theory-informed approaches authorised, and how are dissenting arguments? What does it do to find authority by arguing for a relationship between Joyce's texts and theory? In the reception of Gabler and Derrida, what is being communicated about authority – and who wields it – in Joyce studies?

Joyce studies was very quick to evaluate the field's interaction with poststructuralist theory: as monographs engaging with or influenced by theory proliferated in the late 1980s and early 1990s, two retrospective studies swiftly appeared.[25] Alan Roughley's 1991 overview, *James Joyce and Critical Theory*, gives a clearly pro-theory – and specifically pro-Derridean deconstruction – introduction to structuralist, semiotic, Anglo-American feminist, French feminist, psychoanalytical, Marxist, and poststructuralist encounters within Joyce studies. Roughley does not doubt 'the intriguing relationships which exist between Joyce's fiction and a variety of critical theories'.[26] His certitude, enthusiasm, and positive overview of deconstructive Joyce finds an alternative in Lernout's *The French Joyce*, published in 1990. Lernout's influential but resoundingly negative critique of theoretical Joycean criticism particularly singles out deconstruction, managing to both homogenise all deconstructive criticism and attack it for lacking a unified approach. His 'disagreements with the theory and practice of poststructuralism' more generally are in part due to his belief that poststructuralists see theirs as 'not just another methodology but the only way in which texts can meaningfully be read' (15 and 10) (though Lernout could be accused of the same in the pages of *The French Joyce*). Lernout holds the early enthusiasts of theory accountable for not properly explaining themselves (a conclusion based,

I'll point out again, on 'reading between the lines' of the Paris Symposium proceedings); his view of the 1988 Venice Symposium is no less damning. Targeting the younger scholars who adopted new approaches, Lernout cries careerism: 'poststructuralism and feminism sell well', he concludes, apparently dismissing any other reasons a critic might have to engage with either school of theory (17). *The French Joyce* eventually recommends readings informed by historical context, and also promotes a 'view of the producer of literature that comes closer to Joyce's self-understanding'. Lernout describes 'Joyce's view of himself as a highly self-conscious demiurge, the godlike creator of an oeuvre that is a challenge to the divine creation' (212). This Stephen-ism (cf. 'like the God of the creation') is given plainly as Joyce's view of himself, a claim made without citation or evidence: presenting as unquestionable both the conflation of Joyce and Stephen and the authority of Joyce's presumed understanding of the producer of literature.

Despite the efforts of Lernout and others, work increased to affirm Derrida's place in literary studies, and defend the connection between Derrida and Joyce. The field of Derridean Joyce studies has resulted in numerous works, predominantly focused on *Finnegans Wake*.[27] These studies established a continued interaction of Derridean thought and Joycean texts despite, as Roughley details in his 1999 study *Reading Derrida Reading Joyce*, the attempts of Joyce criticism to move past Derrida and Joyce 'by closing off or ignoring the conceptual ruptures and textual spaces opened up in the writings of both'.[28] This continued activity is also, however, due to a complex manoeuvring of critical and authorial authority. Derrida's deconstruction is, to an extent, authorised by its invocation of Joyce; and Joycean critics' use of Derrida's work is authorised by both that proclaimed link and by the authority of Derrida himself. Derrida was not alone in placing Joycean texts at the root of his approaches to reading: when critics hang arguments from references to Kristeva's use of Joyce's work as an example of the '*polyphonic*' novel in her writings on intertextuality, or Wolfgang Iser's reliance on Joyce's texts in his formation of reader response criticism, these critics are using the same mode of authorisation that combines the authority of the theorist and Joyce himself. Critics find their own relationships between theory and Joyce, too, making their case by reiterating a theorist's arguments, delving into argued links with Joyce's work, or simply flagging a relationship between Joyce and theory without detail. This last method of citation is occasionally framed within a more general view of poststructuralism as a development of essentially modernist ideas: as, for example, in this reference to 'challenges (inspired by modernist thought and by authors like Joyce) to the foundations of the idea of authorship, such as those of Heidegger, Barthes, Foucault, and so on'.[29] Such statements imply a well-known and accepted relationship between 'authors like Joyce' and poststructuralism's 'challenge' to authorship – and suggest this 'inspiration' is not even worth questioning.

Simultaneously, relationships between Joyce and literary theory continue to be queried and refuted: one particular early 2000s critical back-and-forth serves as a useful example. In a 2002 article 'The Fidelity of Theory: James Joyce and the Rhetoric of Belatedness', Joseph Brooker derides 'the naturalization of the relation between theory and Joyce', focusing specifically on the British reception of poststructuralism.[30] He repeats his argument in his 2004 study *Joyce's Critics*, in which he also worries over Joyce giving theory 'status', but aligns himself with Lernout's sceptical view of theory (claiming Lernout 'need not be rehearsed here').[31] In the earlier article Brooker pulls at the 'central dialectic' of British poststructuralism: that it was 'propelled at its very origin' by Joyce's 'textual politics'. Sidestepping a detailed engagement with either Joyce's texts or the theory in question, Brooker claims that placing Joyce at the roots of theory 'allows theory to be "applied" to Joyce on the grounds that it is not really being applied, because it has been, so to speak, secreted by the text as its own self-understanding' (210 and 219).

On the same topic, Laurent Milesi shifts the emphasis of this debate in his 2004 introduction to *James Joyce and the Difference of Language*:

> What the multi-faceted resilience of Joyce's fabrications has made possible – and why his novels have long been a privileged testing ground for new theoretical agendas and thus themselves stood the test of time – is his readers' (self-)empowerment through the very medium and fabric of his works, beyond the mere academic mapping of different theoretical grids onto his fiction.[32]

Milesi's notion of a reader's self-empowerment did not convince Paul K. Saint-Amour, who pointedly cites Brooker's work on 'belatedness' in a review of Milesi's edited collection. Saint-Amour pushes Brooker's argument, naming efforts to suggest Joyce pre-empted theory as 'a self-authorizing move within Joyce studies'.[33] Critics taking a position like Brooker and Saint-Amour's cannot accept an argument like Milesi's: that Joyce's text is the source of empowerment or authority for the reader, whether that reader is a theorist developing their own work or a critic using literary theory with their reading of Joyce. For such sceptics, this is but a deceptive ruse to cover up self-authorisation on the part of the reader/critic. The implication is that self-authorisation is not good enough: the self-empowered reader is not a sufficient source of authority. What is, then?

The debate over whether *Ulysses* and *Finnegans Wake* are, to use Lawrence's useful and perhaps more neutral term, 'hospitable' to theory (*Who's Afraid of James Joyce?*, 5), has not addressed at length the activities of Joycean criticism that predates or ignores literary theory. Do Joyce's works anticipate all readings or readers themselves, and therefore specific literary theories? Are arguments in favour self-authorised, authorised by theorists, authorised by Joyce, or a product of the reader's empowerment? In the various versions of debates around these questions, it is difficult to find a discussion of how the behaviour and focuses of 'pre-theory' Joycean criticism shares qualities with the work of theoretical Joyceans and theoretical texts themselves. What are the implications of resemblances between the work of so-called traditionalists and theoretical approaches in terms of authority? What do we do with critical sniping over whether the text has 'secreted' theory, when writers like Kenner and Derrida reach corresponding conclusions from reading *Ulysses*? Ideas are pre-empted, as is the debate itself: the self-reflexivity of early Joyce studies means that the question of how best to read a literary text – and how such readings are authorised – has been a prominent feature of the field since the 1920s.

Early critics were concerned, if often indirectly, with the issue of what literary criticism should aim for, and with questions related to the relationships between author, reader, and text. As I showed in Chapter 2, the shift in Joyce studies from 'what was the author trying to do?' to 'how do we read this?' was prompted by *Ulysses* criticism and *Ulysses* itself. Questions of authorship were implicitly explored in Joyce studies before the challenges of poststructuralist and deconstructive theoretical approaches, but only explicitly interrogated after the 'arrival' of theory. Pointing out echoes between early Joyce studies and deconstructive criticism contributes to an argument I examine above: that Joyce studies and deconstructive criticism are the same thing, that 'this is what we have been doing for years'.[34] As I suggested earlier, the comparison gives authority to both sides of the argument, both validating and invalidating deconstructive criticism of Joyce's texts. But if we look again at this comparison with a specific focus on how Joyce studies has engaged with questions of authorship, it begins to matter considerably whether the 'new approaches' were a pointless novelty or a pertinently Joycean activity.

Issues of how to analyse literary origins, the role of the reader, the nature of the text, and the relationships between all three, are present and gestured towards in early or 'pre-theory' Joyce studies, but these issues only became explicit inquiries in work 'post-theory': work that cited poststructuralist and deconstructive theory. Theory's 'arrival' therefore did contribute something significant, even if only a framework, language, or method to aid the further exploration of extant concerns of authorship and authority. Joycean critics were prompted to directly consider questions of authorship, and the resultant work has had a significant impact on how the author is perceived in Joyce studies.

The Author in Joyce Studies

In the 1980s and early 1990s a handful of Joyce critics engaged directly with questions of authorship: some prompted by the provocations of poststructuralist theory, and others by an idea of poststructuralist theory's impact. The author was a site for critical investigation in small flurries of important work during this period; however, Joyce studies' engagement with questions surrounding how readers perceive the author, how the interrelations of authorial and readerly roles or activities function, or how concepts of the author's authority affect reading and criticism, was and remains limited. Some authorial queries have been taken up again more recently, in line with modernist studies' interests in authorial self-fashioning. This recent work updates and adds valuable detail to the few major 1980s and 1990s texts of Joycean authorship and authority, but does little to rethink or question the overwhelming preference for author over reader in such foundational studies. In this section I will consider how the field has dealt directly with the relationships between author, reader, and text, looking at work which discusses the author via narrative, intertextuality, Stephen Dedalus, authority, and self-fashioning. I'll begin with the criticism of the 1980s and 1990s, much of which argues for a return of the author; a curiosity in retrospect, as it is not apparent that the author was ever lost or abandoned in Joyce studies.

By the early 1980s, poststructuralist theory had made only limited inroads to Joyce studies, yet its perceived threat to the author appears to have prompted swift responses. As early as 1982, two Joyceans already seek or identify the author's return. Brook Thomas asks, in his theory-embedded study *James Joyce's 'Ulysses': A Book of Many Happy Returns*, how the author might 'return to his text' (5), while in 'Joyce and the Displaced Author' Christopher Butler argues that a removal of the author for a freedom of reading is 'doomed to failure' – that texts 'lead back to the author as origin, and our notions of him'.[35] Joycean work on author questions continued to focus on an authorial return across the 1980s and early 1990s: Joyce is a key figure in Susan Stanford Friedman's 1991 article on the dead and then 'insistently returned' author, 'Weavings: Intertextuality and the (Re)Birth of the Author', and Joyce returns – after death – as a 'bogeyman' in Jean-Michel Rabaté's *James Joyce, Authorized Reader*.[36] Rabaté's classic study, still generally seen as the key Joycean text on authority and the author, has an interesting publication and translation history: after first publishing the study in French in 1984, by the time Rabaté's English translation appeared in 1991 his critical approach had significantly changed. Declaring in his preface that he has 'since systematically situated myself' in genetic criticism, Rabaté distances himself from *Authorized Reader*'s 'theoretical response to Joyce as read in a Lacanian and Derridian perspective' (xii). This stated difference brings to mind Stephen's lack of belief in his own reading of Shakespearean authorship – a topic of Rabaté's study – and is redolent of how quickly some Joyceans moved on from poststructuralism. There is no suggestion in Rabaté's corrective preface, furthermore, that the conclusions of *Authorized Reader* are incompatible with his new critical interests and methods: authorial return and genetic criticism, we might infer, coexist comfortably.

Before I come back to the arguments of *Authorized Reader* and returns of (or to) the author, it is important to consider the efforts during this period to engage with debates of authorship without – as it were – taking sides. By this I mean arguing for neither a death nor a return of the author, and attempting to avoid privileging the authority of author or reader. John Paul Riquelme seeks to achieve this by rooting his theory-informed discussions in narrative: in his 1983 study *Teller and Tale*, Riquelme identifies a 'teller' in Joyce's works, a narrator figure that 'can be no more absolutely distinguished from author than from tale'.[37] Riquelme proposes an author whose 'ineluctable presence during the writing' and 'necessary absence during the reading' are contained within 'a single term: *narrator*' (132). Insistently locating his arguments in narrative, Riquelme describes an unseeable writer for whom we find 'figures' in the text: 'figures *for* the writer' in language, styles, personae (133). Gillespie's 1989 study *Reading the Book of Himself* also focuses on narrative, analysing narrative strategies with the aim to refuse notions of either correct or unlimited meanings in Joyce's texts. Gillespie argues for balance, for 'a both/and condition that does not assign either to the author or to the reader the position of sole arbiter of meaning'.[38] These arguments stumble, however.

Looking for ways to allow readings that 'deviate' from 'a single privileged interpretation', Gillespie turns to Stephen's ideas of authorship in *Portrait*, and to Joyce's words as quoted in Arthur Power's 1974 memoir *Conversations with James Joyce* (164). Acknowledging a level of irony in Stephen's words, Gillespie nevertheless claims it is possible to 'derive from them an understanding of the delicate balance that must exist in the relationship between author and reader' (5). He treats Stephen not as an ironic figure of an author within the text, but as an authorised representative of Joyce in the text. Hanging his argument thus from Stephen, Gillespie goes on to inform us that Joyce's reader can hold a position of control, but within limiting boundaries – and that, referring to Joyce's own thoughts on *Ulysses* quoted by Power, 'that was what Joyce aimed to do' (172). In referring to Joyce via Power, and a sort of Stephen-as-Joyce, Gillespie underwrites his argument against 'privileged interpretation' with the author's authority: with the author's interpretation. *Reading the Book of Himself* contradictorily maintains an author-over-reader hierarchical power structure: Gillespie's proposal for a balance of interpretive power between author and reader is based on Joyce's texts and informed by theoretical notions of an active reader (he cites Barthes, Derrida, Bakhtin, Fish throughout), yet his suggestions are then authorised by the author. Gillespie's work does not examine such contradictions, nor were they picked up by others – *Reading the Book of Himself* is far from the only piece of Joycean criticism in which an authorial return undermines arguments which seek to challenge the author's authority.

In the context of critical and theoretical debates surrounding the death of the author, referencing Joyce's opinions signals a return to the author: these allusions to letters or Joyce as quoted by others give and promote interpretive value and authority to the words of the author. Where critics reach out for Joyce's words within critical work which otherwise proclaims allegiance to anti-authorial approaches to literature, the results are confusing. MacCabe's *James Joyce and the Revolution of the Word* is an early example: MacCabe's use of Joyce's words to authorise political readings, in a study which positions itself within a movement away from the author as a root of meaning, shows how easy it is for the author to creep back in to the discussion and continue to enjoy authority. Such issues crop up again in later work, for example by Kevin Dettmar in 1996: in his Lyotard-informed study *The Illicit Joyce of Postmodernism: Reading Against the Grain* he takes a death-of-the-author stance, yet refers to tales of Joyce's life and Joyce's composition. His head turned by such anecdotes, Dettmar maintains more traditional critical habits – and betrays the strength of this tendency towards the author.

Rabaté discusses the use of Joyce's own words in criticism, aptly, as Rabaté too turns to Joyce's letters and Power's Joyce in *Authorized Reader*. He focuses on a critical reader's ability to question Joyce, specifically Joyce's denial of believing the theories of Vico – relating his discussion of biographical references to 'Stephen's denegation' (183). Given his argument for an author 'coming back like a bogeyman to scare critics and readers', Rabaté's turn to Joyce does not contradict the general shape of his critical endeavour (153) (unlike Gillespie, Dettmar, and MacCabe). *Authorized Reader* does not address, however, its use of the schemata – or any other critic's use thereof. Whether or not references to the schemata are seen as betraying an interest and investment in Joyce's own view of *Ulysses*, the schemata are inarguably extra-textual authorial documents. The discussion of *Authorized Reader* is solidly rooted in the relationships between critics and authority, yet Rabaté does not explore the ramifications of using the authorially approved schemata – or of their dissemination by Joyce and his critic friends. Rabaté also reads Stephen's words as unironically Joyce's own: 'Joyce, it is true', he claims, 'does not say that the author has died, preoccupied as he is with dead mothers and dying fathers, but states that he has been "refined out of existence"' (3). Elsewhere, he claims Stephen's discussions in 'Scylla and Charybdis' to be where 'Joyce approaches most closely his concept of an author's authority' (155). Ultimately, Rabaté defines the author in his study by following Stephen, and thus, by the logic of *Authorized Reader*, following Joyce's own definition. The arguments of *Authorized Reader* for a returning author who has not 'died' are therefore aligned with Joyce's presumed view of authorship, and Rabaté invokes the authority of Stephen-as-Joyce to endorse this position.

The majority of the articles, chapters, and books on Joyce and authorship sprinkled across the 1980s and early to mid-1990s argued for a return to or of the author, and focused on Stephen. While work on Stephen and Joyce from this period does not necessarily involve conflating Stephen as Joyce, where it does the implications of that blurring in terms of critical or authorial authority are rarely raised or queried. A notable exception is Christine Froula's 1996 reappraisal of Joycean self-portraiture, *Modernism's Body: Sex, Culture, and Joyce*. Froula's analysis of ironic autobiography and the artist's subjectivity draws on deconstructive, feminist, and psychoanalytic approaches, signalling Stephen's 'continuity with his maker' with her term 'Stephen/Joyce'.[39] Vicki Mahaffey's 1988 study *Reauthorizing Joyce*, meanwhile, discusses monological authority in broad terms, spending far less time than Rabaté on authorship specifically. Mahaffey combs Joyce's texts to find different forms of authority, related in *Ulysses*, for example, to gender, politics, language, and specific characters. Mahaffey's approach emphasises the activity of readers, and, in a marked departure from her contemporaries working on similar topics, brings in feminist literary theories and critics – prefiguring Friedman's slightly later work 'Weavings'. Friedman's 1991 article develops Nancy K. Miller's assertion of the necessity for feminist criticism to find a way of 'reintroducing the spider – as author, as subject, as agent, as gendered body, as producer of the text'. Reading *Portrait*, Friedman hopes to extend Miller's rejection of 'the concept of anonymity that Barthes, Foucault, and Kristeva promote in their versions of intertextuality' from women writers to all writers; she argues, further, that there is already a 'reinsertion of the author' in how the theories of intertextuality have been received in literary criticism (158–9 and 173).

Movements away from the death of the author took place for a variety of reasons in literary studies; as I reference for example in Chapter 1, the author's identity became central to several critical approaches. The majority of early arguments for an authorial return in Joyce studies, however, were not underpinned by critical and theoretical approaches for which an author's gender, race, sexuality, nationality, or class are important. So what quality, attribute, or function can we ascribe to the author that kept drawing critics back? Some valuable candour comes from outside Joyce studies: Leo Bersani's 1988 article 'Against *Ulysses*' sets out a provocative reading of the novel, Joyce, and 'the extraordinarily prosperous Joyce industry'.[40] Better known for his contributions to queer theory, in this article Bersani embraces quite a clear non-Joycean position. Exploring if we read or decipher *Ulysses*, if interpretation of the novel is possible, and if perhaps it is not as complex as we think it is, Bersani argues that 'Where *Ulysses* really leads us is to Joyce's mind; it illuminates his cultural consciousness' (225). With references also to how the text 'also includes, or at least alludes to, the anxiety from which we escape in our exegetical relocation of the work itself within the masterful authorial consciousness at its origin', Bersani nevertheless insists *Ulysses* is nothing less than 'modernism's most impressive tribute to the West's long and varied tribute to the authority of the Father' (225 and 228).

The whole of *Ulysses*, Bersani argues, points to its creator; even further, 'the book gives birth to its author' (227). As its title suggests, 'Against *Ulysses*' has a fairly confrontational tone – yet Bersani's argument that it is the text itself that leads us to the author is not dissimilar from arguments made by those embedded within Joyce studies, who identified or demanded a return to or of the author. And the quiet presence of the author in studies which otherwise sought to turn away from the author's authority further suggests the strength of that pull towards the text's origin (or an idea of its origin). Even further, these contradictory turns to the author within anti-authorial criticism expose a strange confusion surrounding the perception of the author and authorial authority in Joyce studies. The author's 'return' drew an extraordinary amount of attention, considering it is unclear the author ever 'left'.

The field's muddled demands for authorial return in work of the 1980s and early 1990s did not turn into fodder for critical work on the author in the decades that followed. This contradictory episode of author criticism instead gave way to useful work focused on intertextuality, errors, and celebrity: topics for which questions of authorship are only one facet. The relationships between author, reader, and text are often sites for discussion in studies of Joycean intertextuality and literary relations, and critics including Lucia Boldrini, Patricia Novillo-Corvalán, and Scarlett Baron have continued to effectively explore how best to situate Joyce's intertextual practices within existing theoretical frameworks of influence and intertextuality.[41] When exploring the literary relationship between Joyce and an earlier author, critics must decide what sort of agency to attribute to Joyce – who in such studies is both Joyce-the-author and Joyce-the-reader. Is the relationship one of passive influence, active reference, or one where textual boundaries dissolve? Are such categories useful? The authorial connotations of literary relations come back often to questions of intention: must, for example, inter-literary references found by a reader be intentionally placed there by the author?

Readings of Joycean intentions frequently return to the idea that Joyce intended for us to not worry ourselves too much with his intentions; an idea first expressed coherently by Kenner (as I discussed in Chapter 2) but also similar to Derrida's readings of Joyce. Kenner argues in his 1980 study *'Ulysses'* that we as readers are 'liberated' from any anxiety over the author's intention, as part of our role as collaborators in the text – but that this is due to Joyce's own efforts to hide his intentions.[42] While Kenner is not always cited (nor any congruence with Derrida observed), many others have taken this stance on intention. Tim Conley's 2003 study *Joyces Mistakes: Problems of Intention, Irony, and Interpretation* unsurprisingly picks up on this paradox of Joycean intention, referencing M. Keith Booker (and a similar point by Vicki Mahaffey): 'often his authorial intention is apparently that one should not grant interpretive authority to authorial intention'.[43] Conley, furthermore, opens his study by quoting Arthur Power's Joyce's concession, when asked if his intentions have been misunderstood: 'Which of us can control our scribblings?'[44] The original paradox, critics arguing that it is the author's intention that we do not place too much emphasis on authorial intention when reading – a paradox these critics enjoy – is then further authorised apparently by Power's Joyce. In this frequently reiterated concept of Joycean intention, critics give the greatest credence to Joyce's own idea of intention. I will pick up this tangle in the next two chapters, but here it is vital to reiterate the centrality of the author that is repeated with the doctrine of Joyce intending for us to ignore his intentions. Disregarding intentions using this logic, as Conley and others suggest we do, is not due to a decentring of the author in criticism, or a formalist approach to literature, or a prioritisation of the activity of the reader: it is the result of endowing the author with the upmost authority.

The most recent sustained academic engagement with questions of authorship provides strong evidence of a continued preference for authors over readers. The author in celebrity studies, a field that has made significant inroads to Joyce studies, explores how authors formed themselves as authors: the personas they cultivated, promotional techniques they employed, author-foils they wrote into their work. The reader, in such approaches, is merely the receptacle for the author's views on authorship. Work on the author in modernist studies has, for the last twenty years, been firmly focused on authorial self-fashioning – on modernist authors' knowing manipulations of authorial personas or brands. Joyce figures prominently in Aaron Jaffe's 2005 *Modernism and the Culture of Celebrity* and Paul K. Saint-Amour's 2003 monograph *The Copywrights*, which both, through their respective lenses of literary celebrity and intellectual property, consider Joyce's own ideas of authorship. Work by Jonathan Goldman on Joyce and authorial branding, and by Eleni Loukopoulou on Joyce's authorial self-promotion in London, also develops insight into Joyce's authorship – as perceived by Joyce. Jaffe's analysis of Joyce in *Modernism and the Culture of Celebrity* is firmly focused on Stephen in *Portrait*. His interest is in Joyce's notion of authorship, which he reads as Stephen's; but he also appraises such readings of the relationship between Stephen and Joyce. Jaffe picks apart critical readings which conflate Joyce and Stephen, and those which ironise Stephen and separate the character and the author; he argues that both readings seek 'Joyce's authoritative voice', finding it either in Stephen or in determining 'Joyce's intelligence' in his 'ironic distance'.[45] Promoting the concept of authorial self-fashioning, Jaffe claims everything returns to the author. His approach – though insightful – undermines a reader's agency, and insists not only that what an author 'is' can be controlled, or authorised, by the author, but perhaps also that this holds more value than how the author is perceived by the reader.

The Copywrights, Saint-Amour's study of literature and intellectual property, considers Joyce's own awareness of literary copyright, finding tensions in

Joyce between collective authorship and the single genius, between intertextuality and originality.[46] Saint-Amour's Joyce is aware of, and in 'Oxen of the Sun' and beyond, responding to, an idea of authorship informed by copyright law: from the link between copyright and an author's life, to the notion of 'fair use and infringement' (166–8 and 170). Eleni Loukopoulou also examines self-conscious authorship in *Up to Maughty London*, her important 2017 study of London as a site for Joyce's authorial self-promotion, while additionally extending earlier work such as John Nash's on the cultural and political context of Joyce's reception.[47] Jonathan Goldman's 2014 work on 'authorial branding' of Joyce and by Joyce himself, meanwhile, also considers both the author aware of his own reception, and that reception itself.[48] In recent work within Joyce studies, then, ideas of the author are presented as malleable: but this malleability is primarily (or often even exclusively) in the hands of the author. Critical interest overwhelmingly revolves around Joyce's own understanding of authorship, giving value to Joyce's view of authorship over any other. The author is well and truly present in Joyce studies.

The critical texts I have picked at in this section have formed vital contributions to Joyce studies; I am not attempting in my readings to perform some sort of nit-picking 'gotcha!'. But unanswered questions remain: missed, or deemed unimportant. What could an 'absent' author mean for Joyce criticism – what would criticism look like and how would it work, if the author *had* 'died'? Why is preference given by critics to Joyce's view of intention, or a Stephen/Joyce's view of authorship? Why has Joyce studies not explored the idea of an author as malleable in the hands of the reader? Such queries, raised explicitly and implicitly by work bred from the Joycean engagement with poststructuralist and deconstructive theory, have been left behind. The field's preference for the author's authority preps the way for the critical approaches that have gained popularity and strength since the 1990s, to which I now turn.

How to Read Joyce

What position does the author occupy in Joyce studies today? In the last thirty years, historicist readings have increasingly gained dominance. Critics underpin a variety of approaches with the methods of genetic criticism, and, in certain corners of the field, continue to discuss the usefulness of theory-informed literary criticism. Growing bodies of research examine Joyce's texts through the useful lenses of feminist, queer, posthuman, ecological, and disability studies, or detail the literary interrelations between Joyce and other artists. In this final section, I will consider what recent and current Joyce criticism communicates about the relationships between author, reader, and text. After first looking at the ongoing debate over the validity of theory, I will turn to perhaps the most prevalent critical approaches in Joyce studies: genetic, historical, and political. These approaches create and position themselves within their own histories of Joyce studies, but few examine or even touch upon questions of authorship and authority. The author's identity, historical context, and compositional processes carry differing but persistent levels of authorising clout in today's popular approaches. The author, in other words, is important in contemporary Joyce studies, but that importance has been neither considered in the context of the field's development nor sufficiently analysed in terms of authority.

Joyce studies continues to produce work asking openly how to read Joyce's texts: not only new guidebooks and annotations of vital practical use, but also considered and ambitious work such as Margot Norris's *Virgin and Veteran Readings of 'Ulysses'*. Norris's 2011 study uses Possible Worlds theory in a narrative context to hypothesise a new reader encountering *Ulysses* for the first time, underscoring how the text requires readers to continually fill in gaps, infer, discover the implicit. She argues that the first-time reader participates with the text more than their veteran counterpart;[49] a welcome emphasis on different kinds of active, creative reading, rooted by Norris in narrative theory. Elsewhere, the field has continued to question the relevance and fecundity of relationships between Joyce and theory, particularly the literary and philosophical links between Joyce and deconstruction. David Vichnar's 2010 study *Joyce Against Theory: James Joyce After Deconstruction*, for example, returns to, promotes, and complicates the idea 'that Joyce's writing is itself theoretical through and through', by assessing several theoretical approaches within Joyce studies since Derrida's 'Ulysses Gramophone'.[50] Vichnar situates his study in relation to his obvious precursors, Roughley and Lernout – unsurprisingly favouring Roughley – and staunchly opposes Joseph Brooker's historical analysis of the impact of theory within Joyce studies in Brooker's *Joyce's Critics* (2004). Vichnar disagrees particularly, and tellingly, with an aside of Brooker's: '(Strictly, the Derridean claim refers to the operation of Joyce's writing, not the man himself: but this makes little practical difference.)' (*Joyce's Critics*, 169) As Vichnar points out, 'the distinction between Joyce-the-man and Joyce-the-writer matters a good deal' (5). This comment, in what is otherwise predominantly a round-up of other work, outlines an issue that remains significant: what do we mean by 'Joyce', and how should we read Joyce the man, the writer, or any distinction or relationship between the two?

One of Joyce studies' most outspoken non-theorists describes these dilemmas in 'Joyce the Verb', first given as a talk at the 1988 Symposium. In the essay Senn, who has for decades got away with claiming little to no knowledge of theory (but enough knowledge, apparently, to dismiss it wholesale), determines that 'It is equally true to say "Joyce has been dead for forty-five years", as to claim "Joyce is alive." "Joyce" does not equal "Joyce".'[51] The arguments of 'Joyce the Verb', if we believe Senn's claims of ignorance, exist in a critical world without literary theory. Exploring how naming and knowing are not etymologically linked, Senn observes how we use Joyce's name in phrases such as 'reading Joyce' without meaning Joyce-the-person – while at other times doing the opposite. 'At one extreme', he continues, 'the word does duty for a life lived in various cities in the course of almost sixty years; at the other possible ends of the scales it suggests writing, thinking, creating, developing, intending – you name it, and you name it appropriately by verbs'. Senn acknowledges the likelihood 'that someone has already put this into a system of trendy abstractions' (8–9). Arguably, someone has: Foucault's 'What is an Author?' explores remarkably similar ground.

Derek Attridge, a pioneer of theory-informed criticism of Joyce who has been at the forefront of changing attitudes towards different theoretical approaches, has asked across his work what we mean by and how we read 'Joyce'. In his discussion, and cheering on, of deconstructive criticism at the 1984 Symposium, Attridge notes that by 'Joyce' he means a 'name to stand for the group of texts bearing that signature' (*Augmented Ninth*, 85). In his 1990 chapter 'Reading Joyce', Attridge introduces the experience of reading that group of texts, of enjoyment and 'pleasures' which 'rely on qualities of inexplicability, unpredictability, inexhaustibility'.[52] Attridge relishes 'an endlessly repeated failure' to 'end' reading, and warns readers to mistrust

> Any critical text which claims to tell you (at last) what a work of Joyce's is "about", or what its structure, or its moral position, or its symbolic force, "is" [. . .] because it is making a claim that, taken literally, would exclude all other ways of reading the work. (3)

Senn similarly is 'sceptical' of statements such as '*Ulysses* is', preferring '*Ulysses* does . . . acts . . . performs'.[53] Senn's distaste for theory has been a feature of the field for decades, so the similarities between his and Attridge's approaches to definitive critical statements are curious. Senn could even be the focus of Attridge's response in *Joyce Effects* (2000) to critical tendencies which deride the shifts of theoretical criticism from each new novelty to the next:

> Those who complain most loudly [. . .] usually imply that obscured by the frenetic musical chairs of critical fashion is some solid, abiding, dependable approach to literature [. . .] The problem with that position is that the approach it favours is necessarily itself historical, the product of specific social, economic, and cultural forces.[54]

There is no limit, Attridge continues in *Joyce Effects*, to what can be read in a text or said about that text (17). Warnings against conclusive statements of what *Ulysses* 'is' come thus from both pro- and anti-theory sources; common ground amid such differing attitudes. There is no one consistently correct way to read Joyce critically, nor one mode that is best, ultimate, or definitive. Any approach is valid, save that which announces itself the 'only' approach.

Such egalitarian critical values can falter. In 1997 the question of how to read the Joyce of manuscripts, letters, notes, and a reader's own construction returned to the fore: as in 1984, this was due to the work of an editor rather than a critic. Danis Rose's *Ulysses: The Reader's Edition* pushed the role of editor to its limits, resulting in a trial four years later in which the Joyce estate charged Rose with both infringement of copyright and 'passing off' – a charge that accused Rose of changing *Ulysses* so much that it could no longer be considered an edition of Joyce's text. John Kidd reappeared in *The New York Review of Books*, describing Rose's edits as 'so anti-Joycean that the author is Danis Rose, not James Joyce'.[55] Rose changed spelling, inserted hyphens, amended perceived 'errors', and punctuated the unpunctuated. Critics raced to respond. Though ostensibly a *Finnegans Wake* special issue, the Summer 1997 *James Joyce Quarterly* includes reviews of Rose's *Ulysses* by Gabler, Senn, Gillespie, and Lawrence Rainey.[56] These reviews point out errors in Rose's reading, challenging Rose's decisions with a combination of evidence from manuscripts, previous readings, and each critic's own judgement – methods remarkably similar to Rose's own. Defending Danis Rose against this massed response, Joseph Kelley proposes that the disagreements between Rose and others are really about a difference in belief in how much meaning was 'intended' in *Ulysses*, and that critics use a faith in Joyce's genius to authorise their own interpretations.[57] The authority of copyright law succeeded, lending authority to the fury of the critics: *A New Reader's Edition* appeared in 2004, altered after the Joyce estate's success in court put a stop to the distribution of *A Reader's Edition* – winning over copyright but not the 'passing off' charges.[58] Following the logic of Kelley's argument, each critic's response to Rose's edited *Ulysses* was determined by a reading of Joyce the author; the resultant spat indicates some unease on the part of the critics whose idea of Joyce was briefly unsettled.

The study of manuscripts, notebooks, proofs, revisions, and margin notes informs a strand of Joyce studies that started to gain significant strength and influence in the 1990s. Distinct from textual editing, though involved in much of the same material, as the name suggests genetic criticism examines a text's genesis. It focuses on process and development, prioritising the drafts, notes, and worksheets – or *avant-texte* – over the final published text. What is sometimes called 'applied' genetic criticism involves using this mode of analysis to better understand not only how the text came to be, but also elements of its final form.[59] In its focus on the author's processes and scrutinising of the author's handwritten notes to inform an interpretation of the final text, applied genetic criticism suggests authorial intent; or, more cautiously, suggests an author's interest in a particular topic. While working in clear opposition to the authority of the published, final text, genetic criticism's relationship to the authority of the author is more complicated. Furthermore, while in many respects the methodology emphasises endless opportunities for new and varied readings of Joyce's texts, genetic criticism's touch of scientific method can lead its advocates to claim they have, for example, found 'concrete proof'.[60]

Issues of intent, proof, and interpretation feature heavily in the first (of four, so far) *European Joyce Studies* edited collection on genetic criticism, published in 1995. The editors David Hayman and Sam Slote include an introduction to the methodology, in which Hayman carefully claims the materials of genetic criticism can 'clarify both intent and content without dictating interpretation'.[61] Hayman describes genetic critics as 'few in number and still learning our trade' (12); the next *European Joyce Studies* collection on genetic criticism appeared just a few years later in 1999, no longer introducing the field to a novel method but already speaking from a position in which apparently 'genetic criticism has come of age'.[62] The positioning of the author in Joycean genetic criticism declares an investment not necessarily in authorial authority but in the authority of authorial process, method, writing. The separation of writing from writer often wavers, however. In Michael Groden's 1997 study *'Ulysses' in Progress*, which continues the work started by A. Walton Litz in *The Art of James Joyce*, Groden proudly informs us that 'Wherever possible I have used Joyce's own words to support my statements.'[63] The edited collection *How Joyce Wrote 'Finnegans Wake'*, published in 2007, opens meanwhile with a preface from Groden which includes the claim that 'Genetic studies start with Joyce himself.'[64] While Dirk van Hulle, in his detailed 2008 work *Manuscript Genetics*, denies genetic criticism is 'a new form of biographism', other genetic work explicitly links historical moments of composition with events in Joyce's biography in order to authorise readings.[65] Opinions on intention, biographism, positivism, interpretation, and evidence or proof differ between genetic critics, just as critics differ over whether or not genetic study should be used to underpin literary interpretations or focus purely on how a text was written without extrapolating further.

While the methodology of genetic criticism is in some respects anti-intention, as it looks past an intended 'final' text, that same methodology also seeks knowledge of why or by what logic an author put this or that spelling, word, phrase, or passage here or there in the text. Furthermore, genetic critics often assign significance to *when* this or that was added or changed in the text. Back in 1961, Litz argued that the lateness of Homeric additions to *Ulysses* proved their unimportance; more recent genetic critics imply that elements of Joyce's texts added later matter more or less, while others see incessant return and revision as key to Joyce's aims and methods. So, are Joycean genetic critics interested in the author's actions, but not the author himself? Writing in 2002 on literary criticism more broadly, Oliver Davis accuses genetic critics of carefully and deliberately masking their need for 'special – intimate – access to the author'.[66] Davis holds 'that the repression by genetic critics of desires for authorial intimacy' creates stand-ins for the author, most particularly 'the cult of work' (both their own labour and that of the author) (92). In a comprehensive article of the same year, however, Wim van Mierlo shows little of this repression: he openly and enthusiastically encourages critics to 'recuperate the author' in Joyce studies through historicising and genetic research.[67] Van Mierlo adeptly positions both historicist and genetic criticism as the underdogs of Joyce studies, ignored primarily in favour of theory. The history he presents from the early 2000s is one in which theoretical and formalist approaches have apparently reigned over all others, and it promotes – like the histories offered by Brooker and Lernout – the importance of historicist literary criticism as a corrective measure against the stranglehold of theory. For van Mierlo at the time, manuscript genetics offers further protection from theory's excesses by focusing on 'the interface between author and text' (57).

Before genetic criticism achieved the popularity and authority it enjoys today, genetic critics positioned their approach as long ignored and vitally important; thus employing a similar strategy to the early advocates of literary theory in Joyce studies. Furthermore, just as deconstruction was in part authorised by a link to Joyce, genetic criticism's oblique links to the author are a source of its authority. It has morphed from a small, highly specialised part of Joyce studies to a common, even expected, method. Popular in modernist studies more broadly, genetic criticism is also part of a strong turn towards archival and material approaches in the wider field of literary studies. The Centre of Manuscript Studies at the University of Antwerp hosted the 2018 Symposium, titled – in appreciation of Litz – 'The Art of James Joyce', and notes, drafts, manuscripts, and proofs held at libraries in Europe and North America continue to be picked through by students and critics. Davis suggests, back in 2002, a link between the 'scientistic rhetoric of the genetic critic' and funding criteria for literary research projects (99). Twenty years later, funding proposals often benefit from including proposed research trips – which in literary studies tend often to only be necessary for visiting archives – and it is possible that genetic criticism's 'scientific' approach to literary studies might appeal more to generalist grant committees, perhaps even promising definite and quantifiable outcomes.

Interest in the history of Joycean texts has been matched – and predated – by a far broader historical turn. Foundational texts of historicist and political Joyce criticism were published in the 1990s, from James Fairhall's Fredric Jameson-inflected 1993 work *James Joyce and the Question of History* to Emer Nolan's 1995 study *James Joyce and Nationalism*. Nolan's approach is explicitly remedial and with political motivations, seeking to recontextualise Joyce as an Irishman and 'offer a corrective to pervasive and systematic misreadings of Joyce'.[68] The growth of Irish Studies as a field, and the renewed interest in Joyce as Irish, has been key to the increasing popularity of historical and political readings of Joyce. Lernout's wish for a return to historical reading methods was granted; to historicise Joyce became, and remains, a standard critical manoeuvre in Joyce studies. Historicist critics in the 1990s and 2000s set out the position and importance of historicising Joyce by describing a field in which historical context and political issues had been disregarded: from the 1940s through to the end of the 1990s 'any type of reading that questions the text historically became increasingly outdated', and 'Joyce studies has tended from its inception to consider Joyce's texts without much recourse to extratextual matters'.[69]

Adding urgency to one's approach is not unusual; I've noted it several times in this book (and could be accused of it myself). The claims above, however, risk occluding earlier and contemporaneous work by scholars exploring readings of Joyce informed by feminist and queer theory. The author's biography and the context of writing is important to much of feminist Joyce criticism, and was explicitly discussed in the pioneering 1980s and 1990s collections *Women in Joyce* and *Ulysses: En-Gendered Perspectives*.[70] Historical, political, and biographical contexts were also essential for example to Joseph Valente's early work on Joyce and queer studies in the 1990s, which sought indispensably to 'redress the compulsory heterosexuality' of Joyce studies.[71] Feminist and queer approaches to literature also rely on theoretical frameworks; perhaps it is for this reason they were excised from leading historicists' histories of the field. Yet great swathes of historicist criticism are underpinned by, for example, Marxist, post-colonial, and/or new historicist theory. The proclaimed turn away from theory by early 2000s Joyceans suggests that, for some, 'theory' had become shorthand for ahistorical or formalist approaches only.

The author – or an idea, a construction, of the author – as a figure who drafts, writes, rewrites; a person who existed at a specific time and place, a gendered being with a certain sexuality, is of fundamental relevance to approaches which use the methodology of genetic criticism or historicism. As such approaches, rich in archival materials and context, continue now to gain strength in Joyce studies, questions of authorship – of the relationship between the author, reader, and text – have fallen away. Though the author is important in myriad ways to popular approaches in contemporary Joyce studies, this importance is not queried or defended. The question of criticism's relationship to or view of the author has been lost in an abundance of work on other topics – but the author, and aspects of the author's identity and history, have become absolutely key to these other topics and to how work is authorised in Joyce studies today. Critical readings of Joyce's texts are now frequently authorised genetically or with biography; with 'extra-textual matters' that relate to the author. Are the relationships between author, reader, and text no longer queried because Joyce studies has solved such issues? If so, what was the solution?

In one of the more depressing critical comments of recent years, Lernout gripes 'When today somebody claims to have found something new in *Ulysses*, it usually means that they have failed to consult all of the necessary secondary literature.'[72] Yes, Joyce studies is cumulative and collaborative and requires knowledge of the critical work that has gone before. But I have to disagree with Lernout's 2018 suggestion that it is more likely to under-research than it is to form novel readings – which almost implies that there is a limit to what we can 'find' in *Ulysses*. Lernout is grieving for what he calls 'a more innocent time' (105), but his attitude communicates the notion that we will one day run out of things to find in *Ulysses*.[73] The critic who told me there was 'nothing more to say' about Joyce and Homer comes to mind once more. This negative outlook does two things: first, it diminishes the potential for new readers to rethink, discover, create new readings. It overlooks the possibility that a reader whose gender, race, class, or sexuality differs from the critics who have written the majority of Joycean criticism might have a perspective on Joyce's texts that differs too. Second, it places great authority with extant critical readings, ignoring the critical history of revision and reappraisal that defines Joyce studies.

Traces of Stuart Gilbert's authorially authorised work still remain, an instance of how Joyce's authority functions within the criticism of his texts. Many of the above critics repeat Gilbert's suggestions and ideas, including Iser, Lawrence, Senn, and Rabaté. Gilbert's readings also prompted work by Levin, Kain, Litz, and Kenner exploring issues such as the role of criticism, the polysemy of text, the activity of reading, the relevance of intention, playfulness, intertextuality, the potential within language, and who or what lies behind the text. These issues arose from critical disagreements, but also from the text of *Ulysses* itself – from the way its specificities continue to provoke us to consider how to read the text. The similarities between the concerns of 'pre' theory Joyce criticism and poststructuralism or deconstruction suggest that such questions and interests do arise from reading *Ulysses* or the *Wake*, and are not arbitrarily pulled from theory to be applied or mapped onto Joyce's texts. My discussions in Chapter 3 make the same argument, showing how queries often associated with poststructuralism are also provoked and complicated by the relationship between *Ulysses* and Homeric scholarship.

Something of the text of *Ulysses* prompts a search for authority, for help, for something to pin down. This reveals not only an effect of *Ulysses*, but a more pervasive critical attitude: Joyce studies is not alone in seeking authorised exegesis. The autobiographical elements do not justify the use of Joyce's letters to 'explain' an episode's style, or Stephen's words (as Joyce's) to find an overarching theory of art to unravel what the novel is trying to achieve. The letters, Stephen, the author's notes and manuscript scribbles, literary theory: all could be characterised as places readers and critics go for assistance. Where we seek help is caught up in questions of authority: underwriting a critical reading by referring to an author's biography or their extra-literary words promotes the idea of authorial authority. Turning to a claim that Joyce intended for us to ignore his intentions, or arguing that a theoretical approach is apt because Joyce is at its roots, or focusing on authorial self-fashioning:

these are also manoeuvres that place authority with the author. Using the methodologies of genetic criticism, furthermore, promotes the authority of process, genesis – and thus, though many might disagree, of origin and author over reception and reader.

Questions of how to read the author have become sidelined in Joyce studies, though questions of how to read Joyce's texts continue to garner detailed attention. The link between these two areas of enquiry is everywhere, yet goes largely unexplored. Joyce studies is a collection of readings each formed by attitudes towards the author-reader-text relationship. It is a history of self-conscious shifts in reading, an argument in itself for the limitless ways in which one can read a literary text. Yet the author is woven throughout, glinting in the background behind episode titles, nudging Gilbert, chased by genetic critics, contextualised, politicised, and deified. While Barthes describes how an awareness of the polysemia of texts, the active role of the reader, and language as a source of meaning precludes a turn to the authority of the author, it is clear that in Joyce studies the threat of a closure of possible readings is rarely located at the author. Joyce studies confirms that authorial authority can coexist with a freedom of reading, but it has stopped asking how.

The author has continued to be perceived, invoked, promoted, and constructed as a source of authority since the boom of Joyce studies. This has persisted despite changing approaches, trends, movements towards and away from different literary theories. This does not confirm the author's authority: it confirms that critics choose this mode of authorisation, and argue for it. Critics invoke the author to serve their own critical purposes – so then does authority really lie with the author, or with the critic? Or reader? Exploring how this works is the task of the next chapter, in a return to *Ulysses*.

Notes

1. And on that mountain: it follows that this chapter of metacriticism is reference heavy. To avoid excessive notes, I will cite all texts in full in the first instance and where possible give further references after quotations in the text.
2. Umberto Eco, 'Joyce, Semiosis and Semiotics', in *The Languages of Joyce: Selected Papers from the 11th International James Joyce Symposium, Venice, 12–18 June 1988*, ed. Rosa Maria Bollettieri Bosinelli, Carla Marengo Vaglio, and Christine van Boheemen (Philadelphia, PA and Amsterdam: John Benjamins, 1992), 19–38.
3. For excellent recent work on the risks of 'Seeing the Theory era as a single period', see Eric Hayot, 'Then and Now', in *Critique and Post-critique*, ed. Elizabeth S. Anker and Rita Felski (Durham, NC and London: Duke University Press, 2017), 279–95 (287).
4. *The Irish Times*, 17 June 1967, 9. Dublin, National Library of Ireland, Niall Montgomery Papers, MS 50, 118/1/49.
5. '"Bloomsday" finds a new home', *The Irish Times*, 17 June 1967, NLI, MS 50, 118/1/49.

6. Bernard Benstock, 'Introduction', in *James Joyce: The Augmented Ninth, Proceedings of the Ninth International James Joyce Symposium, Frankfurt 1984*, ed. Benstock (Syracuse, NY: Syracuse University Press, 1988), 3–24 (5–6).
7. Geert Lernout, *The French Joyce* (Ann Arbor: University of Michigan Press, 1990), 13.
8. The Caucus's first occurrence was a year earlier, at a 1983 conference in Massachusetts. Karen Lawrence, 'Women Building the Foundation', in *Who's Afraid of James Joyce?* (Gainesville: University Press of Florida, 2010), 90–6 (92–5).
9. Colin MacCabe, *James Joyce and the Revolution of the Word* (London: Macmillan, 1978), 1–12.
10. Lawrence, *The Odyssey of Style in 'Ulysses'* (Princeton: Princeton University Press, 1981), 7, 9, and 63.
11. MacCabe, 'Uneasiness in Culture', *Cambridge Review*, vol. 93, no. 2208 (2 June 1972), 174–7 (176). Brook Thomas, *James Joyce's 'Ulysses': A Book of Many Happy Returns* (Baton Rouge and London: Louisiana State University Press, 1982), 13.
12. Jennifer Levine, 'Rejoycings in "Tel Quel"', *James Joyce Quarterly*, vol. 16, no. 1/2, 'Structuralist/Reader Response Issue' (Fall, 1978–Winter, 1979), 17–26 (17).
13. *Post-Structuralist Joyce: Essays from the French*, ed. Derek Attridge and Daniel Ferrer (Cambridge: Cambridge University Press, 1984), 7 and 8.
14. Jonathan Culler, *On Deconstruction: Theory and Criticism after Structuralism* (London: Routledge and Kegan Paul, 1983), 7.
15. Jacques Derrida, 'Two Words for Joyce', in *Post-Structuralist Joyce*, ed. Attridge and Ferrer, 145–59 (145).
16. Margot Norris, 'Review: *Post-Structuralist Joyce: Essays from the French*', *James Joyce Quarterly*, vol. 23, no. 3 (Spring, 1986), 365–70 (370), and Fritz Senn, 'Letter to the Editor', *James Joyce Quarterly*, vol. 24, no. 1 (Fall, 1986), 115–16.
17. Derrida, 'Ulysses Gramophone: Hear Say Yes in Joyce', in *Acts of Literature*, ed. Attridge (New York and London: Routledge, 1992), 253–309 ('Ulysses' is not italicised).
18. Attridge, 'Signature/Countersignature: Derrida's Response to *Ulysses*', in *Derrida and Joyce: Texts and Contexts*, ed. Andrew J. Mitchell and Sam Slote (Albany: State University of New York Press, 2013), 265–80 (268–70).
19. I refer throughout this chapter to the translation of Derrida's talk given in the 1992 collection of his work, *Acts of Literature*, which its editor, Attridge, describes as 'editorially modified in the light of the published French text' (from the translation by Tina Kendall, revised by Shari Benstock, in *The Augmented Ninth*) (256). However, in the 1987 French publication *Ulysse Gramophone: Deux mots pour Joyce* the word 'directly' is in fact written as '*indirectement*', and in every other English translation (including the first, in *The Augmented Ninth*) one finds 'indirectly'. Whether an 'editorial modification' unrelated to the French, or a misunderstanding corrected elsewhere, I have retained this oddity as I enjoy the concept of knowing *Ulysses* both directly and incompetently, at first- and second-hand, with full access to the text yet no complete reading.
20. Attridge, 'Signature/Countersignature', 277.
21. Michael Patrick Gillespie, 'Past its Sell-by Date: When to Stop Reading Joyce Criticism', in *Bloomsday 100: Essays on 'Ulysses'*, ed. Morris Beja and Anne Fogarty (Gainesville: University Press of Florida, 2009), 213–27 (217).

22. Lernout, 'Controversial Editions: Hans Walter Gabler's *Ulysses*', *Text*, vol. 16 (2006), 229–41 (229), and C. George Sandulescu and Clive Hart, eds, *Assessing the 1984 'Ulysses'* (Gerrards Cross: Colin Smythe, 1986), xix and xx.
23. John Kidd, 'The Scandal of *Ulysses*', *The New York Review of Books*, 30 June 1988 <http://www.nybooks.com/articles/1988/06/30/the-scandal-of-ulysses-2/> [accessed 10 May 2021].
24. For adeptly summarised details – editorial, textual, and historical – of this altercation, see for example Sam Slote, '*Ulysses* in the Plural: The Variable Editions of Joyce's Novel', The National Library of Ireland Joyce Studies 5 (Dublin: 2004), 26–32.
25. For example: Michael Patrick Gillespie, *Reading the Book of Himself* (1989); Suzette Henke, *James Joyce and the Politics of Desire* (1990); and Hélène Cixous, *Readings: The Poetics of Blanchot, Joyce, Kafka, Kleist, Lispector, and Tsvetayeva*, Sheldon Brivic, *The Veil of Signs: Joyce, Lacan, and Perception*, and Bernard Benstock, *Narrative Con/Texts in Joyce* (all 1991).
26. Alan Roughley, *James Joyce and Critical Theory: An Introduction* (Hemel Hempstead: Harvester Wheatsheaf, 1991), xi.
27. These include Claudette Sartiliot, *Citation and Modernity: Derrida, Joyce, and Brecht* (1993); Murray McArthur, 'The Example of Joyce: Derrida Reading Joyce', a *James Joyce Quarterly* article from 1995; *Reading Derrida Reading Joyce* by Alan Roughley (1999); Christine van Boheemen-Saaf, *Joyce, Derrida, Lacan, and the Trauma of History: Reading, Narrative, and Postcolonialism* (1999); Peter Mahon, *Imagining Joyce and Derrida: Between 'Finnegans Wake' and 'Glas'* (2007); and *Derrida and Joyce: Texts and Contexts*, ed. Andrew J. Mitchell and Sam Slote (Albany: State University of New York Press, 2013).
28. Roughley, *Reading Derrida Reading Joyce* (Gainesville: University Press of Florida, 1999), xii.
29. Tim Conley, *Joyces Mistakes: Problems of Intention, Irony, and Interpretation* (Toronto: University of Toronto Press, 2003), 10. Another good example is in Phillip F. Herring's *Joyce's Uncertainty Principle*: a single footnote claiming without detail or qualification that a line of the *Wake* anticipates Barthes, Foucault, and Derrida (Princeton, NJ: Princeton University Press, 1987), 197.
30. Joseph Brooker, 'The Fidelity of Theory: James Joyce and the Rhetoric of Belatedness', in *Joyce's Audiences*, ed. John Nash, European Joyce Studies 14 (Amsterdam: Rodopi, 2002), 201–21 (202).
31. Brooker, *Joyce's Critics: Transitions in Reading and Culture* (Madison: University of Wisconsin Press, 2004), 168–9 and 149.
32. Laurent Milesi, 'Introduction: Language(s) with a Difference', *James Joyce and the Difference of Language*, ed. Milesi (Cambridge: Cambridge University Press, 2003), 1–27 (10).
33. Paul K. Saint-Amour, 'Review: *James Joyce and the Difference of Language* by Laurent Milesi', *South Atlantic Review*, vol. 70, no. 1 (Winter, 2005), 189–93 (192).
34. Senn, quoted by Norris in 'Review: *Post-Structuralist Joyce*', 370.
35. Christopher Butler, 'Joyce and the Displaced Author', in *James Joyce and Modern Literature*, ed. W. J. McCormack and Alistair Stead (London: Routledge, 1982), 56–76 (70).

36. Susan Stanford Friedman, 'Weavings: Intertextuality and the (Re)Birth of the Author', in *Influence and Intertextuality in Literary History*, ed. Jay Clayton and Eric Rothstein (Madison: University of Wisconsin Press, 1991), 146–80 (173), and Jean-Michel Rabaté, *James Joyce, Authorized Reader* (Baltimore, MD: Johns Hopkins University Press, 1991), 153.
37. John Paul Riquelme, *Teller and Tale in Joyce's Fiction: Oscillating Perspectives* (Baltimore, MD and London: Johns Hopkins University Press, 1983), 246 n. 7.
38. Gillespie, *Reading the Book of Himself: Narrative Strategies in the Works of James Joyce* (Columbus: Ohio State University Press, 1989), 6.
39. Christine Froula, *Modernism's Body: Sex, Culture, and Joyce* (New York: Columbia University Press, 1996), 1.
40. Leo Bersani, 'Against *Ulysses*', in *James Joyce's 'Ulysses': A Casebook*, ed. Attridge (Oxford: Oxford University Press, 2004), 201–29 (202–3).
41. Scarlett Baron, *'Strandentwining Cable': Joyce, Flaubert, and Intertextuality* (Oxford: Oxford University Press, 2012); Lucia Boldrini, *Joyce, Dante, and the Poetics of Literary Relations: Language and Meaning in 'Finnegans Wake'* (Cambridge: Cambridge University Press, 2001); and Patricia Novillo-Corvalán, *Borges and Joyce: An Infinite Conversation* (London: Legenda, 2011).
42. Hugh Kenner, *'Ulysses'* (London: George Allen and Unwin, 1980), 155.
43. M. Keith Booker, *Joyce, Bakhtin and the Literary Tradition: Toward a Comparative Cultural Poetics* (Ann Arbor: University of Michigan Press, 1995), 219. Quoted by Conley, *Joyce's Mistakes*, 57. See also, on intention within an editorial context, Vicki Mahaffey, 'Intentional Error: The Paradox of Editing Joyce's *Ulysses*', in *Representing Modernist Texts: Editing as Interpretation*, ed. George Bornstein (Ann Arbor: University of Michigan Press, 1991), 171-91 (referenced by Conley, *Joyces Mistakes*, 61–2).
44. Arthur Power, *Conversations with James Joyce*, ed. Clive Hart (London: Millington, 1974), 89.
45. Aaron Jaffe, *Modernism and the Culture of Celebrity* (Cambridge: Cambridge University Press, 2005), 34–5.
46. Saint-Amour, *The Copywrights: Intellectual Property and the Literary Imagination* (Ithaca, NY and London: Cornell University Press, 2003), 160.
47. Eleni Loukopoulou, *Up to Maughty London: Joyce's Cultural Capital in the Imperial Metropolis* (Gainesville: University Press of Florida, 2017), and John Nash, *James Joyce and the Act of Reception* (Cambridge: Cambridge University Press, 2006).
48. Jonathan Goldman, 'Afterlife', in *The Cambridge Companion to 'Ulysses'*, ed. Sean Latham (New York: Cambridge University Press, 2014), 33–48 (35).
49. Margot Norris, *Virgin and Veteran Readings of 'Ulysses'* (New York: Palgrave Macmillan, 2011), 10.
50. David Vichnar, *Joyce Against Theory: James Joyce After Deconstruction* (Praha: Univerzita Karlova v Praze, 2010), 1.
51. Senn, 'Joyce the Verb', in Senn, *Inductive Scrutinies: Focus on Joyce*, ed. Christine O'Neill (Dublin: Lilliput, 1995), 7–34 (7). For an example of his attitude to theory, see his 1988 interview included in *Inductive Scrutinies*, xvi, and the introductory 'The Creed of Naiveté' that follows.

52. Attridge, 'Reading Joyce', in *The Cambridge Companion to James Joyce*, ed. Attridge (Cambridge: Cambridge University Press, 1990), 1–30 (2).
53. Senn, *Joyce's Dislocutions: Essays on Reading as Translation*, ed. John Paul Riquelme (Baltimore, MD and London: Johns Hopkins University Press, 1984), x.
54. Attridge, *Joyce Effects: On Language, Theory and History* (Cambridge: Cambridge University Press, 2000), 13.
55. Kidd, 'Making the Wrong Joyce', *The New York Review of Books*, 25 September 1997 <http://www.nybooks.com/articles/1997/09/25/making-the-wrong-joyce/> [accessed 10 May 2021].
56. It has also for some time been listed on *JSTOR* as a '*Finnegan's Wake*' issue, as if a vengeful re-punctuator had hacked *JSTOR* (Roses's *Ulysses* is infamous for its inserted apostrophes in 'Penelope').
57. Joseph Kelley, 'A Defense of Danis Rose', *James Joyce Quarterly*, vol. 35/36, vol. 35, no. 4–vol. 36, no. 1 (Summer–Fall, 1998), 811–24. See also Erwin R. Steinberg and Christian W. Hallstein on Kelley, in 'Probing Silences in Joyce's *Ulysses* and the Question of Authorial Intention', *James Joyce Quarterly*, vol. 40, no. 3 (Spring, 2003), 543–54 (549).
58. Slote, '*Ulysses* in the Plural', 35.
59. 'Applied' in this context is used, for example, by Alison Lacivita in her innovative study *The Ecology of 'Finnegans Wake'* (Gainesville: University Press of Florida, 2015), 25.
60. A term used by Lacivita, 25.
61. Hayman, 'Genetic Criticism and Joyce: An Introduction', in *Probes: Genetic Studies in Joyce*, ed. Hayman and Slote, European Joyce Studies 5 (Amsterdam: Rodopi, 1995), 3–18 (6). Daniel Ferrer and Jean-Michel Rabaté's essays in this volume also wrangle with questions of intention.
62. Slote and Wim van Mierlo, 'Genitricksling Joyce: An Introduction', in *Genitricksling Joyce*, ed. Slote and van Mierlo, European Joyce Studies 9 (Amsterdam: Rodopi, 1999), 3–11 (6).
63. Michael Groden, *'Ulysses' in Progress* (Princeton, NJ: Princeton University Press, 1997), 11.
64. Groden, 'Preface', in *How Joyce Wrote 'Finnegans Wake': A Chapter-by-Chapter Genetic Guide*, ed. Luca Crispi and Slote (Madison: University of Wisconsin Press, 2007), vii–xi (viii).
65. Dirk van Hulle, *Manuscript Genetics, Joyce's Know-How, Beckett's Nohow* (Gainesville: University Press of Florida, 2008), 4.
66. Oliver Davis, 'The Author at Work in Genetic Criticism', *Paragraph*, vol. 25, no. 1, Giorgio Agamben (March 2002), 92–106 (92).
67. Wim van Mierlo, 'Reading Joyce in and out of the Archive', *Joyce Studies Annual*, vol. 13 (Summer 2002), 32–63 (58).
68. Emer Nolan, *James Joyce and Nationalism* (London and New York: Routledge, 1995), xiii.
69. Van Mierlo, 'Reading Joyce', 39, and Slote and van Mierlo, 3.
70. Suzette Henke and Elaine Unkeless, eds, *Women in Joyce* (Urbana, Chicago, London: University of Illinois Press, 1982), and Kimberly J. Devlin and Marilyn Reizbaum, eds, *'Ulysses': En-Gendered Perspectives. Eighteen New Essays on the Episodes* (Columbia: University of South Carolina Press, 1999).

71. Joseph Valente, 'Joyce's (Sexual) Choices: A Historical Overview', in *Quare Joyce*, ed. Valente (Ann Arbor: University of Michigan Press, 1998), 1–16 (1).
72. Lernout, 'Nabokov on Joyce and *Ulysses*', in *Vladimir Nabokov's Lectures on Literature: Portraits of the Artist as Reader and Teacher*, ed. Ben Dhooge and Jürgen Pieters (Amsterdam: Brill, 2018), 101–20 (108).
73. Norris's *Virgin and Veteran Readings* is an apt balm for this.

5

JOYCE'S READER

As Molly narrates and is narrated in the final episode of *Ulysses*, 'Penelope', a barely punctuated meandering in eight sentences and forty-odd pages, we can read in her narrative an intertextual relationship between her role and a Barthesian understanding of textuality and reading. Loose with syntax, grammar and (if only seemingly) logic, the episode presents itself as simultaneously a prose falling apart and a prose of astonishing density. Molly provides some of the most self-referential lines of the novel – 'I dont like books with a Molly in them', 'O Jamesy let me up out of this pooh', and 'they all write about some woman in their poetry' – and this, along with her misreading of 'metempsychosis', gives Molly a metatextual position in the novel: as one who responds to texts (18.657–8, 18.1128–9, 18.1333–4, 4.339). The evocation of the Homeric Penelope, implicit in the character of Molly throughout *Ulysses*, becomes explicit in the final tangled episode – and the correspondence between Molly and Penelope's nighttime roles is particularly clear. Having promised her suitors to choose one to marry once she has woven a shroud for her father-in-law Laertes, she weaves by day and unravels by night to buy herself much-needed time. While Penelope's deception can be read in terms of female writing (along with the weaving of other mythical mortals such as Arachne and Philomela), we can also view her activity as an intertextual link between Molly Bloom (née, nicely, Tweedy) and the reader of *Ulysses*. Understanding 'text' as a metaphor for a 'network', as 'etymologically [. . .] a tissue, a woven fabric', lends a satisfying significance to the presence of Penelope ('Text', 159). The roots of 'text' are emphasised by Roland Barthes in 'From Work to Text', in which he argues that the nature of text 'asks of the reader a practical collaboration' ('Text', 163). This develops, as I have discussed before, 'The Death of the Author': 'everything is to be *disentangled*, nothing *deciphered*; the structure can be followed, "run" (like the thread of a stocking) at every point and at every level' ('Author', 147). As readers of *Ulysses* we are given licence to unravel and weave the text anew, forming and undoing our readings.

While this chapter will refer to and complicate ideas expressed in both 'The Death of the Author' and 'From Work to Text', it interacts more specifically with two essays from *The Rustle of Language*, a collection of Barthes's essays written between 1967 and 1980. 1970's 'Writing Reading' discusses *S/Z*, and develops Barthes's approach to both the author and the reader. The latter is detailed further in 'On Reading', an idea from which echoes a focus of this chapter:

> In the field of reading [. . .] there is not only no pertinence of *levels*, there is no possibility of describing *levels* of reading, because there is no possibility of closing the list of these levels [. . .] we do not know where to halt the depth and the dispersion of reading: at the apprehension of a meaning? Which meaning? Denoted? Connoted? [. . .] I can decide that in the depths of every text, however readable its conception, there is, there remains a certain measure of the unreadable. ('Reading', 35)

Barthes's arguments read like the lessons learnt by readers of *Ulysses* or *Finnegans Wake*; these could be the words of Joyce critics. This chapter will begin by exploring these ideas of limitless yet incomplete reading, before addressing how such a reading affects, and is affected by, our attitudes towards authorship. The question of authority will run through the chapter, as I discuss how our readings are authorised by the way we understand the figure of the author.

My argument is that the manner in which we read *Ulysses* provokes attitudes towards the author which are seemingly incompatible: that the ways we learn to read *Ulysses* re-enact a Barthesian concept of 'authorless' reading, while the same textual intricacies that prompt such ways of reading simultaneously affirm the activity and control of an author. After the previous chapter on 'post-theory' Joycean criticism, I wish to make it clear that it is not only the recent decades of the discipline that affirm the pertinence to Joyce studies of questions of authorship, but also the text itself. I want to track how the form and content of *Ulysses* demands we move through and beyond the text. This chapter is also in some ways a response to and a querying of one focus of the previous chapter: the relationship between Joyce's texts and poststructuralist theory. The paradox of reading that I argue for and scrutinise here reaches back both to my discussions of 'Eumaeus' in Chapter 3, and to what I hope Chapters 1, 2, and 4 established: a sense of extremes of opinion, coexisting clashing approaches, and the dual presence in Joyce studies of a corrective urge and a faith in a multiplicity of readings. By continuing my discussion of narrative in *Ulysses* from Chapter 3 I will be able to look at the concept of *Ulysses* as 'difficult': this will enable me to link this conversation back to critical and popular notions of Joyce as author. The overall aim of this chapter is to explore the ramifications of how reading *Ulysses* prompts us to become aware of our own activity of reading, and to slot those explorations into my wider analysis of the looping relationships between author, reader, text, and critic.

In order to discuss reading *Ulysses* I have chosen a scope and focus both specific and general: my starting points will be one sentence from 'Calypso', and 'Wandering Rocks' as a whole episode – enabling me to discuss reading in the requisite detail, engage with the way one sentence is woven into the rest of the text, and extend my readings to the text in full. My choices may need a little clarification. 'Wandering Rocks' engenders discussions of narrative and difficulty through its form, or rather through how we react to its form. I think its stylistic effects offer an experience of stymied reading that is hard to read our way out of. This then links to 'Eumaeus': unanswerable questions that inevitably lead us to look further. The single sentence from 'Calypso', however, is tougher to justify. I chose 'The sluggish cream wound curdling spirals through her tea' (4.366) by chance, as an experiment – it was elected because it seemed innocuous and understated, but happened upon because it is intriguing and striking. The more I have read it the less like 'chance' this choice seems, and the less coincidental my selection of a sentence of such fecundity (though coincidences of reading, and coincidences in *Ulysses*, are relevant here). An important part of my argument is that it could be any sentence, that we can read any part of this novel with such intensity. However, my interest in the less usual modes by which *Ulysses* narrates Bloom's thoughts, and in all the unsaids of 'Calypso' – both explored in Chapter 3 – perhaps made my selection predictable. A final clarification: for the purposes of my discussion, I have decided to conflate cream and milk, as the former is an element of the latter and used similarly in the novel (this could be an error – there may be subtleties at play in *Ulysses* that I am overlooking).[1]

This chapter will open with a close reading of 'The sluggish cream wound curdling spirals through her tea'. I will read and reread the sentence, tracing associations, resonances, and echoes throughout the text. I hope to illustrate how far this can be pushed, how elaborate the reading of an innocuous sentence can be, and analyse my own reading of the sentence: an interrupted, far-ranging, active, and creative reading. With Barthes's help I will argue that this exaggeration of reading is not dissimilar from any reading – it is rather making apparent what is inherent to any act of reading. Arguing thus that the manner in which we are encouraged by *Ulysses* to read *Ulysses* is similar to the reading described by Barthes in his anti-authorial work (and in this, linking back to and developing the arguments of Chapter 3), I will begin to unpick the alternative, and make it as clear as I can how entwined are these opposing views of the author for the reader. This mightily plotted, intricately mapped novel drags our focus to its creator. 'Wandering Rocks', mapped and plotted both more and less than we might want, will aid my discussion of this aspect of reading *Ulysses* – and pick up an analysis of the difficulties we face as readers. Looking at how narrative functions in 'Wandering Rocks' – or rather, how 'Wandering Rocks' make us question the purposes and functions of narration – will lead me to examine the ways in which the episode changes our perceptions of how significance is attributed via narration, setting us up to perceive the significance of the unnarrated, and how our complicated, far-reaching readings allow us to 'read' these 'unwritten' parts of the text.

From 'Wandering Rocks' I want to home in on two linked ideas. These are the idea of difficulty and the idea that a reading which is difficult can lead us somewhere affecting, a moment or moments of pathos, development of character, for example – and that in this way intricate 'plotting' takes on further meaning. Following a textual echo, unravelling a network of intra- or intertextual references, or piecing together something that is unnarrated can lead us to the human warmth of the novel. In this way our creative, 'limitless' reading follows paths that are in all senses 'written': an experience which emphasises the activity of the author. This informs my argument that the activity of the author is highlighted via our activity of reading, and leads into an investigation of how this difficult text can spark a deifying approach to the author. Discussing 'genius' or 'god-like' Joyce, and reaching back to (yet pushing past) the 'double laughter' of Derrida's 'Ulysses Gramophone: Hear Say Yes in Joyce', the final parts of this chapter link back to my earlier analysis of the author in and beyond Joyce studies. Noting the similarities of how a 'genius' author can authorise a critic's readings and how a 'dead' author allows for the same authority of reading, I will show how the back-and-forth of reader and author prompted by *Ulysses* prefigures the debates of anti-authorial and author-centric theory and criticism that I investigated in earlier chapters. Finally, I will return to our opening sentence from 'Calypso' and Barthes's 'levels of reading' to test out and describe the critical and readerly authority we gain through reading *Ulysses*. In this chapter I will show how a freedom of authorless reading and a god-like genius author coexist within the reader's activity. Crucially, it is the reader who comprehends this teetering, useful, provocative balance – and thus, ultimately, the reader who holds authority.

'Thumbed pages. Read and read' (10.845–6): 'Calypso' and an Absent Author

'The sluggish cream wound curdling spirals through her tea.'

'Sluggish' is a word that immediately seems to refer to more than the cream. It reaches out to Molly, rising late, lazily reclining in bed; associations which perhaps echo Bloom's own thoughts as he brings her breakfast. Bloom's mind too, however, is sluggish this morning in the 'Gelid light and air' of the kitchen (4.7). He strains to define metempsychosis for Molly, burns his breakfast kidney, forgets what he did with his hat, and fails to get his latchkey from his other trousers. Of course, Molly's own mind is sluggish as well – she forgets the word she wishes to understand, the word we know from Bloom's later recollections she sounds out as 'met him pike hoses'. 'Sluggish' becomes a description, then, of the characters and the time of day. As for the cream (aside from its endowment with slightly too much of an adjective) it could lead us back to the mewling 'pussens' given 'warmbubbled milk' already that morning – back to the confusions of the pronoun 'she' that Bloom uses interchangeably for his wife and the cat, and back to that affectionate interaction between Bloom and an other (4.24, 4.37, 4.11–59). In 'wound' there are traces of a manipulation, a trapping even, in its suggestion of a gradual surrounding, wrapping, tying. 'Curdling' adds to this, with its connotations of forcibly changing a state, of metamorphosis – not necessarily for the better. It adds a sour taste to the sentence, a taste of something going wrong. 'Spirals' disorient, twisting and confusing, and a journey of cream through tea gains the weight of a more mystical descent: these winding curdling spirals of cream describe a forced and disorienting change, and thus bring us back to Molly's unknown word. This startling parallel of making tea with the transmigration of souls brings into this sentence the associations of metempsychosis in the episode: of Patrick Dignam's funeral happening later that morning, but also of Molly's book in which she finds the word and Bloom's first offered definition of it – 'It's Greek' (4.341). We might be forgiven for seeing this – a feminine, winding entrapment, a change in form, and another text with Greek words in it – as an invocation of the *Odyssey*'s Calypso and Circe. Dragging ourselves back to the tea, it is of course very much 'her tea' – it is linked to Molly in the first description earlier in this episode of her sitting up in bed, 'The warmth of her couched body rose on the air, mingling with the fragrance of the tea she poured' (4.305–7). This tea punctuates the narrative of 'Calypso' at various points, creating occasional little pauses of detail. Perhaps 'the sluggish cream wound curdling spirals through her tea' is a pause in conversation as well as the text, a moment for Bloom to think before going on to give another definition of metempsychosis. We could then read this sentence as a description of Bloom's pause for thought, the words coloured by his current preoccupation, by a mind full of reincarnation.

Quickly we find ourselves following traces beyond 'Calypso'. Bloom has just told Molly of the forgetfulness inherent to this concept of rebirth, 'frowning' as he himself forgets (4.341). He does not mention the river Lethe and the role drinking its waters plays in such mythic renewal – erasing past lives for the reborn – but while Molly drinks her tea a reader might find themselves looking forward to the 'waters of oblivion' in the next episode 'Lotus Eaters', and the corresponding amnesiac properties of the lotus in the *Odyssey* (5.365).[2] If not distracted by a descent into Greek myth, we might be similarly brought out of 'Calypso' by a recollection of that other breakfast in *Ulysses*: tea is had by Stephen Dedalus, Buck Mulligan, and the Englishman Haines three episodes earlier at the same time of day (a trinity to match that of Bloom, Molly, and Boylan). The arrival in 'Telemachus' of the milkwoman providing the necessary companion for their cups is imbued with a particular sense of importance:

> Old and secret she had entered from a morning world, maybe a messenger. She praised the goodness of the milk, pouring it out. Crouching by a patient cow at daybreak in the lush field, a witch on her toadstool, her wrinkled fingers quick at the squirting dugs. They lowed about her whom they knew, dewsilky cattle. Silk of the kine and poor old woman, names given her in old times. A wandering crone, lowly form of an immortal serving her conqueror and her gay betrayer, their common cuckquean, a messenger from the secret morning. To serve or to upbraid, whether he could not tell: but scorned to beg her favour. (1.399–407)

When Stephen and Bloom are together in the early hours of the next morning, several hundreds of pages later, the narrative again ascribes a strange weight and ritual to their consumption of hot drinks, and Molly's cream reappears as Bloom makes cocoa:

> Relinquishing his symposiarchal right to the moustache cup of imitation Crown Derby presented to him by his only daughter, Millicent (Milly), he substituted a cup identical with that of his guest and served extraordinarily to his guest and, in reduced measure, to himself the viscous cream ordinarily reserved for the breakfast of his wife Marion (Molly). (17.361–5)

The pomposity of the three young men (along with Stephen's idea of Mother Ireland) tints the description of the milkwoman, while the ridiculous tone of Bloom's cocoa-making is typical of 'Ithaca'. But without our description of Molly adding cream to her tea might we notice this coincidence of ceremony, the importance of dairy, permeating these book-ending cups of tea and cocoa? This odd significance neatly prefigures the importance ascribed by critics to the third, unwritten breakfast made the next day at 7 Eccles Street – clung to by some as an indicator of the future of the Blooms' marriage.[3]

Associations come and go in our paused reading of this pause in conversation. The Blooms' cat is here not only with the cream but with the 'purr' heard in 'curdling' (though she of course does not only purr, making her variety of 'Mkgnao!' noises and a 'Gurrhr!' (4.16, 4.25, 4.32, 4.38). There's more purring, later in *Ulysses*, from a librarian, a drum, and two lawnmowers.)[4] A recollection of the 'sluggish bile' of Stephen's mother is less pleasant but forges another link between 'Telemachus' and 'Calypso', as the only two instances of the word 'sluggish' appear at the same time of day in North and South Dublin (1.109). The 'cream' has still more disparate connections: 'Two sheets cream vellum paper' in 'Sirens', 'the cream of the joke' in 'Eumaeus', Molly's memory in 'Penelope' of Bloom saying 'it was sweeter and thicker than cows then he wanted to milk me into the tea well hes beyond everything', and Lenehan's claim in 'Wandering Rocks' that sitting next to Molly he was 'lost, so to speak, in the milky way' (11.295, 16.179, 18.577–8, 10.570). The tea lingers in Bloom's thoughts as he views the 'Bath of the Nymph' print on the wall of their bedroom a few lines later in 'Calypso' as being perhaps the colours of 'Tea before you put milk in it', and tea and its warmth stay in his thoughts in 'Lotus Eaters' (4.370–1). The tea could even be read as infusing the text beyond Bloom – the schematically assigned colour of 'Lotus Eaters' is 'dark brown' (think again of tea before you put milk in it).[5] 'The prison gate girls', meanwhile, kindly spell out 'See you in tea' much later, in 'Circe' (15.1895).

As previously noted, in 'Calypso' the warmth of Molly's body is perceived by Bloom as 'mingling with the fragrance of the tea she poured', and perfumes continue to connote Molly's warm physicality for Bloom throughout *Ulysses*. The question asked in his letter from Martha Clifford in 'Lotus Eaters', 'Do tell me what kind of perfume does your wife use', is repeated in full and in part throughout the novel (5.258). In 'Lestrygonians', a couple of hours after reading the letter, the question continues to repeat in Bloom's mind and is followed shortly by a hinted-at memory: 'A warm human plumpness settled down on his brain. His brain yielded. Perfume of embraces all him assailed. With hungered flesh obscurely, he mutely craved to adore' (8.637–9). Within three lines this develops into many mingled experiences: 'Perfumed bodies, warm, full. All kissed, yielded: in deep summer fields, tangled pressed grass, in trickling hallways of tenements, along sofas, creaking beds' (8.642–4). A few pages later the key memory is identified: Bloom and a 'warmfolded' Molly lying on Howth Head, in each other's arms and surrounded by rhododendrons and ferns (8.898–916). The importance of this memory to the Blooms and the novel is confirmed by Molly in 'Penelope'. She also remembers 'the day we were lying among the rhododendrons on Howth head in the grey tweed suit and his straw hat the day I got him to propose to me yes first I gave him the bit of seedcake out of my mouth' (18.1572–4). Molly closes the text by recalling,

> and then I asked him with my eyes to ask again yes and then he asked me would I yes to say yes my mountain flower and first I put my arms around him yes and drew him down to me so he could feel my breasts all perfume yes and his heart was going like mad and yes I said yes I will Yes. (18.1605–9)

As ever in *Ulysses*, humour both cruel and affectionate is close at hand. Beyond the mingling of Molly's warmth and the tea's fragrance Bloom picks up the 'foul flowerwater' of old incense in their bedroom (4.316). I would surely not be the only reader drawn backwards and forwards to two other close-by references to 'flower water', which when brought together form an illuminating comparison of the preoccupations of Stephen and Bloom. A description of the sea moving amongst low rocks, coloured by Stephen's thoughts and ways of thinking, occurs towards the end of 'Proteus': 'It flows purling, widely flowing, floating foampool, flower unfurling' (3.459–60). Meanwhile 'Lotus Eaters' describes at its close Bloom foreseeing himself in the bath: 'He saw his trunk and limbs riprippled over and sustained, buoyed lightly upward, lemonyellow: his navel, bud of flesh: and saw the dark tangled curls of his bush floating, floating hair of the stream around the limp father of thousands, a languid floating flower' (5.568–72). Juxtaposing Stephen's literary pretentions (seen in the narrative's habit in 'Proteus' of echoing Stephen as he tries out words) with Bloom's mental image of his own 'limp father of thousands' results in a slight but not unkind mocking of both men. This in turn reveals the more serious and essential concerns of each character: Stephen's anxieties over his own talents and aspirations, and Bloom's worries over his roles as man, father, and sexual being. (There is also a similarity rumbling away under this comparison, however: Stephen's dreams of writing and Bloom's self-contemplation reveal a common preoccupation with creation, legacy, making a mark. They did not need to worry about permanence.) And, with less humour, part of the cause of Bloom's disquiet perhaps hovers amongst 'The sluggish cream wound curdling spirals through her tea.' That sour note of 'curdling' is unpleasant, connoting a splitting or going too far. Just a page earlier as Bloom carries Molly's breakfast into the bedroom they briefly discuss the letter she has received, now badly hidden under the 'dimpled pillow'. 'O, Boylan' wrote the letter to 'Mrs Marion' to arrange their meeting later that day (4.312). As eventually becomes clear, Molly and Boylan are meeting at four o'clock to have sex for the first time; the thought of another man with his wife is on Bloom's mind, curdling the marital domesticity of the morning. In 'Ithaca' he even finds 'soured adulterated milk' complete with 'semisolidified curds' in the kitchen dresser just before he notices Boylan's betting slips close by, and shortly before he gives Molly's cream away to his guest Stephen (17.312–14, 17.320). He is preoccupied enough in 'Calypso' to directly cause another unpleasant sensation just a few lines later: the smell of burnt kidney from the kitchen downstairs (4.380–1).[6]

Following the traces of this sentence we read widely, this focus affecting our other readings and bringing together disparate moments of text. The satisfying results of such excessive reading encourage us to push further: if one description of adding cream to tea draws out the ever-circled memory of Howth Head then where else might it take us? Placing limits feels inappropriate, dealing as we are not just with the far-reaching possibilities of our own minds but with those of the characters. As I mentioned, the narrative's brief focus on Molly's transforming tea can be read as a description of a character's pause for thought. Such a reading provides an explanation for how fertile this seemingly innocuous sentence is. If it describes Bloom thinking, then to discover traces of his thoughts within it is no surprise.[7] The presentation of human thought in *Ulysses*, is complexly and unorthodoxly mimetic, a scattered web of fragments served both by form and content that the reader must draw together in reading the novel. In this one sentence a Ulyssean mimesis can be seen. On the pages of another novel we might read 'while she added cream to her tea Bloom/I thought of metempsychosis, his/my mind wandering to the day ahead'. Instead we have a curiously finely wrought yet economic description of the cream's journey through the tea, catching our attention by being slightly too much yet not enough. This encourages us to pause with Bloom, to return, to read-over or 'overread'. In doing so we mimic the possible cognitions of Bloom at that moment and at later moments in the day, unable to fix the links we find and so allowing them to shift and change. We work hard to create something which can be seen as a mapping of Bloom's thought, as we do from start to finish in *Ulysses*, reading back and forth, skipping and repeating. Layered over this, of course, are our own associations that function beyond Bloom – such as the breakfast of 'Telemachus', which he does not know about – our understanding being constantly altered or adjusted by further reading. It's satisfying that both a moment of contemplation colouring one's other thoughts and opinions, and a new or developed reading adjusting one's previous and later readings, could also be compared to how tea is changed by adding milk.

Mimicry of the movements and functions of human thought cause much of the active reading we perform in *Ulysses*, flicking back and forth through the book as we bring together threads of the characters' internal lives. Form and content work in harmony, and result in a gradually increased understanding of the characters and the day we move through with them – further mirroring how we 'know' or 'comprehend' people and events in our own lives; 'a secondary mimetic technique', as Leo Bersani notes in 'Against *Ulysses*'.[8] This encourages us to enter into a mode of reading which contributes to perceptions of *Ulysses* as 'difficult' (as I will discuss further below), in which to catch up with a character's thoughts we must make connections between repetitions and gestures separated by tens or hundreds of pages, relying on our own notes and folded page corners. This mode of reading itself encourages a liberated, active, creative reading in which finding resonances can become our primary activity. We can have great fun testing the limits of how much significance can be assigned to such traces and relationships, and reading with our ears metaphorically pricked up can predictably affect our reading beyond *Ulysses*. What am I to do when, reading as *Ulysses* prompts, I find tea and curdling, spiralling cream in other texts? I read it in this unsuspecting description of adding milk to tea in Stella Gibbons's 1932 novel *Cold Comfort Farm*: 'The opaque curve purred softly down into the teak depths of the cup.'[9] It begs to be noticed in these words, said by Valentine in Tom Stoppard's 1993 play *Arcadia*: 'The ordinary-sized stuff which is our lives, the things people write poetry about – clouds – daffodils – waterfalls – and what happens in a cup of coffee when the cream goes in – these things are full of mystery, as mysterious to us as the heavens were to the Greeks.'[10] If I were to use these intertextual links to form a critical reading of any of the three texts in question I would be relying only on the authority of my own reading; would this constitute a valid argument? Is the similarity of sentence form and a thread between 'purred' and 'curdling' enough to argue for the presence of *Ulysses* in *Cold Comfort Farm* or for any effect of such presence? How would I compose an argument that 'what happens in a cup of coffee when the cream goes in' is a reference to *Ulysses*, or what that reference could mean in either *Arcadia* or *Ulysses*? I am goaded by the way in which I read *Ulysses* to question what my reading authorises, and what authorises my reading.

This performance of close reading could be seen as 'overreading', as an excessively extensive if not absurd or indulgent act typical of and specific to *Ulysses*.[11] This mode of reading is specific to *Ulysses*, and yet simultaneously not. Barthes opens 'Writing Reading' with the following question:

> Has it never happened, while you were reading a book, that you kept stopping as you read, not because you weren't interested, but because you were: because of a flow of ideas, stimuli, associations? In a word, haven't you ever happened to *read while looking up from your book?* (29)

He continues, defending *S/Z*: 'It is such a reading, at once insolent in that it interrupts the text, and smitten in that it keeps returning to it and feeding on it, which I tried to describe' (29). Following this approach, we can see our physical back-and-forth page-turning and note-making as an enactment of any reading in which one's mind wanders yet remains in the text – which is in turn a conscious active re-enactment of reading itself. As Barthes continues: 'composition *channels*; reading, on the contrary (that text we write in ourselves when we read), *disperses*, disseminates' (30). This concept of writing a text in ourselves as we read, a familiar Barthesian marriage of reading and writing as a 'single signifying practice', rings true with the way we read *Ulysses*, constructing a text as we manoeuvre our way through the parallactic narrative. The so-called difficulties we face in *Ulysses* – the presentation of the characters' minds, the differing styles, the echoes of and references to other texts – cause us as readers to make apparent that which is inherent in any act of reading: a dispersion of 'ideas, stimuli, associations'. As we read one sentence of the novel and follow its threads within and without the text of *Ulysses* we find that its traces in turn affect other readings – it infuses throughout, colouring the places where it leads. The reading of an episode, sentence, word, winds curdling spirals through one's reading of the entire text, and beyond.

The intertextuality of the novel feeds into this along with the intratextuality: part of the dispersion, the dissemination, of our reading is structurally, thematically, and linguistically woven into the text of *Ulysses* through its references to other texts, and as Bersani notes it is our intratextual wanderings that teach us to leave the text in order to keep reading (212). Openly and obliquely, *Ulysses* is referential from its title to its core, and one way of understanding what we might call an 'exaggeration' of reading could be to appreciate the novel as an 'exaggeration' of what constitutes a text. *Ulysses* makes explicit that which Barthes argues is implicit to all texts: the text is 'a tissue of quotations', 'a network' asking 'of the reader a practical collaboration'. Most pertinently:

> a text is made of multiple writings, drawn from many cultures and entering into mutual relations of dialogue, parody, contestation, but there is one place where this multiplicity is focused and that place is the reader, not, as was hitherto said, the author. The reader is the space on which all the quotations that make up a writing are inscribed without any of them being lost; a text's unity lies not in its origin but in its destination. ('Author', 148)

This contributes to Barthes's declaration that an author limits text: closes reading ('Author', 147). My interrupted, far-ranging, active, and creative reading is not dissimilar from any reading – it, again, is rather making explicit what is implicit to all acts of reading. As my exaggerated mode of reading an exaggerated text suggests a form of writing, and a limitlessness and creativity which proscribe an author and prioritise the reader, it implies the same of any reading of any text.

'Very large and wonderful and keeps famous time' (10.828): 'Wandering Rocks' and the Genius Author

The process of reading described above results also in a more tangible form of writing: annotation. Our copies of *Ulysses* become overwritten with notes, the margins crammed with questions and reminders, page numbers listed as a record of echoes tracked, the names of authors and works visited marked down next to circled words. Though active and engaged, there is an element of catching up at play in this mode – and I am again reminded of Hugh Kenner's alignment of the reader of *Ulysses* with the scholiasts of Alexandria.[12] This sensation of catching up is particularly clear for the reader faced with 'Wandering Rocks', the tenth and central episode of the novel. Divided into eighteen sections with a final coda, 'Wandering Rocks' follows to some extent the structure of *Ulysses*.

Its central scene focuses on Bloom, though he is only one of roughly fifty characters who move around Dublin between three and four in the afternoon in the episode. A directory's worth of street and building names pinpoint the movements of these characters across the nineteen scenes, which are often interrupted by unmarked interpolations: snatches of observation from some other place, some other scene in the episode occurring at the same time. Identifying these inferences of simultaneity is much easier for those with an in-depth knowledge of Dublin's geography, and readers without this knowledge may find themselves plotting the movements of the characters on a map of the city. We can only understand why, in the first scene of the episode, Father Conmee greets and is greeted by all whom he meets apart from Mr Denis J. Maginni, if we know that Mountjoy Square East, where Father Conmee 'smiled and nodded and smiled and walked', is roughly ten minutes' walk away from Mr Maginni at 'the corner of Dignam's court': Conmee and Maginni are near each other in the text, not in Dublin (10.54–60). Figuring out this first interpolation encourages us to believe that mapping the characters across the city may reveal something of importance. With either glosses and critical annotations or our own scrawled-on map (or some time spent searching an online map) we can be assured that the movements of and encounters between the characters have been perfectly worked out and timed – but our endeavours reveal little beyond the exactitude of the plotting.

In his 1974 chapter on the episode, Clive Hart notes that it 'is [also] in fact full of verbal echoes and thematic connexions which are, so to speak, potential interpolations made by the reader himself'.[13] We can understand this concept of 'potential interpolations' as describing the sort of reading I've discussed above; the text on the page is interpolated by our wandering minds, by our reading as we look up from the page. Two passages of 'Wandering Rocks' even interpolate 'Calypso' and continue our tracing of milk and cream. As mentioned before, walking along Wellington Quay Lenehan tells his friend M'Coy a story of sitting next to Molly Bloom (obnoxiously miming 'ample curves of air'), joking that while 'Bloom was pointing out all the stars and the comets in the heavens [. . .] I was lost, so to speak, in the milky way' (10.556–70). Very close by in the Dublin Bread Company tearooms ('We call it D. B. C. because they have damn bad cakes') a Panama-and-'primrose waistcoat'-clad Buck Mulligan and the Englishman Haines have coffee and scones while Charles Stewart Parnell's brother plays chess near a window (10.1058, 10.1065). Discussing Stephen Dedalus's plan 'to write something in ten years', Haines tastes his creamy *mélange* coffee: '– This is real Irish cream I take it, he said with forbearance. I don't want to be imposed on' (10.1089–90, 10.1094–5). With a pomposity that reaches back to Buck that morning and forward to the cocoa of 'Ithaca' that night, colonial tourist Haines demands to be sure he has an authentic Irish experience, while in the coda of the episode the British rule imposed on Ireland is displayed in the procession of the Viceregal cavalcade through the streets of Dublin. Either Lenehan or Haines could interpolate our reading of tea in 'Calypso'. The interpolations that take us across the city in 'Wandering Rocks', however, are directed wanderings, plotted for us, and though we can make arguments for the effect or meaning of individual interpolations, their significance *en masse* seems only to be their precision.[14] Hart's definition of 'potential interpolations' as being 'made by the reader themselves' implies that, conversely, the actual interpolations of the 'Wandering Rocks' narrative are instead authorial, made by Joyce. They thus raise awareness of the author's activity, and we are rewarded for our efforts with a reminder of how skilfully and intricately plotted the text is.

Tracking the interpolations and the movements of the characters does not, however, offer us a greater understanding of the strangeness of 'Wandering Rocks'. Such strangeness is caused by a series of structural, stylistic, linguistic, and narrative oddities. Jeri Johnson dubs these 'disorienting effects', a turn of phrase which gestures towards a reader's sense of being lost in this episode despite being able to pinpoint each of its events on a map.[15] Interpolations are examples of these bizarre quirks in the episode, all of which also interrupt and confuse our reading in some way. Repetitions, moments of wordplay, and a continued thwarting of narrative momentum cause us to question the focus of the narrative. As discussed above, repetitions are a standard characteristic of *Ulysses*; in 'Wandering Rocks', however, we find repetitions which occur confusingly close together and with unusual similarity. We are used to repetitions having significance in the novel, but this stutters when we are told twice within seven lines that Father Conmee 'stepped on to an outward bound tram' and 'stepped into an outward bound tram' (10.108–9, 10.113–14) or that Almidano Artifoni 'trotted on stout trousers after the Dalkey tram. In vain he trotted, signalling in vain' (10.364–5). Searching for some logic behind these repetitive moments, we can at times find echoes of the effects of 'Sirens' or Stephen's wordplay in 'Proteus'. The latter makes some sense and suggests significance in scenes where Stephen is present, such as during his conversation with Artifoni: his linguistic touch seems to reach 'pigeons roocoocooed' and 'swaying his ashplant in slow swingswong' (10.343, 10.348–9). We can also see Stephen's linguistic experimentation affecting the opening of his scene with Dilly Dedalus, with three different attempts to describe what dust does, each more elaborate than the last:

> Stephen Dedalus watched through the webbed window the lapidary's fingers prove a timedulled chain. Dust webbed the window and the showtrays. Dust darkened the toiling fingers with their vulture nails. Dust slept on dull coils of bronze and silver, lozenges of cinnabar, on rubies, leprous and winedark stones. (10.800–4)

Why, then, does the narrative use a similarly alliterative style in its central scene, describing the shopman showing books to Bloom? 'Onions of his breath came across the counter out of his ruined mouth. He bent to make a bundle of the other books, hugged them against his unbuttoned waistcoat and bore them off behind the dingy curtain' (10.596–8). And why are we told that Cashel Boyle O'Connor Fitzmaurice Tisdall Farrell has his 'stickumbrelladustcoat dangling' twice in two short paragraphs (10.1101–8)?[16] The cumulative effect is of narrative inattention or forgetfulness. This is heightened by the repetition of 'a onelegged sailor', an example used by both Hart and Karen Lawrence in their analyses of 'Wandering Rocks' (10.7 and 10.228). Giving the impression that the narrative has either forgotten that it and we have encountered the sailor already or that the narrative does not recognise its own previous narration of the sailor, the repetition of '*a* onelegged sailor' disrupts our reading. Lawrence argues that 'The narrative inability to progress from the indefinite to the definite article illustrates a strange failing in the "narrative memory." A crucial component of the development of narrative is precisely this ability to synthesize knowledge while accumulating it.'[17] We expect to be told of 'the onelegged sailor' once we have read of 'a onelegged sailor': for that encounter to cause a change in article. Later he is given as 'the sailor' and 'the onelegged sailor' (10.239 and 10.1063), and the definite article does appear comfortably elsewhere – such as when 'A constable on his beat' becomes 'the constable' (10.98–9). With consistency, we could argue for some rule or stylistic choice. The inconsistency emphasises Lawrence's argument for a 'strange failing': the effect is of something not working, of something having gone wrong (curdled?). The onelegged sailor seems unworthy of the narrative's attention, divided as it is between its nineteen scenes.

Non-human objects, however, seem to catch the narrative focus at random. Just as when the language seems to take on Stephen's mode of playing and trying out ways of expression in scenes which focus on him, something akin to the Uncle Charles Principle occurs elsewhere in the episode. Characteristics and emotions seep into inanimate objects, and an apparently random selection of items find themselves curiously detailed. Innocent peaches become 'shamefaced' and later 'blushing' in the company of Blazes Boylan, as if when painting Boylan guilty (on his way to meet Molly) the narrative's brushstrokes catch the fruit, 'fat pears' 'bedded' with the peaches in a basket (10.299–336); Kenner dubs these 'Boylan-verbs' and 'Boylan-epithets'.[18] In the coda, the excitement of the cavalcade reaches tens of characters, and even 'the salute of Almidano Artifoni's sturdy trousers' is acknowledged (10.1281–2). And while Father Conmee greets and is greeted on his walk he also passes 'cabbages, curtseying to him with ample underleaves' (10.180–1). We could argue that the result of this particular disorienting effect is that Boylan's flirting, the cavalcade's impact, or Conmee's ego are emphasised. However, when Conmee sees an old woman stepping off the tram, and sees 'the conductor help her and net and basket down', why are woman and objects placed oddly on an equal footing by the absence of possessive pronouns (10.136–7)? And if this narrative is capable of a complex trope in which objects are swept up in emotional tides in order to emphasise the self-importance of Boylan, the Viceroy, and Conmee, then why is it incapable of recalling what or who it has already narrated? As much as we can try to argue for some significance in the embarrassed peaches, deferential trousers, and curtseying cabbages, the overwhelming impression is of an illogical narrative focus. Furthermore, the briefness of each scene cuts short any effect these characterised objects might impart, as the attention of the narrative shifts thoughtlessly. This also halts much of the momentum of pathos in the episode: Dignam's son's grief and Stephen's perception of his younger sister as 'drowning' at home are both cut cruelly short, as the interior life of a character appears insufficient to keep the narrative interested.

'Wandering Rocks' is uncomfortable because much of what we expect as readers, even as readers of *Ulysses*, is thwarted. We expect a narrative to keep track of its characters, of some of their inner lives, of its own narration, language, decisions – even as far in as 'Eumaeus' we expect the narrative to keep track of its own jokes too, such as Bloom's L-less misnomer (in fact, we expect an unusually high level of this. As Kenner argues, 'Novelists don't normally know where characters' hats are' (*'Ulysses'*, 46).). We expect 'plot' to be more than marks on a map, 'realism' to be more and less than precise timing. We expect important occurrences to garner narration: as Johnson points out, '*Wandering Rocks* teasingly hints that it is the fact of the narrative frame which bestows significance on narrated events, not vice versa'.[19] The purpose of the narrative comes into question, and, as when reading 'Eumaeus', the narrative's oddities suggest a personality behind the strangeness. Hart describes the narrator's 'difficult personality [as] the most salient thing about the chapter'.[20] Johnson reacts to the narrative's intrusions and seemingly forgetful omniscience by referring to its 'capriciousness', while Lawrence responds to the same effects by discussing 'the narrative mind':[21]

> Reality is "defamiliarized," to borrow a phrase from the Russian formalists, a process due to the type of narrative mind in the chapter. This narrative mind exhibits what I would call a "lateral" or paratactic imagination: it catalogues facts without synthesizing them. It documents the events that occur but fails to give the causal, logical, or even temporal connections between them.[22]

Again, as in 'Eumaeus', we might find ourselves reading the narrative failures of 'Wandering Rocks' as indicative of a mind, a character. The lack of a consistent central character rules out a possible extended version of the Uncle Charles

Principle in this episode, but the idea of the narrator as personified overseer may bring us back to Kenner's version of the Arranger: only here the Arranger has little idea of or interest in what it has 'said before'. Kenner argues that 'Wandering Rocks' is indeed 'Joyce's earliest explorations of the Arranger – the captions of "Aeolus" extended his presence retroactively at a late stage of revision – and it is noteworthy that in "Wandering Rocks" the Arranger's difficult personality manifests itself in snares for the reader' (*'Ulysses'*, 65). An inefficient Arranger, or personality-laden narrator; we are again seeking some logic, some system behind the oddities of 'Wandering Rocks'. A 'distracted narrator' theory carries some credence: the narrator is sophisticated but attempting too much, and finds its attention easily grabbed by, for example, the gleam of what we infer is Molly's 'generous white arm from a window in Eccles street' which interpolates Corny Kelleher's brief scene (10.222–3). The idea of an observing, even voyeuristic, narrator is similarly convincing: looking at all of Dublin and making sure to include mention that

> A flushed young man came from a gap of a hedge and after him came a young woman with wild nodding daisies in her hand. The young man raised his hat abruptly: the young woman abruptly bent and with slow care detached from her light skirt a clinging twig. (10.199–202)[23]

We could even argue for a narrator who is easily influenced by its characters: with an overall episode style that takes on Father Conmee's concerns with noticing, greeting, and recognising others and being noticed, greeted, or recognised in return; Bloom and Boylan's preoccupations with illicit sex; Stephen's linguistic experimentation and play; Master Dignam's attempt to reach truth through language ('Pa is dead. My father is dead' (10.1170)); and even the cavalcade's showy procession and display of power through and over all of Dublin.

So, what is the function of a narrative that encourages such theorising? We are desperately seeking a reason not only for why the events of 'Wandering Rocks' are narrated in this manner, but for why they are narrated at all. In Chapter 3 I described how and with what effect the style of 'Eumaeus' draws our attention to the 'act' of narration and its potential perpetrators; here we are faced with confusion over, to refer again to Johnson, the 'fact' of narration: '*Wandering Rocks* teasingly hints that it is the fact of the narrative frame which bestows significance on narrated events, not vice versa'.[24] As our efforts fail to find reasons for how or why the episode is narrated, it is our efforts that are spot lit. This prompts questions of what is not narrated: if the causality we presume exists between significance and narration is far less certain, it follows that what is not included in the narrative can be of great relevance and import – that its 'not'ness is as pointed as Molly's holding of a cup 'by nothandle' (4.333). This is, of course, something that we have begun to glean from previous episodes – and that we become increasingly aware of throughout *Ulysses*.

To return to 'Calypso': Molly's pronunciation of metempsychosis as 'met him pike hoses' is not included in the narrative, and neither is the conversation had by Molly and Bloom which reveals the specific time of Molly and Boylan's meeting – both are narrated only later in retrospect. As we are so aligned with Bloom and Stephen in the novel it is unsurprising that Molly and Boylan's meeting also goes unnarrated – but it is left to us to figure out why, for example, we are not witness to Bloom's visit to Patrick Dignam's widow in between 'Cyclops' and 'Nausicaa' (and to comprehend in the first place that there was a missed conversation or visit). Kenner gives a lot of attention across his work to these gaps; his explanation of Bloom's unnarrated visit is that Bloom does not want to think about it. Kenner develops this reading between *Joyce's Voices* and *'Ulysses'*, labelling the gap 'an especially eloquent chapter' and concluding that Bloom's mental avoidance of it is due to more than a sadness around Dignam's death: that rather Bloom suspects Cunningham brought him along on the visit for anti-Semitic reasons (that he would be of help with a 'sticky' financial situation).[25] After what Bloom goes through in 'Cyclops', it is perhaps unsurprising that this has such an impact on the structure of the novel's narrative. In my extended reading of the cream spiralling through Molly's tea in the first part of this chapter my wanderings suggested that the pause for detail is coloured by Bloom's thoughts: those thoughts are at once unnarrated and narrated, as we find we still read his preoccupations in the short description of the cup of tea. We might think too of Kenner's argument that the musical style of 'Sirens' plays on Bloom and Molly's tacit agreement to refer to her meeting with Boylan as a singing rehearsal; the style itself tells us of Bloom's concerns, it adds to the story of how he is around four o'clock, it narrates his misery as he fails to avoid thinking about what might be happening in his home at that time (*'Ulysses'*, 90–1). In *Virgin and Veteran Readers of 'Ulysses'* Margot Norris also focuses on 'textual incompleteness and implicature'; she relates this more clearly to the act of reading, by emphasising the risks these skips and gaps invite readers to take as we make inferences and search for what is implicit.[26] As Kenner notes, 'There is much the Blooms do not say to each other, much also that the book does not offer to say to us' (*'Ulysses'*, 48). We grow accustomed in *Ulysses* to reading the unnarrated, as we fill in gaps, make associations, tie together disparate threads. If our tracing of the threads of one short sentence about tea can function as an act of narrating the inner life of Bloom, then what we mean by 'narration' in this novel is not something contained within the words on the page. Are we, then, reading unwritten text?

Reading 'unwritten text' may seem to be the least of our problems when reading *Ulysses*. The fabric of this 'usylessly unreadable Blue Book of Eccles' (*FW*, 179.26–7), from its language to its intertextuality to its structure, makes for difficult reading. It demands a great deal from the reader in terms of memory, concentration, and further reading (of the novel itself and its many reference points). To borrow Leonard Diepeveen's definition of difficulty in *The Difficulties of Modernism*: the reader's expectations, including their desire for comprehension, are thwarted.[27] 'It is customary to note', with Kenner, 'that Joyce makes very severe demands of his reader'.[28] The text's difficulty returns us to its transformation from Homeric oral epic to printed novel: Joyce's 'demands' work successfully only because we hold the book, and thus 'the whole conception of *Ulysses* depends on the existence of something former writers took for granted as simply the envelope for their wares: a printed book whose pages are numbered'.[29] Yet it is the aspects of the text that make it difficult that also cause the modes of reading I have been exploring: active, creative readings that seek and form theories; understandings of the text that shift and alter as we read and reread.[30] There is, however, a further effect of the difficulty of *Ulysses*: our attention is drawn through the text to its creator – the writing being who crafted such complexity. As Bersani argues, with reference to the character Odysseus, 'trickery, cunning, and ruse are the novel's first connotations' and 'they define an authorial strategy' (202). The perfectly timed 'Wandering Rocks' and its confusing, unfulfilling interpolations encourage a great deal of work on the part of an engaged reader; our reward is the ability to grasp how well-wrought the episode is. A 'Bloom' mentioned at one point in 'Wandering Rocks' is revealed, hundreds of pages later, to be a dentist of no relation; a reader who, as encouraged by the text, reads carefully to identify this dentist Bloom gets little in return.[31] Elsewhere, intratextual references make little to no sense at all, such as when a joke of Lenehan's is referred to in Bloom's thoughts though Bloom was absent when the joke was told.[32] These, for want of a far better term, 'false leads', act like bright spotlights on the complexity of the text. The difficulty of reading that prompts an active and creative reading role also encourages an awareness of the text as 'authored': an awareness of the author.

The author is also brought to our attention when confronting difficulties leads us somewhere: when close reading and effort have a revelatory effect. Trying to find some narrative logic behind that single sentence of 'Calypso' took a convoluted route to an affecting place: the act of making tea coloured by Bloom's preoccupations. My reading brought a moment of understanding, and, though fleeting and suggestive, that moment offered character and narrative development along with a mimetic effect of getting to know Bloom better. The complicated and in-depth reading Kenner applies to 'Sirens' unravels narrative and stylistic confusion – answering the challenge of a strange style – and arrives again at an affecting understanding of Bloom's mind. When we fill in the gaps of what goes unnarrated in 'Calypso' we have a similar experience, learning more about Bloom as we learn more about how the narrative works.

Molly holds her cup 'by nothandle', hand wrapped around the heat of her tea in the cold morning air; in the 'not-narrated' of the novel we likewise grasp its warmth. Our own acts of reading deliver pathos, and complete plot; while plotting the movements of 'Wandering Rocks' on a map may feel fruitless, 'plotting' is an activity we engage in throughout *Ulysses*. However, just as the concrete gaps in narration – the skipping of events or conversation – are written into the remaining text with oblique and obvious reference, are we not also following trails set up for us when we unpick an episode or a sentence or a moment of confusion? Is our reading written into the text – is it part of the plot? Are we following written paths? Does the remarkableness of finding narrative development at the end of an hour's close reading make us congratulate ourselves for our reading skills, or marvel at the creator who can guide our reading – even when we leave the text – to a useful place? As Mark A. Wollaeger points out,

> Readers of Joyce are familiar with the experience of following out an interpretive lead, an allusion, say, or an inter-textual echo, only to discover that one's ingenuity has all the time been in service of returning to a place where Joyce has long been expecting us.[33]

What we find is as a result of our own reading, but we read in a manner prompted by the text itself. This is akin to the 'double-laughter' of Derrida's 'Ulysses Gramophone', which I will return to and expand on below. Both exist: our creativity of reading and the author's ability to pre-empt us. It is Barthes's 'limitless' text, but it does not preclude the author. Rather, our own activity of reading highlights the author's activity. The text provokes inventive, active reading, and that reading brings our attention back to the author.

Difficult Authors, Difficult Readers

These difficulties – this filling of gaps and pitching of answers and theorising of solutions – lead to a heightened awareness of our own reading, of our own activity of reading. Reading as understanding, as temporarily fixing meaning (or fixing openness), as 'that text we write in ourselves'; the processes and effects of such reading, of our reading, are drawn to our attention. Our activity becomes part of what we read, pulling not only at the text on the page but also at the unsettled text in our minds and the relationship between the two. This awareness of our reading leads to an awareness of the author, one carefully crafted step ahead of us, able to write a text which pre-empts all responses without refusing inventive interpretation. Comprehending or identifying difficulty (whether when forming theories of reading *Ulysses* or just trying to find out from the novel that 16 June is a Thursday) leads us not only to the author but perhaps to a certain attitude towards the author. One such attitude, seen in criticism and beyond, results in a deification of sorts; a reading of genius, of exceptionalism.

Much of this is light-hearted: in 'Ulysses Gramophone' Derrida, for example, refers to Joyce and other 'finite divinities'.[34] Kenner, meanwhile, occasionally uses biblically tinged, if tongue-in-cheek, phrasing to describe Joyce's opinion of his own work: 'the author inspecting what he had been writing for seven years, and seeing that it was good' (*'Ulysses'*, 157). Inherited from Budgen ('he looks on his handiwork when he has done it and finds it good'), this recurrent deifying quirk perhaps makes a joke of Joyce's sense of self-worth more than it outlines a critical attitude.[35] Such deification, however, can be taken more seriously.

In 'Survivors of Joyce', John Banville remarks on Joyce's legacy:

> The greatness, or part of the greatness, of an *Aeneid*, of a *View of Delft*, of a *Don Giovanni*, of a *Ulysses*, rests in the fact that they are, in an essential way, *closed*. By this I do not mean to say that these works of art are difficult, or obscure – what could be more limpid than the light that hovers over Delft? – but that they are *mysterious at their core*. There is something uncanny about such art. It does not seem to have been produced by human hands, but to have created itself out of nothing by some secret, unknowable means.

Banville elaborates:

> He is one of those writers . . . or should I say, *he is a writer* (for he is probably unique) whose work is utterly free of solecisms, of errors of judgement, of mistakes: for such things, should they seem to appear, are immediately transformed, by a sort of continuous chain reaction, into *inventions*.[36]

Banville's short commentary on the creation of Joyce's texts reveals how perceived greatness affects views of an author. It is also very much from the perspective of a later literary writer, and, if we follow Anne Enright, specifically of a male writer:

> It's male writers who have a problem with Joyce; they're all 'in the long shadow of Joyce, and who can step into his shoes?' I don't want any shoes, thank you very much. Joyce made everything possible; he opened all the doors and windows.[37]

Enright's omnipotent Joyce, however, is more than a touch divine too. In defence of his opinions, Banville notes that 'it will be no good my pointing out that Joyce himself held that the artist should stand disengaged from his art, off in the background somewhere, paring his nails – no one pays much attention any more to *that* piece of piety': a confusing conflation, familiar to *The Reader's Joyce*, of

Stephen and Joyce's words. Banville's argument, instead, is that we can only 'know about' *Finnegans Wake* or *Ulysses*, rather than 'understand'. He grasps the oddly 'biblical' quality given to these texts, claiming that such a quality is 'conferred' due to 'the quality of *closure*': 'great art, I am convinced, does not "reveal" itself to us, does not open outwards to our needs; on the contrary, it is great precisely because it is closed against us'.[38] Banville almost removes the author in his reading of greatness – calling Joyce 'the supreme escape-artist, a Houdini of the word, who used every possible rhetorical device in order to bury himself', and finding an author incapable of mistakes.[39] This describes our reading of Joyce's texts more than it describes Joyce; we have a faith in the completeness and perfection of *Ulysses* that *is* biblical – this enables our close readings – and we can see in our own reading and in Joycean criticism a refusal to accept error or failure in Joyce's texts.[40] From Kenner's corrections of Wyndham Lewis's conclusions; to Hart and Lawrence's reading of 'a onelegged sailor'; to my own reading of '(*sic*)': all rely on a particular level of faith in the text – that it is without flaws, as it is meant to be, or even (oh no) as it was intended. Our free and interpretive, creative reading relies upon a perfect text (once we have checked the errata!), which itself implies a particular level of faith in the author's talent ('Bosh!'), and in the author.

'The element of performance and exhibition in the writing itself', observes Lawrence, 'is too great to allow the reader to receive all the applause'.[41] Critics including Bersani, Vicki Mahaffey, and Michael Patrick Gillespie note that our reading, and criticism, of *Ulysses* celebrate its author; Bersani goes so far as to claim that 'Exegesis reveals that *Ulysses* signifies Joyce's multitudinous stylistic and structural intentions; it demonstrates that the work glorifies its creator just as Christ – concentrating and purifying in His Person a universal human truth – glorifies the Father' (227–8). This critical viewpoint is perhaps one reason why critics continue to return and give non-ironic credence to Stephen's idea of an author-god; it also describes an effect of Kenner's work – for all its tongue-in-cheek references to a godly author. By identifying, across several pieces of criticism, author-foils such as the Arranger Kenner looks away from the author for answers, yet glorifies the author who created such a complicated, slippery, novel piece of narrative trickery; he refers often and significantly to a 'grand design' (three times, for example, in *Joyce's Voices*). Acts of criticism can confirm, reiterate, and rely on a very high opinion of the author; true even for Bersani, who confesses that 'Even in writing "against *Ulysses*," we can only feel a great sadness in leaving it' (228). And as Jonathan Goldman argues, the 'authorial branding' of *Ulysses*, Joyce's fame, and the cultural status of Joyce and his works 'announce the author's renown and connote his genius'.[42]

Such attitudes towards the author affect our reading, as they are also affected by our reading. How we read the text and its author is determined within a looping relationship between reader, author, text, and critic, which takes no heed of incompatibilities or contradictions. An active mode of reading presupposes an absent author, yet is prompted by the text's difficulties. These difficulties in turn draw our attention to the text's creator – and furthermore to the creator's skill. This genius author is emphasised too by our faith somehow in the text as perfect, which both deifies and removes the author. Our reading leads us to questions of authorship, as I made clear in Chapter 3: reading the absence of an author behind the name Homer as providing a space for both authorially seeking scholarship and a freedom of creative reading. The far-reaching – distrustful – mode of reading encouraged by the difficulties of 'Eumaeus' develops our attempts to identify an author-figure in the narrative. Reading the 'genius' of Joyce, we find again Barthes's 'birth of the reader'; here in the service of not just locating, but exalting the author. Retaining our focus on the activity of reading: what practical difference does it make to face a Barthesian 'dead' author or a genius? I can read Circe and Calypso, metempsychosis and the river Lethe, the milkwoman of 'Telemachus', Ithacan hot cocoa, the Blooms' pussens, Molly on Howth Head, Stephen's wordplay, Bloom's 'father of thousands', and his approaching cuckoldry in one short description of adding milk to tea because I, as reader, am where the multiplicity of the text is gathered; because there is no author and therefore no limit to the text, which is open and has no possible 'final signified'. Or, do I find such richness in a stream of milk because Joyce was a genius, because *Ulysses* is infallible – because such wealth of meaning is written into the text by an unfathomable literary mind?

Coincidentally, this is not the first reading of *Ulysses* to find itself 'spinning in milk': in 'Ulysses Gramophone' Derrida laments the Joyce-authorised French translation of the novel, due to its alteration of 'galaxy of events' to 'gerbe des événements' or 'sheaf of events'. As he complains, 'that loses all the milk and thus also the milky tea that constantly irrigate *Ulysses* to precisely make of it a milky way or "galaxy"'.[43] This coincidence is appropriate, given Derrida's interest in 'Ulysses Gramophone' in coincidence as one way in which reading *Ulysses* spills over into our own lives, as a contributing factor to the sensation that everything is contained within the novel.[44] Moving in circles away from the irrigating milk, Derrida presents in 'Ulysses Gramophone' his reading of the 'double laughter' in *Ulysses*:

> nothing can be invented *on the subject* of Joyce. All that can be said of *Ulysses*, for example, is already anticipated, including, as we saw, the scene of the academic competence and the ingenuity of meta-discourse. We are caught in this net. We find all the gestures to take the initiative of a movement announced in a superpotentialized text that will remind you, at a given time, that you are caught in a network of language, writing, knowledge, and *even of narration* [. . .] Everything that happened to

me, including the narration that I would attempt to make of it, was said in advance, narrated in advance in its dated singularity, prescribed in a sequence of knowledge and narration: within *Ulysses*, to say nothing of *Finnegans Wake*, by this hypermnesic machine capable of storing in a giant epic work, with the memory of the West and virtually all the languages of the world, *the very traces of the future*. Yes, everything has already happened to us with *Ulysses*, and in advance signed by Joyce.[45]

Read in one way, Derrida's reading of *Ulysses* finds the novel and 'the event signed Joyce' as near-mythical, even fantastic – the same Joyce as Enright's, who 'made everything possible'.[46] The text is 'superpotentialized' and pre-empts not only its reading but also the life of its reader: it and Joyce have caught us 'in this net', and contain 'the very traces of the future'. This is, after all, a text which seeps into our own world when it requires 7 Eccles Street's vacancy on the real 16 June, or keeps a late library book on Bloom's shelves from ever being returned (in *'Ulysses'* Kenner reports in a footnote that *The Stark-Munro Letters* by Arthur Conan Doyle, listed in 'Ithaca' as borrowed from the Capel Street Library and '13 days overdue', was never returned in the real world. The discovery that the book was declared 'missing' by the library in 1906 was revealed at the Sixth Symposium in 1977 (143)). Derek Attridge further clarifies Derrida's 'two laughters':

> A double laughter, he argued, runs through the text: a sardonic, triumphant laughter that takes pleasure in the work's totalizing power, and a light, dancing laughter that opens the work to otherness. The former arises from the encyclopedic ambition of the novel, its appearing always to preempt any response made by the reader; the latter to its ceaseless undermining of any such ambition, opening fresh spaces for inventiveness, what we might call a deconstructive laughter. The two laughters presuppose one another, ventriloquize one another, put one another at risk, make each other possible; they correspond to the two types of criticism, the mechanical analysis of a text and the countersignature of unique affirmation [. . .] *Ulysses*, then, is a work of such complexity and richness that it seems to preempt all critical manoeuvres, yet that very complexity makes possible unpredictable coincidences, connections, and insights – not just within the work, but, as Derrida's personal narrative reveals, between the work and the lives of its readers.[47]

As I explored in the fourth chapter of this book, the significance of 'Ulysses Gramophone' is generally seen as its position within Derrida's arguments for the importance of Joyce's texts to deconstruction. The extent to which we can contend that Joyce's texts prefigure the concerns associated with poststructuralist theory underpins the discussions of this chapter: arguing that the way we are provoked into reading *Ulysses* is later described by Barthes as, simply, reading; that his definition of 'text' is writ large in Joyce's novel; and how the opposing attitudes to the author that we form in our active reading find an important role in Derrida's work. This pre-empting, and contradiction, is echoed by Joyce studies itself – as my reliance on Kenner's modes of reading emphasises. The happy coexistence of incompatible readings that this chapter has detailed can be seen in Joyce studies: an openness to multiplicity, a faith in infinite interpretations, in difference, alongside a need to correct, improve, read better, find the 'best' approach, invoke authority. Reading *Ulysses* prefigures the critical-theoretical debates played out in Joyce studies and beyond: we find in our own readings a contradictory response to the author. In order to pull at and develop what Derrida's 'double laughter' *does* in terms of how we read and how we write criticism, I need now to ask how this contradictory response relates to authority.

Authorise This

The way in which *Ulysses* prompts me to read dares me to test out my own reading authority. What I require to authorise readings has shifted and altered in Joyce studies (reflecting changes within and beyond the field): the personal involvement of Joyce, a fashionable critical focus, an established theoretical framework, access to the author's notes and drafts. How would I validate my own readings, were I to follow up on the milk and cream and tea and coffee I find beyond 'Calypso', beyond *Ulysses*, in the unwritten links I read with *Cold Comfort Farm* and *Arcadia*? Would my argument be authority enough? Gibbons's *Cold Comfort Farm* is known for parodying other novels, such as those of D. H. Lawrence, in its presentation of the Starkadders. Its intratextual response to other literature is more complex, however, as the books read by the protagonist Flora Poste appear to then inform events beyond her control that drive her story forward. In Stoppard's *Arcadia*, meanwhile, there is tension between being read as a real person and read as a character – as historical persons appear alongside the fictional counterparts who read them in turn. Perhaps in both texts we can read an interest in being the subject in, or focus of, literature: in the effects of being read, explored through metaleptic reading characters.[48] Furthermore, Bloom and Stephen share flower water-soaked worries of what will be left of them when they are gone, of their legacy – unaware of their permanence as characters in a text. Linking these three texts are the curdling spirals of dairy in Molly's tea, but also perhaps a shared interest in how characters are formed by fiction, and the effects of reading. How would I justify this connection? Pure coincidence carries some weight – as does its treatment in Derrida's hands, arguing that *Ulysses* contains within it 'traces of the future'. This is significantly similar to the 'genius' route: the text of *Ulysses* is so totalising and adept that any later literary exploration in modern literature of anything similar to its concerns will by definition be pre-written by it. Do I need something more concrete? Stoppard wrote elsewhere on Joyce, turning him into one of his characters twenty years before writing *Arcadia* (as I will explore in the next chapter). Gibbons, meanwhile, wrote a novel that played with the novel form, ten years after *Ulysses* – can influence, inspiration, or direct response be inferred? Do I need to find a line in drafts or notes of *Cold Comfort Farm* or *Arcadia*, or a statement in letters or interviews with either author to find traces of intentions? An alternative is to be the authority as the reader, to remove the authors so as to authorise my own readings. This extends – perhaps to absurdity – Barthes's arguments that 'In the field of reading [. . .] there is not only no pertinence of *levels*, there is no possibility of describing *levels* of reading, because there is no possibility of closing the list of these levels': that we 'do not know where to halt the depth and the dispersion of reading' ('Reading', 35). Do I authorise my readings with the authority of author, reader, or critic? Can they be separated?

Critical acts which invoke the authority of the author rely often on a (sometimes veiled) determination of intention; attempts to do this within Joyce studies have been predictably complicated. As I have discussed before, the idea that Joyce did not intend for his readers to worry about intentions is well-established in Joyce studies. The author's intention, and authority, is maintained in this movement – we are only allowed to kid ourselves we have interpretative freedom because he planned this all along. Self-effacement, or mock-self-effacement, affirms the Dedalean model of authorship: impersonal, yet ultimately in control. We are trapped in an author's game; as Jean-Michel Rabaté warns, 'A writer who pretends to dispossess himself of his traditional prerogatives' will return 'like a bogeyman to scare critics and readers'.[49] Attempts to ignore the author are pre-empted, authorially authorised, and thus neutered. The author's authority functions too, as I explored in earlier chapters, in references to his authorised exegesis, to Gilbert, Budgen, or even *Our Exagmination*; to the schemata, letters, the reported conversations with friends; to notesheets and manuscripts. This last is the most prevalent mode of authorial authorisation in Joyce studies today. In her 2012 study on intertextuality, Joyce, and Flaubert, for example, one way in which Scarlett Baron authorises links between the two authors is by citing 'David Hayman's momentous discovery of three "Flaubert" jottings in one of the *Finnegans Wake* notebooks. One of these states: "G. F can rest having made me".'[50] Genetic criticism in this mode places a high premium on what the author thinks, or is presumed to mean. When we invoke authorial authority like this, including via Stephen's theories, we reach towards something akin to the romantic authorial attitudes explored by M. H. Abrams, where the author is the key to the work.

In the absence of either Gibbons's or Stoppard's authorising statements, my alternative is a reader's authority, Barthes's anti-authorialism, and particularly models of intertextuality which deny or remove filiation.[51] The agency of the author is removed in both Barthes's and Julia Kristeva's models of intertextuality – forged in opposition to the concept of influence – with the reader taking on the active role. In such conceptions of intertextuality, is there any need to find or prove a link between *Cold Comfort Farm*, *Arcadia*, and *Ulysses* stronger than the link of my own comprehension? In various hands, intertextuality has been treated as a mode of reading in which the author or any authorial intention is irrelevant. By critics such as Susan Stanford Friedman and more recently Baron, intertextuality is also figured as insistently Joycean; furthermore, in both Friedman's and Baron's reappraisals of intertextuality, the author is included. Baron does not only include the author in Joycean intertextuality, she claims Joyce and Flaubert as 'surely the prime movers behind intertextual theory, as well as its paradigm cases'.[52] Likewise, critics such as Gillespie link Stephen's Flaubertian authorial theories in *Portrait* to a removal of the author, using this to read Joyce's later texts: 'In effect the novel consciously shifts the terms of engagement from the subject-centred consciousness to the language-centred discourse described by Roland Barthes and by Michel Foucault.'[53] Yet, as Baron points out, in *Portrait* 'paradox arises because Stephen's borrowed declaration consists of a denial of intertextuality as a modus operandi of literary creation': rather than Barthes's 'intertextual author' Stephen describes a 'figure of God at the origin of creation, creating out of nothing'.[54] And if we seek to authorise our readerly authority of intertextuality by noting Joyce's importance to and citation by Kristeva (or Derrida) we maintain the same power structures of agency and causation found in ideas of influence. Which is the same as arguing that Joyce intended we ignore intention.

Critics do pitch middle grounds between readerly and authorial authority; we can see this for example in Gillespie's argument (discussed in Chapter 4) for 'a both/and condition that does not assign either to the author or to the reader the position of sole arbiter of meaning'.[55] His response to *Ulysses* gives great weight to the reader's role, but by claiming this was what Joyce wanted Gillespie keeps the reader's movements within a limited frame set by the author. Thus, though seemingly striking a balance between the authority of each, Gillespie's argument in fact maintains and affirms the author's authority. His approach outlines the implicit attitude of most Joycean criticism (often despite proclaimed theoretical allegiances): drawing on both authorial and readerly authority, but prioritising the former. The construction of a critic's authority is a complicated manoeuvre, in part as the critic straddles both reader and author roles. In *James Joyce, Authorized Reader* Rabaté notes a similar sort of anxiety to my own, worrying that 'when the text keeps referring to its own problematic origins, the reader turned critic has either to invoke another writer or critic as an instance of authority or to produce his own theory of authority'. Rabaté then argues that the text itself authorises our shift from reader to critic: it 'puts an end to the dichotomy between reader and author by abolishing the opposition between text and commentary, novel and criticism'.[56] He refers here to *Finnegans Wake*, yet as I have explored above *Ulysses* provokes the same questions. In Rabaté's reading, there is a 'price to pay for the death of the author' in Joyce's texts: that 'such a birth of the reader-as-writer can only be founded on a philosophy of authority'.[57] His 'death of the author', however, as I highlighted in Chapter 4, is Stephen's-read-as-Joyce's, which traps Rabaté's discussions in an extra layer of authorial authority that he does not examine. But his argument, that in gaining authority the reader becomes critic, is also rooted in the texts of Joyce; as are, for example, Laurent Milesi's proposal that Joyce's 'readers' (self-)empowerment [is made possible] through the very medium and fabric of his works', referring to critical empowerment as much as readerly, and Umberto Eco's suggestion that an interpretation can be deemed 'acceptable' if we 'check it against the text as a coherent whole'.[58]

Responses outside Joyce studies to the theories of the death of the author also debate critical authority: blurrings of reader and critic, for instance, are inferred by Susan Sontag's reading of Barthes's 'notions of "text" and "textuality" [which] translate into criticism the modernist ideal of an open-ended, polysemous literature; and thereby make the critic, just like the creators of that literature, the inventor of meaning'.[59] Within this, the roles of critic and author blur too. While Michael Moriarty may argue that of his own study 'All the reader has to bear in mind is that when statements are made here about Barthes's attitudes, priorities, and values, "Barthes" is a kind of theoretical fiction, a device of exposition',[60] Adrian Wilson declares that not even anti-authorial theory can escape the invocation of authorial authority, let alone critical responses to those theories: 'the author's death', he argues, 'was itself an *authored* event, requiring the authorial signatures of Barthes and of Foucault'.[61] Seán Burke, meanwhile, points out that through the massive response to their theoretical works Barthes, Foucault, and Derrida transformed themselves from critics to authors; 'great' authors, in fact.[62]

As I explored in Chapter 4's account of Joycean disagreements, claiming one's criticism is authorised by Joyce's texts can ruffle the feathers of those who claim the same for their own, opposing work. It also, as touched upon above, runs the risk of simply mirroring the movements of critics who seek authorial authorisation and of glorifying the author who wrote such a text. Discussing authorial intent in a 2003 article, Erwin R. Steinberg and Christian W. Hallstein reference Joseph Kelley's response to the Danis Rose scandal, emphasising how in the ensuing editorial argument critics authorised their readings by a belief in the author's skill:

> "Since most of us believe that Joyce did everything by design, we perpetuate fictions about his intentions." In making his argument, Kelley

demonstrates how Joyce scholars are simply privileging their own personal readings by declaring Joyce a genius and then self-righteously deciding what his intentions were.[63]

This is again reminiscent of one of Abrams's observations: that romantic critical modes – exemplified in the work of John Keble – create images of the author which serve their own purposes and contexts; an endeavour we have seen also in Homeric scholarship.[64] These responses intimate that critical authority comes from elsewhere, from 'fictions' created by the critic themself. R. G. Collingwood explores similar possibilities of created authority in *The Idea of History*: in his chapter 'The Historical Imagination' Collingwood investigates authority in the sphere of historical scholarship, a field in which 'authority' frequently refers to a source or a person.[65] Collingwood details why and how a historian might however 'tamper' with an authority, and the consequences of these 'emergency measures' (235 and 236). This leads him to

> the discovery that, so far from relying on an authority other than himself, to whose statements his thought must conform, the historian is his own authority and his thought autonomous, self-authorizing, possessed of a criterion to which his so-called authorities must conform and by reference to which they are criticized. (236)

Collingwood argues that the historian 'is relying on his own powers and constituting himself his own authority; while his so-called authorities are now not authorities at all but only evidence' (237). Collingwood is at pains to show he is not trying to undermine historical scholarship; he is instead revealing yet another 'discovery':

> that the historian himself, together with the here-and-now which forms the total body of evidence available to him, is part of the process he is studying, has his own place in that process, and can see it only from the point of view which at this present moment he occupies within it. (248)

Collingwood's discussions, though from a different field, are relevant to acts of literary criticism and the processes by which literary critics validate their readings. A critic's aims or agenda, perhaps, provide their own authority. The critic becomes here, in part, strangely aligned with Barthes's reader: the final arbiter of meaning, authorised by their own act of writing through reading, able and required to 'play'. Yet the critic is 'part of the process,' and critical authority in Joyce studies also relies on the critical authority of others. As in perhaps all fields of scholarship, certain critics gain canonical status; we signpost their work, their discoveries, authorising our own with such references whether in agreement or opposition. These established Joyceans and theorists are, nevertheless, also readers. Whether we view Joyce studies as collaborative or corrective, it is a catalogue of readings and readers.

Let's return to 'The sluggish cream wound curdling spirals through her tea.' I have mentioned overreading, but we could push that further: following the motion described in the sentence and twisting downwards into the roots of these words, their etymologies.[66] 'Sluggish' has grown from the Middle English *slugge*, a lazy person, and the obsolete verb *slug*, to 'be lazy' – it shares its roots with 'sluggard', and was first connected to people, a human trait, which gives some credence to reading the word as referring to Bloom and Molly as much as it refers to the cream. 'Cream' has Latin and Greek roots, reaching English via Old French; etymologies also detail from the 1500s the use of 'cream' to refer to the absolute best part of something, as it is used in 'Eumaeus's 'cream of the joke'. This use of cream draws the mind back to the 'adulterated milk', and to Bloom's doling out of the cream 'reserved' normally for Molly; revenge, perhaps, if Bloom views Molly's adultery in misogynistic terms of her giving away or sharing something 'special'. And one synonym for 'cream' when used to describe the best of a group is the 'flower', a reminder that our Henry Flower is not entirely guiltless. Reading 'wound' in isolation from the rest of the sentence we might think of its homograph, of hurt or injury – as perhaps Boylan's letter, and Molly's tucking of it under the pillow, wounds Bloom. 'Wound' in terms of 'wind' comes from the Old English *windan*, meaning to turn, twist, plait, curl, brandish, swing. Its Proto Germanic origin *wendan* stems from the Proto-Indo-European root *wendh-*, which suggests turning, winding, and weaving. This root is also the source of the Latin *viere*, to twist, plait, weave, and of *vincere*, to bind. Furthermore, 'wind' is related to 'wend' – to proceed or, in more modern usage, to meander – which is from the Old English *wendan*, to turn, go, direct; and also to convert, or translate. 'Wander' is also from the PIE root *wendh-*; the use of 'wandering' in terms of one's mind or affections dates back to the 1400s, with the myth of the 'wandering Jew' dating from the previous century. Bloom wanders through Dublin, winding through its streets, as his mind – and wife – wanders too. And caught up in the word 'wound' I find that which contains all this: a twisted, plaited, woven text. Arguably the connotations of 'text' are backed up within 'spirals' too, coming via Middle French from the Latin *spiralis*: winding around a fixed centre, or coiling. *Spira* in Latin suggests a coil, fold, or twist as well as spiral, and the Greek *speira* refers to a winding, coil, twist, wreath, or anything wound or coiled. Calypso, Circe, and their 'braided tresses' spring to mind, as does the weaving of Calypso ('she fared to and fro before the loom, and wove with a shuttle of gold');[67] our own twisting 'plotting' when reading; and Penelope, Molly, and the woven text. I could even argue the difficulty of a complexly twisting woven text is referred to in 'curdling' as a word for thickening; in the etymological connotations of crossing over, or overcoming, that 'through' contains; and even in that deeply embedded trace of translation in 'wound': fighting our way through something resistant, heavy, dense, and from that making new but coexisting, palimpsestial versions of the text.

Reading, Barthes reminds us, '(that text we write in ourselves when we read), *disperses*',[68] like cream or milk in tea. The movement described in this sentence of *Ulysses* describes reading *Ulysses*: as we flip back and forth, each rereading colours those that precede it. Our readings of the text are altered with the addition of newer readings, from revisiting a page, following up an intertext, browsing the work of a critic, or digging into etymologies. The etymological suggestions of this sentence, of braiding and weaving, further describe the text we read and the continually metamorphosing text we write in reading: our activity, our agency, and our play. That we might then wander off in spirals to *Cold Comfort Farm* or *Arcadia* tells us more about *Ulysses* than these later texts, or any others in which *Ulysses* can be found. Goldman touches upon this on his own meander through potential Ulyssean reference: finding traces of the novel in an Elvis Costello lyric, he asks,

> Are such resonances intentional, and if so, how do they affect our understanding of these works? For some, intentionality is irrelevant; any echo of Joyce inflects the text's meaning, regardless of the author's aims. With this in mind, we can consider the impulse to find such references, and see that this approach imposes Joyce as a reading filter over other cultural products. *Ulysses* is known as a hunting ground for literary allusions; in turn, the world has become a hunting ground for *Ulysses* allusions.[69]

This 'impulse' or 'reading filter' encourages unlimited readings. We gain this authority of reading – if a self-analysing, worrying sort of authority – from *Ulysses*. We do so in spite of Joyce, as Joyce is not effaced in this authorising: he is more than Barthes's 'paper-author', allowed to return to the text only as a guest ('Text', 161). This is possible because, as the novel repeatedly upholds, opposites can be simultaneously true in *Ulysses*. The way in which we are encouraged by the text to read the text affirms an authorial presence while maintaining the need for creative and active reading, and this pre-empts, or writes in advance, the back-and-forth of author-centric and anti-authorial critical debate. *Ulysses* prefigures debates of intention or authority, as it prefigures Gibbons and Stoppard or the Homeric scholarship of Milman Parry; it uncannily takes up more space than it should, knows more than it should, seeping into the real world in vacant homes and missing library books. This, in turn, affirms Joyce the creator as some sort of divine genius, but also the reader as a free agent and final arbiter of meaning. Within this pre-empting gesture, even the debate of whether *Ulysses* has limits or can infinitely pre-empt is itself prefigured, written in advance in the text which prompts such debate.

The unfathomable genius with totalising power and an inability to err, and an absence, a space for inventiveness, initiative, and creativity coexist within the reader's activity, the reader's text. Our act of reading makes this coexistence possible: *we* comprehend it. It is this emphasis that is missing in Derrida's 'double laughter'. Our authority as readers is temporary and partial – and this is key – not because it is superseded by the authority of the author, but because it is built by the necessarily and wonderfully unstable text in our minds. While words for 'to read' in many European languages have origins in 'to gather' – and our own *Ulysses*es continue to shift and sway in response to what we gather within and without its printed pages – the English word 'to read' shares the Proto-Germanic source *redan* with the German *raten*: 'to advise', or 'to guess'. Though now an obsolete usage, 'to read' meaning 'to guess, make out, or tell by conjecture' has Old English roots. Guessing is a creative act, informed by and responding to evidence, yet transitory and subjective; 'best guesses' assume authority in the absence of definites, and several can coexist – just as Joyce studies affirms there can be no one correct reading of *Ulysses*. A 'lucky guess' is deemed successful, and connotes (often suspect) coincidence – an important part of reading Joyce for multiple critics and anyone who has ever found something revelatory in the text by accident. Our moments of unstable clarity created while reading *Ulysses* are informed guesses, useful because they are temporary, responding to the way the novel re-enacts itself as text: woven, intertextual, difficult or unreadable, for disentangling not deciphering, demanding 'play, activity, production, practice' ('Text', 162). A freedom of authorless reading and a god-like genius author coexist in the text we create while reading *Ulysses*, and through this fecundly changeable text we derive authority.

Notes

1. In my defence, milk can behave like the cream described in 'Calypso' – when added into tea.
2. The river Lethe is mentioned just once, in 'Oxen of the Sun' (14.1114).
3. Austin Briggs details critical readings of breakfast on 17 June in 'Breakfast at 7 Eccles Street: *Oufs Sacher-Masoch*?', in the proceedings of the Eighteenth Symposium, *Joyce in Trieste: An Album of Risky Readings*, ed. Sebastian D. G. Knowles, Geert Lernout, and John McCourt (Gainesville: University Press of Florida, 2007), 195–209.
4. 'the quaker librarian purred' in 'Scylla and Charybdis', '*The drum turns purring in low hesitation waltz*' in 'Circe', and the lawnmowers of Siamese twin Oxford dons Philip Drunk and Philip Sober in the same episode '*purring with a rigadoon of grasshalms*' (9.1, 15.4017, 15.2537).
5. According to Petr Skrabanek, the Liffey is 'described by Joyce as having the colour of tea without milk, "Tea" in slang means both "whiskey" and "urine". *Le thé*

in French is "tea". But the Lethe is also the river of forgetting, the river of death.' Skrabanek, '*Finnegans Wake* – Night Joyce of a Thousand Tiers', in *The Artist and the Labyrinth*, ed. Augustine Martin (London: Ryan, 1990), 229–40 (232). On that note: 'When I makes tea I makes tea, as old mother Grogan said. And when I makes water I makes water [. . .] *So I do, Mrs Cahill*, says she. *Begob, ma'am*, says Mrs Cahill, *God send you don't make them in the one pot*' (1.357–62).

6. We could even argue for an alternative reading, that it is Molly's mind that tinges this sentence – Molly who 'poured more tea into her cup, watching it flow sideways' (4.359). It could be Molly who observes the spirals curdling through her tea, pondering both her husband's description of reincarnation and her imminent first act of adultery. Such a reading would be a radical departure from the standard interpretation that Molly's interior world is kept from the reader until 'Penelope', and could be refuted by the use of 'her' in the context of the surrounding text – such as the words that follow, 'Better remind her of the word: metempsychosis', which are surely Bloom's.
7. In the BBC's 1988 documentary 'James Joyce's *Ulysses*', in the first episode of the series 'The Modern World: Ten Great Writers', several sections of *Ulysses* are dramatised. One such is Bloom's and Molly's conversation in 'Calypso', including a zoomed-in shot of white cream, poured slowly via the back of a spoon, spiralling into Molly's dark tea as Bloom explains reincarnation. In an otherwise fairly straightforward dramatisation of the scene, the swirling cream stands out visually – as does the immediately preceding illustration from Paul de Kock's book *Ruby*. Molly's sexuality and the meaning of metempsychosis – Bloom's thoughts – are visually layered over the image of the tea. Nigel Wattis, dir. (*BBC*, 10 January 1988).
8. Leo Bersani, 'Against *Ulysses*', in *James Joyce's 'Ulysses': A Casebook*, ed. Derek Attridge (Oxford: Oxford University Press, 2004), 201–29 (205). Further references to this edition are given after quotations in the text. A similar point is made by Hugh Kenner in *'Ulysses'*, the results of 'Joyce's aesthetics of delay' (London: George Allen and Unwin, 1980), 81. Further references to this edition are given after quotations in the text, too.
9. Stella Gibbons, *Cold Comfort Farm* (Harmondsworth: Penguin, 1949), 82.
10. Tom Stoppard, *Arcadia* (London: Faber, 1993), 47.
11. Nancy K. Miller uses the term 'overreading' very differently in her essay 'Arachnologies: The Woman, The Text, and The Critic'. Miller's concept opposes Barthes's authorless reading; she defines 'The goal of overreading, of reading for the signature' in her reading of Arachne as 'to put one's finger – figuratively – on the place of production that marks the spinner's attachment to her web'. I am here using the term 'overreading' without Miller's connotations of reaching for the writing subject, but rather as an exaggeration of the reader's role. In *The Poetics of Gender*, ed. Miller (New York: Columbia University Press, 1986), 270–95 (288).
12. Bersani stretches the word 'simply' when noting that 'The exegetical work to be done is enormous, but in a sense it has already been done by the author, and we simply have to catch up with him' (225), but then so does Barthes in claiming we are 'simply' holding together all traces of a text.
13. Clive Hart, 'Wandering Rocks', in Hart and David Hayman, eds, *James Joyce's 'Ulysses': Critical Essays* (Berkeley: University of California Press, 1974), 181–216 (193).

14. Hart attempts to find reasons for each of the interpolations, recording his findings in a table at the end of his chapter on the episode. The reasons given for three interpolations are listed, wonderfully, as just '?'. Hart, 'Wandering Rocks', 207, 212, and 214.
15. *Ulysses: The 1922 text*, ed. Jeri Johnson (Oxford: Oxford University Press, 2008), 866.
16. And what of the differences? Father Conmee steps 'onto', then 'into', while Farrell's dangling belongings only gain the determiner 'his' when mentioned a second time.
17. Karen Lawrence, *The Odyssey of Style in 'Ulysses'* (Princeton, NJ: Princeton University Press, 1981), 84–5.
18. Hugh Kenner, *Joyce's Voices* (Berkeley, Los Angeles, and London: University of California Press, 1978), 27. Kenner notes also the later repetition of 'bedded' and the description of a 'disrobed' bottle at the end of that day; I would add the 'soured adulterated milk' Bloom also finds at home.
19. Johnson, ed., *Ulysses: The 1922 text*, 866.
20. Hart, 'Wandering Rocks', 186.
21. Johnson, ed., *Ulysses: The 1922 text*, 866.
22. Lawrence, *The Odyssey of Style in 'Ulysses'*, 83.
23. Parallactically, this story is told again in 'Oxen of the Sun': 'And in your ear, my friend, you will not think who met us as we left the field. Conmee himself!' (14.1153–4).
24. Furthermore, where significance is not immediately apparent we usually presume that what is included in the narrative will be important at a later point in the text.
25. Kenner, *Joyce's Voices*, 91 and 117–18; and '*Ulysses*', 101–3.
26. Margot Norris, *Virgin and Veteran Readings of 'Ulysses'* (New York: Palgrave Macmillan, 2011), 4.
27. Leonard Diepeveen, *The Difficulties of Modernism* (New York and London: Routledge, 2003), x.
28. Kenner, *Flaubert, Joyce and Beckett: The Stoic Comedians* (London: Dalkey Archive Press and Normal, 2005), 32.
29. Kenner, *The Stoic Comedians*, 34.
30. The consonance between Molly, Penelope, and text extends to include the relationship between the text'ness' of *Ulysses* and its difficulty if we note a modern scholarly approach to Penelope. As described by Tim Whitmarsh, this involves seeing Penelope as 'an embodiment of the Odyssean virtue of self-concealment, as inscrutable to us as she is to Odysseus'. 'Introduction', in Samuel Butler, *The Authoress of the 'Odyssey'* (Bristol: Bristol Phoenix Press, 2003), vii–xxv (xxi).
31. 'Mr Bloom's dental windows' (10.1115) solved by Kenner ('*Ulysses*', 65).
32. The boundaries between characters' minds dissolve for the sake of the 'Rose of Castile / rows of cast steel' joke, told first by Lenehan in 'Aeolus' and then referenced by Bloom in 'Circe' (7.588–91, 15.740) – in the interim, however, Michael William Balfe's 1857 opera of that name is frequently on Bloom's mind in 'Sirens'.
33. Mark A. Wollaeger, 'Stephen/Joyce, Joyce/Haacke: Modernism and the Social Function of Art', *ELH*, vol. 62, no. 3 (Fall, 1995), 691–707 (691).
34. Jacques Derrida, 'Ulysses Gramophone', trans. François Raffoul, in *Derrida and Joyce: Texts and Contexts*, ed. Andrew J. Mitchell and Sam Slote (Albany: State University of New York Press, 2013), 41–86 (59).

35. Frank Budgen, *James Joyce and The Making of 'Ulysses'* (Bloomington: Indiana University Press, 1961), 48. In perpetuating the myth of Joyce spending one day writing the aforementioned 'Perfume of embraces' etc., Budgen does much to mythologise the skills of Joyce – but more on this in the following chapter.
36. John Banville, 'Survivors of Joyce', in *James Joyce: The Artist and the Labyrinth*, ed. Augustine Martin (London: Ryan, 1990), 73–81 (74 and 80).
37. Quoted in David Mehegan, 'For this writer, identity is subject to change', *Boston Globe*, 27 February 2008 <http://archive.boston.com/ae/books/articles/2008/02/27/for_this_writer_identity_is_subject_to_change/?page=2> [accessed 16 June 2021].
38. Banville, 75–7.
39. Banville, 80.
40. Kenner explores 'our sense of the book's integrity' explicitly in *The Stoic Comedians* (see 60), but more generally in much of his work on Joyce. A further note: my use of 'biblical' here refers to only certain textual approaches to the Bible.
41. Lawrence, *The Odyssey of Style in 'Ulysses'*, 7–8.
42. Jonathan Goldman, 'Afterlife', in *The Cambridge Companion to 'Ulysses'*, ed. Sean Latham (New York: Cambridge University Press, 2014), 33–48 (35).
43. Derrida, 'Ulysses Gramophone', 43.
44. A similarity between Derrida and Kenner, who notes that '*Ulysses* welcomes coincidence' (Kenner, '*Ulysses*', 156).
45. Derrida, 'Ulysses Gramophone', 60.
46. Derrida, 'Ulysses Gramophone', 61.
47. Derek Attridge, 'Signature/Countersignature: Derrida's Response to *Ulysses*', in *Derrida and Joyce*, 265–80 (277).
48. I am referring again to Gerard Genette's notion of 'metalepsis' in *Narrative Discourse: An Essay in Method*, trans. Jane E. Lewin (Ithaca, NY: Cornell University Press, 1980), 236.
49. Jean-Michel Rabaté, *James Joyce, Authorized Reader* (Baltimore, MD: Johns Hopkins University Press, 1991), 153.
50. Scarlett Baron, '*Strandentwining Cable': Joyce, Flaubert, and Intertextuality* (Oxford: Oxford University Press, 2012), 15. Baron's reference is to Joyce, *Finnegans Wake* notebook, VI.B.8, 42.
51. Barthes defines the text – which as I have explored above *Ulysses* so embodies – as working against 'the myth of filiation'. The text 'reads without the inscription of the Father' ('Text', 160–1).
52. Baron, 280.
53. Michael Patrick Gillespie, *Reading the Book of Himself: Narrative Strategies in the Works of James Joyce* (Columbus: Ohio State University Press, 1989), 98.
54. Baron, 92.
55. Gillespie, *Reading the Book of Himself*, 6.
56. Rabaté, 151 and 191.
57. Rabaté, 152.
58. Laurent Milesi, 'Introduction: Language(s) with a Difference', in *James Joyce and the Difference of Language*, ed. Milesi (Cambridge: Cambridge University Press, 2003), 1–27 (10); Umberto Eco, 'Joyce, Semiosis and Semiotics' in *The Languages*

of Joyce: Selected Papers from the 11th International James Joyce Symposium, Venice, 12–18 June 1988, ed. Rosa Maria Bollettieri Bosinelli, Carla Marengo, and Christine Van Boheemen (Philadephia: John Benjamins, 1992), 19–38 (35).
59. Susan Sontag, 'Writing Itself: On Roland Barthes', in *A Barthes Reader*, ed. Sontag (London: Vintage, 2000), vii–xxxviii (xi).
60. Michael Moriarty, *Roland Barthes* (Cambridge: Polity, 1991), 3.
61. Adrian Wilson, 'Foucault on the "question of the author": A Critical Exegesis', *The Modern Language Review*, vol. 99, no. 2 (April, 2004) 339–63 (342).
62. Seán Burke, *The Death and Return of the Author: Criticism and Subjectivity in Barthes, Foucault and Derrida*, 3rd edn (Edinburgh: Edinburgh University Press, 2008), see 171–2.
63. Erwin R. Steinberg and Christian W. Hallstein, 'Probing Silences in Joyce's *Ulysses* and the Question of Authorial Intention', *James Joyce Quarterly*, vol. 40, no. 3 (Spring, 2003), 543–54 (549).
64. This is not the same as Alexander Nehamas's postulated author, the notion that 'No reading can fail to generate an author.' Nehamas differentiates between the text-manifesting-author and real-life-writer; as I will discuss in Chapter 6, this distinction does not work. (See Nehamas, 'What an Author Is', *The Journal of Philosophy*, vol. 83, no. 11, Eighty-Third Annual Meeting American Philosophical Association, Eastern Division (November, 1986), 685–91 (690), and 'The Postulated Author: Critical Monism as a Regulative Ideal', *Critical Inquiry*, vol. 8, no. 1 (Autumn, 1981), 133–49).
65. R. G. Collingwood, *The Idea of History* (Oxford: Oxford University Press, 1961), 234–5. Though first published in 1946, this was written in the 1930s. Further references to this edition are given after quotations in the text.
66. The etymologies here and at the end of this chapter are taken from John Ayto, *Word Origins: The Hidden Histories of English Words from A to Z*, 2nd edn (London: A&C Black, 2005), first published in 1990; T. F. Hoad, ed., *The Concise Dictionary of English Etymology* (Oxford: Oxford University Press, 1986); Walter W. Skeat, *The Concise Dictionary of English Etymology* (Ware: Wordsworth, 2007); the online version of *An Anglo-Saxon Dictionary*, ed. Joseph Bosworth and T. Northcote Toller <https://bosworthtoller.com/>; and the *OED Online* (Oxford University Press, July 2021) <www.oed.com> [both accessed 29 July 2021].
67. S. H. Butcher and A. Lang, *The Odyssey of Homer: Done into English Prose* (London: Macmillan, 1924), 78.
68. And the spiral, remember, is according to Moriarty an important form in Barthes's writing (Moriarty, 102).
69. Goldman, 40.

6

'THE JAMES JOYCE I KNEW': LEGACIES AND *TRAVESTIES*

> I never knew you could write so well. It must be due to your association with me.
>
> *Joyce to Frank Budgen*[1]

Writing in 1841, Thomas Carlyle reads the works of Shakespeare as 'so many windows, through which we see a glimpse of the world that was in him'.[2] In his Homeric scholar role of 1897, Samuel Butler declares that 'art is only interesting in so far as it reveals an artist'.[3] And in response to Hugh Kenner's reading of *Ulysses* 'not as the expression of Joyce himself but of a *persona*', in 1961 S. L. Goldberg sighs: 'It sounds – one must say – remarkably boring.'[4] Though written seventy years ago, Goldberg's view is not out of date in Joyce studies. Joyce's life and work are both of interest to critics, and often treated together: it's not unusual for Joyce critics today to make efforts to prove the author's interest in a particular topic through reference to his life – or records thereof. Thematic studies – such as recent work on Joyce and betrayal or exile – frequently attempt to underpin an interpretation of a given theme's importance to Joyce's texts with alleged evidence of that theme's importance to Joyce's life.[5] This positioning is often now carefully framed and self-aware: critics might acknowledge the limits of reading the work via the life, while arguing the life is of interpretive value. Some refuse the implication that they are in fact reading Joyce's texts in order to reach the author, or that they are conflating Stephen and Joyce.⁶ The way in which one reads the ambiguously autobiographical elements of Joyce's texts can enhance or lessen the romantic link between an author's life or personality and their works, but Stephen is not the only reason Joyceans study the author's life.

For this is, of course, not a Joycean-specific tendency: while autobiographical touches might encourage a critic to delve into letters and biographies, so will an author's status, as will the general fascination with the lives of authors which exists within and without literary academia to this day. Literary biographies, collected letters, memoirs from friends, and an ongoing exchange of anecdotes result from this interest, and as an author gains more fame or celebrity, the demands for biographical works increase – in turn enhancing the author's renown. These works are in no short supply in Joyce studies, a part of what Loren Glass labels 'a bombardment of gossipy memoirs'; linking literary celebrity to modernism's contradictory belief in ostensibly impersonal authors who yet became wildly famous.⁷ Joyce studies is as full of gossip about Joyce as *Ulysses* is of gossip about Dubliners. Among many 'gossipy memoirs' and biographical texts are Frank Budgen's Joyce-assisted 1934 work *James Joyce and the Making of 'Ulysses'*; the authorised and authorially controlled 1939 biography by Herman Gorman; Stanislaus Joyce's 1957 *My Brother's Keeper*; Richard Ellmann's 1959 biography *James Joyce*, and its new edition in 1982; Arthur Power's 1974 recollections *Conversations with James Joyce*; Stan Gébler Davies's *James Joyce: A Portrait of the Artist* of the following year; Alessandro Francini Bruni's 'Joyce Stripped Naked in the Piazza', a 1922 lecture published in the *James Joyce Quarterly* in 1977; Edna O'Brien's short 1999 biography, *James Joyce*; John McCourt's 2000 text *The Years of Bloom: James Joyce in Trieste 1904–1920*; Gordon Bowker's *James Joyce: A Biography* of 2011; and Edna O'Brien's 2020 *James and Nora: A Portrait of a Marriage*. The texts by Budgen, Ellmann, and Power arguably have canonical status in Joyce studies, and their effect in the field goes beyond the transmission of biographical information. In this chapter I will read this canon of three written Joyces, alongside and through one more (definitely non-canonical): the Joyce of Tom Stoppard's play *Travesties*.

Stoppard's Joyce debuted in 1974, the same year as Power's. He shares a stage with several fictional and historical characters in a play which, in my reading here, opens up connections between works of literary biography, their critical uses, and *Ulysses* itself. The fictionalisation of historical figures, including of authors, has been the subject of extensive criticism. It is one of several far-reaching areas of criticism which the discussions of this chapter could encounter – along with criticism of (auto)biography, (auto)biographical fiction, the *Künstlerroman* and 'the artist as hero' genre more generally, biographical literary criticism, and theoretical approaches to the use of biography in criticism. While I have looked a little at the last in Chapter 1, and touch on the other areas here and elsewhere, they must lie predominantly outside the scope of this present chapter. This chapter functions as a preamble to my conclusion, a response to the rest of *The Reader's Joyce* – and I therefore do not want to draw in too many new elements, but rather bring together and play with my earlier explorations and conclusions. What I present here is eventually a comparative reading of *Travesties* and *Ulysses*; it is also a reading of yet another area of Joyce studies, but one under the influence of Chapter 5's conclusions and this book's interest in literature as criticism. What I aim for is an irreverent reading of how Joyce's life has been read and written, rather than a comprehensive analysis of how biographical criticism intersects Joyce studies. Many earlier questions will recur in this chapter – including the question of the life and the work, of Roland Barthes's view of a culture strictly centred around the author. I am exploring the texts used in Joyce studies in that 'powerful mode [. . .] of endowing a reading with authority' Michael Moriarty describes, where we 'explain it by reference to the author's life' and thus uphold 'the notion of an authoritative reading against which other readings could be judged for deviance' – the mode Barthes railed against.[8] In what follows I argue that (when read with a little productive impertinence) the texts which facilitate a Joycean critical interest in and use of the author's life raise questions of truth, authenticity, useful fictions, genius, and authority.

Budgen's *The Making of 'Ulysses'*, Ellmann's *James Joyce*, and Power's *Conversations with James Joyce* have been among the most cited works of biography in Joyce studies (though only Ellmann's is, strictly, a biography), but it is not only for this reason that I will discuss them here. Joyce's involvement in the writing of Budgen's text adds a nice extra element to the Joyce the text promotes, while the status of Ellmann's biography (described by Davies as having, 'to my taste, too much of the monument about it')[9] suggests the Joyce Ellmann presents is particularly fit for purpose. Both texts do much to enhance the perceived exceptionalism of Joyce-the-man, as befits Joyce-the-author. They also laid the ground for Power's memoir, the form of which begs close attention. The long, detailed, and didactic speeches Power cites as Joyce's – presented as recollected truth – benefit juxtaposition with *Travesties* and its games of memory, history, and literary fame. By looking at the personality of Joyce crafted by each of these three works of anecdote, biography, and memoir, I can continue my ongoing discussion of how the way we read an author affects how we read a text, and vice versa. This picks up several threads from my chapters on Homeric ideated authorship, Joycean criticism, and authority, as I note how these three texts are used by critics. In writing the 'real' Joyce these biographical works conversely contribute to a mythic Joyce – the out-of-reach genius discussed in my previous chapter – an effect that doubles when anecdotes are then also cited by critics. An intertextual narrative of Joyce exists beyond, yet influenced by, his semi-autobiographical novels: it is collaboratively written by biographers, memoirists, and critics. *Travesties*, to which I turn to at length as a primary text of this chapter, plays with and laughs at this mythic Joyce, and at many of the questions raised by my discussions here and elsewhere in *The Reader's Joyce*; it also aids my emphasis on how authors are constructed. Budgen, Ellmann, Power, and Stoppard present written Joyces, and the way in which we read these Joyces has a variety of implications. The unstable, ludic Joyce of *Travesties* holds my attention, drawing this chapter back through Joyce studies and *Ulysses*.

'James Joyce was an artist. He has said so himself': Biographies and Anecdotes[10]

Clive Hart describes Budgen's *The Making of 'Ulysses'* as a 'partly fictionalised biography', not intended to be 'everywhere literally true': 'memory being fallible and fragmented, [Budgen] deliberately fictionalised to approach truth indirectly'. *The Making of 'Ulysses'* was written with Joyce's help; he gave Budgen letters and notesheets from which Budgen formed several of 'the remembered conversations' which populate the text and a multitude of Joycean critical works, and helped him to write some small sections of textual discussion.[11] Its indirect truth works for Hugh Kenner: in his 1960 introduction to a new edition of *The Making of 'Ulysses'* he argues that Budgen 'gives us the only coherent image we possess of any portion of Joyce's life', before clarifying: 'the only one, that is, in which the man we are shown seems compatible with the major fact, the facts [sic] that justifies our interest in him: the fact that he was a very great writer'.[12] Budgen's text 'took', as Kenner notes in *'Ulysses'*, 'a long time to have much effect', perhaps for the reasons Kenner gives in a 1987 preface to his 1956 study *Dublin's Joyce*: 'Budgen? He was "anecdotal" and "too close to his subject." One got warned against overreliance on a book like that. (But how manifest his enthusiasm! And how alive his Joyce was!).'[13] Kenner played a significant role in bringing Budgen into the critical tradition, embracing and developing his text's emphasis on 'the centrality of Bloom' and clearly taking no notice of New Critical objections to a text so involved with its subject.[14]

The Making of 'Ulysses' is a memoir, semi-fictionalised biography, and web of anecdotes mixing memories and constructed conversations to present the reader with commentaries on individual episodes and the novel as a whole, Joyce's thoughts on writing, Budgen's own thoughts on art, and recollections of Zurich. Within its narrative are some of the most-quoted Joyceisms – '"I want [. . .] to give a picture of Dublin so complete that if the city one day suddenly disappeared from the earth it could be reconstructed out of my book"', '"But I want the reader to understand always through suggestion rather than direct statement"', Odysseus as the '"complete man in literature"'– and detailed descriptions of Joyce's relationship to *Ulysses*, writing, and language (Budgen, 67–8, 21, and 15–17). In his 1972 introduction to the text Hart describes it as 'matching biography to criticism in a way that not only allows each to illuminate the other but shows their fundamental interdependence' (another example of mainstream critical attitudes in the Joycean early 1970s).[15] This 'matching' results in a picture of Joyce that is pointedly human yet mystical, emphasising the extraordinariness of the 'very great writer'.

Budgen, an artist himself, shows a particular interest in Joyce's relationship with words: with the artist's relationship to their material. He details Joyce's enjoyment of the German word 'Leib', for example, describing how Joyce 'spoke of the plastic monosyllable as a sculptor speaks about a stone' (13). He later gives an evocative outline of Joyce's understanding of language, of words:

> They are quick with human history as pitchblende with radium, or coal with heat and flame. They have a will and a life of their own and are not to be put like lead soldiers, but to be energised and persuaded like soldiers of flesh and blood. The commerce of life new mints them every day and gives them new values in the exchanges, and Joyce is ever listening for living speech from any human lips. (175)

To Joyce, Budgen summarises, words are 'mysterious means of expression as well as an instrument of communication' (175). While in part Mallarméan, with notes of 'the poet-speaker who yields the initiative to words' moving like 'a trail of fire over precious stones',[16] this approach to language also however emphasises a human historicism embedded within each word: mysterious yet communicative. A tension between otherly strangeness and prosaic humanity runs through much of Budgen's account of Joyce. His Joyce advocates the primacy of the very human Bloom over the technical or Homeric, and as a result Budgen's reading of, for example, 'Wandering Rocks', is refreshingly down to earth: it is teatime in Dublin, and at teatime everyone moves around (123). Yet Budgen argues that

> Some human mood must invest the work of every poet, for every poet is himself a human being. Joyce is a keen-sensed stranger, a delicate recording instrument, an artificer as ingenious, patient and daring as the hawklike man whom Stephen invokes at the end of *A Portrait of the Artist*. (71)

Human – yet delicate instrument, mythical artificer; Joyce and his relationship to his work extend beyond the typical.

Despite attempting to perhaps salve the excesses of Stuart Gilbert's emphasis on the symbolic aspects of *Ulysses*, Budgen imbues the text and its author with yet more of the unusual. Marvelling at Joyce's enjoyment in and knowledge of his own work, he remarks: 'Joyce composes with infinite pains, but he looks on his handiwork when he has done it and finds it good' (48). As I discussed in the last chapter, this jokey deifying quirk is most obviously repeated by Kenner – while the view of Joyce as exceptional is widely declared and implied. Budgen's accounts of Joyce's memory, of his knowledge of his own work – that unlike 'Most human memories' Joyce's does not 'begin to fail at midnight' (176) – establish Joyce's exceptionalism, as do moments where descriptions of the artist's relationship to their materials give way to exalting portraiture. Budgen's Joyce does not only hold huge swathes of his work in his mind after writing, able to recall any phrase of the mammoth *Ulysses*; he also does so before the text forms on the page: 'The words he wrote were far advanced in his mind before they took shape on paper [. . .] He was always looking and listening for the necessary fact or word; and he was a great believer in his luck. What he needed would come to him' (171). The uncanniness of Joyce's compositional methods, veiled in part as 'luck', grows with Budgen's observation that 'Something in Joyce's head suggests to me an alchemist' (12).

Combining an epic mind with an ancient, rare, unbelievable, transformative skill, Budgen's Joyce has fate on his side and can rely on luck. Thus, another set of incompatibles arises: this lucky writer is yet also a fervently toiling perfectionist, working hard to finish just two peerless sentences. Budgen's most famous story, of Joyce 'seeking [. . .] the perfect order of words' (20), refers to 'Perfume of embraces all him assailed. With hungered flesh obscurely, he mutely craved to adore' (8.638–9). As Kenner details in his introduction to *'Ulysses'*, this is a little piece of fiction: Joyce – Kenner finds in the Rosenbach manuscript – came up with another version of these sentences that he deemed good enough.[17] Budgen's synecdochal anecdote for the care with which Joyce composed *Ulysses* sustains the impression of an obsessive hard-worker, a realism at odds somewhat with an author who also 'ascrib[es] to the words he writes a singular force of prophecy' – a comment on Joyce's 'superstition': Budgen tells stories about the 'originals' of three characters from Joyce's texts, who met unfortunate ends in real life after publication, linking these to Joyce's belief in his own power of foresight (193). Budgen then moves swiftly on, without saying more on the divining potential of Joyce's written words. This is the anecdotal equivalent of a Joyce 'in advance': these coincidences gain significance as they are grouped together and repeated – and as they are deemed revelatory by Joyce.

Described by Kenner as a 'mentor' and 'the ideal reader for whom Joyce was writing',[18] Budgen's value in Joyce studies lies beyond the contributions of anecdotes – though it is for these that his study is perhaps most often referenced. His text has had a critical influence, confirming with Kenner's help the central role that Bloom occupies in *Ulysses*. In this, *The Making of 'Ulysses'* has enjoyed the same success as Gilbert's *James Joyce's 'Ulysses'*: Joyce has got his message into the critical tradition, even if via a complicated and delayed route. What Budgen's study has also achieved is the continuous presence in

Joyce criticism of biographical details and stories that are repeated to the point of a mythology. Joyce's opinions of his work are anecdotally given as reported speech and critically received, and continue to reach all readers of *Ulysses*. Many of these comments also appear in Richard Ellmann's 1959 biography *James Joyce*.

First published not long after the 1957 publication of Joyce's selected letters, Ellmann's biography collates information from published and unpublished letters, the personal memories of various people, notes, and documents to form a detailed, epic compendium of biographical insight. It creates an enduring impression of Joyce's mind, portraying an extraordinary character from youth to adulthood. Joyce's letters home from school, his lists of things needed, 'sounded like grocer's lists': an observation linked both to Joyce's comment in a letter to Budgen that he has '"a grocer's assistant's mind"', and to his father's summation that '"If that fellow was dropped in the middle of the Sahara, he'd sit, be God, and make a map of it."'[19] The young Joyce described his age as '"half past six"', and performed a charade of 'sunset' by sitting 'in a rounded chair with just the top of his head showing over its top' (27 and 53).[20] In 1902, Ellmann tells us, George Russell describes Joyce the young man to W. B. Yeats as 'The first spectre of the new generation [. . .] I have suffered from him and I would like you to suffer' (100).[21] Ellmann's remarkable, difficult, youthful Joyce parades the traits of a writing genius, a perfect fit even as a child for what we expect of one who could author *Ulysses* and *Finnegans Wake*. His fully grown, published, reflective Joyce – post-*Wake* – claims that the purpose of that work is just '"to make you laugh"' (703).[22] Yet, famously, this Joyce also wants two things: that his reader '"should devote his whole life to reading my works"', and '"to keep the critics busy for three hundred years"' (703).[23]

Ellmann's Joyce is pleasingly compatible with what we want our writers of remarkable novels to be, fulfilling a desire created by the texts themselves for their author to be extraordinary. He is also an older version of an un-ironic Stephen Dedalus, and the existence of this other written-Joyce results in some confusion. Ellmann tells us of Joyce's first day at the school Clongowes: 'his father reminded him that John O'Connell, his great-grandfather, had presented an address to the Liberator at Clongowes fifty years before' (27–8). Ellmann's cited source for this story is *Portrait*. In the passages that follow, though Ellmann details the odd discrepancy, he continues to describe Joyce's early life with reference to *Portrait*. At one point, John Joyce's words are from the novel, and at the opening of Ellmann's fourth chapter we are told about Joyce at Belvedere: 'As he said in *Portrait*, his soul threw off the cerements that covered it and spurned the grave of boyhood' (33 and 42). This works in reverse too, as Ellmann draws direct lines from life to work, suggesting that Nora Barnacle's 1908 miscarriage 'helped to make Bloom's chief sorrow, in *Ulysses*, the death just after birth of his son Rudy' (268–9). Ellmann is a reader of both Joyce's life and work, and in *James Joyce* we find analysis of Joyce's early and fragmentary or late and fully realised writings. As I have explored, several critics (early and recent) use *Portrait* to infer Joyce's aesthetic views. This is followed through to its logical conclusion in Ellmann's use of the novel as an illustration of the author's early life. His use emphasises a close relationship between life and autobiographically informed fiction – close, and perhaps simple too. Ellmann's other efforts to separate Stephen and Joyce are undermined, as his reading of their school days leaves little room for complexity, parody, or irony. The (pseudo- or semi-) autobiographical elements of Joyce's fiction are of course part of the reason a biography was such an important milestone in Joycean criticism. Ellmann's *James Joyce* is, after all, the only scholarly work to have its own standardised abbreviation in the *James Joyce Quarterly*, used also by most critical texts in Joyce studies. Reading Stephen as an un-ironic Joyce makes a literary critical statement. Ellmann's combination of biography and criticism in *James Joyce* contributes to an enduring presence of biographical criticism in Joyce studies, which has survived shifts away from or debates over such modes.

Budgen's *The Making of 'Ulysses'* includes a particularly careful reading of self-portraiture – one which does not seem to have got into the critical tradition despite the ongoing need to evaluate the relevance of the biographical in Joyce studies. As I touched upon in Chapter 2, across *The Making of 'Ulysses'* Budgen reports Joyce's comments about Stephen. Observing that '"I haven't let this young man off very lightly, have I? Many writers have written about themselves. I wonder if any one of them has been as candid as I have?"', Budgen's Joyce describes a high level of honesty in his portrayal of Stephen (51). This is then carefully, if subtly, undermined: '"Some people who read my book, *A Portrait of the Artist* forget that it is called *A Portrait of the Artist as a Young Man*."' Joyce stresses the last four words, leading Budgen to attempt an interpretation. Perhaps the emphasis means that Joyce is now older, changed; or that there is a great stretch of time through which he looked back to write; or both (60–1). Not knowing how better to interpret Joyce's words, Budgen then develops his own reading of self-portraiture – of the implied distance between Joyce and Stephen. To paint a self-portrait, he argues, one 'is fatally bound to paint himself painting himself [. . .] something of objective truth gets lost in the process'. Furthermore, the artist 'is not only painting himself painting himself; he is also painting himself posing to himself'. Pulling apart differences, Budgen suggests that 'All the psychological inducements to fictify his portrait are present in greater measure for the writer than for the painter.' The writer's 'medium is not an active sense, but memory, and who knows when memory ceases to be memory and becomes imagination?' (61–3). Budgen's reading of the act of self-portraiture suggests a fundamental distance between the writing and written self: unless one were able to resist fiction, and be very self-aware. He uses these ideas to compare the 'portrait' Stephen to the 'all-round' Bloom, but we can also find here some sort of accidental self-reflexive acknowledgement that the point where memory shifts to imagination is a crucial issue of the genre in which Budgen himself writes: memoir.

'MY MEMORIES, IS IT, THEN? LIFE AND TIMES, FRIEND OF THE FAMOUS. MEMORIES OF JAMES JOYCE. JAMES JOYCE AS I KNEW HIM. THE JAMES JOYCE I KNEW': ARTHUR POWER AND TOM STOPPARD[24]

In 1974 Arthur Power's *Conversations with James Joyce* was published as a book-length memoir, and Tom Stoppard's play *Travesties* premiered at the Aldwych theatre in London.[25] Power's memoir is a detailed account of conversations had with Joyce in Paris in the 1920s, while Stoppard's play presents Henry Carr's memories of Joyce (among others) in Zurich in 1917. Power opens *Conversations* with an admission:

> In these conversations I have tried to reconstruct some of the talks I had with Joyce at different times from notes taken when I returned home after spending an evening with him.
>
> I realise how inadequate much of it is, for much that was said has been forgotten or is inadequately expressed, while to give an impression of a man of such talent one would have to have talent equal to his own, as deep a consciousness of the social and psychological changes of his time as he had, and the same almost agonized gift for expressing it.[26]

Power's Joyce is openly reconstructed, yet still his extended speeches – despite Power's defence of rushing home to take notes – request a significant amount of faith from the reader. Though Power confesses that 'I was very talkative, while Joyce was naturally silent' (9), his Joyce gives his opinions in long, detailed, pages-long monologues stretching the anecdotal 'he said' to its limits and beyond. This Joyce spouts his thoughts on what an author must do, on the difference between classical and modern literature, on Irish genius. He describes how he is approaching 'Work in Progress', contrasting emotional, creative, unpredictable writing and intellectual, fact-based, planned writing (the full passage runs over a page):

> The more we are tied to fact and try to give a correct impression, the further we are from what is significant. In writing one must create an endlessly changing surface, dictated by the mood and current impulse in contrast to the fixed mood of the classical style [. . .] A book, in my opinion, should not be planned out beforehand, but as one writes it will form itself, subject, as I say, to the constant emotional promptings of one's personality. (95)

As one might expect, Power's Joyce's lengthy opinions often concern his own writing or the reception of his work:

> Then in your opinion, I said, the critics and the intellectuals have boggled the issue, have not seen your intention clearly, and have put meanings into it which did not exist, which they have invented for themselves.
> Yes and no, replied Joyce, shrugging his shoulders evasively, for who knows but it is they who are right. What do we know about what we put into anything? Though people may read more into *Ulysses* than I ever intended, who is to say that they are wrong: do any of us know what we are creating? Did Shakespeare know what he was creating when he wrote *Hamlet*; or Leonardo when he painted 'The Last Supper'? After all, the original genius of a man lies in his scribblings: in his casual actions lies his basic talent. Later he may develop that talent until he produces a *Hamlet* or a 'Last Supper,' but if the minute scribblings which compose the big work are not significant, the big work goes for nothing no matter how grandly conceived. Which of us can control our scribblings? (89)

When quoted at length (though neither of the above passages are even in full), the disparity between the form of Power's memoir and his admission of attempted reconstruction is particularly apparent: following the conceit of perfect recall one finds in such texts, we are encouraged to forget that Power's Joyce's epic aesthetic theses were formed from notes taken retrospectively decades earlier. While the image of an acolyte trying to write down every word that Joyce utters tells us something of Joyce's authorial standing, it also paints a picture of Power himself.

In a detour from his subject, Power describes his disappointment at reading the diary of Madame Hastings, Amedeo Modigliani's mistress (otherwise known as Beatrice Hastings, the pen name of Emily Alice Haigh, an innovative feminist author): 'I was prepared for a revelation as I opened the leaves of her manuscript [. . .] But as I read on I was disappointed' (84). The diary was more about Hastings than about her famous lover, and leaves Power dissatisfied. This story echoes the risks of Power's own endeavour, however: that his memoir tells a reader more about its author, than its subject. Modigliani's mistress, defined by her relationship, might also prompt us to consider the cachet of fame: her diary is of interest only, apparently, for its association with Modigliani. Power is safe from the misogyny that has led Beatrice Hastings to be overlooked by some, but he is aware that his time in Paris might be of interest only for its 'revelations' concerning Joyce. He is careful not to disappoint the reader, and he has been rewarded with multiple citations and new editions.

In his 1991 essay 'Writer as Hero', Michael McKeon draws a striking image from Samuel Johnson 'of the biographer as pickpocket'. Teasing apart the implications of this 'monetary figure' in terms of James Boswell's 1791 *The Life of Johnson*, McKeon offers two possibilities. The first is that 'if Boswell aims to become a man of letters through the artistic construction of Johnson as a man of letters, the interests of the two cannot be expected to coincide always'. The second complicates this, suggesting instead that such 'conflict' might not exist:

> If the biography is about Johnson, it must also be about him who perceives Johnson [. . .] And in this respect, the reciprocity of writer and writer's author must be very close. This is perhaps only to repeat the modern truth that all biographies are in a sense also autobiographies . . .[27]

This correlates with M. H. Abrams's reading of biographical criticism, in how it aligns with the critics themselves: of romantic scholars on Milton – 'each of these portraits of Milton bears a notable likeness to the portraitist'[28] – or the narcissistic criticism of John Keble. Given the use of Power's Joyce within literary criticism, these romantic modes of criticism are relevant here. Abrams's response to Keble returns us to McKeon's first reading of the pickpocketing biographer, who variously profits from their subject: Keble's Homer is an authorial figure both Keble-esque and serving Keble's critical purposes (as I discuss in Chapter 3). The same could be true of Power's Joyce: he provides Power with a subject, with the benefits of association, and with the authority needed to pull off a biographical memoir. In turn, he serves the purposes of a generation of Joyce scholars – providing them with a fresh source of authorial quotations.

Power's Joyce is quoted by critics in much the same way as Budgen's, or as Joyce's letters; his attitude to planning quoted above, for example, is regularly cited in books on *Finnegans Wake*.[29] Critics including Michael Patrick Gillespie and Tim Conley, as I've noted, reference Power's Joyce's thoughts on intention, using his quoted words to give further credence to a notion of intentional anti-intentionalism that existed with Kenner before the publication of Power's memoir. These words are also quoted by critics seeking to authorise their own methodologies: by, for instance, Kevin Dettmar in *The Illicit Joyce of Postmodernism*, to argue he can read as much or as little postmodernism in *Ulysses* as he likes; by Jean Kimball in *Odyssey of the Psyche: Jungian Patterns in 'Ulysses'*, to defend analysing the text for Jungian secrets; and by Daniel Bristow in *Joyce and Lacan: Reading, Writing, and Psychoanalysis*, making the same defence 'as Joyce himself said'.[30] The questions that such citations raise feed into a complex web of interlinked critical issues: Power himself describes his text as 'an impression', so is Power's Joyce authentic? What does that mean? Does it matter that, unlike Budgen's text, *Conversations* was written without Joyce's help? Could we argue that the author of these long speeches constructed from old notes and memory is Power himself? And in making such an argument, and thus undermining the use of Power's Joyce by critics, wouldn't we be in turn affirming the validity of using direct authorial commentary as authority in criticism? One thing is clear: Joyceans do not seem interested. Even in Conley's sharp study of author and reader intentions and mistakes – an otherwise intensely self-reflexive piece of criticism – Power's Joyce is quoted without query.

Stoppard's *Travesties* has great fun with the authenticity of memoirs, the reliability of memory, and how proximity to 'genius' affects 'normal' people. It portrays Henry Carr's memories of Dadaist Tristan Tzara, distinctly-non-Dadaist Vladimir Lenin, and Joyce; the fictionalised recollections of Carr merge with literary and biographical texts in an account of an apparently very real encounter between Joyce and Carr, a consular employee. In a story told by both Budgen and Ellmann, after Joyce and Carr were involved in a production of *The Importance of Being Earnest* in Zurich they engaged in a legal dispute over the cost of a pair of trousers bought by Carr for his role. Carr reportedly irritated Joyce sufficiently to warrant inclusion in *Ulysses* as the Private Carr of the 'Circe' episode: 'I'll wring the neck of any fucking bastard says a word against my bleeding fucking king' being one of his better lines (15.4644–5). Stoppard doubles this abuse by portraying Carr in *Travesties* as a doddery old man who unreliably remembers and re-remembers Zurich 1917 in such a way that 'the story (like a toy train perhaps) occasionally jumps the rails and has to be restarted at the point where it goes wild', as a stage direction explains (27). In performance, abrupt changes in lighting and a loudly chiming cuckoo-clock make the sudden shifts clear and easy to comprehend, if a little startling at first.[31] These resets allow Carr to edit his recollections and acknowledge that he has gone wrong somewhere; they also emphasise the influence of several texts on his memories as they are told and retold in differing idioms. The plot of *The Importance of Being Earnest* gives structure to much of Carr's recollections; *Travesties* also lifts from Wilde's play some character names, modes of speaking, phrases, and jokes. The opening of the second act quotes from *Memories of Lenin* directly, and a whole section of the first act mimics the catechistic question and answer form of the 'Ithaca' episode of *Ulysses*. Mistaken and adopted identities extend beyond the importance of being, or not being, Tristan Tzara, as Carr gives several versions of the characters. So, as Carr is damned to fiction in *Ulysses*, Joyce is damned here: reduced variously to 'an Irish nonsense' parody of the stage Irishman, to the questioner of Tzara in the style of 'Ithaca', and to a magician – and in each incarnation trying to borrow a little money and wearing the mismatched halves of two suits (which at one point swap: 'My wardrobe got out of step in Trieste, and its reciprocal members pass each other endlessly in the night') (33 and 96).

Both as an old man remembering and a young man remembered, Carr has a gloriously patchy memory of Joyce. Carr calls Joyce Doris, Phyllis, Deidre, and Bridget, and in his guise as 'Irish nonsense' Joyce and every other character speak in limericks for a scene (49, 53, and 95). *Ulysses* also has quite an impact on Carr's memory: in the Ithacan section, for instance, Joyce carefully requests copyright-swerving biographical information in the cool yet ridiculous tones of scientific enquiry:

> Quote judiciously so as to combine maximum information with minimum liability.
> [. . .]
> Quote discriminatively from Ball's diary in such a manner as to avoid forfeiting the goodwill of his executors.
> [. . .]
> Corroborate discreetly from any contemporary diarist whose estate is not given to obsessive litigation over trivial infringements of copyright. (58–9)[32]

As Joyce works on 'Oxen of the Sun' in the library ('Deshill holles eamus [. . .] Thrice', 'And is it a chapter, inordinate in length and erratic in style, remotely connected with midwifery?') his endeavour is mocked by several characters ('what possible book could be derived from reference to Homer's *Odyssey* and the Dublin Street Directory for 1904') – including by Carr in a particularly Wildean joke (18, 97, and 44). Asked where he is from, Joyce replies: 'Dublin, don't tell me you know it?' 'Only from the guidebook', sneers Carr, 'and I gather you are in the process of revising that' (47).

Joyce is only one of several characters, and in no way directly involved in the central romance plot, but his presence provides much of the best humour of *Travesties*. While some of this is at his own expense, or at Carr's, it is at times directed at retrospective anecdotal memoirs by those who knew great artists. *Travesties* harks back to a time before Joyce's celebrity or fame was established, and Carr's recollections are openly revisionary:

> It is true I knew him well at the height of his powers, his genius in full flood in the making of *Ulysses*, before publication and fame turned him into a public monument for pilgrim cameras more often than not in a velvet smoking jacket [. . .].
> [. . .]
> To those of us who knew him, Joyce's genius was never in doubt. To be in his presence was to be aware of an amazing intellect bent on shaping itself into the permanent form of its own monument – the book the world now knows as *Ulysses*! Though at the time we were still calling it (I hope memory serves) by its original title, *Elasticated Bloomers*.

Carr goes on to describe Joyce as:

> in short, a complex personality, an enigma, a contradictory spokesperson for the truth, an obsessive litigant and yet an essentially private man who wished his total indifference to public notice to be universally recognised – in short a liar and a hypocrite, a tight-fisted, sponging, fornicating drunk not worth the paper, that's that bit done. (22–3)

Joyce's personality (even when not confused with a smoking jacketed Wilde) is unfixed in Carr's memory and in the play as a whole: it varies to serve different purposes, is influenced by Joyce's own texts, and depends greatly on the tone of the play at any given moment. It also mimics the contradictory images of and statements about Joyce we find in Joycean criticism and biography; or perhaps Joycean critical opinions mimic Henry Carr – he is not the last to read *Ulysses* as a self-conscious monument to Joyce's intellect.

Stoppard's Joyce (or Carr's) fulfils his role of recollected artist by putting forth his views on art – as does Tzara, and, with different cause, Carr himself. Amongst the mistaken identities, pastiches, and resets, there is ongoing discussion of the validity of art – lent a particular edge by the First World War context and the Zurich location: 'My dear Tristan', says Carr, 'to be an artist *at all* is like living in Switzerland during a world war. To be an artist *in Zurich, in 1917*, implies a degree of self-absorption that would have glazed over the eyes of Narcissus' (38). Carr and Tzara's arguments about art and artists cause some notable scene resets, usually where Tzara's chanting or screaming of 'dada dada dada' coincides with Carr's fury over the self-worth of artists: 'The idea of the artist as a special kind of human being is art's greatest achievement, and it's a fake!' (46–7). Towards the end of Act One, when Tzara and Joyce discuss Dadaism while Joyce conjures silk hankies and flags from his hat, Tzara reaches another pitch of hysteria:

> Your art has failed. You've turned literature into a religion and it's as dead as all the rest, it's an overripe corpse and you're cutting fancy figures at the wake. It's too late for geniuses! Now we need vandals and desecrators, simple-minded demolition men to smash centuries of baroque subtlety, to bring down the temple, and thus finally, to reconcile the shame and the necessity of being an artist! Dada! *Dada! Dada!!*
>
> (*He starts to smash whatever crockery is to hand; which done, he strikes a satisfied pose.* JOYCE *has not moved.*) (62)[33]

Joyce's response is worth quoting in its entirety:

> You are an over-excited little man, with a need for self-expression far beyond the scope of your natural gifts. This is not discreditable. Neither

does it make you an artist. An artist is the magician put among men to gratify – capriciously – their urge for immortality. The temples are built and brought down around him, continuously and contiguously, from Troy to the field of Flanders. If there is any meaning in any of it, it is in what survives as art, yes even in the celebration of tyrants, yes even in the celebration of nonentities. What now of the Trojan War if it had been passed over by the artist's touch? Dust. A forgotten expedition prompted by Greek merchants looking for new markets. A minor redistribution of broken pots. But it is we who stand enriched, by a tale of heroes, of a golden apple, a wooden horse, a face that launched a thousand ships – and above all, of Ulysses, the wanderer, the most human, the most complete of all heroes – husband, father, son, lover, farmer, soldier, pacifist, politician, inventor and adventurer ... It is a theme so overwhelming that I am almost afraid to treat it. And yet I with my Dublin Odyssey will double that immortality, yes by God *there's* a corpse that will dance for some time yet and *leave the world precisely as it finds it* – and if you hope to shame it into the grave with your fashionable magic, I would strongly advise you to try and acquire some genius and if possible some subtlety before the season is quite over. Top o' the morning, Mr. Tzara!

(*With which* JOYCE *produces a rabbit out of his hat, puts the hat on his head, and leaves, holding the rabbit.*) (62–3)[34]

There is more than a hint of Wilde in this Joyce's reference to 'the season', and a final flourish of 'Irish nonsense', yet also a view of the character Ulysses we know from Budgen's Joyce. Amongst all the silliness, parts of Joyce's speech – and of Carr's and Tzara's earlier – have the weight of seriousness about them, allowing the play to explore art's relationship with and responsibility to history, politics, and war. *Travesties* asks what art should be, what genius means, and how real-life people are presented within fictional and biographical texts, playing in its self-consciousness with the tropes of friend-of-the-author-memoir, a genre of writing which raises the same questions.

WRITTEN JOYCES

Stoppard's Joyce is formed of historical and biographical information taken primarily from Ellmann's *James Joyce* and mixed with quantities of *Ulysses*;[35] he is thus constructed in response to and from his own literary texts, and from personal anecdotes, memories, biographies, and letters. From a facetiously formal perspective, Stoppard's Joyce is constructed in the same way as Budgen's, Ellmann's, or Power's: an obscure combination of texts, facts, memory, and fiction. And Stoppard's Joyce, in this, is formally similar to *Travesties* itself – which is in turn reminiscent of *Ulysses*: fiction populated by real people, historical events, and a multitude of literary and non-literary texts. *Travesties*' relationship to *The Importance of Being Earnest* echoes *Ulysses*' with the *Odyssey*: the characters unknowingly play more than one role, the plots are layered over one another, and the later text exists in parallel with its precursor. At times in *Travesties*, as Clive James nicely points out, it even appears *The Importance of Being Earnest* is being concurrently performed off-stage: such as when Tzara leaves the stage and is heard '(*voice off*)' exchanging lines with Carr playing Algernon (63), 'so that exit becomes an entrance in a play (the *other* play)'.[36] We can see the infectious intertextuality of Joyce's texts in another self-conscious story of his life: Mary M. Talbot's and Bryan Talbot's 2012 graphic novel *Dotter of Her Father's Eyes* layers Mary Talbot's childhood (as the daughter of Joyce scholar James S. Atherton) over the life of Joyce's daughter Lucia, and borrows lines from the films *The Red Shoes* and *The Graduate* in its telling.[37]

In *Travesties*, such intertextuality and Joyce's proclamations on artistic genius and importance are – unsurprisingly – undercut. The hat from which Joyce pulls handkerchiefs, flags, and a rabbit plays an important role. Before his interrogation by Joyce, Tzara is seen composing poetry by pulling out and replacing pieces of paper in a hat (echoing an earlier scene in which Joyce locates his own notes on '*tiny scraps of paper*' in his pockets (19)). When Joyce later enters the stage with paper in his hair and on his shoulders, it becomes apparent whose hat Tzara was using. While Joyce fires Ithacan questions at Tzara he slowly replaces these pieces of paper in his hat, before conjuring out of it a white carnation made of the scraps. Joyce's conjuring parodies the 'magician' artist of his later speech, and perhaps also his own work: the white carnation is made of the scraps of another's art, of Tzara's, a collage of previous texts worked anew. The paper flower, which ends up in Tzara's buttonhole, is a small and silly version of the woven or mosaic text, of the activities of the scissors and paste men Joyce and Stoppard.

Travesties bears further comparison with *Ulysses*: both texts, for example, explore subjectivity by allowing a character's thoughts to structure the narrative. Carr's badly controlled, restarting, confused memory gives *Travesties* its structure, and, as I have variously shown in Chapters 3 and 5, the form of *Ulysses* is affected by Bloom's mental meanderings in a multitude of ways. Bloom's thoughts lead to gaps and errors in *Ulysses*, from the missing visit to Dignam's widow, to incorrectly detailed finances, to the adjusted account of his day he gives to Molly. Carr's memories form – we find out at the end of the play – an impossible situation, as Joyce and Lenin were actually in Zurich a year apart. This final exchange between Old Carr and his correcting wife Old Cecily reveals *Travesties* to be another adjusted account by husband to wife. Furthermore, by being drawn thus irresistibly back to *Ulysses* through *Travesties* we find yet more consonance between each text and the genres of literary memoir, biography, and autobiography. Exploring subjectivity is one way in which *Ulysses* and *Travesties* raise questions of reliability, of truth, of the borders between reality and fiction; questions also raised by the extended biographical anecdote of a memoirist. A memoir written by an author's acquaintance is concerned with the personality of the artist, the life and work of the artist – and the relationships between them – as is *Travesties*, and, particularly through Stephen, *Ulysses*. In order to explore the personality, life, and work of the artist, Power's *Conversations*, *Travesties*, and, to an extent, *Ulysses* create author characters. These texts write an author, and in doing so they engage in writing authorship.

The written authors that are the subject of memoir and anecdote rely on the trust with which we invest in each 'she said'; this is reinforced each time a critic references the words of Power's Joyce. To determine the authenticity of 'Joyce said' we look to the scribe of those words, to the memoirist: that Power knew Joyce appears sufficient, given we have no other way of ascertaining whether Joyce spoke thus. This doubles the effect of the preterite tense which, as I discussed in Chapter 3, Roland Barthes describes in *Writing Degree Zero*: the preterite tense, or 's/he said' function of third person narration, '*signifies* a creation' and 'is a lie made manifest, it delineates an area of plausibility which reveals the possible in the very act of unmasking it as false' (46–7). This inherent aspect of third person narration is, in a way, an act of concealment; as Barthes claims, 'Behind the preterite there always lurks a demiurge, a God, or a reciter' (46). As we turn to Power to determine the validity of his Joyce's words, remaining unable to fully unveil what combination of truth and fiction we are reading, we double Barthes's description of writing – 'Its task is to put the mask in place and at the same time point it out' – and though Barthes's analysis relates to writing in the third person 'in the novel' here we find the same effect in the reported speech of a first person memoir (48).

Masks and concealment provide yet another thread between Power's memoir and its contemporaneously published counterpart *Travesties*, if we unpick the title of the latter. A travesty is a literary burlesque of a serious work. Etymologically, 'travesty' comes from an adjective with specific connotations of being dressed up: from the French *travesti* (past participle of *travestir*) – to be dressed in disguise – and the Italian *travestire* – to disguise by clothing. Its Latin roots are *trans*, across or over, and *vestire*: to dress or clothe.[38] *Travesties* is heavily populated with dressing up and disguise, along with fake, confused, and forgotten names and roles. Carr repeatedly refers to his character in *The Importance of Being Earnest* as 'the other one', forgetting the role of Algernon while to some extent playing it in *Travesties*. The name-swapping and elements of disguise from Wilde's play are doubled in Stoppard's as Tristan Tzara and Henry Carr pretend to be Jack Tzara and Tristan Tzara respectively; *Travesties* itself dresses up as *The Importance of Being Earnest*. Joyce's name is forgotten and mistaken by Carr, and we learn eventually that not only did Carr never hold the role of Consul in Zurich as he pretends – but that a 'Bennett' did. Bennett, furthermore, is the name with which Carr refers to his butler, who not only apes the Wilde character Lane (Algernon's butler), but is revealed to have yet another part to play. Displaying vast knowledge of the Russian Revolution in an early, reset scene, Bennett is revealed later to at least have 'radical sympathies' and at most be a disguised, undercover Bolshevik; spies are mentioned often – if suitably subtly – in *Travesties* (95). Carr, meanwhile, is greatly concerned with clothing – he unknowingly plays Algernon in his obsessions with which suit and studs he will wear, he is convinced to knowingly play Algernon in Joyce's production by the promise of two costume changes, and he is much offended by Joyce's mismatched suits. And punning away in the background: the legal suit and countersuit brought by Carr and Joyce over the cost of some costume trousers.

In Chapter 3 I discussed disguise and textual dressing up in *Ulysses*: they are defining features of the form, content, styles, and characters of the novel. To refer back to the Latin roots of 'travesty' – *trans* and *vestire*, or across/ over and to clothe – we might think particularly of M'Intosh, whose identity is confused with the overclothes he wears. John Paul Riquelme even argues 'that all the book's styles, including the initial one, are disguises, personae, masks',[39] and there is something of this stylistic dress-up in *Travesties* too. The scenes reset, styles are borrowed from other texts, parts of plot and sections of dialogue are repeated in new modes. Yet despite the 'resetting' of such scenes some plot and information survive across stylistic hops: Bennett's secret identity, for instance, or Carr's knowledge of Joyce's christened middle name (Augusta). In this way these resets have a little essence of *Ulysses*' episodic shifts, clothed in styles which alter their contents to a variety of extents. We might even think of Kenner's suggestion that in *Ulysses* Homer 'educates us still, not least when we glimpse him in the mocking mirrors of a novel that was not long ago thought to *travesty* him, but that in fact soberly, exuberantly pays him intricate homage'.[40] *Ulysses* is a complicated reading of its precursor; perhaps we can argue the same of *Travesties*. Though the obvious precursor to Stoppard's play is *The Importance of Being Earnest*, in that playful intertextual relationship between the two texts *Travesties* points more to *Ulysses*. It perhaps does still travesty Joyce's novel, but while also paying it homage: it pulls at and admires it, mocks and echoes it, exploring concerns which are relevant to the questions reading *Ulysses* raises.

In the fun *Travesties* has with disguised characters and text, role-playing and playfulness, lies and truth, fiction and reality, it asks questions about authors: about their personalities, their genius, their responsibilities to society, the stories we tell about them, and their relationship to their texts. Even the joke of Doris, Phyllis, Deidre, Bridget, Joyce relies upon the impossibility of forgetting Joyce's name: upon a Foucault-esque awareness that 'Joyce' does far more than refer to the man James Augustine/Augusta Aloysius Joyce. We can therefore read another form of writing woven into the mixture of biography, history, fiction, and rewriting that forms the play: that of literary criticism. *Travesties* reads and responds to *Ulysses*, asking and exploring questions the novel raises that have implications beyond its pages: it reads and responds to literary memoirs and biographies, and to cultural interest in authorial genius and authorial commentary; to the treatment of art and artists under Lenin; to Dadaism and what it reacted against; and even (if we want) to the class divides of *The Importance of Being Earnest*, subverting the small role of a 'lowly' butler. Finally, *Travesties* reads, responds to, and rewrites Joyce.

Both Budgen's and Power's texts acknowledge their elements of fiction, reaching towards authenticity by merging the white lie with the 'truth'. In this their texts mirror their Joyces: contradictory combinations of otherly and real, of mythical and human. Budgen's question, 'who knows when memory ceases to be memory and becomes imagination?', applies to his own text as well as to Joyce's *Portrait*. It is of course relevant also to Power's *Conversations*; yet while it is usual to note the less-than-honest presentation of Budgen's conversations with Joyce, the same caveats are not applied to Power's. In his own introduction Power calls his memoir 'inadequate', arguing that 'to give an impression of a man of such talent one would have to have talent equal to his own'. He acknowledges an impossibility in his endeavour, that he can at most only attempt to write Joyce. Yet the authority given to Power's Joyce by critics infers a completeness, a Joyce so utterly Joyce his words are treated like those in his letters. The formal similarities between Power's and Stoppard's Joyce beg a playful but useful question: what if a critic were to reference Stoppard's Joyce in the same way? What stops us from using *that* Joyce's words about the relationship between art and history, for example? The reason critics will reference Power's Joyce and not Stoppard's relies, as I've observed, on a pact of authenticity. Power is authentic because he knew Joyce, even if fifty years previously, and the critic is then not only authentic in referencing him but also reaffirms Power's authenticity through the act of citation. That agreement, to give faith to the written Joyces of a Power or a Budgen, contains within it a reiteration of much of criticism's continuous seeking of the author's authority and ceaseless investment in a link between the life and the work. This search is hard to avoid, and can be difficult to identify. My own use of Samuel Butler's Homeric theory in Chapter 3, for example, is in part authorised by previous Joycean critics – those critics in turn were authorised by Stanislaus Joyce, who 'kindly informed' the critic W. B. Stanford that *The Authoress of the 'Odyssey'* was important to his brother.[41] In Chapter 5 I reference the authorially provided schematic colour of 'Lotus Eaters'. Even my reliance in this book on etymologies could be read as authorised by Joyce: his fascination with words is detailed in many texts, including in the caricatured 'Joyce Stripped Naked in the Piazza'.[42]

There remains, however, an identifiable instability to these written Joyces. They are products of writing, like 'scores' of inferred, ideated, critically written Homers – and could thus be treated as if as unstable as text: each being temporarily altered by acts of reading. In 'Joyce the Verb' Fritz Senn clarifies 'Reading Joyce (you see, we use the name but don't mean the person)'[43] – yet when reading Joyce's texts, Joyce the 'event', there *is* often a reading of the person, the author. Readings of Joyce the author and Joyce the biographical man do often have an impact on critical readings of Joyce's texts, and thus are a part of them; one further way in which asking how we read the text involves asking how we read the author. The characters presented by Budgen, Ellmann, Power, and Stoppard are also readings of Joyce – his life and texts. Jacques Derrida argues in 'Two Words' against the phrase 'reading Joyce': the idea of 'having "read" Joyce' amuses him, and he suggests instead that we 'stay on the edge of reading Joyce'.[44] Derek Attridge, meanwhile, in 'Reading Joyce' describes the 'pleasures' which 'rely on qualities of inexplicability, unpredictability, inexhaustibility'.[45] As textual constructions, are the Joyces of memoir, biography, and anecdote as constantly in flux as the Joyce of *Travesties*, as the text of *Ulysses*? Are the Joyces of literary criticism?

I am not advocating a form of hypothetical intentionalism, nor do I wish to quantify the difference between the real-life writer and some implied or postulated author.[46] I seek rather to emphasise the unsteadiness of any idea of Joyce. We cannot reconstruct a complete Joyce, cannot finish reading him, nor fix a permanent image of him. Discussing the author is to discuss instabilities: we must attempt to perceive and pick apart a layering of acts of reading and writing, all of which are positioned in changeable relation to one another. Happily, we are prepared for this by *Ulysses* – more than ready to understand conclusions are malleable, to conclude understandings are temporary, and to enjoy how the strength and usefulness of both are enhanced by their mutability. I propose that for the reader or critic all Joyces are unstable, flexible, and in crucial part formed by our activity of reading. Our ideated Joyces, then, are not our source of authority: we are, as readers.

Notes

1. In Frank Budgen, *James Joyce and The Making of 'Ulysses'*, with an introduction by Hugh Kenner (Bloomington: Indiana University Press, 1961), 317. This is part of the 'Further Recollections', an appendix to the 1961 edition. Further references to this edition are given after quotations in the text.
2. Thomas Carlyle, *On Heroes, Hero-Worship and the Heroic in History*, quoted in M. H. Abrams, *The Mirror and the Lamp: Romantic Theory and the Critical Tradition* (Oxford: Oxford University Press, 1971), 249.
3. Samuel Butler, *The Authoress of the 'Odyssey': Where and when she wrote, who she was, the use she made of the Iliad, and how the poem grew under her hand* (Bristol: Bristol Phoenix Press, 2003), 6.

4. S. L. Goldberg, *The Classical Temper: A Study of James Joyce's 'Ulysses'* (London: Chatto and Windus, 1961), 104 and 107.
5. James Alexander Fraser's deft study *Joyce & Betrayal* is a recent example, carefully establishing the importance of betrayal in Joyce's life (London: Palgrave Macmillan, 2016). With a slightly different emphasis Michael Patrick Gillespie, in *James Joyce and the Exilic Imagination*, attempts to show how important Joyce saw the theme of exile to his own life (Gainesville: University Press of Florida, 2015).
6. Yet others openly conflate Stephen and Joyce, and attempt to separate, like Christine Froula, 'the life of Joyce-the-artist' and 'Joyce's life as actually lived'. *Modernism's Body: Sex, Culture, and Joyce* (New York: Columbia University Press, 1996), 2.
7. Loren Daniel Glass, *Authors Inc: Literary Celebrity in the Modern United States, 1880–1980* (New York and London: New York University Press, 2004), 5.
8. Michael Moriarty, *Roland Barthes* (Cambridge: Polity, 1991), 2.
9. Stan Gébler Davies, *James Joyce: A Portrait of the Artist* (London: Davis-Poynter, 1975), 7.
10. Flann O'Brien, 'A Bash in the Tunnel', in *Stories and Plays* (New York: Penguin, 1977), 201.
11. Clive Hart, 'Frank Budgen and the Story of the Making of *Ulysses*', in *Re-Viewing Classics of Joyce Criticism*, ed. Janet Egleson Dunleavy (Urbana and Chicago: University of Illinois Press, 1991), 120–30 (128). This is a modified version of Hart's introduction to *The Making of 'Ulysses'* published by Oxford University Press in 1972.
12. Hugh Kenner, 'Introduction', in Budgen, ix–xv (xiv). This comment was made the year after Ellmann's biography was first published.
13. Kenner, *'Ulysses'* (London: George Allen and Unwin, 1980), 170, and *Dublin's Joyce*, Morningside Edition (New York: Columbia University Press, 1987), xi.
14. Kenner, *'Ulysses'*, 5.
15. Hart, 'Frank Budgen', 124.
16. Stéphane Mallarmé, 'From "Crisis in Verse"', in Seán Burke, ed., *Authorship: From Plato to the Postmodern. A Reader* (Edinburgh: Edinburgh University Press, 1995), 51–3 (51).
17. Kenner, *'Ulysses'*, 5 fn. 12.
18. In his introduction to Budgen, ix and xi.
19. Richard Ellmann, *James Joyce: New and Revised Edition* (Oxford: Oxford University Press, 1982), 28. Quoting Father Conmee (*Letters of James Joyce*, vol. I, ed. Stuart Gilbert (New York: The Viking Press, 1957, new edn 1966), 393), John Joyce ('Interview with Mrs. Eileen Shaurek, 1953'), and James Joyce (Letter to Budgen, 2nd May 1934, *Letters*, vol. III, ed. Ellmann (New York: The Viking Press, 1968), 304). Further references to this edition are given after quotations in the text, with further bibliographic detail in notes.
20. The first story is from Herbert Gorman, *James Joyce* (New York: Farrar Rinehart, 1939), 27, and Stanislaus Joyce, *My Brother's Keeper*, ed. Ellmann (New York: The Viking Press, 1975), 40, and the second from 'Interview with Mrs. Kettle, 1953'.
21. George Russell, 'Some Characters of the Irish Literary Movement', shown to Ellmann by Alan Denson.

22. Letter to Ellmann from Terence White Gervais, 1954.
23. 'Interview with Jacob Schwartz, 1956', and Max Eastman, *The Literary Mind* (1931), 100.
24. Tom Stoppard, *Travesties* (London: Faber, 1975), 22. I am using what was my father's copy; it is printed both upside down and back to front, and signed by the author. Further references to this edition are given after quotations in the text.
25. A shorter text 'Conversations with Joyce' first appeared in the *James Joyce Quarterly*, vol. 3, no. 1 (Fall, 1965), 41–9. It reports conversations had in 1921, many of which run over several pages. Much of the discussion revolves around other writers, and though there are traces of some of the conversations presented in the full memoir, many of the more quoted passages of the latter are absent.
26. Arthur Power, *Conversations with James Joyce*, ed. Hart (London: Millington, 1974), 9. Further references to this edition are given after quotations in the text.
27. Michael McKeon, 'Writer as Hero: Novelistic Prefigurations and the Emergence of Literary Biography', in *Contesting the Subject: Essays in the Postmodern Theory and Practice of Biography and Biographical Criticism*, ed. William H. Epstein (West Lafayette, IN: Purdue University Press, 1991), 17–41 (37–8).
28. 'It would appear, then, that a biographical interpretation of a work may, on its own principles, be interpreted by the biography of the interpreter; and this opens up the vista of an infinite regress.' Abrams, 254.
29. See for example Finn Fordham in *Lots of Fun at 'Finnegans Wake': Unravelling Universals* (Oxford: Oxford University Press, 2007), 9; Kevin J. H. Dettmar in *The Illicit Joyce of Postmodernism: Reading Against the Grain* (Madison: University of Wisconsin Press, 1996), 167; John Bishop in the notes of *Joyce's Book of the Dark: 'Finnegans Wake'* (Madison: University of Wisconsin Press, 1986), 454 n. 7.
30. Dettmar, 50; Jean Kimball, *Odyssey of the Psyche: Jungian Patterns in 'Ulysses'* (Carbondale: Southern Illinois University Press, 1997), 137; and Daniel Bristow, *Joyce and Lacan: Reading, Writing, and Psychoanalysis* (Oxford: Routledge, 2017), 83.
31. These extra effects are also suggested in the stage directions (27). In the Apollo Theatre production in 2017 (dir. Patrick Marber), the lights dimmed or coloured slowly as the scene lost its way, suddenly returning to full brightness with an extremely loud cuckoo-clock noise as the scene reset (seen 14 February 2017).
32. We also must wonder whose estate caused Stoppard enough trouble to warrant reference in the play itself.
33. At the Apollo Theatre performance, Tzara began this speech with real, affecting seriousness and anger – lasting right up until his final pose.
34. In both the 2017 Apollo Theatre production and a 2011 production by the Birmingham Repertory Theatre Company (dir. Philip Wilson), Joyce conjured a live rabbit.
35. In his 'Acknowledgements' Stoppard lists Ellmann's *James Joyce* and John Gross's *Joyce* (London: Fontana/Collins, 1971) as amongst the texts from which he has 'profited variously – and gratefully' (15).
36. Clive James, 'Count Zero Splits the Infinite', in *Encounter*, November 1975, on James's website – an archive of his works. <https://archive.clivejames.com/books/stoppard.htm> [accessed 19 March 2021]. The Birmingham Rep even staged both plays with the same cast for a season in 2011.

37. Mary M. Talbot and Bryan Talbot, *Dotter of her Father's Eyes* (London: Jonathan Cape, 2012). Many source texts are listed in this graphic novel, which also includes a sort of visual intertextuality: photographs of real artefacts are included in the illustrations, along with Atherton's copy of *Wake*, with annotations and pressed flowers in its pages. *The Red Shoes* and *The Graduate* are not listed as source texts, but are quoted. 'Why do you want to dance?' 'Why do you want to live?' 'Well, I don't know exactly. But I *must*' 'That's *my* answer too' are lines from *The Red Shoes*; in *Dotter*, the exchange is between Lucia Joyce and Beckett (71). 'Will you kiss me? Will you marry me?' 'I don't know' is from *The Graduate*, and in *Dotter* is spoken by Bryan and Mary Talbot (61).
38. Etymologies taken from John Ayto, *Word Origins: The Hidden Histories of English Words from A to Z*, 2nd edn (London: A&C Black, 2005), and the *OED Online* (Oxford University Press, July 2021) <www.oed.com> [accessed 29 July 2021].
39. John Paul Riquelme, *Teller and Tale in Joyce's Fiction: Oscillating Perspectives* (Baltimore, MD and London: Johns Hopkins University Press, 1983), 220. Karen Lawrence makes a similar point across *The Odyssey of Style in 'Ulysses'* (Princeton, NJ: Princeton University Press, 1981).
40. Kenner, *Joyce's Voices* (Berkeley, Los Angeles, and London: University of California Press, 1978), 95. My emphasis.
41. Kenner, among many others, references this in *Joyce's Voices*, 111. W. B. Stanford, *The Ulysses Theme: A Study in the Adaptability of a Traditional Hero* (Oxford: Basil Blackwell, 1954), 276 fn. 6.
42. Or do I take my authority for the relevance of etymological analysis from Roland Barthes, from his continued references to the metaphorical roots of the word 'text'?
43. Fritz Senn, 'Joyce the Verb', in Senn, *Inductive Scrutinies: Focus on Joyce*, ed. Christine O'Neill (Dublin: Lilliput, 1995), 7–34 (8).
44. Jacques Derrida, 'Two Words for Joyce', in *Post-Structuralist Joyce: Essays from the French*, ed. Derek Attridge and Daniel Ferrer (Cambridge: Cambridge University Press, 1984), 145–59 (148).
45. Attridge, 'Reading Joyce', in *The Cambridge Companion to James Joyce*, ed. Attridge (Cambridge: Cambridge University Press, 1990), 1–30 (2).
46. Alexander Nehamas separates the postulated author from the real, historical writer. As this chapter makes clear, I find such a separation reductive.

CONCLUSION: THE READER'S JOYCE

In a history of changing attitudes towards the author, Roland Barthes's essays 'The Death of the Author' and 'From Work to Text' constitute the most extreme movements away from the author as either arbiter of meaning or source of authority. They also most explicitly emphasise the importance of the reader and of the text. These essays pit author against reader, conceiving the authority of each as mutually exclusive: the open, limitless text can have no author. They also describe modes of reading and qualities of text which strongly resonate with *Ulysses*. The ways in which *Ulysses* draws attention to our activity of reading, and the involvement of Joyce in the novel's reception, have made Joyce studies a highly self-reflexive field, and one which variously pre-empted questions explored by literary theorists from the 1960s onwards. Discussing how to read *Ulysses* became an inescapable aspect of Ulyssean criticism at a very early stage in its reception, and the question of how to read the author is caught up in questions of how to read the text. In part through authorially authorised studies, a key enquiry of early criticism became that of how one should handle the novel's intertextual relationship with the *Odyssey*. That enquiry has fallen wildly in and out of fashion, and the far-reaching effects of how *Ulysses* rewrites not only the *Odyssey* but also scholarly readings of Homer have been missed. These effects create a complex web of authorial and readerly roles, strands of which confirm that explorations of authorship manifest not only in poststructuralist theory and pre-theory Joyce criticism, but in both Homeric scholarship and the Homeric games of *Ulysses*.

There was, however, a sustained resistance to poststructuralist theory in Joyce studies. Anti-authorialism and the birth of the reader were given little credence and had little impact, and – curiously – several critical studies argued for a return of the author in a discipline which had never quite abandoned the author's authority. In its endless expansion, the discipline continues to advocate a freedom of reading that somehow coexists with an ongoing reliance on authorial authority. This contradiction has arisen in response to the way in which *Ulysses* makes us read, but it is also pre-figured within that activity of reading. Reading *Ulysses* puts the reader in an active and creative role, while also highlighting the uncanny talents of its author. In reading *Ulysses*, however, we create our own authority as readers. We can also create an author, one not unrelated to the author described in anecdotal works of biography: informed by and informing such constructions of the biographical author. The author is thus not an authoritative source of meaning, but an unstable part and product of our reading. The limitless text and the author coexist, comprehended in our reading.

I'm not a poststructuralist, and my conclusions are not those of the death of the author, though I do maintain a prioritising of the reader. Like Barthes, furthermore, I find answers in literature. In the introduction to this book, I looked briefly at the ways in which other literary texts have explored questions of authorship. I returned to this focus in my third chapter, arguing for the fictive potential of the Homeric Question, and again in my final chapter's reading of textual representations of Joyce. By emphasising the capacity of fiction to both prompt and answer challenges to received notions of the relationships between author, reader, and text, *The Reader's Joyce* responds directly to any limitation of such discussions to theoretical or philosophical spheres. However, it was necessary to begin this book with a chapter focusing on theoretical and critical shifts in how the author has been understood, and how this has affected understandings of the reader's role, the properties of text, and the interconnections between all three. This was both to contextualise Barthes's anti-authorialism within an ongoing shifting debate, and conversely to – in a way – remove it from its context, to be free to then allow elements of it to chime with a number of my observations. I followed thus the request for playful, open reading, and have been able to compare aspects of anti-authorialism with the work of pre-poststructuralist and anti-theory Joyceans, and with straight-faced and tongue-in-cheek Homeric scholars; with the ways in which we read texts without authors, and texts which exalt their author; and with *Ulysses* itself.

Barthes's death of the author remains a relevant site of enquiry for literary studies today, despite its near-caricature reputation. It informed the pre- and post-theory hinge of Chapters 2 and 4, which together analyse how Joyce studies has engaged with questions of authorship, reading, and textuality. Chapter 2 focuses on three aspects of early Joyce studies: Joyce's involvement and the effects of authorially authorised criticism, readings of Stephen Dedalus as Joyce, and the habits of Joycean criticism which resulted from each. Criticism of *Ulysses* quickly became as much about how to read the text as it was about the text itself, and, as criticism is an act of reading, became self-reflexive. It grew into a discipline with a corrective urge yet – at its best – an openness to multiplicity, traits that we can trace back to the reception of the Homeric in *Ulysses* and Joyce's own role in that reception. Joyce studies' treatment of the *Odyssey* in *Ulysses* has ramifications in terms of the author, as well as for the critic and reader. By pulling at an intertextual link many think fully explicated, Chapter 3 is a close reading in retaliation to the idea that there can be 'nothing more to say' – and the attitudes it reveals. Finding Samuel Butler's *The Authoress of the 'Odyssey'*, and its response to Homeric scholarship, between 'Eumaeus' and the *Odyssey* exposes ways in which the episode plays with oral and written performances of narrative and of authorship. Authorially seeking Homeric scholarship is rewritten in *Ulysses*, and that rewriting is completed by our activity of reading: our efforts are the echo, as we mimic a creative role of authorless reading which searches for and constructs an ideated author.

An element of Chapter 3 is how Barthes's descriptions of text and reading resonate with the text and reading of *Ulysses*' interactions with the *Odyssey*. Though the chapter also emphasises how poststructuralist theory is only one manifestation of questions of how author, reader, and text function, the relevance of Barthes's work sets up the focuses of Chapter 4. Reaching back to Chapter 2, it continues to assert that Joyce studies has always asked and provoked questions about the author-reader-text relationship. Across Joyce studies, critics choose how to read the relationship between author, reader, and text – but rarely acknowledge or examine these choices. Even studies interested in issues of authorship can overlook the implications of their own critical modes and tendencies. Questions prompted by this relationship are thus everywhere in Joyce studies, but the field has ceased to ask what causes its contradictory attitudes to the author.

Chapter 5 is my response to this unexplored area, returning once more to a reading of the text of *Ulysses*, and a close reading of how we read it. Chapter 3 examined the unknown suggested by a misplaced '(*sic*)', which referred back to 'Calypso' and the word 'metempsychosis'. It is to 'Calypso' that Chapter 5 also returns to investigate the ways in which *Ulysses* prompts us to read. I argue that the novel provokes limitless, authorless reading, where the reader gains authority in their active, creative endeavours. By then bringing 'Wandering Rocks' into a discussion of narrative games, the chapter asks how the ways in which *Ulysses* gives authority to the reader – and demands we test the limits of our reading – also glorify the author. Again, the reading and the text resonate with Barthes's description of both, but go further too: the 'birth of the reader' is not 'at the cost of the death of the author'. In Chapter 3 I read a 'birth' of the reader strangely in the service of finding or constructing an author; in my arguments of Chapter 5, through the birth of the reader the author is not only located but deified. A freedom of authorless reading and a god-like genius author coexist within the text we create while reading *Ulysses*, and through this fecundly unstable text we derive authority.

Chapter 6 brings together conclusions of 1 through 5. In particular, through its analysis of the biographical Joyce in Joyce studies via the fictional Joyce in *Travesties*, it plays with the notion that we the readers construct the author. Referring back to performances of authorship and creative author-hunting I discussed in Chapter 3, and the suggestion that convenient versions of the author are crafted to suit a critic's purposes, Chapter 6 proposes that for the reader or critic all Joyces are text based. They are thus unstable, flexible, and in crucial part formed by our activity of reading. Biographical Joyces are also constructions, and therefore are figures in flux rather than of unarguable authoritative permanence. This argument takes a concept and tests it: that there is a particular mode of reading which *Ulysses* prompts, and that it is one which ignores boundaries, chronology, and perceived hierarchies of authority – thus gaining its own creativity and authority.

Creative reading is a response to *Ulysses*: in our activity of reading, as *The Reader's Joyce* shows, we complete for example a fertile aspect of the novel's rewriting of the *Odyssey* and perform the final steps of forming an ideated genius author that some use to authorise interpretations. Questions about our role as readers, the role of the author, and how both interact with the text have always been present in Joyce studies – along with their resultant contradictions. These questions are formed by our reading, and are therefore not exactly *in Ulysses*, but rather present in the text and intertexts we create when reading. The extent to which we refer to an authorial authority is therefore determined by us.

I asked several questions in the introduction to this book, finding the following responses through my readings of *Ulysses*, criticism, and reading itself. The novel encourages a reader to question the authority of an author by emphasising the reader's activity and the text's intertextuality and openness. It draws attention to the reader's role through an intertext of Homeric scholarship, through the difficulties caused by the ways in which characters' thoughts are narrated, and by ensuring that 'how to read *Ulysses*' is a constant query for both reader and critic. These effects work together by both undermining and affirming the author's skill and authority. Revisiting the Homeric intertextuality of *Ulysses* is germane to questions of authorship and reading for several reasons. The reception of that textual connection prompted several key traits of Joyce studies, still functioning today. The interaction of 'Eumaeus' with the *Odyssey* and the Homeric Question makes the reader mimic authorially seeking Homeric scholars, and this reveals a way in which we as readers create further intertextual echoes through our activity of reading. Questions of the roles and relationships of author, reader, and text have been inconsistently acknowledged and responded to in Joyce studies, despite the self-awareness of the field. Joyce studies is complexly and significantly involved in the upkeep of the genius author. This author-centric scholarly environment affects reading and criticism by undermining particular theory-aligned responses, keeping biography consistently important to criticism throughout a number of critical shifts, and providing critics with a god-like author with whom to authorise their own readings. Despite this, Barthesian anti-authorialism is pertinent to *Ulysses* as it describes both how we read and the text itself, and resonates curiously with aspects of Joycean criticism. Questions such as these have been put on a back burner in the field, not only because of general changes in interest and focus, or the unfashionableness of poststructuralism, but also because of the strength of the author's perceived authority and the authority of the critic-authors who invoke it, affirm it, and are invested in it.

There are final questions to answer. Is *Ulysses* a special case, an unusual text? It is of course, in that it is an exaggeration of text demanding an exaggerated mode of reading and thus dragging the implicit out into the open. So, are the questions *Ulysses* prompts of author, reader, and text relevant to the wider literary field? How? The wonderful specificities of *Ulysses*, its idiosyncrasies, excesses, and difficulties, are what makes it relevant to any literary encounter. The complexity of the text, its overt intertextuality, styles of narrative, extra-textual authorial hints, and adoring critics are extremes of the norm: all literary texts are formed of networks of associations and previous texts, all require us to navigate narrative in order to grasp character and event. Many carry authorial advice and commentary on book jackets, in introductions, collections of letters, interviews in magazines, or social media – and those that do not are marked for that lack. Critics will seek these comments out, and to varying degrees determined by fame, celebrity, and canonical status, critics will establish the significance of the link between the texts and the name of their author. These exaggerations contained within the pages of *Ulysses* and formed by our responses to it are what makes it more universally relevant: its extremes of text, reader, and author. *Ulysses* and our reading of it make the inherent apparent, how all texts are formed of other texts, all readings are creative, and yet all authors are given authority, and how – as confirmed by criticism and popular culture – the link between an author's life and work continues to fascinate many. Reading *Ulysses* is an activity germane to any literary encounter because it draws attention to how we read and how that relates to our notions of the author; it is relevant because it raises questions which have remained in the background of literary studies, and affirms their continuing significance. My answer to those neglected questions is that there can be something of a reversal, where a coexistence of author and reader is possible without reinforcing a hierarchy of author over reader: where the author is in crucial part created by the reader, and given a role or an authority of the reader's choosing.

New methods respond to the old, developing, altering, or simply adding more resources, more options. In non-sequential fits and starts, *The Reader's Joyce* has described authorship as an intrinsically changeable mode: my readings of *Ulysses* have led me to flashpoints in the development of the author in contemporary culture. In 'Eumaeus' I find the transition from oral to written composition and transcription, but I also find a phase of absolute division between nineteenth-century classical scholars, split over their interpretations of Homer. In 'Calypso' and 'Wandering Rocks' my readings enact a debate over two extreme understandings of the author, aping twentieth-century challenges to the author question. I have been prompted to read and reference readings of the end of literary patronage, the shift towards intellectual property, modernist modes of celebrity, the death of the author, the return of the author, and the author online. Interrogating the author-reader-text triad, as I have, emphasises these re-modellings and highlights the importance of sifting through histories of notions, readings, challenges, and retreats. Querying the relationships between author, reader, and text is relevant to readings for which context is less important, and to readings in which context is crucial: all involve inherent assumptions about such relationships, and future research in either mode could gain much by paying attention to those fundamental attitudes. Unpicking an episode, passage, sentence, word, is an activity that will produce richness again and again. It is not pedantic; nor is returning to the formation of critical responses anything to do with a desire to seek historical curiosities. Those earlier encounters are present in our own, and returning to them is a way of asking how we read now. This approach, the critical method of *The Reader's Joyce*, responds to *Ulysses*: to how the novel goads us into questioning what reading is, what it entails, and where it ends.

BIBLIOGRAPHY

Abrams, M. H., *The Mirror and the Lamp: Romantic Theory and the Critical Tradition* (Oxford: Oxford University Press, 1971).
Ackroyd, Peter, *Notes for a New Culture* (London: Alkin Books, 1993).
Adair, Gilbert, *The Death of the Author* (New York: Melville House, 2008).
Alderton, Dolly, 'Kristen Roupenian, author of Cat Person, is dating a woman', *Sunday Times*, 13 May 2018 <https://www.thetimes.co.uk/article/kristen-roupenian-author-of-cat-person-is-dating-a-woman-fghsfn02g> [accessed 5 July 2021].
Altieri, Charles, 'Modernist Innovations: A Legacy of the Constructed Reader', in *Modernism*, ed. Ástráður Eysteinsson and Vivian Liska (Amsterdam and Philadelphia, PA: John Benjamins, 2007).
Anker, Elizabeth S., and Rita Felski, eds, *Critique and Post-critique* (Durham, NC and London: Duke University Press, 2017).
Attridge, Derek, ed., *The Cambridge Companion to James Joyce* (Cambridge: Cambridge University Press, 1990).
—— 'Criticism's Wake', in *James Joyce: The Augmented Ninth, Proceedings of the Ninth International James Joyce Symposium, Frankfurt 1984*, ed. Bernard Benstock (Syracuse, NY: Syracuse University Press, 1988), 80–7.
—— ed., *James Joyce's 'Ulysses': A Casebook* (Oxford: Oxford University Press, 2004).
—— *Joyce Effects: On Language, Theory and History* (Cambridge: Cambridge University Press, 2000).

—— *Peculiar Language: Literature as Difference from the Renaissance to James Joyce* (London: Methuen, 1988).

—— 'Signature/Countersignature: Derrida's Response to *Ulysses*', in *Derrida and Joyce: Texts and Contexts*, ed. Andrew J. Mitchell and Sam Slote (Albany: State University of New York Press, 2013), 265–80.

Attridge, Derek, and Daniel Ferrer, eds, *Post-Structuralist Joyce: Essays from the French* (Cambridge: Cambridge University Press, 1984).

Attridge, Derek, and Marjorie Howes, eds, *Semicolonial Joyce* (Cambridge: Cambridge University Press, 2000).

Ayto, John, *Word Origins: The Hidden Histories of English Words from A to Z*, 2nd edn (London: A&C Black, 2005).

Baldick, Chris, *Criticism and Literary Theory from 1890 to the Present* (London: Longman, 1996).

Banville, John, 'Survivors of Joyce', in *James Joyce: The Artist and the Labyrinth*, ed. Augustine Martin (London: Ryan, 1990), 73–81.

Barker, Egbert J., *Pointing at the Past: From Formula to Performance in Homeric Poetics* (Cambridge, MA: Harvard University Press, 2005).

Baron, Scarlett, *'Strandentwining Cable': Joyce, Flaubert, and Intertextuality* (Oxford: Oxford University Press, 2012).

Barthes, Roland, 'The Death of the Author', in *Image-Music-Text*, trans. Stephen Heath (London: Fontana, 1977), 142–8.

—— 'From Work to Text', in *Image-Music-Text*, trans. Stephen Heath (London: Fontana, 1977), 155–64.

—— 'From *Writing Degree Zero*', trans. Annette Lavers and Colin Smith (1977), in *A Roland Barthes Reader*, ed. Susan Sontag (London: Vintage, 2018), 31–61.

—— *Image-Music-Text*, trans. Stephen Heath (London: Fontana, 1977).

—— 'On Reading', in *The Rustle of Language*, trans. Richard Howard (Berkeley and Los Angeles: University of California Press, 1989), 33–43.

—— *The Pleasure of the Text*, trans. Richard Miller (Oxford: Basil Blackwell, 1990).

—— *The Rustle of Language*, trans. Richard Howard (Berkeley and Los Angeles: University of California Press, 1989).

—— *S/Z*, trans. Richard Miller (Oxford: Basil Blackwell, 1990).

—— 'Writing Reading', in *The Rustle of Language*, trans. Richard Howard (Berkeley and Los Angeles: University of California Press, 1989), 29–32.

Bayard, Pierre, *How to Talk About Books You Haven't Read*, trans. Jeffrey Mehlman (New York: Bloomsbury, 2007).

Beck, Harald, and John Simpson, *James Joyce Online Notes* <http://www.jjon.org/joyce-s-words/eatondhp> [accessed 29 July 2021].

Beckett, Samuel et al., *Our Exagmination Round his Factification for Incamination of Work in Progress* (London: Faber, 1961).

Beja, Morris, and Shari Benstock, eds, *Coping with Joyce: Essays from the Copenhagen Symposium* (Columbus: Ohio State University Press, 1989).
Beja, Morris, and Anne Fogarty, eds, *Bloomsday 100: Essays on 'Ulysses'* (Gainesville: University Press of Florida, 2009).
Benjamin, Walter, 'The Author as Producer', in *Understanding Brecht*, trans. Anna Bostock (London: Verso, 1998), 85–103.
—— *One-way Street and Other Writings*, trans. J. A. Underwood (London: Penguin, 2009).
Benstock, Bernard, 'The Fabulous Voyaging of Richard M. Kain', in *Re-Viewing Classics of Joyce Criticism*, ed. Janet Egleson Dunleavy (Urbana and Chicago: University of Illinois Press, 1991), 8–22.
—— ed., *James Joyce: The Augmented Ninth, Proceedings of the Ninth International James Joyce Symposium, Frankfurt 1984* (Syracuse, NY: Syracuse University Press, 1988).
—— *Narrative Con/Texts in Joyce* (Basingstoke: Macmillan, 1991).
Bersani, Leo, 'Against *Ulysses*', in *James Joyce's 'Ulysses': A Casebook*, ed. Derek Attridge (Oxford: Oxford University Press, 2004), 201–29.
Best, Stephen, and Sharon Marcus, 'Surface Reading: An Introduction', *Representations*, vol. 108, no. 1 (Fall, 2009), 1–21.
Binet, Laurent, *The Seventh Function of Language*, trans. Sam Taylor (London: Harvill Secker (Vintage), 2017).
Birrioti, Maurice, and Nicola Miller, eds, *What is an Author?* (Manchester and New York: Manchester University Press, 1993).
Bishop, John, *Joyce's Book of the Dark: 'Finnegans Wake'* (Madison: University of Wisconsin Press, 1986).
Boheemen-Saaf, Christine van, *Joyce, Derrida, Lacan, and the Trauma of History: Reading, Narrative, and Postcolonialism* (Cambridge: Cambridge University Press, 1999).
—— 'Joyce in Theory/Theory in Joyce', in *James Joyce*, ed. Sean Latham (Dublin: Irish Academic Press, 2010), 153–69.
Boldrini, Lucia, *Joyce, Dante, and the Poetics of Literary Relations: Language and Meaning in 'Finnegans Wake'* (Cambridge: Cambridge University Press, 2001).
Bollettieri Bosinelli, Rosa Maria, and Franca Ruggieri, eds, *The Benstock Library as Mirror of Joyce*, Joyce Studies in Italy 7 (Rome: Bulzoni Editore, 2002).
Booker, M. Keith, *Joyce, Bakhtin and the Literary Tradition: Toward a Comparative Cultural Poetics* (Ann Arbor: University of Michigan Press, 1995).
Booth, Wayne C., *The Rhetoric of Fiction*, 2nd edn (Chicago and London: University of Chicago, 1961, 1983).
Borges, Jorge Luis, *Labyrinths: Selected Stories and Other Writings*, ed. James E. Irby and Donald A. Yates (London: Penguin, 2000).

Bosworth, Joseph and T. Northcote Toller, *An Anglo-Saxon Dictionary* <https://bosworthtoller.com/> [accessed 29 July 2021].

Brannon, Julie Sloan, *Who Reads 'Ulysses'? The Rhetoric of the Joyce Wars and the Common Reader* (New York and London: Routledge, 2003).

Braun, Rebecca, *Constructing Authorship in the Work of Günter Grass* (Oxford: Oxford University Press, 2008).

Briggs, Austin, 'Breakfast at 7 Eccles Street: *Oufs Sacher-Masoch*?', in *Joyce in Trieste: An Album of Risky Readings*, ed. Sebastian D. G. Knowles, Geert Lernout, and John McCourt (Gainesville: University Press of Florida, 2007), 195–209.

Bristow, Daniel, *Joyce and Lacan: Reading, Writing, and Psychoanalysis* (Oxford: Routledge, 2017).

Brivic, Sheldon, *The Veil of Signs: Joyce, Lacan, and Perception* (Urbana: University of Illinois Press, 1991).

Brooker, Joseph, 'The Fidelity of Theory: James Joyce and the Rhetoric of Belatedness', in *Joyce's Audiences*, ed. John Nash, European Joyce Studies 14 (Amsterdam: Rodopi, 2002), 201–21.

—— *Joyce's Critics: Transitions in Reading and Culture* (Madison: University of Wisconsin Press, 2004).

Bruni, Alessandro Francini, 'Joyce Stripped Naked in the Piazza', *James Joyce Quarterly*, vol. 14, no. 2, Joyce Reminiscences Issue (Winter, 1977), 127–59.

Budgen, Frank, *James Joyce and The Making of 'Ulysses'* (Bloomington: Indiana University Press, 1961).

Burke, Seán, ed., *Authorship: From Plato to the Postmodern. A Reader* (Edinburgh: Edinburgh University Press, 1995).

—— *The Death and Return of the Author: Criticism and Subjectivity in Barthes, Foucault and Derrida*, 3rd edn (Edinburgh: Edinburgh University Press, 2008).

—— *The Ethics of Writing: Authorship and Legacy in Plato and Nietzsche* (Edinburgh: Edinburgh University Press, 2008).

Butcher, S. H., and A. Lang, *The Odyssey of Homer: Done into English Prose* (London: Macmillan, 1924).

Butler, Christopher, 'Joyce and the Displaced Author', in *James Joyce and Modern Literature*, ed. W. J. McCormack and Alistair Stead (London: Routledge, 1982), 56–76.

Butler, Samuel, *The Authoress of the 'Odyssey': Where and when she wrote, who she was, the use she made of the 'Iliad', and how the poem grew under her hand*, ed. Tim Whitmarsh (Bristol: Bristol Phoenix Press, 2003).

—— *The Authoress of the 'Odyssey': Where and when she wrote, who she was, the use she made of the 'Iliad', and how the poem grew under her hand* (London: Jonathan Cape, 1922, republished by Forgotten Books, 2008).

Cain, Sian, 'Cat Person: the short story that launched a thousand theories', *The Guardian*, 13 December 2017 <https://www.theguardian.com/books/2017/dec/13/cat-person-short-story-that-launched-thousand-theories> [accessed 5 July 2021].

Castle, Gregory, 'James Joyce, *Ulysses*', in *The Blackwell Guide to Literary Theory* (Oxford: Blackwell, 2007), 272–4.

Caughie, John, ed., *Theories of Authorship* (London and New York: Routledge and Kegan Paul, 1981).

Cixous, Hélène, 'At Circe's, or, the Self-Opener', in *Early Postmodernism: Foundational Essays*, ed. Paul Bové (Durham, NC: Duke University Press, 1995), 387–97.

—— *The Exile of James Joyce*, trans. Sally A. J. Purcell (London: Calder, 1976).

—— *Readings: The Poetics of Blanchot, Joyce, Kafka, Kleist, Lispector, and Tsvetayeva*, trans. and ed. Verena Andermatt Conley (Minneapolis: University of Minnesota Press, 1991).

Claiborne Park, Clara, 'Author! Author! Reconstructing Roland Barthes', *The Hudson Review*, vol. 43, no. 3 (1990–1), 377–98.

Clarke, Austin, '"Stephen Dedalus": The Author of *Ulysses*', in *Reviews and Essays of Austin Clarke*, ed. Gregory A. Schirmer, Irish Literary Studies 40 (Gerrards Cross: Colin Smythe, 1995), 43–5.

Clayton, Jay, and Eric Rothstein, eds, *Influence and Intertextuality in Literary History* (Madison: University of Wisconsin Press, 1991).

Collingwood, R. G., *The Idea of History* (Oxford: Oxford University Press, 1961).

Conley, Tim, *Joyces Mistakes: Problems of Intention, Irony, and Interpretation* (Toronto: University of Toronto Press, 2003).

—— *Useless Joyce: Textual Functions, Cultural Appropriations* (Toronto: University of Toronto Press, 2017).

Connor, Stephen, 'Authorship, Authority, and Self-Reflection in Joyce and Beckett', in *Re:Joyce'n Beckett*, ed. Phyllis Carey and Ed Jewinski (New York: Fordham University Press, 1992), 147–59.

Cosgrove, Brian, *James Joyce's Negations: Irony, Indeterminacy and Nihilism in 'Ulysses' and Other Writings* (Dublin: University College Dublin Press, 2007).

Culler, Jonathan, *On Deconstruction: Theory and Criticism after Structuralism* (London: Routledge and Kegan Paul, 1983).

Davies, Stan Gébler, *James Joyce: A Portrait of the Artist* (London: Davis-Poynter, 1975).

Davis, Oliver, 'The Author at Work in Genetic Criticism', *Paragraph*, vol. 25, no. 1, Giorgio Agamben (March, 2002), 92–106.

Dederer, Claire, 'What Do We Do with the Art of Monstrous Men?', *The Paris Review*, 20 November 2017 <https://www.theparisreview.org/blog/2017/11/20/art-monstrous-men/> [accessed 5 July 2021].

Derrida, Jacques, *Acts of Literature*, ed. Derek Attridge (New York and London: Routledge, 1992).
—— *Limited Inc* (Evanston, IL: Northwestern University Press, 1988).
—— 'Two Words for Joyce', in *Post-Structuralist Joyce: Essays from the French*, ed. Derek Attridge and Daniel Ferrer (Cambridge: Cambridge University Press, 1984), 145–59.
—— 'Ulysses Gramophone', trans. François Raffoul, in *Derrida and Joyce: Texts and Contexts*, ed. Andrew J. Mitchell and Sam Slote (Albany: State University of New York Press, 2013), 41–86.
—— 'Ulysses Gramophone: Hear Say Yes in Joyce', trans. Tina Kendall, rev. Shari Benstock, in *Acts of Literature*, ed. Derek Attridge (New York and London: Routledge, 1992), 253–309.
Dettmar, Kevin J. H., *The Illicit Joyce of Postmodernism: Reading Against the Grain* (Madison: University of Wisconsin Press, 1996).
Devlin, Kimberly J., and Marilyn Reizbaum, eds, *'Ulysses': En-Gendered Perspectives. Eighteen New Essays on the Episodes* (Columbia: University of South Carolina Press, 1999).
Diepeveen, Leonard, *The Difficulties of Modernism* (New York and London: Routledge, 2003).
Donovan, Stephen, Danuta Fjellestad, and Rolf Lundén, eds, *Authority Matters: Rethinking the Theory and Practice of Authorship* (Amsterdam and New York: Rodopi, 2008).
Dunleavy, Janet Egleson, ed., *Re-Viewing Classics of Joyce Criticism* (Urbana and Chicago: University of Illinois Press, 1991).
Ebury, Katherine, and James Alexander Fraser, eds, *Joyce's Non-Fiction Writings: 'Outside His Jurisfiction'* (London: Palgrave, 2018).
Eco, Umberto, 'Joyce, Semiosis and Semiotics', in *The Languages of Joyce: Selected Papers from the 11th International James Joyce Symposium, Venice, 12–18 June 1988*, ed. Rosa Maria Bollettieri Bosinelli, Carla Marengo Vaglio, and Christine van Boheemen (Philadelphia, PA and Amsterdam: John Benjamins, 1992), 19–38.
Eliot, T. S., *Selected Prose of T. S. Eliot*, ed. Frank Kermode (London: Faber, 1975).
Ellmann, Richard, *James Joyce: New and Revised Edition* (Oxford: Oxford University Press, 1982).
—— *'Ulysses' on the Liffey* (London: Faber, 1972).
Enos, Theresa, 'Reports of the "Author's" Death May Be Greatly Exaggerated but the "Writer" Lives on in the Text', *Rhetoric Society Quarterly*, vol. 20, no. 4, Essays in Honor of George Yoos (Autumn, 1990), 339–46.
Epstein, E. L., 'The Irrelevant Narrator: A Stylistic Note on the Place of the Author in Contemporary Technique of the Novel', *Language and Style*, vol. 2, no. 1 (Winter, 1969), 92–4.

Fairhall, James, *James Joyce and the Question of History* (Cambridge: Cambridge University Press, 1993).
Farrell, John, *The Varieties of Authorial Intention: Literary Theory Beyond the Intentional Fallacy* (Cham: Palgrave Macmillan, 2017).
Fathallah, Judith, *Fanfiction and the Author: How Fanfic Changes Popular Cultural Texts* (Amsterdam: Amsterdam University Press, 2017).
Felski, Rita, *Hooked: Art and Attachment* (Chicago: University of Chicago Press, 2020).
―――― *The Limits of Critique* (Chicago and London: University of Chicago Press, 2015).
―――― *Literature after Feminism* (Chicago: University of Chicago Press, 2003).
Fish, Stanley, 'Transmuting the Lump: *Paradise Lost* 1942–1979', in *Doing What Comes Naturally: Change, Rhetoric, and the Practice of Theory in Literary and Legal Studies* (Durham, NC and London: Duke University Press, 1990), 247–93.
Flack, Leah Culligan, *James Joyce and Classical Modernism* (London: Bloomsbury, 2020).
―――― *Modernism and Homer: The Odysseys of H.D., James Joyce, Osip Mandelstam, and Ezra Pound* (Cambridge: Cambridge University Press, 2015).
Flaubert, Gustave, *Correspondence*, ed. Eugène Fasquelle (Paris, 1900), vol. II.
Folkenflik, Robert, 'The Artist as Hero in the Eighteenth Century', *Yearbook of English Studies*, 12 (1982), 91–108.
Fordham, Finn, *Lots of Fun at 'Finnegans Wake': Unravelling Universals* (Oxford: Oxford University Press, 2007).
Foucault, Michel, *Language, Counter-memory, Practice: Selected Essays and Interviews*, ed. Donald F. Bouchard, trans. Bouchard and Sherry Simon (Ithaca, NY: Cornell University Press, 1977).
Fowler, Robert, 'The Homeric Question', in *The Cambridge Companion to Homer*, ed. Robert Fowler (Cambridge: Cambridge University Press, 2004), 220–32.
Frame, Douglas, 'New Light on the Homeric Question: The Phaeacians Unmasked', included in 'A virtual birthday gift presented to Gregory Nagy on turning seventy by his students, colleagues, and friends', The Centre for Hellenic Studies, Harvard University <https://chs.harvard.edu/CHS/article/display/4453> [accessed 29 July 2021].
Frank, Joseph, 'Spatial Form in Modern Literature', in *Essentials of the Theory of Fiction*, ed. Michael J Hoffman and Patrick D. Murphy, 3rd edition (Durham, NC and London: Duke University Press, 2005), 61–73.
Fraser, James Alexander, *Joyce & Betrayal* (London: Palgrave Macmillan, 2016).
French, Marilyn, *The Book as World: James Joyce's 'Ulysses'* (Cambridge, MA and London: Harvard University Press, 1976).

Friedman, Alan W., and Charles Rossman, eds, *De-familiarizing Readings: Essays from the Austin Joyce Conference* (Amsterdam and New York: Rodopi, 2009).
Friedman, Susan Stanford, 'Weavings: Intertextuality and the (Re)Birth of the Author', in *Influence and Intertextuality in Literary History*, ed. Jay Clayton and Eric Rothstein (Madison: University of Wisconsin Press, 1991), 146–80.
Froula, Christine, *Modernism's Body: Sex, Culture, and Joyce* (New York: Columbia University Press, 1996).
Gallix, Andrew, 'Roland Barthes' challenge to biography', *The Guardian*, 14 August 2015, Books Blog <https://www.theguardian.com/books/booksblog/2015/aug/14/roland-barthes-challenge-to-biography> [accessed 5 July 2021].
Gallop, Jane, *The Deaths of the Author: Reading and Writing in Time* (Durham, NC and London: Duke University Press, 2011).
Garber, Megan, '"Cat Person" and the impulse to undermine women's fiction', *The Atlantic*, 11 December 2017 <https://www.theatlantic.com/entertainment/archive/2017/12/cat-person-is-not-an-essay/548111/> [accessed 5 July 2021].
Gass, William H., 'The Death of the Author', *Salmagundi*, no. 65 (Fall, 1984), 3–26.
Genette, Gerard, *Narrative Discourse: An Essay in Method*, trans. Jane E. Lewin (Ithaca, NY: Cornell University Press, 1980).
Gibbons, Stella, *Cold Comfort Farm* (Harmondsworth: Penguin, 1949).
Gibson, Andrew, *Joyce's Revenge: History, Politics, and Aesthetics in 'Ulysses'* (Oxford: Oxford University Press, 2002).
Gilbert, Stuart, *James Joyce's 'Ulysses'* (London: Faber, 1960).
Gillespie, Michael Patrick, ed., *Foundational Essays in James Joyce Studies* (Gainesville: University Press of Florida, 2011).
—— *James Joyce and the Exilic Imagination* (Gainesville: University Press of Florida, 2015).
—— 'Kenner on Joyce', in *Re-Viewing Classics of Joyce Criticism*, ed. Janet Egleson Dunleavy (Urbana and Chicago: University of Illinois Press, 1991), 142–54.
—— 'Past its Sell-by Date: When to Stop Reading Joyce Criticism', in *Bloomsday 100: Essays on 'Ulysses'*, ed. Morris Beja and Anne Fogarty (Gainesville: University Press of Florida, 2009), 213–27.
—— *Reading the Book of Himself: Narrative Strategies in the Works of James Joyce* (Columbus: Ohio State University Press, 1989).
Gillespie, Michael Patrick, and Paula F. Gillespie, *Recent Criticism of James Joyce's 'Ulysses': An Analytical Review* (Rochester, NY: Camden House, 2000).
Glass, Loren Daniel, *Authors Inc: Literary Celebrity in the Modern United States, 1880–1980* (New York and London: New York University Press, 2004).

Godlin Roemer, Marjorie, 'Which Reader's Response?', *College English*, vol. 49, no. 8 (December, 1987), 911–21.

Goldberg, S. L., *The Classical Temper: A Study of James Joyce's 'Ulysses'* (London: Chatto and Windus, 1961).

Goldman, Jonathan, 'Afterlife', in *The Cambridge Companion to 'Ulysses'*, ed. Sean Latham (New York: Cambridge University Press, 2014), 33–48.

Goodman, Lesley, 'Disappointing Fans: Fandom, Fictional Theory, and the Death of the Author', *The Journal of Popular Culture*, vol. 48, no. 4 (August, 2015), 662–76.

Gordon, John, 'Spot the Author', *James Joyce Quarterly*, vol. 28, no. 1 (Fall, 1990), 291–2.

Gorman, Herbert, *James Joyce* (New York: Farrar Rinehart, 1939).

Graziosi, Barbara, *Inventing Homer: The Early Reception of the Epic* (Cambridge: Cambridge University Press, 2002).

Graziosi, Barbara, and Emily Greenwood, eds, *Homer in the Twentieth Century: Between World Literature and the Western Canon* (London: Oxford University Press, 2007).

Groden, Michael, 'Preface', in *How Joyce Wrote 'Finnegans Wake': A Chapter-by-Chapter Genetic Guide*, ed. Luca Crispi and Sam Slote (Madison: University of Wisconsin Press, 2007), vii–xi.

—— *'Ulysses' in Progress* (Princeton, NJ: Princeton University Press, 1997).

Gross, John, *Joyce* (London: Fontana/Collins, 1971).

Grossman-Heinze, Dahlia, 'The witch hunt is coming for you, Woody Allen', *Bitch*, 27 October 2017 <https://www.bitchmedia.org/article/woody-allen-witch-hunt> [accessed 5 July 2021].

Groth, Helen, 'How to Listen to Joyce: Gramophones, Voice and the Limits of Mediation', in *Sounding Modernism: Rhythm and Sonic Mediation in Modern Literature and Film*, ed. Julian Murphet, Helen Groth, and Penelope Hone (Edinburgh: Edinburgh University Press, 2017), 63–76.

Guertin, Carolyn, *Digital Prohibition: Piracy and Authorship in New Media Art* (London: Continuum, 2012).

Haas, Lidija, 'Roland Barthes: "Author, I'm Sorry"', *The Telegraph*, 12 November 2015 <http://www.telegraph.co.uk/books/what-to-read/roland-barthes-centenary-death-of-the-author/> [accessed 5 July 2021].

Hall, Edith, *The Return of Ulysses: A Cultural History of Homer's 'Odyssey'* (London: I. B. Tauris and Co, 2008).

Harkin, Patricia, 'The Reception of Reader-Response Theory', *Composition and Communication*, vol. 56, no. 3 (February, 2005), 410–25.

Hart, Clive, 'Frank Budgen and the Story of the Making of *Ulysses*', in *Re-Viewing Classics of Joyce Criticism*, ed. Janet Egleson Dunleavy (Urbana and Chicago: University of Illinois Press, 1991), 120–30.

Hart, Clive, and David Hayman, eds, *James Joyce's 'Ulysses': Critical Essays* (Berkeley: University of California Press, 1974).

Hassan, Ihab, '( ): *Finnegans Wake* and the Postmodern Imagination', in *Light Rays: James Joyce and Modernism*, ed. Heyward Ehrlich (New York: New Horizon, 1984).

Hawthorn, Jeremy, 'Authority and the Death of the Author', in *Authority Matters: Rethinking the Theory and Practice of Authorship*, ed. Stephen Donovan, Danuta Fjellestad, and Rolf Lundén (Amsterdam and New York: Rodopi, 2008), 65–88.

Hayman, David, 'Genetic Criticism and Joyce: An Introduction', in *Probes: Genetic Studies in Joyce*, ed. David Hayman and Sam Slote, European Joyce Studies 5 (Amsterdam: Rodopi, 1995), 3–18.

—— *'Ulysses': The Mechanics of Meaning*, revised and extended edition (Madison: University of Wisconsin Press, 1982).

—— Hayman, David, and Sam Slote, eds, *Probes: Genetic Studies in Joyce*, European Joyce Studies 5 (Amsterdam: Rodopi, 1995).

Hayot, Eric, 'Then and Now', in *Critique and Post-critique*, ed. Elizabeth S. Anker and Rita Felski (Durham, NC and London: Duke University Press, 2017), 279–95.

Henke, Suzette, *James Joyce and the Politics of Desire* (London: Routledge, 1990).

Henke, Suzette, and Elaine Unkeless, eds, *Women in Joyce* (Urbana, Chicago, London: University of Illinois Press, 1982).

Herring, Phillip F., *Joyce's Uncertainty Principle* (Princeton, NJ: Princeton University Press, 1987).

Higgins, Charlotte, 'The Lost Books of the Odyssey', *The Guardian*, 15 May 2010 <http://www.theguardian.com/books/2010/may/15/lost-books-odyssey-zachary-mason> [accessed 16 June 2021].

Hirsch Jr, E. D., *Validity in Interpretation* (New Haven, CT: Yale University Press, 1967).

Hoad, T. F., ed., *The Concise Dictionary of English Etymology* (Oxford: Oxford University Press, 1986).

Hollier, Denis, 'Foucault: The Death of the Author', *Raritan*, vol. 5, no. 1 (1985), 22–30.

Homer, *The Odyssey*, trans. Walter Shewring (Oxford: Oxford University Press, 2008).

—— *The Odyssey*, trans. Emily Wilson (New York: W. W. Norton, 2018).

Iser, Wolfgang, *The Act of Reading: A Theory of Aesthetic Response* (London and Henley: Routledge and Kegan Paul, 1978).

—— *The Implied Reader: Patterns of Communication in Prose Fiction from Bunyan to Beckett* (Baltimore, MD and London: Johns Hopkins University Press, 1974).

―――― 'Ulysses and the Reader: Wolfgang Iser Discusses the Importance of Ulysses in the Development of "Reader Response" Criticism', *James Joyce Broadsheet*, no. 9 (October, 1982), 1–2.

Jaffe, Aaron, *Modernism and the Culture of Celebrity* (Cambridge: Cambridge University Press, 2005).

Jaffe, Aaron, and Jonathan Goldman, eds, *Modernist Star Maps: Celebrity, Modernity, Culture* (Farnham, Surrey and Burlington, VT: Ashgate, 2010).

James, Clive, 'Count Zero Splits the Infinite', in *Encounter*, November 1975 <https://archive.clivejames.com/books/stoppard.htm> [accessed 19 March 2021].

Joyce, James, *Finnegans Wake* (London: Faber, 1975).

―――― *A Portrait of the Artist as a Young Man* (London: Penguin, 1974).

―――― *Ulysses* (London: The Bodley Head, 1960).

―――― *Ulysses*, ed. Hans Walter Gabler with Wolfhard Steppe and Claus Melchior (London: The Bodley Head, 2008).

―――― *Ulysses: The 1922 text*, ed. Jeri Johnson (Oxford: Oxford University Press, 2008).

Joyce, Stanislaus, *My Brother's Keeper*, ed. Richard Ellmann (New York: The Viking Press, 1975).

Kain, Richard M., *Fabulous Voyager: James Joyce's 'Ulysses'* (Chicago: University of Chicago Press, 1947).

Kamuf, Peggy, *Signature Pieces: On the Institution of Authorship* (Ithaca, NY and London: Cornell University Press, 1988).

Kelley, Joseph, 'A Defense of Danis Rose', *James Joyce Quarterly*, vol. 35/36, vol. 35, no. 4–vol. 36, no. 1 (Summer–Fall, 1998), 811–24.

Kelly, Dermot, *Narrative Strategies in 'Ulysses'* (Ann Arbor, MI: UMI Research Press, 1988).

Kenner, Hugh, *Dublin's Joyce*, Morningside Edition (New York: Columbia University Press, 1987).

―――― *Flaubert, Joyce and Beckett: The Stoic Comedians* (London: Dalkey Archive Press and Normal, 2005).

―――― *Joyce's Voices* (Berkeley, Los Angeles, and London: University of California Press, 1978).

―――― *The Mechanical Muse* (Oxford: Oxford University Press, 1987).

―――― *The Pound Era* (Berkeley and Los Angeles: University of California Press, 1971).

―――― *'Ulysses'* (London: George Allen and Unwin, 1980).

Kershner, R. Brandon, 'Intertextuality', in *The Cambridge Companion to 'Ulysses'*, ed. Sean Latham (New York: Cambridge University Press, 2014), 171–83.

Kestner, Joseph, 'Virtual Text/Virtual Reader: The Structural Signature Within, Behind, Beyond, Above', *James Joyce Quarterly*, vol. 16, no. 1/2 (Fall, 1978/Winter, 1979), 27–42.

Kiberd, Declan, *'Ulysses' and Us: The Art of Everyday Living* (London: Faber, 2009).
Kidd, John, 'Making the wrong Joyce', *The New York Review of Books*, 25 September 1997 <http://www.nybooks.com/articles/1997/09/25/making-the-wrong-joyce/> [accessed 10 May 2021].
—— 'The scandal of *Ulysses*', *The New York Review of Books*, 30 June 1988 <http://www.nybooks.com/articles/1988/06/30/the-scandal-of-ulysses-2/> [accessed 10 May 2021].
Killeen, Terence, *'Ulysses' Unbound: A Reader's Companion to James Joyce's 'Ulysses'* (Gainesville: University Press of Florida, 2018).
Kimball, Jean, *Odyssey of the Psyche: Jungian Patterns in 'Ulysses'* (Carbondale: Southern Illinois University Press, 1997).
Knight, Diana, ed., *Critical Essays on Roland Barthes* (New York: G. K Hall, 2000).
Knowles, Sebastian D.G., *At Fault: Joyce and the Crisis of the Modern University* (Gainesville: University Press of Florida, 2018).
Koch, Vivienne, 'An Approach to the Homeric Content of Joyce's *Ulysses*', *Maryland Quarterly*, vol. 1 (1944), 119–30.
Koliades, Constantine, *Ulysses Homer; or, a Discovery of the True Author of the 'Iliad' and 'Odyssey'* (Whitfish, MT: Kessinger, 2010).
Kristeva, Julia, *Desire in Language: A Semiotic Approach to Literature and Art*, ed. Leon S. Roudiez, trans. Thomas Gora, Alice Jardine, and Leon S. Roudiez (New York: Columbia University Press, 1980).
Lacivita, Alison, *The Ecology of 'Finnegans Wake'* (Gainesville: University Press of Florida, 2015).
Lamb, Charles, *The Adventures of Ulysses*, ed. John Cook (Edinburgh: Split Pea, 1992).
Larbaud, Valéry, 'James Joyce', in *James Joyce: The Critical Heritage*, ed. Robert H. Deming, 2 vols (London: Routledge and Kegan Paul, 1970), 252–62.
Latham, Sean, ed., *The Cambridge Companion to 'Ulysses'* (New York: Cambridge University Press, 2014).
Latour, Bruno, 'Why Has Critique Run out of Steam? From Matters of Fact to Matters of Concern', *Critical Inquiry*, vol. 30, no. 2 (Winter, 2004), 225–48.
Lawrence, Karen, *The Odyssey of Style in 'Ulysses'* (Princeton, NJ: Princeton University Press, 1981).
—— *Who's Afraid of James Joyce?* (Gainesville: University Press of Florida, 2010).
Lernout, Geert, 'Controversial Editions: Hans Walter Gabler's *Ulysses*', *Text*, vol. 16 (2006), 229–41.
Lernout, Geert, *The French Joyce* (Ann Arbor: University of Michigan Press, 1990).

────── 'Nabokov on Joyce and *Ulysses*', in *Vladimir Nabokov's Lectures on Literature: Portraits of the Artist as Reader and Teacher*, ed. Ben Dhooge and Jürgen Pieters (Amsterdam: Brill, 2018), 101–20.
Levin, Harry, *James Joyce: A Critical Introduction* (Norfolk: New Directions, 1941).
────── *James Joyce: A Critical Introduction* (Norfolk: New Directions, 1960).
Levine, Jennifer, 'Rejoycings in "Tel Quel"', *James Joyce Quarterly*, vol. 16, no. 1/2, 'Structuralist/Reader Response Issue' (Fall, 1978–Winter, 1979), 17–26.
Levitt, Morton P., 'Harry Levin's *James Joyce* and the Modernist Age: A Personal Reading', in *Re-Viewing Classics of Joyce Criticism*, ed. Janet Egleson Dunleavy (Urbana and Chicago: University of Illinois Press, 1991), 90–105.
Lewis, Wyndham, *Time and Western Man* (London: Chatto and Windus, 1927).
Litz, A. Walton, *The Art of James Joyce: Method and Design in 'Ulysses' and 'Finnegans Wake'* (London: Oxford University Press, 1961).
────── 'The Genre of *Ulysses*', in *The Theory of the Novel: New Essays*, ed. John Halperin (New York: Oxford University Press, 1974).
Litz, A. Walton, Louis Menand, and Lawrence Rainey, eds, *Modernism and the New Criticism* (Cambridge: Cambridge University Press, 2000).
Loukopoulou, Eleni, *Up to Maughty London: Joyce's Cultural Capital in the Imperial Metropolis* (Gainesville: University Press of Florida, 2017).
Luce, J. V., *Homer and the Heroic Age* (London: Thames and Hudson, 1975).
Lyotard, Jean-François, *The Lyotard Reader and Guide*, ed. Keith Crome and James Williams (New York: Columbia University Press, 2006).
────── *The Postmodern Condition: A Report on Knowledge*, trans. Geoff Bennington and Brian Massumi (Manchester: Manchester University Press, 1984).
McArthur, Murray, 'The Example of Joyce: Derrida Reading Joyce', *James Joyce Quarterly*, vol. 32, no. 2 (Winter, 1995), 227–41.
MacCabe, Colin, *James Joyce and the Revolution of the Word* (London: Macmillan, 1978).
────── 'The Revenge of the Author', in *Subject to History: Ideology, Class, Gender*, ed. David Simpson (Ithaca, NY and London: Cornell University Press, 1991), 34–46.
────── 'Uneasiness in Culture', *Cambridge Review*, vol. 93, no. 2208 (2 June 1972), 174–7.
McCarthy, Patrick A., 'Stuart Gilbert's Guide to the Perplexed', in *Re-Viewing Classics of Joyce Criticism*, ed. Janet Egleson Dunleavy (Urbana and Chicago: University of Illinois Press, 1991), 23–35.
McCourt, John, ed., *James Joyce in Context* (Cambridge: Cambridge University Press, 2009).

McKeon, Michael, 'Writer as Hero: Novelistic Prefigurations and the Emergence of Literary Biography', in *Contesting the Subject: Essays in the Postmodern Theory and Practice of Biography and Biographical Criticism*, ed. William H. Epstein (West Lafayette, IN: Purdue University Press, 1991), 17–41.
Magalaner, Marvin and Richard M. Kain, *Joyce: The Man, The Work, The Reputation* (New York: New York University Press, 1956).
Mahaffey, Vicki, 'Intentional Error: The Paradox of Editing Joyce's *Ulysses*', in *Representing Modernist Texts: Editing as Interpretation*, ed. George Bornstein (Ann Arbor: University of Michigan Press, 1991), 171–91.
—— *Reauthorizing Joyce* (Cambridge: Cambridge University Press, 1988).
Mahon, Peter, *Imagining Joyce and Derrida: Between 'Finnegans Wake' and 'Glas'* (Toronto and London: University of Toronto Press, 2007).
Marmodoro, Anna, and Jonathan Hill, eds, *The Author's Voice in Classical and Late Antiquity* (Oxford: Oxford University Press, 2013).
Mason, Zachary, *The Lost Books of the 'Odyssey'* (London: Vintage, 2011).
Mehegan, David, 'For this writer, identity is subject to change', interview with Anne Enright, *Boston Globe*, 27 February 2008 <http://archive.boston.com/ae/books/articles/2008/02/27/for_this_writer_identity_is_subject_to_change/> [accessed 16 June 2021].
Melaney, William D., ed., *After Ontology: Literary Theory and Modernist Poetics* (Albany: State University of New York Press, 2001).
Milesi, Laurent, ed., *James Joyce and the Difference of Language* (Cambridge: Cambridge University Press, 2003).
Miller, Nancy K., 'Arachnologies: The Woman, The Text, and The Critic', in *The Poetics of Gender*, ed. Nancy K. Miller (New York: Columbia University Press, 1986), 270–95.
—— 'Changing the Subject: Authorship, Writing, and the Reader', in *Feminist Studies/Critical Studies*, ed. Teresa de Lauretis (London: Palgrave Macmillan 1986), 102–20.
Mitchell, Kaye, *Intention and Text: Towards an Intentionality of Literary Form* (London: Continuum, 2008).
Montgomery, Niall, Papers, MS 50, 118, National Library of Ireland, Dublin.
Moriarty, Michael, *Roland Barthes* (Cambridge: Polity, 1991).
Mullin, Katherine, *James Joyce, Sexuality and Social Purity* (Cambridge: Cambridge University Press, 2003).
Myrsiades, Kostas, ed., *Reading Homer: Film and Text* (Madison and Teaneck, NJ: Fairleigh Dickenson University Press, 2009).
Nabokov, Vladimir, *Lectures on Literature*, ed. Fredson Bowes, intro. John Updike (New York and London: Harcourt Brace Jovanovich, 1980).
Nagy, Gregory, *The Best of the Achaeans: Concepts of the Hero in Archaic Greek Poetry* (Baltimore, MD: Johns Hopkins University Press, 1975).

Nash, John, *James Joyce and the Act of Reception: Reading, Ireland, Modernism* (Cambridge: Cambridge University Press, 2006).
―― ed., *Joyce's Audiences*, European Joyce Studies 14 (Amsterdam: Rodopi, 2002).
Nehamas, Alexander, 'The Postulated Author: Critical Monism as a Regulative Ideal', *Critical Inquiry*, vol. 8, no. 1 (Autumn, 1981), 133–49.
―― 'What an Author Is', *The Journal of Philosophy*, vol. 83, no. 11, Eighty-Third Annual Meeting American Philosophical Association, Eastern Division (November, 1986), 685–91.
Nelson, Stephanie, 'Telling Time: Techniques of Narrative Time in *Ulysses* and the *Odyssey*', in *Reading Joycean Temporalities*, ed. Jolanta Wawrzycka (Leiden: Brill, 2017), 121–36.
―― *Time and Identity in 'Ulysses' and the 'Odyssey'* (forthcoming, Gainesville: University Press of Florida, 2022).
Nolan, Emer, *James Joyce and Nationalism* (London and New York: Routledge, 1995).
―― '"Who's he when he's at home?": Re-reading Joyce and Modernism', *Modernism/Modernity*, vol. 12, no. 3 (2005), 505–9.
Norris, Margot, *The Decentred Universe of 'Finnegans Wake': A Structuralist Analysis* (Baltimore, MD and London: Johns Hopkins University Press, 1976).
―― 'Review: *Post-Structuralist Joyce: Essays from the French*', *James Joyce Quarterly*, vol. 23, no. 3 (Spring, 1986), 365–70.
―― *Virgin and Veteran Readings of 'Ulysses'* (New York: Palgrave Macmillan, 2011).
Novillo-Corvalán, Patricia, *Borges and Joyce: An Infinite Conversation* (London: Legenda, 2011).
O'Brien, Flann, *Stories and Plays* (New York, Penguin, 1977).
O'Doherty, Brian, ed., *Aspen* no. 5 and 6, 'The Minimalism issue' (New York: Roaring Fork, 1967) <http://www.ubu.com/aspen/aspen5and6/index.html> [accessed 29 July 2021].
OED Online (Oxford University Press, July 2021) <www.oed.com> [accessed 29 July 2021].
Osteen, Mark, 'Review: *James Joyce and Critical Theory*, Alan Roughley', *James Joyce Quarterly*, vol. 30/31 (Summer–Fall, 1993), 909–12.
Page, Denys, *The Homeric 'Odyssey'* (London: Oxford University Press, 1955).
Parrinder, Patrick, *The Failure of Theory: Essays on Criticism and Contemporary Fiction* (Brighton: Harvester, 1987).
Peake, C. H., *James Joyce: The Citizen and the Artist* (London: Edward Arnold, 1977).
Peretz, Evgenia, 'James Frey's morning after', *Vanity Fair*, June 2008 <https://www.vanityfair.com/culture/2008/06/frey200806> [accessed 28 July 2021].
Pierce, David, *Reading Joyce* (Harlow: Pearson, 2008).

Platt, Len, *James Joyce: Texts and Contexts* (London: Continuum, 2011).
Plock, Vike Martina, '"The Seim Anew": Joyce Studies in the Twenty-First Century', *Literature Compass*, vol. 7, no. 6 (June, 2010), 477–83.
Porter, James I., 'Homer: The History of an Idea', in *The Cambridge Companion to Homer*, ed. Robert Fowler (Cambridge: Cambridge University Press, 2004), 324–43.
—— 'Homer: The Very Idea', *Arion: A Journal of Humanities and the Classics*, Third Series, vol. 10, no. 2 (Fall, 2002), 57–86.
Pound, Ezra, *Early Writings: Poems and Prose*, ed. Ira B. Nadel (London: Penguin, 2005).
Power, Arthur, *Conversations with James Joyce*, ed. Clive Hart (London: Millington, 1974).
—— *Conversations with James Joyce* (Dublin: Dalkey Archive, 2020).
—— 'Conversations with Joyce', *James Joyce Quarterly*, vol. 3, no. 1 (Fall, 1965), 41–9.
Power, Mary, 'The Discovery of "Ruby"', *James Joyce Quarterly*, vol. 18, no. 2 (Winter, 1981), 115–21.
Pucci, Pietro, *Odysseus Polutropos: Intertextual Readings in the 'Odyssey' and the 'Iliad'* (Ithaca, NY and London: Cornell University Press, 1987).
Rabaté, Jean-Michel, 'James Joyce (1882–1941): Theories of Literature', in *The Continuum Encyclopedia of Modern Criticism and Theory*, ed. Julian Wolfreys (New York: Continuum, 2002), 673–80.
—— *James Joyce, Authorized Reader* (Baltimore, MD: Johns Hopkins University Press, 1991).
—— 'The Joyce of French Theory', in *A Companion to James Joyce*, ed. Richard Brown (Malden: Blackwell, 2008), 254–69.
Remnick, David, 'The war over *Ulysses*', *The Washington Post*, 2 April 1985 <https://www.washingtonpost.com/archive/lifestyle/1985/04/02/the-war-over-ulysses/5bc5964b-0486-4005-beb7-1e56e36590d2/?utm_term=.0245708ccace> [accessed 29 July 2021].
Ridgeway, Ann, 'Two Authors in Search of a Reader', *James Joyce Quarterly*, vol. 1, no. 4 (Summer, 1964), 41–51.
Riquelme, John Paul, *Teller and Tale in Joyce's Fiction: Oscillating Perspectives* (Baltimore, MD and London: Johns Hopkins University Press, 1983).
Robillard, Amy E., and Ron Fortune, eds, *Authorship Contested: Cultural Challenges to the Authentic, Autonomous Author* (New York and London: Routledge, 2015).
Rooney, Ellen, 'Symptomatic Reading is a Problem of Form', in *Critique and Post-critique*, ed. Elizabeth S. Anker and Rita Felski (Durham, NC and London: Duke University Press, 2017), 127–52.
Rose, Steve, 'JT LeRoy unmasked: the extraordinary story of a modern literary hoax', *The Guardian*, 20 July 2016 <https://www.theguardian.com/

film/2016/jul/20/jt-leroy-story-modern-literary-hoax-> [accessed 28 July 2021].

Roughley, Alan, *James Joyce and Critical Theory: An Introduction* (Hemel Hempstead: Harvester Wheatsheaf, 1991).

────── *Reading Derrida Reading Joyce* (Gainesville: University Press of Florida, 1999).

Roupenian, Kristen, *Cat Person And Other Stories* (London: Vintage, 2019).

Saint-Amour, Paul K., *The Copywrights: Intellectual Property and the Literary Imagination* (Ithaca, NY and London: Cornell University Press, 2003).

────── 'Review: James Joyce and the Difference of Language by Laurent Milesi', *South Atlantic Review*, vol. 70, no. 1 (Winter, 2005), 189–93.

Sandulescu, C. George, and Clive Hart, eds, *Assessing the 1984 'Ulysses'* (Gerrards Cross: Colin Smythe, 1986).

Sartiliot, Claudette, *Citation and Modernity: Derrida, Joyce, and Brecht* (Norman and London: University of Oklahoma Press, 1993).

Sartor, Genevieve, ed., *James Joyce and Genetic Criticism: Genesic Fields* (Leiden: Brill, 2018).

Saunders, Max, *Life-writing, Autobiografiction, and the Forms of Modern Literature* (Oxford: Oxford University Press, 2010).

Seidel, Michael, *Epic Geography: James Joyce's 'Ulysses'* (Princeton, NJ and Guilford: Princeton University Press, 1976).

Senn, Fritz, *Inductive Scrutinies: Focus on Joyce*, ed. Christine O'Neill (Dublin: Lilliput, 1995).

────── *Joyce's Dislocutions: Essays on Reading as Translation*, ed. John Paul Riquelme (Baltimore, MD and London: Johns Hopkins University Press, 1984).

────── 'Letter to the Editor', *James Joyce Quarterly*, vol. 24, no. 1 (Fall, 1986), 115–16.

────── 'Review: Prodding Nodding Joyce: The "Reader's Edition" of "Ulysses", Edited by Danis Rose: Some First Impressions', *James Joyce Quarterly*, vol. 34, no. 4 (Summer, 1997), 573–83.

────── *Ulyssean Close-ups* (Rome: Bulzoni Editore, 2007).

Skains, R. Lyle, *Digital Authorship: Publishing in the Attention Economy* (Cambridge: Cambridge University Press, 2019).

Skeat, Walter W., *The Concise Dictionary of English Etymology* (Ware: Wordsworth, 2007).

Skrabanek, Peter, '*Finnegans Wake* – Night Joyce of a Thousand Tiers', in *The Artist and the Labyrinth*, ed. Augustine Martin (London: Ryan, 1990), 229–40.

Slote, Sam, '*Ulysses* in the Plural: The Variable Editions of Joyce's Novel', The National Library of Ireland Joyce Studies 5 (Dublin: National Library of Ireland, 2004).

Slote, Sam and Wim van Mierlo, eds, *Genitricksling Joyce*, European Joyce Studies 9 (Amsterdam: Rodopi, 1999).
Sontag, Susan, ed., *A Roland Barthes Reader* (London: Vintage, 2000).
—— ed., *A Roland Barthes Reader* (London: Vintage, 2018).
—— *Against Interpretation and Other Essays* (New York: Farrar Straus Giroux, 1966).
Spark, Muriel, *The Comforters* (Edinburgh: Polygon, 2017).
Staley, Thomas F., 'Notes and Comments', *James Joyce Quarterly*, vol. 3, no. 1 (Fall, 1965), 1–2.
Stanford, W. B., *The Ulysses Theme: A Study in the Adaptability of a Traditional Hero* (Oxford: Basil Blackwell, 1954).
Steinberg, Erwin R., 'Author! Author!', *James Joyce Quarterly*, vol. 22, no. 4 (Summer, 1985), 419–25.
Steinberg, Erwin R., and Christian W. Hallstein, 'Probing Silences in Joyce's *Ulysses* and the Question of Authorial Intention', *James Joyce Quarterly*, vol. 40, no. 3 (Spring, 2003), 543–54.
Stillinger, Jack, *Multiple Authorship and the Myth of Solitary Genius* (New York and Oxford: Oxford University Press, 1991).
Stoppard, Tom, *Arcadia* (London: Faber, 1993).
—— *Travesties* (London: Faber, 1975).
Talbot, Mary M., and Bryan Talbot, *Dotter of her Father's Eyes* (London: Jonathan Cape, 2012).
Thomas, Brook, *James Joyce's 'Ulysses': A Book of Many Happy Returns* (Baton Rouge and London: Louisiana State University Press, 1982).
Thurston, Luke, ed., *Re-inventing the Symptom: Essays on the Final Lacan* (London: Karnac, 2002).
Tompkins, Jane P., ed., *Reader-Response Criticism: From Formalism to Post-Structuralism* (Baltimore, MD and London: Johns Hopkins University Press, 1980).
Valente, Joseph, ed., *Quare Joyce* (Ann Arbor: University of Michigan Press, 1998).
Van Caspel, Paul, *Bloomers on the Liffey: Eisegetical Readings of Joyce's 'Ulysses'* (Baltimore, MD and London: Johns Hopkins University Press, 1986).
Van Hulle, Dirk. *Manuscript Genetics, Joyce's Know-How, Beckett's Nohow* (Gainesville: University Press of Florida, 2008).
Van Mierlo, Wim, 'Reading Joyce in and out of the Archive', *Joyce Studies Annual*, vol. 13 (Summer, 2002), 32–63.
Vichnar, David, *Joyce Against Theory: James Joyce After Deconstruction* (Praha: Univerzita Karlova v Praze, 2010).
Walker, Cheryl, 'Feminist Literary Criticism and the Author', *Critical Inquiry*, vol. 16, no. 3 (Spring, 1990), 551–71.

Wattis, Nigel, dir., 'The Modern World: Ten Great Writers: James Joyce's *Ulysses*', (*BBC*, 10 January 1988).

Wawrzycka, Jolanta, and Serenella Zanotti, eds, *James Joyce's Silences* (New York: Bloomsbury, 2018).

Wilson, Adrian, 'Foucault on the "question of the author": A Critical Exegesis', *The Modern Language Review*, vol. 99, no. 2 (April, 2004), 339–63.

Wilson, Edmund, *Axel's Castle* (New York: Charles Scribner's Sons, 1950).

—— 'James Joyce's *Ulysses*', in *The Portable Edmund Wilson*, ed. Lewis M. Dabrey (New York: Da Capo Press, 1997), 150–67.

Wolf, Friedrich August, *Prolegomena to Homer*, trans. Anthony Grafton, Glenn W. Most, and James E. G. Zetzel (Princeton, NJ: Princeton University Press, 1985).

Wollaeger, Mark A., 'Stephen/Joyce, Joyce/Haacke: Modernism and the Social Function of Art', *ELH*, vol. 62, no. 3 (Fall, 1995), 691–707.

Woodmansee, Martha, 'The Genius and the Copyright: Economic and Legal Conditions of the Emergence of the "Author"', *Eighteenth-Century Studies*, vol. 17, no. 4 (Summer, 1984), 425–48.

Young, Edward, 'Conjectures on Original Composition in a Letter to the Author of Sir Charles Grandison', in *English Critical Essays. Sixteenth, Seventeenth, and Eighteenth Centuries*, ed. Edmund D. Jones (London: Oxford University Press, 1975).

INDEX

Abrams, M. H., 16–17, 85, 183
Ackroyd, Peter, 30
Adair, Gilbert, 2
Aldington, Richard, 42, 57
Allen, Woody, 32–3
Anderson, Margaret, 40
Ansse de Villoison, J.-B.-G. d,' 82
anti-authorialism
  act of reading, 140, 200
  of Barthes, 5, 14, 162–3, 164
  critical rejection of, 30
  in criticism and theory of the 1980s and 1990s, 29–31
  'The Death of the Author' (Barthes), 1–2, 5, 13, 14, 19, 21–4, 25–7, 29, 33, 34, 139, 197
  deconstruction as, 20
  Joycean criticism of the 1970–80s, 108–9
  limitless reading and authorless texts, 23, 86, 96, 132, 139, 140–1, 156
  term, 10
  theory and criticism, 15, 20–1, 29
Attridge, Derek, 109–11, 112, 113, 126, 160, 192

Aubert, Jacques, 110
author-centrism
  Barthes's view of, 175
  foundational period, 16–17
  term, 10
authority
  authorial authority and the critics, 163–6
  authorially approved readings of *Ulysses*, 6–7, 41–2, 43, 44, 47–8, 62, 131
  authority of 'right' readings in Joyce studies, 6–7, 41–2, 43, 44, 47–8, 62, 102–3, 104, 105, 131, 161–8
  and quotation from biographies, 191
  readerly authority of intertextuality, 146–7, 162–3
  of the self-empowered reader, 116, 161–4, 167–8, 198–9
  sources of interpretative authority in Joyce studies, 105–6, 107, 111, 114, 115, 116–17
  term, 10

author/reader/text relationship
  within criticism and theory, 5–6
  'The Death of the Author' and, 1–2, 13, 14, 21–4, 25–7, 29, 34, 139, 196, 197
  in Joyce studies, 7–8, 104, 105, 116–24, 198
  for *Ulysses*, 1, 4, 28, 198–201
  in works of fiction, 2–3, 87, 91–3, 174, 197
  see also authorship; reading; texts
authorship
  the author as literary subject, 16–17, 18–19, 31
  the author as replaced by language, 19–20, 21
  the author in twenty-first century literary criticism, 31–2
  author-function concept, 21, 28, 86
  authorial authority of the critics, 163–6
  authorial intention, 122–3, 131–2, 162, 167
  authorial return in Joyce studies, 118–21
  authorially approved readings of *Ulysses*, 6–7, 41–2, 43, 44, 47–8, 62, 131
  author-texts, 32
  the 'Butler' figure, 89–91, 94
  capitalist authorship as ownership, 15, 16, 18–19, 32–3
  in celebrity studies, 31–2, 123–4
  critical perspectives, 5–6, 15, 20–1, 28–9
  feminist literary criticism, 31
  fictionalisations of, 2–3, 87, 91
  in genetic criticism, 127–8, 132, 162
  the genius author, 15–16, 17–19, 140, 156–9, 167–8, 175–6, 177–8, 186–7, 188, 199
  histories of, 14–20
  Homer as authoress, 71, 87–91, 94, 191, 198
  how to read the author/text relationship, 41–2, 48, 59–60, 62–3, 124–32
  Joyce as author, 9–10
  the Joyce/Stephen Dedalus relationship, 48–51, 54–5, 58, 119, 120–1, 173–4, 180, 198
  of memoirs and biography, 182–3
  modernist perspectives, 17–18, 30
  of nineteenth-century romanticism, 14, 15–16, 18–19, 85
  as performance, 94–5
  presumptions of autobiography, 12–13
  the return of the author in 1980–90s literary studies, 29–31
  role of the author in *Travesties* (Stoppard), 186–7, 188, 190–1
  scholarship on Homeric authorship, 81–7
  Stephen Dedalus's theories of authorship, 3–4, 7, 18, 41, 119, 123, 158
  term, 10
  see also anti-authorialism
autobiography, 12–13; *see also* biography

Baldick, Chris, 20
Banville, John, 157–8
Baron, Scarlett, 122, 162, 163
Barthes, Roland
  anti-authorialism, 5, 14, 162–3, 164
  authorial authority of, 164
  birth of the reader, 1–2, 5–6, 10, 21, 86, 159, 198–9
  capitalist authorship as ownership, 19
  The Death and Return (Burke) and, 10, 19–20, 23, 29–31, 33
  'The Death of the Author,' 1–2, 5, 13, 14, 19, 21–4, 25–7, 29, 33, 34, 139, 196, 197
  the death of the author in fiction, 2–3
  levels of reading, 139, 141, 162

limitless reading and authorless texts, 23, 86, 96, 132, 139, 140–1, 156
the preterite tense, 75, 91, 93, 94, 96, 189
'On Reading,' 139, 162
The Rustle of Language, 139
S/Z, 24–5, 61, 139, 147
texts as mixed writings and tissues of quotations, 23–5, 26, 31, 56, 86, 138–9, 148
'From Work to Text,' 5, 25–6, 27, 139
Writing Degree Zero, 75, 189
'Writing Reading,' 147
Bayard, Pierre, 1
Beach, Sylvia, 40
Beardsley, Monroe C., 29
Beckett, Samuel, 51
Benjamin, Walter, 27–8, 80
Benstock, Bernard, 106, 112
Bérard, Victor, 43, 88
Bersani, Leo, 9, 121–2, 146, 155, 158
Binet, Laurent, 2–3
biography
  authority and quotation from, 191
  authorship and presumptions of, 12–13
  authorship of, 182–3
  biographical criticism, 119, 120, 123, 174, 175, 183, 191
  Conversations with James Joyce (Power), 119, 120, 123, 174, 175, 176, 181–2, 183–4, 187, 189
  critics quotation of biographies, 119, 120, 123, 183, 189, 192
  elements of fiction, 191
  intersections of literary, critical, theoretical, and biographical reading, 4–5, 33–4, 174–6
  James Joyce and the Making of 'Ulysses' (Budgen), 41, 55, 174, 175, 176–9, 180–1, 187
  James Joyce (Ellmann), 174, 175, 179–80
  Joyce as the genius author, 175–6, 177–8
  the Joyce/Stephen Dedalus relationship, 48–51, 54–5, 58, 119, 120–1, 173–4, 180
  life-art relationship in Joyce studies, 49, 55, 173–4, 192
  readings of self-portraiture, 180–1
  writing the 'real' Joyce, 175
Bleich, David, 20
Boheemen-Saaf, Christine van, 112
Boldrini, Lucia, 122
Booker, M. Keith, 122
Bowker, Gordon, 174
Bristow, Daniel, 183
Brooker, Joseph, 7, 8, 116
Bruni, Alessandro Francini, 174
Budgen, Frank
  centrality of Bloom, 55
  elements of fiction, 191
  James Joyce and the Making of 'Ulysses,' 41, 55, 174, 175, 176–9, 180–1
  Joyce's involvement with *The Making of 'Ulysses,'* 175, 176, 180
  on Joyce's use of language, 177
  the Joyce/Stephen Dedalus relationship, 49, 55
Burke, Seán
  authorial authority of critics, 164
  The Death and Return of the Author, 10, 19–20, 23, 29–31, 33
  on Paul de Man, 30–1
Butler, Christopher, 7
Butler, Samuel
  on the artist, 173
  The Authoress of the 'Odyssey', 6, 71, 87–90, 93, 94, 101 n.64, 170 n.30, 191, 192 n.3, 198
  the 'Butler' figure, 89–91, 94
  Homer as authoress, 6, 71, 87–91, 94, 191, 198
  relationship with Joyce, 87–8, 90

Carlyle, Thomas, 17, 173
celebrity studies, 31–2, 123–4
Cixous, Hélène, 40, 62–3, 107, 110

Collingwood, R. G., 165
Conley, Tim, 97 n.9, 122–3, 183
criticism *see* Joyce studies; literary criticism; *Ulysses* criticism
Culler, Jonathan, 109

Davies, Stan Gébler, 174, 175
Davis, Oliver, 128–9
deconstruction
  as anti-authorialism, 20
  Joyce and the development of, 20, 112–13
  Joyce studies and, 6, 106, 109, 114, 125
  meaning in texts, 109
Derrida, Jacques
  approach to reading Joyce, 9, 110–11
  Derridean Joyce studies, 115, 125
  the 'double laughter' in *Ulysses*, 113, 141, 156, 159–60
  Joyce and the development of deconstruction, 20, 112–13
  Joyce studies' response to, 106, 110
  'Structure, Sign, and Play in the Discourse of the Human Sciences' lecture, 20, 29
  talks at Joyce Symposia, 103–4, 106–7, 111, 112–13
  'Two Words for Joyce,' 9, 106, 110–11, 113
  'Ulysses Gramophone,' 112, 113, 125, 140, 157, 159
Dettmar, Kevin J. H., 120, 183
Diepeveen, Leonard, 155
Donovan, Stephen, 32

Eco, Umberto, 103, 107
Eliot, T. S.
  authorial disappearance, 17–18, 30
  authorially approved readings of *Ulysses*, 69
  corrective attitude to early criticism, 44, 57–8
  '*Ulysses*, Order, and Myth,' 42

Ellmann, Richard
  James Joyce, 174, 175, 179–80
  '*Ulysses' on the Liffey*, 63, 109
Enright, Anne, 100 n.63, 157, 160

Fairhall, James, 129
Felski, Rita, 31, 32
feminist literary criticism, 31, 107, 112, 121, 130
Ferrer, Daniel, 109–11, 112
fiction
  author/reader/text relationship, 2–3, 87, 91–3
  death of the author, 2–3
  fictionalisations of historical characters, 174
  and the Homeric Question, 87, 91–3, 197
Finnegans Wake, 4, 40, 56, 103, 110, 113, 115, 139, 154, 183
Fish, Stanley, 20
Fjellestad, Danuta, 32
Flack, Leah Culligan, 6, 68–70, 94
Flaubert, Gustave, 3, 17, 51, 163
Folkenflik, Robert, 16, 17, 27, 30
Foucault, Michel
  author-function concept, 21, 28, 86
  authorial authority of, 164
  'What is an Author?,' 21, 27–8, 126
Frank, Joseph, 62
French, Marilyn, 63, 109
French theory, 40, 62–3, 106, 107, 108, 109, 112; *see also* deconstruction; poststructuralism
Friedman, Susan Stanford, 7, 31, 118, 121, 163
Froula, Christine, 7, 121, 193 n.6

Gabler, Hans Walter, 107, 112, 113–14, 127
Garber, Megan, 13
genetic criticism, 107, 112, 124–5, 127–9, 132, 162
Genette, Gérard, 75, 81, 93
Gibbons, Stella, 147, 161, 162

Gilbert, Stuart
  authorially approved readings of
    Ulysses, 43, 44, 47–8, 62, 69, 131
  corrective attitude to early criticism,
    44, 57–8
  corrective attitude towards, 45–6,
    47–8, 58–60
  Homeric schema, 40, 43–4, 46–7,
    68–9
  James Joyce's 'Ulysses,' 40, 43, 62, 178
  Joyce's role/authorial presence, 41
  on the Joyce/Stephen Dedalus
    relationship, 48–9
  phrasing in critical texts, 56
Gillespie, Michael Patrick, 55, 61, 119,
  127, 158, 163, 183
Glasheen, Adaline, 40
Glass, Loren, 18, 32, 174
Goldberg, S. L., 50–1, 109, 173
Goldman, Jonathan, 123, 124, 158, 167
Gorman, Herman, 174
Grafton, Anthony, 82, 83
Graziosi, Barbara, 6, 84–7
Groden, Michael, 128
Guertin, Carolyn, 18

Hall, Edith, 87, 89–90
Hallstein, Christian W., 164–5
Hart, Clive, 63, 149, 152, 176–7
Hastings, Beatrice (Emily Alice Haigh),
  182
Hawthorn, Jeremy, 32, 33
Hayman, David
  the Arranger narrative device, 51,
    52–3, 54, 76
  on genetic criticism, 128
  *James Joyce's 'Ulysses': Critical
    Essays*, 63
  Stephen's authorial theory, 54
Heap, Jane, 40
Heath, Stephen, 108
Heyne, Christian Gottlob, 82
Homeric Question
  the absent Homer-author, 86, 159
  birth of the reader and, 86, 91
  Butler's authoress, 71, 87–91, 94, 191,
    198
  etymological analysis, 83
  in 'Eumaeus,' 71
  fictionalisations of authorship, 87,
    91–3, 197
  and ideated authorship, 70, 84–5
  in Joyce studies, 6, 69–71
  multiple Homers, 84–5, 86
  orality of the Homeric texts, 70, 82–3
  questions of authorship, 69, 70–1, 81–7
  relevance of the *Odyssey* to *Ulysses*, 69
  scholarship on Homeric authorship,
    81–7
  term, 69
  Victorian Homeric scholarship, 87–8,
    90, 91
Hulle, Dirk van, 128

identity
  constructions of self by authors as
    celebrities, 32
  disguise and identity in *Ulysses*, 68,
    190
  disguise in *Travesties* (Stoppard),
    189–90
  in the *Odyssey*, 68, 80, 81, 91, 93,
    94–5, 190
intertextuality
  Arcadia's intertextuality with *Ulysses*,
    147, 161, 162
  in 'The Death of the Author'
    (Barthes), 23–4
  Friedman's work on, 31, 121, 163
  Joyce's intertextual practices, 122
  Kristeva's theorisation, 5, 20, 25, 163
  between Molly and the reader, 138
  readerly authority of, 146–7, 162–3
  of *Travesties* with *The Importance of
    Being Earnest*, 184, 187–8, 189–90
  of *Ulysses*, 85–6, 146–7, 148, 161–2,
    163
  Ulysses correspondences with the
    Odyssey, 5, 43, 46–7, 51, 60, 69–70,
    196, 198

Irish Studies, 107, 129
Iser, Wolfgang, 20, 21, 115, 131

Jaffe, Aaron, 7, 32, 123
James, Clive, 188
Johnson, Jeri, 150, 152
Johnson, Samuel, 182–3
Jones, Ellen Carol, 112, 113
Joyce, James
   authorially approved readings of *Ulysses*, 6–7, 41–2, 43, 44, 47–8, 62, 197–8
   biographical texts and gossipy memoirs, 174
   of Budgen, 41, 55, 174, 175, 176–9, 180–1, 187
   dispute with Henry Carr, 184
   of Ellmann's biography, 174, 175, 179–80, 187
   as the genius author, 156–8, 167–8, 175–6, 177–8, 186–7, 188
   involvement with *The Making of 'Ulysses'* (Budgen), 175, 176, 180
   life of in criticism, 173–4
   life-art relationship in Joyce studies, 49, 55, 173–4, 192
   of Power's memoir, 119, 120, 123, 174, 175, 176, 181–2, 183–4, 187, 189
   presentation of Stephen Dedalus, 4
   of Stoppard, 176, 187
   thematic studies on, 173
   in *Travesties* (Stoppard), 181, 184–8
Joyce, Stanislaus, 174
Joyce studies
   authorial return, 118–21
   authority of 'right' readings, 6–7, 41–2, 43, 44, 47–8, 62, 102–3, 104, 105, 131, 161–8
   author/reader/text relationship, 7–8, 40, 104, 105, 116–24, 198
   biographical texts and gossipy memoirs, 174
   conferences, 102, 103–4, 106
   contradictory corrective urge in, 44–8, 57–60, 62
   critical conflation and separation of Stephen Dedalus and Joyce, 41, 48–55, 198
   deconstruction and, 6, 106, 109, 114, 125
   engagement with literary theory, 105–7, 108–12, 114, 116, 126
   feminist Joyce criticism, 107, 112, 121, 130
   French theory, 40, 62–3, 106, 107, 108, 109, 112
   genetic criticism, 107, 112, 124–5, 127–9, 132, 162
   historicist criticism, 107, 115, 120, 124–5, 129–30
   Homeric Question in, 6, 69–71
   Joyce, term, 9–10
   Joycean intention, 122–3, 131–2, 162, 167
   Joyce's role/authorial presence, 41–2
   life-art relationship, 49, 55, 173–4, 192
   metacritical studies, 39
   political approaches, 120, 124–5, 129–30
   poststructuralism and, 6, 104, 106, 107, 109–10, 112, 114, 116, 118, 160–1, 197
   questions of history and politics, 107, 115
   resistance to literary theory, 106–7, 109, 110, 111, 112, 114–15, 116, 125–6
   sources of interpretative authority, 105–6, 107, 111, 114, 115, 116–17
   thematic studies, 173
   women scholars, 40, 107, 112
   see also biography; literary criticism; *Ulysses* criticism
Joyce Symposia, 106–7, 111–12, 129

Kain, Richard M.
   corrective attitude towards Gilbert's study, 45, 58, 60, 131
   Fabulous Voyager, 44, 45

Joyce: The Man, The Work, The Reputation, 39, 40
the Joyce/Stephen Dedalus relationship, 49
non-literary printed paraphernalia, 44–5
phrasing in critical texts, 55–6
role of the reader, 57
Kamuf, Peggy, 23, 30
Keble, John, 17, 85, 165, 183
Kelley, Joseph, 127, 164–5
Kenner, Hugh
  the Arranger narrative device, 51–2, 53–4, 55, 57, 58, 76, 85, 153, 158
  corrective attitude towards Gilbert's study, 58–9
  critical reappraisals of, 61
  critiques of Butler's authoress, 87–8, 90
  on the difficulty of the text, 155
  Dublin's Joyce, 46–7, 53, 55, 176
  Flaubert, Joyce and Beckett: The Stoic Comedians, 51, 52, 53, 79
  Goldberg's critique of, 50–1
  Homeric schema, 40, 46–7, 51, 58, 60, 68, 69
  invisible quotation marks in the narration, 58–9
  Joyce's role/authorial presence, 41, 50–1, 60–1, 122, 131, 173
  Joyce's Voices, 51–2, 53
  the Joyce/Stephen Dedalus relationship, 49–51, 54–5, 58
  on jumbled letters/mistypes, 77
  on *The Making of 'Ulysses'* (Budgen), 55, 176, 178
  narrative gaps, 154
  physicality of the text, 51, 52, 57, 76, 79
  reading of 'Eumaeus,' 74
  role of the reader, 57, 60–1
  shifts from oral to printed texts, 78–9, 85
  'Ulysses,' 40, 53, 57
  the Uncle Charles Principle, 51–2, 55, 57, 58, 74–5, 79, 81, 93, 94, 151, 152–3

Kidd, John, 112, 114
Kimball, Jean, 183
Koch, Vivienne, 43–4
Kristeva, Julia, 5, 20, 25, 107, 115, 121, 163

Lacan, Jacques, 106, 111
language
  the author as replaced by, 19–20, 21
  Bloom's style of speech, 73–4
  in deconstruction, 20
  errors in printed matter, 67–8, 76–81
  the Eumaean narrative style, 67–8, 70, 71–6, 78–9, 80, 81, 89–90, 95–6, 152, 153
  free indirect speech, 74
  of Joyce in *The Making of 'Ulysses'* (Budgen), 177
  on jumbled letters/mistypes, 77
  of Molly in 'Penelope,' 138
  from oral to written text, 77–80, 85
  the preterite tense, 75, 91, 93, 94, 96
  the Uncle Charles Principle, 51–2, 55, 57, 58, 74–5, 79, 81, 93, 94, 151, 152–3
Larbaud, Valéry, 42, 43, 56, 69
Lawrence, Karen, 59, 109, 112, 116, 131, 152, 158
Lernout, Geert, 106, 107, 112, 113, 114–15, 116, 130–1
Levin, Harry
  corrective attitude towards Gilbert's study, 40, 58, 60
  Homeric schema, 50–1
  James Joyce: A Critical Introduction, 44
  Joyce's role/authorial presence, 48–9, 60, 131
  on the Joyce/Stephen Dedalus relationship, 48–9
  phrasing in critical texts, 56
  role of the reader, 56, 57
Levine, Jennifer, 109
Levitt, Morton P., 49
Lewis, Wyndham, 42–3, 50, 57

Linati, Carlo, 41, 69
literary criticism
  the author in twenty-first century literary criticism, 31–2
  authorial authority of, 163–6
  author/text/criticism relationship, 5–6, 15, 20–1, 22, 59, 61–2
  biographical criticism, 119, 120, 123, 174, 175, 183, 191
  corrective criticism, 44–8, 58–60, 62
  feminist literary criticism, 31, 107, 112, 121, 130
  of fictionalisation of historical figures, 174
  genetic criticism, 107, 112, 124–5, 127–9, 132, 162
  historicist criticism, 107, 115, 124–5, 129–30
  interaction with conference talks, 103–4
  New Criticism, 29
  political approaches, 124–5
  the return of the author in 1980–90s literary studies, 29–31
  see also Joyce studies; Ulysses criticism
Litz, A. Walton
  The Art of James Joyce, 44–6, 128, 129
  authority from Joyce's worksheets, 45–6, 60
  corrective attitude towards Gilbert's study, 40, 58
  phrasing in critical texts, 56
Loukopoulou, Eleni, 123, 124
Luce, J. V., 82
Lundén, Rolf, 32
Lyotard, Jean-François, 107

McCabe, Colin, 30, 108, 109, 120
McCarthy, Patrick A., 43, 46, 47, 59–60
McCourt, John, 174
McKeon, Michael, 16, 27, 30, 182–3
Magalaner, Marvin, 39
Mahaffey, Vicki, 7, 121, 122, 158
Mallarmé, Stéphane, 19–20, 21

Man, Paul de, 3, 30–1
Mason, Zachary, 87, 91–3
Menand, Louis, 37 n.45
Mierlo, Wim van, 129
Milesi, Laurent, 116
Miller, Nancy K., 31, 121
modernism, 17–18, 30, 123
Modigliani, Amedeo, 182
Monnier, Adrienne, 40
Moriarty, Michael, 26–7, 30, 164, 175
Most, Glenn W., 82, 83
Mullin, Katherine, 43, 68, 69

Nabokov, Vladimir, 75
Nagy, Gregory, 83, 85
narrative
  active reading and narrative gaps, 154–6
  the Arranger narrative device, 51–4, 55, 57, 58, 76, 85, 153, 158
  author-narrator figures in Joyce, 119
  Bloom within the narrative, 68, 73–4, 75, 78–9, 80, 90, 95, 140
  invisible quotation marks in the narration, 58–9
  language of the Eumaean narrative style, 67–8, 70, 71–6, 78–9, 80, 81, 89–90, 95–6, 152, 153
  the MacGuffin, 82, 95
  the machine beneath the narrative, 50–1, 53
  as a mask, 81, 94, 189
  narrative focus of 'Wandering Rocks,' 140, 141, 148–54, 155
  naturalising style, 59
  third person narration, 75, 91, 93, 94, 96
  the Uncle Charles Principle, 51–2, 55, 57, 58, 74–5, 79, 81, 93, 94, 151, 152–3
Nash, John, 7, 8
Nehamas, Alexander, 30, 172 n.64, 195 n.46
Nelson, Stephanie, 6, 69, 70
Nolan, Emer, 129

Norris, Margot, 7–8, 40, 63, 107, 111, 125, 154
Novillo-Corvalán, Patricia, 122

O'Brien, Edna, 174
Odyssey
  authorship, 81–6
  Butcher and Lang translation, 81, 166
  correspondences with *Ulysses*, 4, 5, 43, 46–7, 51, 60, 69–70, 196, 198
  creative reading of, 86
  disguise and identity in, 68, 80, 81, 91, 93, 94–5, 190
  the narrative, 81, 94–5
  Ulysses as a rewritten *Odyssey*, 68, 80, 82, 96–7
  see also Homeric Question
orality
  of the Homeric texts, 70, 82–3
  shifts from oral to written text in *Ulysses*, 70, 71, 77–80, 85

Peake, Charles, 63, 66 n.43
Porter, James I., 82, 84, 87–8, 90, 94
Portrait of the Artist as a Young Man, A
  as (auto)biography, 49
  in Ellmann's biography, 179–80
  Joyce's role/authorial presence, 48–9
  the Joyce/Stephen Dedalus relationship, 48–50
  Stephen Dedalus' theories of authorship, 3, 7, 41, 48, 119, 123, 158
poststructuralism
  anti-authorialism, 29–30, 31
  author/reader/text relationship, 104
  Joyce studies and, 6, 63, 104, 106, 107, 109–10, 112, 114, 116, 118, 160–1, 197
  Kenner's similarities with, 61–2
Pound, Ezra, 42, 43, 46
Power, Arthur
  Conversations with James Joyce, 119, 120, 123, 174, 175, 176, 181–2, 183–4, 187, 189

  critics' quoting of Joyce-via-Power, 119, 120, 123, 183, 189
  elements of fiction, 191
Power, Mary, 101 n.73

queer theory, 121, 130
Quincey, Thomas de, 83

Rabaté, Jean-Michel, 7, 113, 118–19, 120, 131, 162, 163–4
Rainey, Lawrence, 37 n.45, 127
reader, term, 9
reader response criticism, 6, 20–1
reading
  active reading, 24, 26, 145–8, 154–6, 167, 199–200
  annotation and, 148
  authority of 'right' readings in Joyce studies, 6–7, 41–2, 43, 44, 47–8, 62, 102–3, 104, 105, 131, 161–8
  authority of the critics, 163–6
  authority of the self-empowered reader, 116, 161–4, 167–8, 198–9
  Barthesian levels of reading, 139, 141, 162
  the birth of the reader, 1–2, 5–6, 10, 20–1, 24, 86, 159, 198–9
  of 'Cat Person' (Roupenian), 12–13
  of 'difficult' texts, 1, 140, 141, 146, 147, 154–6
  fictionalisations of, 2–3, 87, 91–3
  how to read the author/text relationship, 41–2, 48, 59–60, 62–3, 124–32
  limitless reading and authorless texts, 23, 86, 96, 132, 139, 140–1, 156
  of narrative gaps, 154–6
  readerly authority of intertextuality, 162–3
  readerly roles in *Ulysses*, 71, 96–7
  'On Reading' (Barthes), 139
  reading approach, 4–5
  the role of 'editor,' 112, 114, 127
  role of the reader in *Ulysses* criticism, 41, 56–7, 60–1, 63

229

reading (*Cont.*)
  of a sentence from 'Calypso,' 140, 141–8, 149–51, 154, 155–6, 161, 166–7, 198
  term 'to read,' 9
  texts as mixed writings and tissues of quotations, 23–5, 26, 56, 138–9, 148
  of 'Wandering Rocks,' 140, 141, 148–54, 155
  'Writing Reading' (Barthes), 147
  see also author/reader/text relationship
Riquelme, John Paul, 119, 190
Rose, Danis, 127, 164–5
Rosenblatt, Louise, 20
Roughley, Alan, 114, 115
Roupenian, Kristen, 12–13
Rowling, J. K., 33

Saint-Amour, Paul K., 7, 18, 27, 116, 123–4
Sandulescu, C. George, 113–14
Schiller, Friedrich, 16–17
Schlegel, Friedrich, 16–17
Schliemann, Heinrich, 87
Seidel, Michael, 6, 43, 47, 69, 81, 88, 90
Senn, Fritz, 6, 47, 69, 111, 125–6, 127, 131, 192
Shakespeare, William, 3–4, 16–17, 173
Shelley, Percy Bysshe, 3, 15, 18
Skrabanek, Petr, 168 n.5
Slote, Sam, 128
Sollers, Phillipe, 109
Solomon, Margaret, 40
Sontag, Susan, 23, 164
Spark, Muriel, 2
Staley, Thomas F., 39
Stanford, W. B., 191
Steinberg, Erwin R., 164–5
Stillinger, Jack, 30
Stoppard, Tom, 147, 161, 162; see also *Travesties* (Stoppard)

Talbot, Bryan, 188
Talbot, Mary M., 188

texts
  annotation of, 148
  authorial ownership, 18–19, 32–3
  author-texts, 32
  Barthes theory of, 25–6
  in 'The Death of the Author' (Barthes), 23–4
  'difficult' texts, 1, 140, 141, 146, 147, 154–6
  genetic criticism, 107, 112, 124–5, 127–9, 132, 162
  how to read the author/text relationship, 41–2, 48, 59–60, 62–3, 124–32
  limitless reading and authorless texts, 23, 86, 96, 132, 139, 140–1, 156
  readerly authority of intertextuality, 162–3
  the role of 'editor,' 112, 114, 127
  in 'What is an Author?' (Foucault), 21, 27–8
  in 'From Work to Text' (Barthes), 25–6, 27
  'writerly' and 'readerly' texts, 24–5
  'Writing Reading' (Barthes), 147
  see also author/reader/text relationship; intertextuality
Thomas, Brook, 109, 118
Topia, André, 110
Travesties (Stoppard)
  comparative reading of *Travesties* and *Ulysses*, 175
  correspondences with *Ulysses*, 188–9
  disguise and identity, 189–90
  Henry Carr's memories of Joyce, 181, 184–7
  intertextuality with *The Importance of Being Earnest*, 184, 187–8, 189–90
  the mythic Joyce in, 174, 176, 181
  role of memory, 184, 189–90
  role of the author, 186–7, 188, 190–1
  title, 189, 190

INDEX

Ulysses
- active reading, 145–8, 155–6, 167, 199–200
- 'Aeolus,' 52, 67, 77, 153, 170 n.32
- Bloom within the narrative, 68, 73–4, 75, 78–9, 80, 90, 95, 140
- 'Calypso,' 8, 45, 53, 60, 65 n.24, 67, 76, 78, 79, 95, 98 n.14, 99 n.25, 140, 141–5, 149, 150, 153, 154, 155–6, 159, 161, 166–7, 169 n.6, 169 n.7, 198, 201
- 'Calypso,' a close reading of a sentence from, 141–8, 149–51, 154, 155–6, 161, 166–7, 198
- 'Circe,' 68, 71, 97 n.12, 144, 168 n.4, 170 n.32, 184
- correspondences with the *Odyssey*, 4, 5, 43, 46–7, 51, 60, 69–70, 196
- correspondences with *Travesties* (Stoppard), 175, 188–9
- 'Cyclops,' 97 n. 12, 154
- as 'difficult,' 1, 140, 146, 147, 154–6
- errors in printed matter, 67–8, 76–81, 85
- 'Eumaeus,' 6, 67–8, 69, 70–80, 81–2, 85, 87, 90–1, 93–4, 95–7, 97 n.12, 99 n.32, 99 n.33, 139, 140, 144, 152, 153, 159, 166, 198, 199–200, 201
- 'Hades,' 74, 76
- Homeric presence in *Ulysses*, 6, 69–71
- intertextuality of, 85–6, 146–7, 148, 161–2, 163
- 'Ithaca,' 74, 143, 145, 149–50, 159, 160, 184, 185
- language of the Eumaean narrative style, 67–8, 70, 71–6, 78–9, 80, 81, 89–90, 95–6, 152, 153
- 'Lestrygonians,' 99 n.25, 144, 178
- 'Lotus Eaters,' 2, 79, 142–3, 144, 145, 191
- the machine beneath the narrative, 50–1, 53
- M'Intosh, 76–7, 80, 91, 190
- the misplaced '(sic),' 78, 95–6, 158, 198
- Molly's misreading of 'metempsychosis,' 78, 95, 138, 142, 146, 154, 159, 198
- narrative focus of 'Wandering Rocks,' 140, 141, 148–54, 155
- 'Nausicaa,' 154
- from oral to written text, 70, 71, 77–80, 85
- 'Oxen of the Sun,' 7, 97 n.12, 124, 168 n.2, 170 n.23, 185
- 'Penelope,' 57, 99 n.25, 136 n.56, 138, 144, 169 n.6
- 'Proteus,' 67, 145, 150
- reader/author relationship, 1–2, 4, 68, 71, 96–7, 199–201
- readings of Shakespeare, 3–4
- repetition in, 76, 146, 150
- as a re-written *Odyssey*, 68, 80, 82, 96–7
- 'Scylla and Charybdis,' 3–4, 7, 35 n.14, 98 n.12, 99 n.26, 120, 168 n.4
- 'Sirens,' 53, 68, 76, 78, 144, 150, 154, 155, 170 n.32
- Stephen Dedalus' theories of authorship, 3–4, 7, 158
- 'Telemachus,' 57, 99 n.26, 143, 144, 146, 159, 169 n.5
- themes of disguise/role-playing/identity, 68, 74–5, 76, 78–80, 91, 93, 190
- 'Wandering Rocks,' 8, 67, 68, 98 n.24, 140, 141, 144, 148–54, 155, 156, 170 n.31, 177, 198, 201

Ulysses criticism
- the Arranger narrative device, 51–4, 55, 57, 58, 76, 85, 153, 158
- authorial return, 121–2
- authorially approved readings of *Ulysses*, 6–7, 41–2, 43, 44, 47–8, 62, 197–8
- corrective attitude of, 44, 45–6, 47–8, 57–60, 198
- as finite, 130–1
- Homeric schema, 42–8, 50–1, 58, 60, 68–9

231

Ulysses criticism (*Cont.*)
  how to read the author/text relationship, 41–2, 48, 55, 59–60, 62–3, 124–32, 196
  Joyce's authorial presence, 43, 44, 50, 60–1
  from Joyce's worksheets, 45–6, 60
  the Joyce/Stephen Dedalus relationship, 48–51, 54–5, 58, 119, 120–1, 173–4, 180, 198
  the machine beneath the narrative, 50–1, 53
  non-literary printed paraphernalia, 44–6
  phrasing in critical texts, 55–6
  physicality of the text, 51, 52, 57, 76, 79
  polysemy of the text, 56, 57, 59, 63
  relationship between *Ulysses* and Homer, 52, 69–70
  role of the reader, 41, 56–7, 60–1, 63

Uncle Charles Principle, 51–2, 55, 57, 58, 74–5, 79, 81, 93, 94, 151, 152–3
  see also Joyce studies
Ulysses: The Corrected Edition (Gabler), 107, 112, 113–14

Valente, Joseph, 130
Vichnar, David, 125
Vico, Giambattista, 43, 82, 85, 120

Welker, F. G., 83, 85
Whitmarsh, Tim, 87, 89
Wilson, Andrew, 164
Wimsatt, W. K., 29
Wolf, F. A., 6, 81, 82–3, 84, 85, 90, 94
Wollaeger, Mark A., 156
Woodmansee, Martha, 15, 18, 27, 30

Young, Edward, 18

Zetzel, James E. G., 82, 83

EU representative:
Easy Access System Europe
Mustamäe tee 50, 10621 Tallinn, Estonia
Gpsr.requests@easproject.com